TAMIL STUDIES

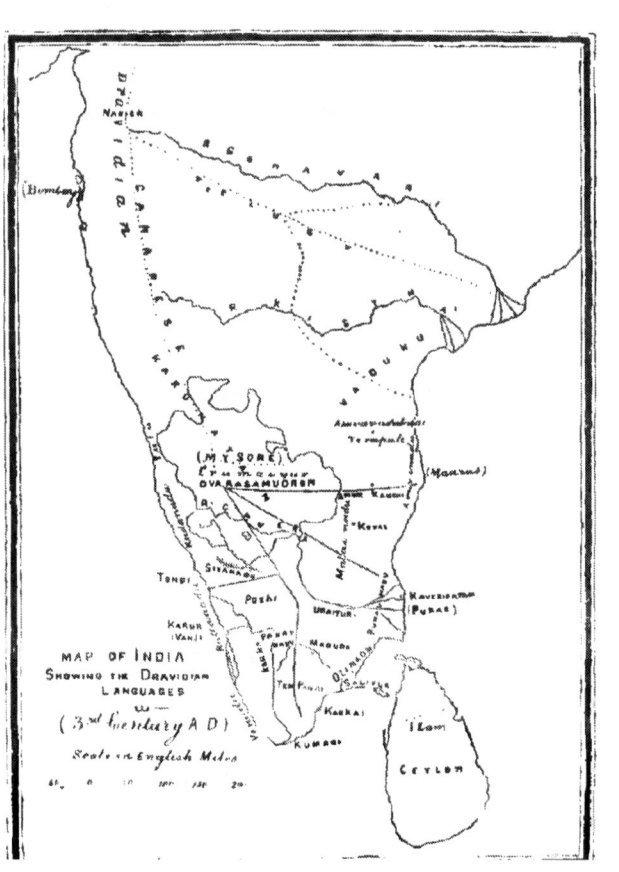

TAMIL STUDIES

OR

ESSAYS ON THE HISTORY OF THE TAMIL
PEOPLE, LANGUAGE, RELIGION
AND LITERATURE

BY

M. SRINIVASA AIYANGAR, M.A.

FIRST SERIES

WITH MAP AND PLATE

MADRAS
AT THE GUARDIAN PRESS

1914

[*All rights reserved*]

G C. LOGANADHAM BROS.
THE GUARDIAN PRESS, MADRAS

To

The Honourable

SIR HAROLD STUART, K.C.V.O., C.S.I., I.C.S.

Member of Council, Madras

This Volume

Is by kind permission most respectfully

Dedicated

By the Author

As a humble tribute of gratitude

PREFACE

A popular hand-book to the history, from original sources, of the Tamil people has been a want. In these essays an attempt has been made for the first time to put together the results of past researches, so as to present before the reader a complete bird's-eye view of the early history of Tamil culture and civilisation. The several topics have been treated from the standpoint of modern criticism, traditions and legends being discarded or utilized with great caution. They are based chiefly upon materials, which have been gathered in the course of my study of Tamil literature, ethnology and epigraphy begun while working under Sir Harold Stuart and Mr. W. Francis, both of the Indian Civil Service, in connection with the Madras Censuses of 1891 and 1901 and the revision of District Gazetteers. Some of the theories explained here might be open to corrections and alterations in the light of further discoveries and investigations. Any criticism calculated to enhance the accuracy and usefulness of the book will be thankfully received.

My obligations to published works especially to the contributions in the *Indian Antiquary* and *Epigraphia Indica* are extensive. A list of the English books consulted in the preparation of this work is given separately to avoid numerous foot-notes and references. My sincere thanks are due to Rao Bahadur M. Rangacharyar, M.A., Professor of Sanskrit and Comparative Philology, Presidency College, Madras, for the introduction to this volume, and to Mr. P. Subba Rao, B. A., of the Madras Record Office, for valuable suggestions while revising the manuscript and correcting the proofs for the press.

ENGLISH WORKS CONSULTED

Bray, Denys —	The Brahui Language.
Buhler, Dr.—	Indian Palæography.
Burnell, Dr. A. C.—	Elements of South Indian Palæography
	On the Aindra School of Sanskrit Grammarians.
Caldwell, Bishop.—	A Comparative Grammar of the Dravidian Languages.
Chitty, Simon Casie.	The Tamil Plutarch.
Colbrooke, H T.	Miscellaneous Essays.
District Gazetteers	(New Edition.)
Epigraphia Indica.	
Farrar, Canon F.W.	Language and Languages.
Forbes, Capt.—	The Languages of Further India.
Francis, W.—	Madras Census Report, 1901.
Gesenius, Dr.—	Hebrew Lexicon.
Grierson, Dr.—	The Languages of India.
	The Linguistic Survey of India.
Gundert, Dr. H.—	The Malayalam Grammar.
	Malayalam Dictionary.
Hasting's Encyclopœdia of Religion and Ethics.	
Hovelacque, M —	The Science of Language.
Hultzsch, Dr. E —	South Indian Inscriptions.
Hunter, Sir W. W.	Non-Aryan Languages of India.
	Imperial Gazetteer.
Haberlandt, Dr. M.	Ethnology.
Imperial Gazetteer	of India (New Edition).
Indian Antiquary.	
Journal of the Royal	Asiatic Society, London.
Liddel and Scott.—	Greek Lexicon.
Kanakasabhai, V.—	The Tamils 1800 years ago.
Keane, A. H.—	Ethnology
Letourneau, C —	Sociology.

Macleane, Dr.—	Manual of Administration.
Madras Christian	College Magazine, The
Max Muller, F.—	The Science of Language.
M'Crindle, J. W.—	Ancient India &c.
Nagamiah, V.—	The Travancore State Manual.
Nelson, J. H.—	The Madura District Manual.
Nesfield, J. C.—	Theory of Indian Castes.
Oppert, Dr. G.—	The Aboriginal Inhabitants of Bharatavarsha.
Pope, Dr. G. U —	The Kural of Tiruvalluvar. The Tiruvachakam.
Quatrefages, A.—	The Human Species.
Rangacharya, M.—	A descriptive Catalogue of Tamil Manuscripts, Vol. I.
Rhys Davids, Dr.—	The Buddhist India.
Rice, L.—	The Mysore Gazetteer. Epigraphia Carnatica.
Risley, Sir H. H.—	The Peoples of India.
Sayce, A. H.—	Principles of Comparative Philology.
Seignobos, Ch.—	History of Ancient Civilisation.
Seshagiri Sastri, M.	Report on Sanskrit and Tamil Manuscripts, Nos. 1 and 2.
Smith, Vincent A.—	Early History of India ; Asoka.
Stuart, Sir H. A.—	Madras Census Report, 1891.
Taylor, Meadows —	History of India.
Thurston, E.—	The Tribes and Castes of Southern India.
Tylor, E. B.—	Primitive Culture.
Vaidya, C. V.—	The Riddle of the Ramayana.
Wallace, A. R.—	The Malay Archipelago.
Whitney, W. D.—	The Life and Growth of Language.
Wijesinha, L. C.—	The Mahawanso.
Williams, Monier,	Sanskrit Dictionary.
Wilson, Prof. H. H.	Glossary of Indian Terms.

INTRODUCTION

It is with very great pleasure that I have, in compliance with the wish of the author, written this short introduction to this volume of really interesting essays on subjects relating to the history of the Tamil people and their culture and civilisation. The history of the famous inhabitants of the ancient Pandya, Chola and Chera kingdoms is in no way less edifying or less valuable as a source of inspiration than the history of the inhabitants of any other part of India, which is throughout highly historic. The progress of Tamil civilisation from its primitive rude restlessness and wild aggressive valour to its ordered sense of humanity and exalted moral and religious aims of a later day is undoubtedly the result of the operation of various momentous influences, the chief ones among which have naturally been religious in origin and character. It is a fact well known to the students of the history of civilisation that, in some of its earlier stages of development, nothing acts so powerfully as an advancingly ethical religion in stimulating and sustaining progress in human communities. Accordingly the virile vitality and undecaying vigour of the Tamil people, subjected to the mellowing influences of Buddhism, Jainism and earlier as well as later Brahmanism gave rise in due time to their sweet, practical and in more than one respect heart-enthralling culture, of which the great Tamil classics, together with their noble Saiva and Vaishnava hymnology—not to mention their mighty and majestic God-aspiring temples—constitute even today the enduring monuments of beauty and glorious divine enthusiasm. To construct and to explain the history of such a people, characterised by such a noteworthy progress in civilisation and possessed of such an enduringly valuable and edifying culture, must indeed be always fascinating; and innumerable avenues of enquiry and research are certain to open out before the watchful eyes of the trained and sincerely earnest student trying to help on this work of historic up-building and exposition. Here in this field of research, criticism and construction, there is ample scope for ethnological, anthropological, and sociological investigations of more than one kind; there is abundant room for the work of antiquarian discovery and illumination in which all the various types of archæologists may take part to their heart's content; and written records of various kinds are also available in quantities large enough to satisfy the hunger of many voracious enquirers after historic truth, or literary beauty or linguistic development. The field for cultivation is both wide and well endowed, but earnest and capable labourers are unhappily as yet too few.

I have no doubt that these essays will act as an eye-opener to many inhabitants of the Tamil land who take a true and cultured pride in the history of their own country. I am far from saying that all the various opinions, which Mr. Srinivasa Aiyangar has expressed on so many topics in this volume, will be found to be absolutely faultless and acceptable to all. It is invariably the fate of opinions, relating to the elements of what may be called constructive history, to undergo more or less rapid modifications as more and more materials become available for examination and subsequent structural utilisation and employment. Moreover, in dealing with problems of constructive history, there arise very often peculiar temptations to base conclusions on insufficient or inaccurate data as well as to adjust the scantily available evidence to preconceived conclusions. My reading of the essays, comprised in this volume of *Tamil Studies*, has led me to feel that their author has earnestly endeavoured to avoid, as far as possible, all such pitfalls, and has calmly and courageously exercised his judgment in the free and clear light of unbiassed reason. That he has had adequate equipment for dealing with the various problems, which he has handled in his essays, comes out well enough from the essays themselves, seeing that they are so well calculated to stimulate thought and bring into existence that curiosity which is the necessary precursor of all true love of scholarly investigation, enquiry and research. The way, in which he has sought and gathered his varied materials and endeavoured to put them together in the spirit of the architect and the interpreter, is assuredly worthy of imitation by many more students of the history of the Tamil people and their culture and civilisation.

M. RANGACHARYA.

TABLE OF CONTENTS

———o———

	PAGE.
PREFACE	VII
INTRODUCTION	XI

ESSAY I.—THE TAMIL PEOPLE.—Introduction—the name 'Dravida' explained—its ethnological meaning—its social significance—Dravida and Gauda contrasted—Dr. Caldwell's use of the term Dravidian—linguistic sense—etymology of the word 'Dravida'—the word Tamil explained—the Tamil country—its ancient limits—the Tamils a mixture of three races according to Tamil literature—Risley's theory examined—data for determining racial varieties—(1) language—(2) anthropometry—(3) archæology—and (4) literary traditions   1

ESSAY II.—THE TAMIL PEOPLE (continued).—The place of the Dravidians in the human family—different views of ethnologists—Risley, Hæckel, Topinard and Keane—Caldwell's aborigines—theories concerning the Dravidian migration—(1) the early Aryans—(2) the Lemurian theory—(a) evidence from ethnology—(b) from philology—(c) from geography—Dr. Hunter's theory—(4) the Mongolian or North-Eastern theory—Kanakasabhai's arguments examined—the Nagas—(3) conclusion... ...   17

ESSAY III.—THE TAMIL PEOPLE (continued).—(5)The North-Western origin—(a) evidence from philology—Mr. Bray's views about the Brahuis—the Brahuis, the Todas and the Vellalas—(b) archæological evidence—the Dravidians and Assyrians—the word Vellala explained—(c) literary evidence—probable date of migration—sea route improbable—commercial relation with the West—no early Tamil words for the ship—the Aryan conquest

	PAGE.

of the South according to the Sanskrit epics—the theories of the neo-Tamil School—the Rakshasas and the Vanaras—their social and religious customs—Summary 33

ESSAY IV.—THE TAMIL CASTES.—The Tamil speaking castes—the Brahmans and the non-Brahmans—the three types of pre-Aryans—the caste system introduced by the Aryans—but it was regional—the Vellalas not included—their occupations—the occupational castes—Tamil and Malayalam castes compared—how the modern castes sprung from the territorial tribes—the hill tribes—the Naga tribes—the Maravas and Eyinas—the Parayas and Idaiyas—the Pallas and Shanars—the fishing castes—the dissolving factors—the Kammalas—the caste system created disputes—the tribal quarters in ancient towns—origin of the Paraiyas—their former greatness—origin of the Kaikolas—the Tamils not good weavers—the Panans and other castes—origin of the Kammalas—the food of the Eyinas—origin of caste pollution ... 58

ESSAY V.—THE TAMIL CASTES.—(continued).—The caste system bred discontent and quarrels—the right and left hand disputes—castes enumerated—the caste privileges—Kammalas and Kaikolas—traditional origin of the division—the social position of the Kammalas and Kaikolas—and Pallis or Vanniyas—suggested origins—Prof. M Rangacharya's theory examined—the distinction not found in Malabar—(1) political origin—(2) supported by social disputes—and (3) confirmed by religion—Summary ... 92

ESSAY VI.—THE TAMIL ALPHABET.—Its importance—the ten heads under which Tamil letters are treated—the Vatteluttu and the Grantha-Tamil characters—the age of Vatteluttu—date of the Tolkapyam—by whom the alphabet was introduced—the two opposite theories—views of Caldwell and Buhler examined—arguments in support of E. Thomas's theory —not derived from Brahmi—Vatteluttu and Brahmi were in use simultaneously—why supplanted by Grantha-Tamil—which was developed from the Pallava characters—how much of modern Tamil characters adapted from Vatteluttu—the shape of vowel-consonants described—why the modern Tamil characters are angular in form—the number and order of letters—pronunciation—letters peculiar to Tamil—accent and emphasis—origin of letters—interchange of letters of similar sounds—how to determine pure Tamil words—initial letters—final letters—and middle letters... 113

Essay VII.—THE PLACE OF TAMIL IN PHILOLOGY.—Where spoken—the Tamil's knowledge of geography—principles of philology—changes in the growth of a language—Tamil an agglutinative tongue—can never become inflectional—traditional origin—it is one of the Dravidian languages—Sanskrit and Tamil compared as regards their vocabulary—Tamil words in Sanskrit—orthography—Dr. Caldwell's views examined—word structure—word formation—coalescence in words or *Sandhi*—compound words or phrases—etymology—differences between Tamil and Sanskrit—prosody in the two languages—other peculiarities of Tamil—the Indo-Germanic affinity—the Dravidian influence on the Sanskrit dialects—affiliation of Tamil—the Dravidian and the Uralo-Altaic languages—causes for the difference—position in the linguistic system—early Tamil (vocabulary, grammar, style and matter)—mediæval Tamil—modern Tamil—need for prose literature. 141

Essay VIII.—PERIODS OF TAMIL LITERATURE.—Tamil literature characteristic of race—insepa-

B

rable from religion—the three classes of Tamil literature—music and the drama—the extent of polite literature—mostly translations—the ethical literature—no Tamil literature without the Aryan influence—history of literature wanting—absence of critical spirit among the Tamils—examination of Damodaram Pillai's classification—of Suryanarayana's—of Caldwell's cycles—of other western scholars—of M. Julien Vinson—proposed classification—(1) the pre-academic period—(2) the academic period—(3) the hymnal period—(4) translations from Sanskrit—(5) the exegetical period—and (6) the modern period—the anti-Brahmanical School—prose literature 185

ESSAY IX.—THE TAMIL ACADEMIES.—Introduction—references to Tamil academies—explanation of the terms *Sangam* and *avai*—the scope of the essay—the upper limit of the Sangam period—the first academy—described—Agastyar and his students—their works—the date of the academy discussed—the location of Dakshana Madura—the second academy described—a continuation of the first—its date—the importance of the third academy—described—when established—and where—its members—(Thiruvalluvamalai, a forgery)—how and when broken up—religion of its members—the value of Nakkirar's account—later academies—literature encouraged by Tamil kings—summary account of the academies—refinement of the Tamil language—how poetical works passed—liberal presents to poets—the French academy and the sangams compared 231

ESSAY X.—THE TEN TENS.—Description of the work—the dates of the several books—of the Chera kings—difficult to get their dates—description of certain ancient Tamil customs—the political condition of the country—the style and language of the work. 264

ESSAY XI.—THE VAISHNAVA SAINTS.—Introduction —religion of the early Tamils—Brahmanization of the Tamils—growth of Brahmanism among the Tamils—the beginning of the Vaishnava sect—the Vaishnava saints—the Guruparamparai—the first Alvars or Saints—their dates—Tirumalisai Alvar—his age—Tiruppan Alvar and Tondaradippodi Alvar—Kulasekhara Alvar and his date—Tirumangai Alvar—his date—Periyalvar and his date—Andal—Nammalvar, the last of the Vaishnava saints—the age of Nammalvar—conclusion 281

ESSAY XII.—THE ORIGIN OF MALAYALAM.—Introduction—etymology of the terms Malayalam and Malabar—people of Kerala were Tamils—the early Tamil poets of Kerala—which was a Tamil country—(1) geographical evidence—(2) from religious literature—the Nambis or Nambudris—and the Bhatta Brahmans—(3) ethnological evidence—(4) archæological evidence —(5) literary evidence—Kannassa Ramayanam—Krishnappattu—Eluttacchan—Unnayi Variyar —(6) linguistic evidence—(a) grammar—(b) vocabulary—formative causes—conclusion ... 340

CONCLUSION.—The Tamil people—the Tamil Brahmans—the Tamil alphabet and language—religion of the Tamils—Tamil literature—Exhortation 377

Appendix. I. The Early Pandya kings ... 387
   ,, II. Note on Agastya's Grammar ... 397
   ,, III. The Age of Manikka Vachakar ... 401
   ,, IV. Note on the word Tiyan ... 411
Index 419

ABBREVIATIONS

Agap.—Agapporul of Iraiyanar
Agat —Agattiyam.
Akam.—Akananuru.
Cher.—Cheraman Perumal
Chin —Cintamani
D. A —Dandi's Alankaram.
Ep. Ind.—Epigraphia Indica.
Ind. Ant —Indian Antiquary.
Ind. Rev.—Indian Review.
J. R. A. S —Journal of the Royal Asiatic Society, London.
Kal.—Kalittogai or Kalladam
Kam —Kamban's Ramayanam
Kap.—Kapilar
Kur.—Kural.
Mani —Manimekalai
Mut —Muttanayanar Antadi.
Nak.—Nakkirar.
Nan —Nannul
Ned.—Nedunalvadai.
Nig —Chudamani Nigandu.
Pat.—Pattuppattu or Pattinappalai.

P. T.—Periya Tirumozhi
Pey.—Peyalvar.
Ping.—Pingalandai
Poi —Poigai Alvar.
P A. —Porunararruppadai.
Pur.—Purananuru.
P. V. M —Purapporul Venbamalai.
Sik.—Sikandiyar
Sil —Silappadikaram.
S. F. P. or Sir.—Sirupanarruppadai.
Siv.—Sivavakkiyar.
S. I. I.—South Indian Inscriptions.
Tat. Sek —Tatva Sekharam.
T T —Tirugnana Sambandar's Tevaram, or Tiruttondar Tiruvandadi
T. V.—Tiruvachakam.
Tol.—Tolkappiyam
Vil.—Villiputtur Alvar

I
THE TAMIL PEOPLE

Who are Dravidians ? Whence and how did they come to South India? These are some of the outstanding problems in Indian ethnology. During the past fifty years various theories have been put forward from the point of view either of philology or anthropology or literature, and it cannot be said that the last word has been pronounced on the subject. It is not intended in these short papers to put forth any new hypothesis, but to bring together all the existing theories bearing on the subject, and to examine them in the light of the evidence furnished by ancient Tamil literature and the labours of reputed scholars and savants.

The word Dravida is widely used as a synonym for Tamil and at the outset it is desirable to explain its origin and meaning. According to Sanskrit pandits 'Dravida' was the name of a particular tract of country in Southern India; and it is so defined in the *Sabdakalpadruma* on the authority of the Mahabharata. The country called 'Dravida' extended along the east coast of India from Tirupati (near Madras) to Cape Comorin and for about sixty miles to the interior. The name is also loosely applied to the south of the Peninsula.

Prof. Wilson and Sir Monier-Williams give three senses in which the word is used— (1) the country in which the Tamil language is spoken; (2) an inhabitant of the country; and (3) a class of Brahmanical tribe called the 'five Dravidas'. In accepting the first meaning western scholars and Indian pandits seem to agree. As regards the second, differences of opinion exist. Whether the name Dravida was applied to all the peoples living in that 'country or only to a particular caste or tribe remains to be settled. The Tamil-speaking non-Brahmans have always called themselves Tamilar but never Dravidas. And the Tamil Brahmans who called themselves the *mahajanam* or the 'great men' were, and even now are, known to the other Brahmans of India as Dravidas. Sankarâcharya (A. D. 820), who was a great Sanskrit scholar and religious reformer, refers to Trignânasambanda, a Brahman Saivite Saint and Tamil poet, as *Dravida Sisu* (Dravida child). This use of the word obtains even to-day. A Tamil-speaking Brahman who has settled down in the Bombay Presidency is spoken of as a 'Dravid' and the word is affixed to the name of the person, *e. g.*, Chintâman *Dravid*, Natesa *Dravid*. But the Tamil-speaking non-Brahmans are known by their caste titles—Mudaliyar, Pillai, and so on. Similarly, the

Telugus of the north call the Tamil Brahmans 'Dravidlu' or 'Dravidas' while the Tamil non-Brahmans are called Sudralu or Dakshanâdi-Sudralu. These clearly show that in practice the ethnological application of the name Dravida was restricted and limited to a particular class, namely, the Tamil-speaking Brahmans.

The significance of the word Dravida in the expression Pancha Dravida has now to be explained. At a very early period in the history of the Indo-Aryan people, the Tamil-speaking Brahmans had developed a system of social and religious customs and practices which became a marked feature of that community.[1] They had a separate ritualistic system; their social code was different from that of the northern Brahmans;[2] and their laws also were

[1]. Baudhayana, Dramidachar and other early commentators on the Brahmasutras, some Aryan reformers and law-givers belonged to the Dravida Brahman community

[2]. The religious ceremonies of the five Dravida Brahmans are more numerous and elaborate. Omission to perform any of them entails degradation or even excommunication. A Dravida Brahman cannot eat fish or meat, and cannot accept food or water from the hands of a non-Brahman without losing his caste. A married woman cannot wear white cloth, and when tying it she must pass it between her legs. A widow should remove not only her ornaments but also her hair, a custom prevalent in the Tamil country at least from the second or third century A. D as will be seen from the following lines of Kalladanar —

ஒண்ணுதல் மகளிர் கைகைம கூர
வயிரால் கடுகுமம்மென
குவையிருங்கூந்தல் கொய்தல் கண்டே

(Trans :—Observed the cutting of the fair, soft, black-sand-like hair of the bright-faced women to enforce their widowhood.)

different. These were generally known as *Dravidasampradaya*. So far as these habits of life, customs, practices and rituals tended to higher spirituality, they were adopted by the other Brahman communities of the peninsula—the Andhras, the Karnatakas, the Maharashtras and the Gurjaras. This accounts for peoples speaking Sanskritic dialects like Marathi and Gujarathi and people speaking non-Sanskritic dialect like Tamil, Telugu and Kanarese being grouped together as Pancha Dravidas or the five Dravidas.

The Dravidas proper were the Tamil-speaking Brahmans. The use of the name for other Brahman communities is an instance of extension of its meaning and application. The term was extended to all Brahmans observing the *Dravidâchârams*, or *Dravidasampradaya*.

In North India the Brahmans, who did not

On the contrary in these matters the Gauda or northern Brahmans are more lax. The Dravida Brahmans are generally very conservative and the strictness in the observance of the above customs is attributed to their natural desire to maintain the purity of their Aryan blood.

Among the Dravida Brahmans, the Nambudris of Malabar form an exception. They seem to have retained some of the original trans-Vindhyan or Gauda customs and resisted the healthy reforms of Sankara, Ramanuja and Ananda Tirtha. Their enforced polygamy, their free intercourse with the non-Aryans, and a few of their *anacharas* or unaryan customs raise some doubt as to the purity of their Aryan descent, a doubt which occurred to our minds in spite of the somewhat rigorous social customs obtaining among them to-day and their fair complexion, which are no doubt due to climatic conditions and their ways of living.

accept these more rigid social rules and practices developed by the Dravida Brahmans of South India, came to be distinguished as *Pancha Gaudas*. From the fact that the Malayalam-speaking Brahmans, the Nambudris, are not mentioned in this classification, it may be inferred that the division of Brahmans into Pancha Dravidas and Pancha Gaudas had taken place long before the evolution of the Malayalam language in the thirteenth century.

From what has been said above it would be clear that the term Dravida had no ethnological significance at first, but this it acquired later on. The definition of the word 'Dravida' quoted by Dr. Caldwell from Sanskrit lexicons 'as a man of out-cast tribe descended from a degraded Kshatriya' is open to question. The genesis of the Dravida castes and tribes given here and that given by Manu cannot be accepted as literally true. It is one of those fictions, familar to Indian sociologists dealing with the question of the origin of caste by which the Brahmans got over the troubles and conflicts between themselves and the numerically stronger and socially more influential sections of the non-Brahmanical tribes on whom they imposed their culture and civilization.

To Dr. Caldwell is due a further extension of the meaning of the term Dravida When the comparative study of the South Indian languages was first started by him, the glossarial and grammatical affinities between them were so marked as to lead him to the conclusion that they were allied languages of the non-Aryan group. He called these languages of South India *Dravidian* and the people speaking them Dravidians. His extension of the word as a generic term for the South Indian group of languages is convenient and has been accepted. Linguistic evidence alone, however, cannot be sufficient, and by itself is unreliable to establish any theory about the origins of castes or the ethnic affinity of peoples. Thus the application of the name Dravidian or Dravida to all tribes, Brahman as well as non-Brahman, inhabiting the extreme south of the Peninsula is unwarranted, inaccurate and misleading.

The derivation of the word Dravida is doubtful. It is purely of Sanskrit origin and may be a compound of two roots *dra*, to run, and *vid*, a piece (of land). It might mean a place to which one runs as a place of retreat, the extreme south of the peninsula being the last place to which any race could betake itself when driven by a stronger race from the north of India. This is only a plausible suggestion. Sanskrit pandits, however, think Dravida is a corruption or Sanskritised form of Tamil. But whether this bold derivation could be supported by any linguistic processes known to philology seems doubtful.

The origin of the word Tamil is not very clear, and native grammarians are silent on this point. Agreeing with certain Tamil and Sanskrit pandits, Dr. Caldwell derives it from Sanskrit *Dravida*. Mr. Dâmodaram Pillai, however, questions the correctness of this etymology and asks—Is it possible for a language to have no native name until one was given to it by Aryans, especially when it was the mother tongue of a tolerably civilised race which had a fairly cultivated literature and which had commercial relationship with the ancient nations of the West? He derives Tamil from the root *Tami* (தமி) lonely, and believes that Tamil means the 'peerless' language. In the *Pingalandai* it is explained thus :—

இனிமையும் நீர்மையுந் தமிழெனலாகும்.
(Tamil means sweetness and mercy).

We find *tamil* used only once in the sense of 'sweetness' in Tamil literature, and that was by the author of Chintamani (about A. D. 950); but we do not see it used in this sense in the earlier Tamil works. Of course the expressions தீந்தமிழ் (the sweet-), கொழுந் தமிழ் (the fat-), தேனுறைதமிழ் (the honeyed-) and தண் டமிழ் (the cool-Tamil) very often occur; but the word Tamil is not by itself used in this sense except in the solitary instance above noted. However, following the *Pingalandai*, the author of the D'avida Prakasika and a few other Indian scholars explain Tamil as meaning the sweet language. This connotation of sweetness seems to have long lingered among Tamil writers, for the royal author of Naishadam speaks of his heroine as one the sweetness of whose speech was sweeter than Tamil, தமிழினு மினியதீஞ் சொற்றையயலாள். Mr. Kanakasabhai thinks it to be an abbreviated form of Tamra-litti, but this etymology seems to be rather fanciful. It may not perhaps be rash to suggest here what appears to be a reasonable derivation. The word Tamil may be taken as a compound of *tam + izh*; *tam* is a reflexive pronoun which has given rise to a very interesting class of words like *tam-appan* (father), *tay* or *tam-ay* (mother), *tam-aiyan* (elder brother), *tam-kai* (younger sister), *tam-akkai* (elder sister), *tam-pi* (n), *tam-piran* &c.; *izh* (which is the root of Izhm or Izhum, Izhudu &c.) means sweetness. Hence Tamizh or Tamil is "that which is sweet" or the sweet language.

It may be observed that this word is used in early Tamil works to denote the language, the people and their country.

That part of the Indian peninsula which the Indo-Aryans called the Dravida was known to ancient Tamils as the *Tamil-akam* or the 'abode of the Tamils'. The extent of this Tamil-akam was not, however, always the same. Tolkâpyar, a Tamil grammarian, probably of the fourth century B. C., Ilangô-adigal, the royal ascetic and reputed author of Silappadikâram, and Sikandiyâr, a pupil of Agastyar and the author of a treatise on music, roughly fix the boundaries of the Tamil country, as may be seen from the following quotations:—

(1) வட வேங்கடம் தென்குமரி யாயிடைத்
தமிழ் கூறு நல்லு லகம்.—*Tol*

(The good world of the Tamils which lies between the northern Vênkatam and the southern Kumari.)

(2) நெடியோன் குன்றமுந் தொடியோள் பௌவமுந்
தமிழ் வரம்பறுத்த தண்புனனுடு.—*Sil.*

(The cool country of the Tamils bounded by Vishnu's hill and the bangled lady's sea—Kumari).

(3) வேங்கடங் குமரி தீம்புனற் பௌவமென்
நின்றனன் செல்ல தமிழது வழக்கே.—*Sil.*

(Tamil prevails within the four limits of Venkatam, Kumari and the seas.)

The Tamil-akam or the land of the Tamils thus seems to have extended east and west from sea to sea, and north and south from the Tirupati hills to Cape Comorin, and to have also included the modern states of Travancore and Cochin and the British district of Malabar.

The Tamils in the west coast who were cut off from the main body and who were much under the control of the Brahman hierarchy, developed a dialect of their own, a patois of Kodum-Tamil and Prakritic Sanskrit, which has been known as Malayalam since the beginning of the thirteenth century. And this isolation accounts also for some of the ancient customs and manners of the Tamils being better preserved to this day in the west coast than in the eastern districts.

The loss of this western strip from the Tamil-akam was, however, soon made up; for, new districts were added to it by the colonisation by the Tamils of the northern portion of Ceylon, beginning from the time of Parantaka Chola (A. D. 907-946) or even from an earlier date. They may be found also in Burma, Sumatra, Java and wherever they could find food and labour.

All the Tamil speaking inhabitants of the southern districts do not belong to one and the same race. Any layman can easily distinguish the Dravidian Tamils from the Aryan Brahmans. The physical characteristics of the hill and forest tribes, such as the Kadars, the Soligas and the Kurumbas differ from those of the Vellalas and the Todas. Dr. A. H. Keane and other ethnologists recognise at least three distinct races in the population of Southern India. This hypothesis seems to receive some countenance and support from ancient Tamil literature and traditions. The well-known classification of rational beings (உயிர்திணை) by the Tamil grammarians into *makkal* (மக்கள்), *devar* (தேவர்) and *narakar* (நரகர்) or *na'gar* (நாகர்) points to the existence of three types of people in the Tamil land, namely, the Dravidian Tamils (Makkal), the Aryan-Brahmans (Devar) and the aboriginal tribes (Na'gar). 'Na'ga' is a word loosely applied to all the aborigines who used to inhabit the forests, the low regions and other unknown realms (Narakam). Even so late as the eleventh century when the process of the capture and absorption of the aboriginal peoples by the superior Dravidians was going on, the more powerful of the Na'ga tribes seem to have struggled hard to maintain their sturdy independence and to preserve their racial integrity.[1] For

1. With this compare the remarks of the Madras Government Epigraphist : " The mythical account of the Epic hero Arjuna marrying a Naga queen and similar stories current about the early Chola kings in Tamil literature, combined with what is stated of the Naga connections with the first Pallava kings . . . confirm

we find in the early Tamil works that the Nagas are described as a race of dark people with curly matted hair. The ancient Tamils were acquainted also with a tribe of naked nomads (நக்கசாரணர்), probably a section of the Nagas living in an eastern Island. They were cannibals and spoke an unknown language.

(1) வாடபசியுழந்த நின்னிரும்பேரொக்கலொடு —*P. A.*
(With your starving, *dark* and large relations)

(2) வலிமுன்பின்வல் லென்றயாகைகைப் புலிநோகிற
சுற்றமை வில்லாசுரி வளர்பித்தையர்
அற்றம பார்த்தல் குங்கடுங் கண்மறவா.—*Kal.*

(The cruel-eyed, curly-haired and able-bodied Maravas (robbers) with tiger-look and banded bows waiting on the roads to harass the travellers).

(3) வென்றிவேற் கிள்ளிக்கு நாசநாடாள் வேவான்
றன் மகள பீலிவளை தான்பயந்த
புனீற்றிளங்குழவி.—*Mani.*

(The tender infant which Pilivalai, the daughter of the ruler of Naganadu, bore for Killi (Chola) who wields the victorious lance)

From the first quotation we learn that the Pânans —the ancestors, or rather, a sub-caste of the modern Paraiyas—were an aboriginal tribe of dark men ; from the second that the Maravas—not the present caste of that name—were a tribe of hunters and robbers with tiger-look and curly matted hair ; while the third

the accepted belief that the Nagas were the original indigenous rulers of Southern India and that they were subdued in course of time by the powerful kings from the north, eventually losing their individuality by intermarriages with the foreigners" Report dated 28-7-1911.

points to the fusion of the Tamils with the aboriginal tribe of Nagas even so early as the first or second century of the Christian era. It might also be learnt from Pattuppattu or the Ten Tamil Idylls and the Mahabalipuram inscriptions of Rajendra Chola (A. D. 1012-1044) that there were among the Nagas at least four sub-divisions, viz , Oli-Nagan, Mugali-Nagan, Sanka-Nagan and Nila-Nagan. The Paraiyas, who constitute nearly a seventh of the Tamil population and who will be shewn hereafter to be the descendants of the ancient Eyina tribe dislike to call themselves Tamils, thus suggesting that they belong to a different race altogether. Further, the various modes of disposing of the dead prevalent among the Tamils of ancient times, namely, cremation, interment and exposure, could not have been practised at the same time by one and the same race. These facts clearly go to prove that there were in the Tamil country at least three distinct races namely, the aborigines (whatever may be their names), the Dravidian Tamils and the Aryan immigrants. Though there was a free intermixture of the aborigines and the Dravidian Tamils and though some isolated instances of the fusion of the second and third are noticeable, the existence of three different types is clear.

Sir Herbert Risley, however, considers that all the South Indians are Dravidians—a dark-complexioned, short-statured people with long head, broad and thick-set nose and long fore-arm. Doubtless this description applies to some of the hill and forest tribes and some low caste Hindus, but it cannot apply to the population of Southern India as a whole. It will be admitted that three types of physical character are observable in the Tamil districts corresponding to the three different races already noticed. First, there are the Aryans with a somewhat fair complexion, tall stature, aquiline nose, small lips, smooth and flowing hair. Secondly, the pure Dravidian like the Todas of the Nilgiris, tall, brown complexioned, with thick prominent nose, hairy body, well-proportioned limbs, receding forehead and of Jewish appearance. And thirdly, we have the aborigines like the Kadars, with African face, flattish and broad nose, thick lips and dark complexioned; and the pot-bellied Kurumbas with wild matted hair, large mouth, prominent outstanding teeth, thick lips and prognathous. Although there must have been intercrossing and shuffling of races from a time long anterior to the Christian era, it is extremely doubtful whether any tribe of the pure Mongolian race had at any time found its way into the Tamil country, as Mr. Kanakasabhai seems to think.

The only data available for determining the racial varieties are, (a) Language, (b) Anthropometry, (c) Prehistoric archæology and (d) Traditions and customs. None of these, however, can independently prove the racial type one way or the other.

(a) No comparative philologist will now admit that language is a safe test of race. Languages have their rise, growth and decay, and languages once well known are entirely forgotten, foreign languages taking their place as though they were native. Thus Keltic is extinct in Cornwall ; Sclavonic has disappeared in Prussia ; Accadian, the home speech of a highly civilised Turanian race in Asia Minor, was completely rooted out by the conquering Semites. Coming to our own country, we find the Brahman settlers in the Tamil land speak only a Dravidian language forgetting their Sanskrit dialects. The entire native population of the Tamil-akam—aborigines, Dravidians as well as Aryans—speak either Tamil or an allied language of the Dravidian family. No successful attempt has yet been made to analyse the Tamil language and to write its history in a purely philological spirit. Dr. Caldwell was the first to trace some distant affinity of Tamil with the Uralo-Altaic languages. Some philologists, however, seem to think that he was not quite successful in the attempt We shall discuss this question more fully in its proper place.

(b) Anthropologists place rather too much confidence in the absolute certainty of the nasal and cephalic indices, of hair and colour as permanent tests of racial distinction. Sir Herbert Risley, Sir William Turner and Dr. Topinard rely on the constancy of cranial measurements, assuming the form of the head as a persistent character that is not liable to be modified by the action of artificial selection. These scientists, however, do not agree among themselves in certain important respects.

Professors Flower, Lydekker and Huxley classify mankind according to the smoothness or roughness of the hair, while others like Quatrefages add to these colour, odour &c. Nevertheless, the value of all these data is being seriously doubted by equally eminent scientists. Professor Cox has brought together all their objections forcibly in a very interesting article that appeared in the *Modern Review (Calcutta)* for 1911. He says 'the cephalic index separates races closely allied and is almost identical for races widely apart.' 'In almost every nation we find almost every cephalic index.' As for the nasal index, M. Colignon after elaborate researches thinks it of minor importance. Professor Sergi of Rome says 'the method of indices is a method only in appearance and it inevitably leads to errors and can produce no satisfactory results.' Professor Ridgeway thinks ' these osteological differences are but foundations of sand.' And above all a writer in the *Muenschener Medizinische* (quoted by Mr. G. A Gait, I.C.S.,) asserts that the numerous head measurements collected with endless assiduity by anthropologists have been shown to be worthless Thus we see that neither the cephalic nor the nasal index is of much value in determining race. The same may be said of hair and colour, as these can be changed in course of time by climate, food and other artificial means and methods. It would therefore be unwise on the part of anthropologists to think they could correctly interpret these physical differences as indications of inferiority or otherwise of a race, especially in a country like India, where there has been for ages past an intermingling of diverse races—autochthonous, Turanian, Semitic or Aryan.

(c) The evidence of pre-historic archæology consists of weapons, implements, and human bones which are found buried in the earth, and the megalithic monuments like the dolmen, cromlech and the kistvaens. Such remains abound in Tamil districts. But in India the science of archæology has not yet advanced, and no excavations on a large scale have till now been undertaken. The finds hitherto brought to light are therefore very limited and do not afford data for any reliable inference concerning ethnic problems.

(d) The fourth source from which we may derive some help for determining racial varieties consists of traditions and ancient customs described in early Tamil works. Some of them may have been distorted, exaggerated or even wrongly stated. The Ramayana and the Mahabharata in Sanskrit, the Tolkapyam, the Purananuru, the Pattuppattu, the Kalittogai and other works in Tamil furnish plenty of evidence. But all these will have to be sifted and considered in the light of other evidences. And this will be attempted in the next chapter.

II

THE TAMIL PEOPLE—*(continued)*.

The original home of the Dravidians and their place in the human family are still subjects of discussion. The various views that have been held by anthropologists in this connection will be passed in review.

'The Dravidian race,' says Dr. Grierson, ' is commonly considered to be the aborigines of India or at least of Southern India, and we have no information to show that they are not the aboriginal inhabitants of the South.' Sir Herbert Risley says, ' Taking them as we find them now it may safely be said that their present geographical distribution, the marked uniformity of physical characters among the more primitive members of the group, their animistic religion, their distinctive languages, their stone monuments and retention of a primitive system of totemism justify us in regarding them as the earliest inhabitants of India of whom we have any knowledge.'

It will be seen from the above extracts that Dr.

Grierson and Sir H. Risley do not take the question deeper than saying that the Dravidians are the aboriginal inhabitants of Southern India The former as a linguist says that the question of the origin and migration of the Dravidian race cannot be solved by the philologist ; and the latter as a leading Indian ethnologist tries to find out some connection between the Dravidians and the Australians; but he is opposed in his conclusion by Sir W. Turner, who has found no cranial connection between the two races. After criticising the other theories concerning the origin and dispersion of the Dravidians, Sir H. Risley comes back to the same ground on which his colleague stood.

According to Hæckel, the Dravidians, the Caucasians, the Basques and the Indo-Germanic races resemble one another in several characteristics, especially in the strong development of the head, which suggests a close relationship between them. Professor Huxley includes them in the smooth-haired division with the North Africans and South Europeans, assuming Australia as the land of their origin. While agreeing with them generally Professors Flower and Lydekker put the Dravidians in the white division of man and observe that in Southern India they are largely mixed with a Negrito element.

This last point is supported by Dr. Topinard who says that the remnants of the black people are at the present day shut up in the mountains and that the ancient inhabitants of the Deccan were identical with the Australians, who probably come from a cross between a leiotrichi race from outside and a Negrito autocthonous race.

Lastly, Dr. Keane thinks that he is able to prove that the Dravidians preceded the Aryan-speaking Hindus and that they are not the true aborigines of the Deccan, they being themselves preceded by dark peoples probably of an aberrant Negrito type.

The question now is ' who are the aborigines ? ' The first scholar who discussed this problem from the stand point of philology was Dr Caldwell; and he arrived at the conclusion that even the lowest castes including the Paraiyas are Dravidians and that they were reduced by conquest to the condition of serfs and jungle tribes. He held also that the Dravidians entered India from the North-West. These two hypotheses of Dr. Caldwell's seem to conflict each other, as it is extremely improbable that a very large body of the so called Dravidians consisting of the dark complexioned Paraiyas, Pallis, Kallas and the several hill and forest tribes could have come from north-western Asia, which has been peopled by the fair complexioned Semitic tribes. There is no philological evidence to show who the aborigines were. Dr. Caldwell does not tell us that there were no people in Southern India before the advent of the Dravidians. If there were no people, the Dravidians should be regarded as the aborigines ; otherwise they are not. He leaves all this an open question. It was, however, taken up by ethnologists, amongst whom Drs. Haddon and Keane are decidedly of opinion that the

Dravidians are not the aborigines, but that they were preceded by a Negrito race akin to the people of the Malay Peninsula and the Australians, the remnants of whom may be found among the jungle and mountain tribes of Southern India. And this is the view accepted by scholars intimately acquainted with the South Indian people, notably by Mr. R. Sewell, who says that ' at some very remote period the aborigines of Southern India were overcome by hordes of Dravidian invaders and driven to the mountains and desert tracts where their descendants are to be found.'

If the Dravidians are not the aborigines, then what was their original home and by what route did they come into Southern India? According to one theory, they were the earliest or the first Aryan settlers. Another theory places their home somewhere in the " submerged Continent " in the Indian Ocean whence they are supposed to have migrated northward to India. According to some, their original home was somewhere in Central Asia and they entered India (a) by the north-east through Assam and Burma, or (b) by both the north-eastern and north-western gates. Yet another makes them immigrants from Western-Asia either by (a) the north-western mountain passes, or direct by (b) the sea route. Each of these may be considered at some length.

The Early Aryan Theory: Like the Celts and Cymri in Ireland, the Tamils were supposed by some to be the representatives of the earliest band of the Aryan immigrants in India. So far as we are aware this theory was never seriously advanced or advocated by any ethnologist. Dr. Caldwell traces some affinity between Tamil and the Indo-European languages, even though their grammar and vocabulary are radically different. Further it was believed for a long time that the megalithic tombs found in some parts of India and England belonged to the ancient Gauls or Celts, which had led to a mistaken idea that the original inhabitants of India, to whom these monuments (dolmens) were attributed, were Aryans akin to the Celts of Europe. But the fact remains that the Tamils themselves called the Aryans *Mlechchas* or foreigners (மிலேச்சராயர். *Ping*, 797) in spite of any social, linguistic and other influences each might have received from the other.

The Lemurian or Sclater's Theory: According to this theory, the original home of the Dravidians was the now submerged continent of Lemuria, which was somewhere in the Indian Ocean before the formation of the Himalaya Mountains. This continent is supposed to have extended from Madagascar in the west to the Malay Archipelago in the east, connecting Southern India with Africa on the one side and Australia on the other. If so, the Dravidians must have entered India from the south long before the submergence of this continent. In support of this theory the following arguments have been adduced:—

Ethnology: The system of totems prevailing

among the half-civilized castes and tribes of India, and the use of the bomerang by the Kallans of South India are found nowhere except among certain Australian tribes; Dr. R. Wallace's description of tree climbing by the Dyaks of Borneo applies equally well to the Kadars of the Anamalai hills; and the chipping of all or some of the incisor teeth by the Kadars and Mala-Vedans may be found among the Jakuns of the Malay Peninsula.

Philology: Linguistic affinities, especially some doubtful resemblance between the numerals in Mundari and in certain Australian dialects have been noticed by Bishop Caldwell and Sir H. Risley. But it may be pointed out that the Munda language is quite independent of the Dravidian tongue and it may be doubted whether the poor similarity in respect of the numerals alone will be enough to establish the theory under discussion.

Geography: The argument under this head has already been stated and more will be said about it further on. However, it may not be out of place to mention here in support of it a tradition which had currency among the early Tamils and has been preserved in their literature. That is,—

பஃறுளி யாற்றுடன் பன்மலே யடுக்கத்துக்
குரிக்கோடுந் தொடுங்கடல் கொள்ள.—*Sil.*

(The cruel sea swallowed up the Pahruli river and the Kumari peak with the chain of mountains).

And the commentary of Adiyârkunallâr on the above lines runs thus: (a) அக்காலத்து அவர் நாட்டுத்

தென்பாலி முகத்திற்கு வடவெல்லே யாகிய பஃறுளி யென்னு
மாற்றிற்கு மிடையே எழுநூற்றுக்காவத வாறும் இவற்றின் நீர்
மலிவாவென மலிந்த ஏழ் தெங்க நாடும் ஏழ் மதுரை நாடும் ஏழ்
முன் பாலே நாடும் ஏழ் பின் பாலே நாடும் ஏழ் குன்ற நாடும் ஏழ்
குணகாரை நாடும் ஏழ் குறும்பனே நாடும் என்னும் இந்த நாற்பத்
தொன்பது நாடும் குமரி கொல்லம முதலிய பன மலே நாடும் காடும்
நதியும் பதியும் தடநீர்க்குமரி வடபெருங்கோட்டின் காறும் கடல்
கொண்டொழிதலாற் குமரியாகிய பௌவமென்றுரைனக—Sil,
198. Cape Comorin is spoken of in early Tamil
literature as a river, a mountain and even as a sea.
And the ancient Tamils, who were acquainted with
the Island of Java and generally with the Eastern
Archipelago, appear to have had some vague notions
about the existence in the remoter past of a vast
country in continuation of Cape Comorin. But, the
geography of this submerged continent as given in
the above excerpt looks very suspicious. And their
tradition about the change of capital of the Pandya
country from South Madura to North Madura (the modern Madura) seems to indicate the Tamilian's theory
of an early migration of some race from the South.

Hunter's Theory: In his account of the
non-Aryan races Dr. W.W. Hunter thinks 'there are
two branches of the Dravidians—the Kolarians and
the Dravidians proper. The former entered India by
the north-east and occupied the northern portion of
the Vindhya table land. There they were conquered
and split into fragments by the main body of Dravidians who found their way into the Punjab through
the north-western passes and pressed forward towards

the south of India'. Yet in another place the same scholar writes as follows : ' It would appear that long before the Aryan invasions, a people speaking a very primitive Central Asian language, had entered by the Sind passes. These were the Dravidas or the Dravidians of later times. Other non-Aryan races from the north pushed them onwards to the present Dravidian country in the south of the peninsula... The extrusion of the Dravidians from northern India had taken place before the arrival of the Aryan-speaking races. The Dravidians are to be distinguished from the later non-Aryan immigrants, whom the Vedic tribes found in possession of the valleys of the Indus and Ganges. These later non-Aryans were in their turn subjugated or pushed out by the Aryan new comers; and they accordingly appear in the Vedic hymns as the 'enemies' (Dasyus) and 'serfs' (Sudras) of the Indo-Aryan settlers. The Dravidian non-Aryans of the south, on the other hand, appear from the first in the Sanskrit as friendly forest folk, the monkey armies who helped the Aryan hero Rama on his march through Southern India against the demon king of Ceylon.'

As Sir H Risley has remarked, the basis of this theory is obscure, and neither philology nor ethnology supports it. It will be shown in the sequel that the Dravidians were not driven from Northern India by later non-Aryan immigrants and that they were not the monkey armies who helped the Aryan hero Rama.

The Mongolian Theory: According to

this theory the Dravidians had lived somewhere on the plateau of Central Asia along with the Mongolians before they entered India by the North-eastern passes from Tibet or Nepal, or by the way of Assam and the Tennaserim provinces. This theory has been very strongly supported by Mr. Kanakasabhai in his *Tamils Eighteen Hundred years ago*. According to him the aboriginal inhabitants of Southern India were the Villavas and Minavas. They were conquered by a highly civilised race called the Nagas who hailed from Central Asia. They were very good weavers and from them the Aryans learnt their alphabet which thenceforth was known as Dêva-Nâgari. He is of opinion that the Maravas, Eyinas, Oliyas, Oviyas, Aruvâlas and the Paratavas mentioned in the Tamil works of the academic period belonged to the above Naga race, and that they had always been hostile to the Dravidian Tamils. Subsequently, these Nagas were in their turn conquered by a Mongolian race called the Tamralittis or the Tamils who had migrated from the Tibetan plateau. They came to the south of India along the east coast in four bands the earliest of whom he considers to be the Mârar who founded the Pandya kingdom. The second were the Thirayar tribe of the Cholas and the third the Vânavar, a mountainous tribe from Bengal, who were the ancestors of the Chera kings ; and the fourth and last, the Kôsar tribe of the Kongu country, In this way he accounts for the origin of the four ancient Tamil kingdoms.

Further on, the same writer observes as follows:—
'As the Tamil immigrants came into Southern India at distant intervals of time and in separate tribes and were fewer in number than the aboriginal Nagas and Dravidians, they had to adopt the ancient Dravidian language and in course of time they modified and refined it into the language now known as Tamil. The peculiar letter *zh* (ழ) which does not exist in the other Dravidian languages was doubtless brought in by the Tamil immigrants. This letter occurs in the Tibetan languages. It indicates most clearly that the primitive home of the Tamil immigrants must have been in the Tibetan plateau'. And in support of his theory that all the Tamils are of Mongolian origin he goes on to say that the existence of very many words in *gn* (ங), *jn* (ஞ) and *n* (ண) in Tamil, Burmese and Chinese, and the similarity between Malayalam and the Mongolian languages, clearly confirm the North-eastern or the Mongolian origin of the Tamil people.

In attributing a Mongolian origin to the Tamils Mr. Kanakasabhai relies partly on literary evidence and partly on the similarity of sound in certain words. He seems to misinterpret some passages in Tamil works and distorts current traditions so as to support his preconceived theories; and it would be fallacious and unwarrantable to draw any inference from words like Tamra-litti and Tamil, Mrânmar and Maran, Kôshan or Kushan and Kosar &c., which are similar only in sound. He has entirely ignored the testimony of archæology, philology and anthropology. It is necessary to examine his statements more fully.

He says the Villavâs and the Minavās were the aborigines of Southern India, citing the Bhils and the Minas of Central India in support of his assertion. Villavan is a bowman and Minavan is a fisher-man and these are some of the titles applied honorifically to the Chera and Pandya kings. There is no caste or tribe bearing either name in the Tamil districts. Further, the Bhils and the Minas do not speak a Dravidian language. How they were ethnically related to the Tamils and to what race they had belonged he quietly passes over.

Again, he says that the Nagis were a highly civilised aboriginal race from whom the Aryans learnt their Sanskrit alphabet. Before entering upon any criticism of these statements we shall enquire who these Nagas were. There were Nagas in Northern India as well as in Southern India. About the former Capt. Forbes writes as follows in his *Languages of Further India*:—' It is now acknowledged that prior to the irruption of the Aryans into India from the west across the Indus, the valley of the Ganges was occupied by various races of Turanian origin. The Aryans came in contact with two races : one of fierce black degraded savage tribes whom they called *Asuras, Rakshasas, &c.;* the other a people who lived in cities and possessed wealth, and whose women were fair, whom they termed the Nagas or serpent worshippers, and who doubtless belonged to the great Takshak or 'Serpent race' of Scythia. Under the continued pressure of the advancing Aryan invaders, these Turanian tribes were driven back carrying before them in their turn the feeble and scattered remnants of the black aboriginal race, who were either exterminated or found a last refuge in the most inaccessible forests and mountains' Nothing definite is known about the South Indian Nagas except what is mentioned in the Manimekalai and the occasional references in the Pattuppattu and in the inscriptions. In the early Buddhistic Tamil literature the name of this tribe occurs very often.

நாக நன்னுட்டு நானூறு யோசனை
வியன்பாதலத்து வீழ்ந்து கெடும்தும்.—*Sil.*

(The four hundred *yojanas* of the good country of the Nagas will be destroyed by sinking into the broad nether world).

நக்க சாரணா நாகா வாழ்மலை —*Sil.*

(The mountain inhabited by the naked nomads and the Nagas.)

The Naga Nadu or the country of the Nagas is described as a vast island situated in the east or rather south-east of the Tamil country ; and the Nagas were a half civilised tribe, some of whom were naked nomads while others were cannibals. They spoke a language not understood by the Tamil people. From this description it might be easily surmised that the country referred to was Ceylon and that the people were the Veddas or Vedas. Nîlan and Nâgan were names quite familiar among the Kallan and the Vedan or Vettuvar tribes of the Tamil districts. Nilan was the name of the Vaishnava saint Tirumangai Alvar, a Kalla by caste, and of the donor of the fine cloth to Ay a hill king ;

நீல நாகன நல்கிய கலிங்கம் —S.P.P.

(The fine cloth presented by Nilan of the Naga tribe) Nagan was the name of a Veda chieftain and the father of the famous Saiva saint Kannappa Nayanar. From these it will be seen that the Nagas were not so highly civilised as is represented by Mr. Kanakasabhai ; but doubtless they were a martial tribe of hunters from whom, as we have shown elsewhere, the Pandyas, the Cholas and the Pallavas recruited their armies. It seems, therefore, that 'Naga' was the name given by the Aryans to any aboriginal tribe in Southern India and Ceylon, and it might be remarked that the Nagas of the south were distinct from the Nagas of Northern India who are described by Capt. Forbes in the above extract. The South Indian Nagas were probably the aborigines, while their North Indian namesake were Turanian or Scythian immigrants from Central Asia belonging probably to the Mongolian race.

As regards the origin of the Nagari alphabet the conclusions of Dr. G. Buhler and other eminent authorities on Indian Paleography are certainly opposed to the bold assertion of Mr. Kanakasabhai that the Aryans learnt it from the Nagas. The word Nagari' is derived from *nagar*, a city, but not from

'Naga' the name of a tribe, as he seems to think and the Nagari or the Deva Nagari was the alphabet formerly used by the Aryan city folk.

Again, Mr. Kanakasabhai says the Tamil immigrants were a Mongolian tribe quite independent of the 'aboriginal Nagas and Dravidians'; and in support of his theory he cites the existence of the peculiar letter ழ (zh) in Tamil and in some of the Tibetan languages, but which 'does not occur in the other Dravidian or Sanskrit languages.' Eliminating the Nagas and the Mongolian tribe of Tamils from the population of the Tamil districts, one would be anxious to know who these Dravidians were. Were they his Villavar and Minavar aborigines or some other tribe which had its existence only in his imagination? Then, adverting to the peculiar letter ழ we must say that it did exist in the ancient Kanarese and Telugu languages though it had disappeared owing to the continuous Sanskrit influence for centuries. In modern Kanarese and Telugu it has been dropped or its place taken by ள (l) and ட (d). As Dr. Caldwell has rightly said this letter has sometimes the sound of ள (l) or ய (y) or is even omitted as in modern colloquial Tamil. And it might further be remarked that ழ which has the sound approaching the English zh (as in pleasure) or the French J (as in J'ai) may be found in some of the languages of the Uralo-Altaic group. The mere fact therefore that it is found to prevail equally in Tamil and throughout the aboriginal Indo-Chinese

THE TAMIL PEOPLE 31

tongues of the Himalayas and Tibet is by itself insufficient to establish an ethnic relationship between the two races, especially when there are so many and so strong arguments to the contrary. Further, there is not the slightest affinity between Tamil and the Tibetan tongues, nor the least resemblance in the physical characters of the Tamil people and the Mongolian tribes.

We have already stated that 'Tamra-litti' had no connection with 'Tamil'. Kosar seems to have been a hill tribe more or less akin to the Koyas and the Eyinas (Paraiya) of the Tamil districts, which name is still preserved in the word Koyan-puttur (Coimbatore) meaning the new village of the Koya or Kosar sribe. It is not connected with that powerful and civilized race, the Cushites of antiquity, as Mr. Kanakasabhai seems to think, but rather allied to the Telugu speaking hill tribe of that name. Maran is he who barters; it is a title assumed by the Pandya kings on account of their earliest commercial relationship with the Egyptians, Chaldeans, ancient Arabs and other Western nations. The traditional origin of this word from *Maru* (to beat with a tamarind switch) given in the Madura Tiruvilayadal-Purana, in order to connect it with one of the Siva's 'sacred sports'

மாருன மாறனெனமுகரும் பெயர் பெற்றுன்,

betrays the imaginative flights of the Brahman Purana writers. And we may say that this word Mâran has greater connection with the Hebrew *Mara* to sell or barter, than with the Burmese Mrân-mar.

The weightiest of all objections to Mr. Kanakasabhai's theory seems to come from the pen of Sir H. Risley. He says 'It is extremely improbable that a large body of a very black and conspicuously long-headed type should have come from the one region of the earth which is peopled exclusively by races with broad heads and yellow complexion. With this we may dismiss the theory which assigns a trans-Himalayan origin to the Dravidians.' This objection seems sound, although it is too much to admit that all the inhabitants of Southern India belonged to a ' very black and conspicuously long headed-type' of the human species.

Of the several theories set forth above, those of the Early-Aryan and Mongolian origins may be dismissed as altogether untenable, as they are supported neither by tradition nor by science. The feeble support which Sir William Hunter's theory has received at the hands of scholars in spite of his magic name shows what little substratum of probability there is under it. The Lemurian theory can cover, if at all, only a very small part of the problem and apply only to the primitive aboriginal sections of the people. The bold conclusions of Mr. Kanakasabhai seem to be based on fanciful philological musings and a feverish desire to show originality. In the following chapter an attempt will be made to collect together a few facts and ideas that may constitute what appears to be a more probable solution of this interesting question.

III

THE TAMIL PEOPLE.—*(continued)*.

The one other theory that remains to be considered is that a large number of emigrants from Western Asia came into the country either by a direct sea-route or by land through the Western mountain passes, and became superimposed on the aboriginal stock, probably of the Lemurian origin, before there was any Aryan influence in South India. The original home of these people should have been Assyria and Asia Minor and they should have lived with the ancient Accadians and other Turanian races before they migrated to India through the Northwestern passes. This theory seems to have much to be said in its favour, although apparent objections have been raised against it by Mr. D. Bray, Sir H. Risley and other scholars. We shall as in the case of the other theories collect together all the arguments regarding it under the three main heads of philology, archæology and literary tradition.

Linguistic evidence: Dr. Caldwell thinks that

the Dravidian languages may be affiliated morphologically to the Uralo-Altaic or the Finno-Tartaric family of tongues which comprise the Samoyedic, the Finnic, the Turkic, the Mongolian and the Tungusian groups. To the same family belonged Accadian —a fully developed language spoken by a highly civilised Turanian race that had lived in Assyria, Chaldea, Susiana and Media. The learned bishop after indicating the points of resemblance in grammar and vocabulary between Accadian and the Dravidian languages, comes to the conclusion 'that the Dravidian race though resident in India from a period long prior to the commencement of the Christian era, originated in the Central tracts of Asia—the seed plot of nations—and that from thence after parting company with the Aryans and the Ugro-Turanians, and leaving a colony in Baluchistan, they entered India by way of the Indus.'

In the language of the Behistun tablets (Accadian) we find largely used the consonants of the cerebral class, t, d, n; the genetive termination a அ as in *na, nuna,* or *inna,* and dative *ikka* or *ikki* (Tam. கு, *ku*); ordinals ending in *in* (Tam. ஆம் *am*); and the second person pronoun *ni, nin* (Tam. நீ, நின்). There are other points of linguistic affinity between Tamil and the Altaic languages and the reader is referred to Dr. Caldwell's invaluable *Comparative Grammar* which ought to be in the hands of every student of the Dravidian languages. The connection of the Tamils with Asia Minor is further confirmed by the identity in form and meaning of several important words in the Semitic, Altaic and Tamil languages. For example,—Tam. *akkan*, Ugr. *iggen*=elder sister ; Tam. *annai*, Fin. *anya*=mother; Tam. *appan*, Fin. *appi*, Hung. *ipa*=father ; Tam. *amma*, Samoy. *amma*=mother ; Tam. *attal*, Fin. *atta*=mother : Tam. *am*, Vogoul. *am*=yes ; Tam. *auvai*, Mordvin. *ava*=mother ; Tam. *kattu*, Hung. *kot*=to bind, to tie ; Tam. *kel*, Fin *kul-en*=to hear ; Tam. *ko*, Behistun tablets, *ko*=a king ; Tam. *kozhi*, Vogoul. *kore*=a cock; Tam. *ti*, Samoy. *ti*=fire ; Tam. *tol*, Vogoul. *towl*=skin ; Tam. *jnayiru* (the sun) Hung. *nyar*=summer; Tam. *pidi*,Fin. *pidan*=to catch; Tam. *pira*, Fin *pera*=after; Tam *manai*, Sam. *man*=a house; Tam. *mar-am*, Lap. *mor*=a tree ; Tam. *velich-am*, Hung. *velega*=light &c. We may trace similar affinities with Turkic languages also, both in grammar and vocabulary.

Of course, we must bear in mind the axiom that no account should be taken of mere resemblances in sound and meaning of words for linguistic considerations ; but in the above case such coincidences do not seem to be so purely accidental as to vitiate our conclusions, as there are other collateral evidences to strengthen them, notwithstanding the opinion of M. Hovelacque that ' Dr. Caldwell has not been more successful with his assumed Dravidian affinity.'

It was for a long time supposed that the cradle of the Aryans was somewhere in Central Asia,which was likewise considered the original home of the Dravidians. Dr. Caldwell must have held this view when he said that the Dravidians ' after parting company with the Aryans in the Central tracts of Asia entered India by the way of the Indus'. He has also proved some Dravidian influence in Sanskrit and *vice versa* in order to support his theory that the Dravidians and Aryans lived together before their dispersal from Central Asia. But scholars are now agreed that the original home of the Aryans was somewhere in the Scandinavian Peninsula and that no traces of any Aryan influence can be found in the Accadian language.

And this must afford us a clue to determine the approximate date of the Dravidian migration to Southern India. As pointed out by Dr. Caldwell, the Dravidian languages have had some influence from the Aryan languages It should have taken place only after the Dravidians had left Central Asia and settled in the Punjab, before the arrival of the Aryans. The migration of the Tamils to Southern India should have taken place long after their sojourn in Upper India with the Sanskrit-speaking Aryans; and it will be shown in the sequel that the Dravidians had separated from the Aryans in the trans-Vindhyan Aryavarta sometime after the Mahabharata war about the eleventh century B. C.

The North-Western origin and migration of the Dravidians receive an additional support and confirmation from the Brahui language which has been the home speech of a Dravidian tribe in Baluchistan. The latest verdict on that language is that of Mr. Denys Bray, I. C. S. In his monograph on that tongue he says that 'it is sprung from the same source as the Dravidian language group; it has freely absorbed the alien vocabulary of Persian, Baluchi, Sindhi and other neighbouring languages; but in spite of their inroads its grammatical system has preserved a sturdy existence.' Mr. Bray goes on to give us a word of advice so that we may not identify the Brahuis with the Dravidians. He says ' We can no longer argue with the child-like faith of our forefathers from philology to ethnology, and assume without further ado that this race of Baluchistan whose speech is akin to the languages of the Dravidian peoples of Southern India is itself Dravidian ; that it is in fact the rear guard or the van-guard according to the particular theory we may affect of a Dravidian migration from North to South or from South to North.'

The term ' Dravidian ' means one thing for an ethnologist and another for a philologist. Sometimes both are confounded. The peoples whose home-speech at the present day is a Dravidian language, are not necessarily Dravidians by race ; and there are non-Aryan tribes who speak an Aryan language. To avoid further confusion and misapprehension which have unnecessarily led to conflicting theories, it must be said once for all here that the term 'Dravidian ' does not include the very black hill and forest tribes, the low castes of Southern India who had migrated thither from the submerged continent and the Tamil speaking Aryan Brahmans, but only the high class Tamils—the Vellalas and the Chetti castes —who were more or less brown complexioned, fairly civilized, of good physique and of martial habits like the Semitic or Iranian tribes of North-Western Asia. These people, we presume, are now represented by the Todas of the Nilgiris, though there had been on the plains a complete fusion with the aboriginal races and the later Aryan immigrants, as the proverb says,

கள்ளன் மறவன் கனத்ததேதா ரகம்படியன்
மென்ன மென்ன வெள்ளாளன்.

(A Kallan became a Maravan, the Maravan became an Agambadiyan, and the Agambadiyan became a Vellalan.)

Further, the mental and physical characteristics of the Brahuis as described by Mr. D. Bray agree so well with those found in the literature of the early Dravidian Tamils, that one will be justified in regarding both as ethnically related to each other. Thus, we see that this theory is supported by philological as well as ethnological evidences, and we cannot observe any contradiction between them. The Brahuis must, therefore, be regarded as the rear guard in the Dravidian migration and the Todas its van-guard. We may say that the connection between Brahui and Tamil is so great that no other inference than that of the ethnic relationship between the two peoples seems possible, in spite of Dr. Grierson's assertion that the Brahuis do not belong to the Dravidian race but are anthropologically Iranians. And the existence of such words as *ba*, வாய், vay, (mouth) ; *pu*, புழு, puzhu, (worm) ; *bei*, வை, vai (straw); *khal*, கல், kal, (stone) ; *bil*, வில், vil (bow); *khan*, கண், kan, (eye) ; *mus*, மூக்கு, mukku (nose); *telh*, தேள், tel (scorpion) ; *palh*, பால், pal, (milk); *tugh*, தூங்கு, tungu, (sleep); *gal*, கள், kal- (plural termination) ; *irat*, இரண்டு, irandu, (two) ; &c., and the sentences like, *I mumto bareva*, நான் நும் போடு வருவேன், irresistably lead us to the same conclusion.

Arachæological Evidence : 'The Indian oblong sarcophagi,' says Mr. V. A. Smith, 'discovered at various places in the Madras districts of Chingleput, Nellore, North and South Arcot, are practically identical in form with similar objects found at Gehrareh near Bagdad. This fact is one of many indications connecting archaic Indian civilization with that of Babylonia and Assyria, which suggest tempting ethnological speculations.' The author of *Manimekalai* enumerates five methods of disposing of the dead as prevalent in his days among the Tamils, that is about the third century A. D. They were (1) cremation, (2) exposure in an open place to be eaten by jackals and vultures, (3) burial, (4) stuffing the corpse in natural pits, and (5) covering it up with big earthen jars, (தாழி).

சுடுவோர் நிடுவோர் தொடுகுழிப படுபோர்
தாழ்வயி னடைபோர் தாழியிற் கவிப்போர்.

So far as we know, the only early nation who exposed the dead in this fashion was the ancient

Persians. The Tamil Dravidian, in his march towards India, must have lived in Persia, and moved with Persians sufficiently long to adopt the above custom.

Again some of the Tamil districts abound with peculiar tomb stones called 'Virakkals.' They were usually set up on the graves of warriors that were slain in battle, chiefly in skirmishes following cattle raids.[1] The names of the deceased soldiers and their exploits are found inscribed on the stones, which were decorated with garlands of peacock feathers or some kind of red flowers. Usually small canopies were put up over them.

(1) உடம்பே...
அம்பொடு துளங்கி யாண்டொழிந் தன்றே
புயரிசை வெறுப்பத தோன்றி பெயரே
மடஞ்சான் மஞ்ஞை பணிமயிர் குட்டி
யிடமபிறர் கொள்ளாச் சிறுவழிப்
படஞ்செய் பநதர்க் கன்மிசை யதுவே.—*Pur.*

(2) பட்டோர் பெயரு மாற்றலு மெழுதி
நட்டகல்லு மூதூர் நத்தழும்.—*Cher.*

We give below a specimen of such an epitaph dated 936 A. D. 'Prosperity! In the twenty-ninth year of King Parakesari Varman who conquered Madura when cattle were lifted at Muttukur by the Perumanadigal, Vadunavaran Varadan Tandan having recovered them fell.'

A careful study of the Purapporul Venbamalai will doubtless convince the reader that the ancient

1. In ancient India the lifting of the enemy's cattle usually announced the commencement of hostilities between neighbouring tribes or provinces.

THE TAMIL PEOPLE

Tamils were, like the Assyrians and Babylonians, a ferocious race of hunters and soldiers armed with bows and lances making war for the mere pleasure of slaying, ravaging and pillaging. Like them the Tamils believed in evil spirits, astrology, omens and sorcery. They cared little for death. The following quotations from the above work will bear testimony to the characteristics of that virile race:—

(1) கூடலர் குடர் மாலைகுட்டி
வேறிரித்த விரும்பியா டின்று

(2) சேராதார் வளநாட்டைக
கூரா கொளியன்று.

(3) கூடார் முனைகொள்ளே சாற்றி
வீடறக் கவாந்த வீனெமொழிந்தன்று.

(4) முடித் தலைய பெபிற் பிடர்த்தலைத்தாழித்
தொடித தோட்டு பெப்பிற் றுழைஇய ஆன்சோறு
மறபேய் வாலுவன் வயினெறிந் தூட்ட.—*Sil.*

(1) Garlanded with the entrails of enemies they danced with lances held in their hands topside down. (2) They set fire to the fertile villages of their enemies; (3) and plundered their country and demolished their houses. (4) The devil's cook distributed the food boiled with the flesh of the slain, on the hearth of the crowned heads of fallen kings and stirred with the ladle of the bangled arm.

With these compare some passages from the Assyrian stories of compaigns. 'I had some of them flayed in my presence and had the wall hung with their skins. I arranged their heads like crowns and their transfixed bodies in the form of garlands ... I raised mountains of bodies before his gates. All his villages I destroyed, desolated, burnt ; I made the country desert. I changed it into hills and mounds of debris'.

And yet the early Dravidians are considered by Dr. Caldwell as the framers of the best moral codes, and by the new school of non-Aryan Tamil scholars as the inventors, independent of the slightest Aryan or other influence, of grammar, philosophy, theology and in fact of every science and art. It is enough for the present to remind them that the earliest grammarians of Tamil were Brahmans, their first spiritual instructors were Brahmans, and their first teachers of philosophy were also Brahmans.

The first Tamil grammarian, an Aryan sage, found the customs, polity and even thought of the ancient Tamils so completely at variance with those of the Aryans that he thought it prudent to leave a description of them for the information of their posterity ; and with a view, no doubt, to satisfy the incorrigible and refractory early Tamils and to give them a permanency at least in books, he codified and varnished them with a thin veneer of Aryan religious sanction. These now form the subject matter of the third book of the Tolkapyam.

We have said that the Vellalas were pure Dravidians and that they were a military and dominant tribe. If so, one would naturally ask ' How could the ancestors of peaceful cultivators be a warlike race ?' The term ' Vellalan ' is ordinarily derived by some from *vellam*, flood, and *alan*, a ruler, hence a cultivator; while others derive it from *vellammai*, cultivation. Neither seems to be quite correct, for the right form of this word is Vellân and it occurs in early Tamil inscriptions. In Tamil the words allied to it are *vel*, the god of war; *vel-ir*, the ruling class among the ancient Tamils; *vel-akkaran*, a foot-soldier (now obsolete, but found in the inscriptions of Raja-raja Chola); *vel*, help; *vel-anmai*, truth; and *Vell-alan*, a cultivator. The last two are rarely to be met with in early Tamil literature, while in the others we hear the sound of the war-drum. Compare the word *padai* (படை) which meant an army, a weapon of war and a plough; and to distinguish 'a plough' from the other implements it is now called உழுபடை or a ploughing weapon. And it may be pointed out that all the modern cultivating castes—the Bants, the Nayars, the Pallis and the Telagas or Velamas—were formerly martial tribes like the ancient Vellalas.

Literary evidence: (a) The artificial irrigation of the soil by constructing large reservoirs and canals on an extensive scale was encouraged by the early Tamils.

நிலனனி மருங்கி னீர்நிலைபெருகத்
தட்டோரம் மவிவட்டட்டோரா.—*Pur.*

(Verily, he who has turned the bent (low) land into a reservoir to arrest the flow of the running water is one who has established a name in this world.)

This system, says Meadows Taylor, 'existed probably in no other country except Babylon.'

(*b*) The kings of all the three Tamil dynasties traced their ancestry to one or the other of the North-Indian kings. The Pandyas claimed to be an offshoot of the Pandavas and styled themselves the 'Panchavans'; and the Cholas called themselves 'Sembyan' or the descendants of Sibi, a North-Indian Emperor. These kings are said to have assisted the Pandavas in the Great War.

பெருஞ் சோறுபயந்த பெருநாளிருக்கைப
பூம்புனற் பழைய புகார்நகர் வேந்தன்.—*Sil.*

(The king of Pukar—Cauveripatnam—the city of lovely gardens and sweet water, who from on his throne of audience distributed the 'great food')

ஈரைம பதின்மரும்பொருதுகள த்தொழியப்
பெருஞ்சோற்று மிகுபதமவரையாதுகொடுத்தோய்.—*Pur.*

(Thou art the king that gave the 'great food' liberally at the battle field till the 'one hundred' fell.)

This they could have done only when they were reigning over small districts somewhere in Upper India; because, it would be improbable and impossible that the Cheras, Cholas and Pandyas, had they actually been in the south at the time of the war, could have sent their large contingents all the way to Kurukshetra in the Punjab through impenetrable forests, rivers and mountains. And in support of the above statement we may quote an extract from Mr. J. W. M'Crindle's *Ancient India.* 'The kingdom of Pandion, which was situated on the southern extremity of the Indian peninsula, was founded by an Aryan race whose ancestors had occupied the regions watered by the Jamna. This may be inferred both from the name of the king and that of his capital which was called *Madura* after the celebrated city which adorned of old, as it does still the banks of that great tributary of the Ganges.' The kingdom is mentioned by Pliny (A. D. 77), by the author of the *Periplus of the Erythrœan Sea* and by Ptolemy.

'In his commentary on the prefatory *sutra* to the Tolkapyam, Nacchinarkiniyar describes a tradition relating to the migration of the Dravidian race, which is as follows:—The sage Agastya repaired to Dwarka (*Tam.* Tuvarapati) and, taking with him eighteen kings of the line of Sri Krishna, eighteen families of Vels or Velirs and others, moved to the South with the Aruvalar1 tribes. There, he had all the forests cleared and built up kingdoms settling therein all the people he had brought with him. One of the principalities thus founded by him was Dwarasamudram in the Mysore State. Kapilar, a Brahman poet probably of the second century A. D., addresses the reigning

1. The Aruvalars seem to have been the ancestors of the Kurumbas. They were not liked by the Velirs or Vellalas as will be evident from the bad meanings which these Tamil words acquired in later times and from the following quotation.

வடக ரருவாளா வானகரு நாடா
சுடுகாடு பேயெருமை யென்றிவையாறும்
குறுகா றறிவு டையார்.

(The wise will not approach the Vadugas, Aruvalas, Karnatas the burning ground, the devil and the buffalo.)

chief of this place as the forty-ninth in descent from the original founder of that dynasty.

உவரா வீகைத் துவரை யாண்டு
நாற்பத் தொன்பது வழிமுறை வநத
வேளிருள் வேளே.—*Pur.*

(O! The Velir of Velirs that governed Tuvarai—Dwarasamudram—for forty-nine generations.)

Allowing the usual twenty-five years for each generation, the above kingdom must have been established about B.C. 1075; and this may be assumed as the probable date of the migration of the Tamils to Southern India.

Within the last fifteen years a new school of Tamil scholars has come into being, consisting mainly of admirers and castemen of the late lamented professor and antiquary, Mr. Sundaram Pillai of Trivandram. Their object has been to disown and to disprove any trace of indebtedness to the Aryans, to exalt the civilisation of the ancient Tamils, to distort in the name of historic research the current traditions and literature, and to pooh-pooh the views of former scholars, which support the Brahmanization of the Tamil race. They would not even admit that the early Tamils had ever lived in Upper-India by the side of the Aryans. One of them writes thus: 'It is my view that Tamilians were not derived directly from the settlers in the north during the Indian Vedic days, and that the Tamilians did not immigrate from the north of India to the south by choice or by force; that they are not to be identified with the people whom the Vedic settlers encountered and called Dasyus ; that if they did settle in the south from outside, they did so by *the sea and not by land and through mountain ranges*, and that they came from Assyria and Asia-Minor, the oldest seat of ancient civilisation. I further think, that once they entered India by the Western sea-gate they spread themselves rapidly over the whole of South India up to the Dandakaranya and the Vindhya, which at that time must have been impassable, and that they developed their letters, and arts, and sciences, and law, and government which at the time they came in contact with the Northern settlers must have been in a sense perfect'.

If the above theory be correct, the migration must have taken place earlier than the twelfth century B. C.; and to accomplish such a huge undertaking the Dravidian Tamils must have had an immense navy. But we know of no ancient nation who had it at this remote period.[1] The Egyptians were an agricultural race ; the Assyrians were mountaineers; the Hebrews were shepherds and the Phœnicians alone, but of later date, were a maritime race of merchants. As a matter of fact we know that these last, the Ionians and the Romans and very lately

1. Prof. Sayce believes he has proved the existence of commerce by sea between India and Babylon so early as 3000 B.C by the finding of Indian teak in the ruins of Ur. But this conclusion is not accepted by all scholars. Mr. J. Kennedy has decisively shown in a very learned paper that he can find no archæological or literary evidence for a maritime trade between India and Babylon prior to the seventh century B. C.

the Arabs had commercial intercourse with the early Tamils. Their ships came to South India with gold, wine and lamps and bartered them with the Tamils for pepper, pearl, peacock-feathers and *agil* as the following quotations will show:—

யவனர் தந்த விண மாணன கலம்
பொன் ஒறுடிவந்து கறியொடு பெயரும்.—*Akam.*

(The stately vessel of the Yavanas (Ionians) will come with gold and go with pepper.)

யவன ரியற்றிய விண மாண் டாவை
கையேந்த கனிறைய நெய்சொரிந்து —*Ned.*

(Poured oil in the lamp held by the statue made by the Yavanas.)

யவனா
நன்கலம் தந்த தண்கமழ் தேறல்.—*Pur.*

(The cool sweet-scented wine brought by the fine ship of the Yavanas.)

When their acquaintance with the Tamils had become closer the Romans began to settle in some of the principal Tamil cities. A Pandya king in return sent an embassy to Augustus Cæsar in B. C. 20. He might have been Mudu-Kudumi-Peruvaludi whose name occurs both in Tamil literature and inscriptions. The Roman settlement in Madura probably continued till about 450 A. D. There was also a Greek colony at Kaveripatam in the second century A. D.

The words used in ancient Tamil literature to denote the 'ship' are *navay* (நாவாய்), Gr. Naus, Lat. Navis, Skt. Nav, and *kalam* or *kalan* (கலம்), Ion.

Kalon (a wooden house) These are not Tamil words,[1] and they might have been borrowed from the Ionians or Greeks who had, as already stated, commercial relationship with the ancient Tamils. We know that foreign nations carried on trade with the Tamils and settled in the Tamil countries; but we do not find it said anywhere that the Tamils ever visited any foreign countries for the purpose of commerce, though in later times they had ships and were experts in navigation. Their voyages, however, seem to have been confined mostly to the East as the following extract will show :—

வடமலை பிறந்த மணியும் பொன்னுங்
குடமலை பிறந்த வாரமு மகிழுங்
தென்கடல் முத்துவ குணகடற் றுகிருவ
கங்கை வாரியுங காவிரிப பயனு
மீழத்துணவுங காழகத் தாக்கமும.—*Pat.*

(The gold and gems of the Himalayas, the sandal and *agil* of the Western ghats, the pearls of the Southern ocean, the coral of the Eastern sea, the productions of the Ganges and the Cauvery, the eatables from Ceylon and the spices from Burmah).

As Mr. Vincent Smith has rightly observed, 'Ancient Tamil literature and the Greek and Roman authors prove that in the first two centuries of the Christian era the ports on the Coromandal or Chola

1. The Tamils had words to signify a boat, but not a ship; *Palai, padaku* (Gael. *bala*), *punai,* a catamaran, *tollai* (that which is made hollow), &c. The Tamil lexicographers made no distinction between a raft, a boat and a merchantman.

coast enjoyed the benefits of active commerce with both the West and East. The Chola fleets did not confine themselves to coasting voyages, but boldly crossed the Bay of Bengal to the mouths of the Ganges and the Irrawaddy, and the Indian Ocean to the islands of the Malay Archipelago'. Dr. Caldwell thinks that the ancient Tamils 'had no foreign commerce, no acquaintance with any people beyond the sea except Ceylon, and no word expressive of geographical idea of island or continent'. We might say that Dr. Caldwell was not altogether just in his estimate of the ancient Tamil civilisation. But he might be correct with regard to the Tamils before they had come in contact with the Aryans either in Upper India or in the extreme South.

In this connection it may be observed that most of the capitals of the ancient Tamil kingdoms were inland towns, a fact which militates against the theory of their having been of a daring sea-faring stock.

Again if we believe in the theory that the Tamils migrated to Southern India by the sea and not by the land, how are we to account for the location of the Brahuis—a tribe allied to the Dravidian Tamils—in Baluchistan? And how are we to explain the Aryan elements in the early Tamil language? History and traditions are against it, philology is against it, and in fact everything is against it.

Some glimpses of the Aryan conquest and

colonization of Southern India will be obtained from the two great Sanskrit epics the Mahabharata and the Ramayana. The evidence furnished by them on minute details is, however, extremely questionable. Neither of them has come down to us in its original form. Additions, interpolations and alterations seem to have been made from time to time to the Mahabharata till the tenth or eleventh century A.D., and to the Ramayana at least up to the second or third century, which have given rise to many contradictory statements and anachronisms. It would, therefore, be hazardous to start any theories from incoherent statements, or to cite them in support of one's preconceived theories concerning the civilisation of the aboriginal tribes and the geography of the tracts they inhabited, as has been done recently by the members of the New School of Tamil Research whose love of their language is more than their regard for historic truth.

The present writer cannot pretend to have the boldness or the requisite scholarship in Sanskrit to derive the name 'Rama' from Tam. *Irul*, darkness, to say that the Rakshasas and Vanaras were more civilized than the Aryans, to call the ancient Tamilians Asuras, to assert that Svayamvaram was the form of marriage prevalent among the aborigines, and to proclaim from the house-tops that 'the Rakshasas were monotheists' and worshipped Siva and Siva only with incense and flowers ; while ' the Aryan worship of natural phenomena and their unmeaning sacrifices appeared to the philosophical Tamils—Rakshasas of the Ramayana—to be sacreligious.'

Leaving these theories severely alone, it is our duty in the interest of scientific truth to set forth what we have gleaned from the two great epics and the writings of the ancient Tamils.

Of the two grand epics, the Mahabharata alone seems to have been widely known and regarded, in the Tamil country, as a sacred work Some of the Mahabharata stories and the divine personages mentioned therein like Sri Krishna and Bala Rama occur very often in the early Tamil works of the academic period prior to the fifth or sixth century A. D. On the other hand, the Ramayana was almost unknown to them, except probably to certain Tamil poets of that period as a quasi-historical composition. The author of Silappadikaram (A.D. 220) while describing Kaveripatam, after it was left by Kovalan and Kannaki, compares it to Ayodhya after its desertion by Rama and Sita as in the following lines :—

அரசேதஞ்சமென் றருநகா னனடைந்த
வருந்திறல் பிரிந்த வயோத்தி போல.

And Ravana is mentioned by the author of Madurai Kanji (A. D. 150). He says that owing to the diplomatic skill of Agastya, the royal priest of the Pandya, their Tamil country was saved from being conquered by Ravana.

தென்னவற பெயரிய துன்னருநதபயிற்
றொரூன் முது கடவுட் பின்னர் மேய
வரைத்தா முருவிப்பொருப்பிற் பொருந.

Again both the names Rama and Ravana occur in an example for the logical method of immediate inference cited by Sattanar.

மீட்சியென்ப திராமன் வென்று எனன
மாட்சியி விராவணன் ஏேற்றமை மதித்தல்.—*Mani.*

(To infer that 'Ravana suffered defeat' from the proposition ' Rama won ' is what is called *mitchi*)

Thus we see that Ravana was not a Tamilian and that he and Rama had been regarded by the early Tamils as pure historical personages, till we come to the Puranic period, when the Vaishnava Saints (ஆழ்வார்) following the impetus given to Brahmanism in Upper India, began to deify Rama as an Avatar of Vishnu. And the Ramayana of Valmiki, in which Rama is described as a great national hero—a typical Aryan of noble, pure and sublime life worthy of divine respect—appears to have been recast with vast additions in imitation of the Mahabharata, probably, during the third or fourth century A.D. Even so late as the seventh century, the Ramayana did not secure such a hold on the Tamil mind as the Mahabharata. The following extract from the Kuram grant of the Pallava king Paramesvara Varma I.(A D. 660) will be to the point :

இமமண்டகத்தே பாரதம் வாசிபபதற்குஒருபகு.

(One share to the reader of the Mahabharata at this mantapam.)

And it was one century later that the first Tamil translation of the Mahabharatha was made by

Perum-Devanar, the celebrated compiler of the Eight Tamil anthologies. The Ramayana was translated for the first time in A. D. 1185 by the immortal Kamban.

Now the Ramayana is a quasi-historical epic poem which describes the migration of the Aryans to Southern India prior to the fifteenth century B.C. It gives an account of the tribes that were living in the various regions of the Indian Peninsula. The description of the Pandya and other countries given in the modern recensions of that epic are only later interpolations. The Tamil kingdoms did not come into existence during Rama's time. These provinces were then dense forests inhabited by wild and savage tribes, whom Valmiki called Rakshasas, Yakshas and Vanaras (monkeys) on account of their strange, unfamiliar non-Aryan physical features and customs. In later Sanskrit works the Asuras are sometimes confounded with the Rakshasas; but it is not correct, as the Asuras were a section of the fair-skinned Aryans, now represented by the Parsis, while the Rakshasas were a dark-complexioned cannibal race of hunters and fisherman like the modern Andamaners and the Australian aborigines. The Yakshas of Ceylon and the Rakshasas of Southern India belonged to the same race of people called Yatudanas in the Vedas and Nagas in the later Buddhistic and other literatures. They might have been the ancestors of the modern Paraiyas, Pallas, Idaiyas, Maravas and Kallas. It will be interesting to note that one of the

Marava chieftains under a Pandya king was called Iyakkan or Yakshan.

They were demonolators and hated Siva, an Aryan deity, and their king Ravana who treated Siva with contempt had his ten heads cut off by that deity.

(b) வானெயிநிலநக நக்குவளர் சயிலாயநதன்னே
யாளவலி சருதிச்சென்ற வரககணே வரைக்கீழுன்று
தோளொடு பததுவாயுந் தொலேசததட னழுநதலுன்றி
யாண்மையும் வலியுந் தீர்பபாரவா வலம்புரவளுரே.

The custom of carrying off women for wives was prevalent among them, hence this kind of marriage has come to be known as Rakshasam. This form of sexual alliance which is very common among some of the modern hill tribes and largely practised by the ancient Tamils has left its trace in the social rules called the 'begging for a girl' மட்டாநாஞ்சி and 'refusal to give a girl' மசண்மறுதத பொழிதல். They are explained in the Venbamalai thus:—

எநதிழை யாட்டரு கென்னும
வேநதனேடு வேறு நின்றனறு.

(To see an enemy in the king who begged the gift of a jewelled maiden.)

வெமமுரா ணன்மகள் வேண்ட
வடமதிலாா உறுததுரைத தன்று.

(They in the fort refusing the hand of a damsel to a bitter foe.)

This kind of marriage by capture seems to have led to frequent bloody quarrels between neighbouring villages. As to their cannibalism and excess of flesh-eating and drinking of liquor more will be said in the following pages. So much for the Rakshasa ancestors of our non-Aryan friends.

We shall now enquire who the Vanara or monkey allies of Rama were. Even the early Tamils of the second or third century believed that they were actually monkeys. A poet of that period has said,—

(c) கடுநெடுந்தேரி ராமனுடன் புணர்ச்சிலைதலை
வலித்தகை யரகசன வெளவியஞான்றை
நிலஞ்சேரும தாணிகண்ட குரங்கின்
செம்முகப் பெருங்கிளை—*Pur.*

In reality they were not monkeys, but only an aboriginal race, dark complexioned, short statured, but strong and of monkey-like appearance like the Negritos. They lived upon roots and fruits; and they used only stones and clubs in their fights with the Rakshasas whom they always disliked. This description of the Vanaras leads us to infer that they should have been the ancestors of the modern hill and forest tribes like the Malasars, Soligas, Paliyas, Kadars and the Irulas. We have said before that these hill and forest tribes had their own kings like Vali and Sugriva, the monkey chieftains of the Ramayana.

All that we have discussed in the preceding pages may be summarized thus. The present population of the Tamil districts is composed of four distinct races, namely (1) the Negritos, (2) a mixed leiotrichi race allied to the Veddahs of Ceylon and the aborigines of Australasia, whom, for the sake of brevity, we may call the Nagas, (3) the Dravidian race, and (4) the Aryans. The first two—the Vanaras and the Rakshasas of the Ramayana—had had their original home in the submerged continent before they entered India from the south. Of these the Negritos must have been the earlier immigrants, and they must have been driven to the hills and forests by the mixed race of Nagas who came after them and occupied mostly the maritime districts. The date of their migration cannot be given as we have no data for it. Thirdly, came the Dravidians from Upper India about eleven hundred B.C., who carved out three or four small kingdoms by subduing the petty chieftains of the Naga tribes. Their original home seems to have been Asia-Minor, and they entered India by the North-Western gate long before the arrival of the Aryans; and before they marched southward both the races should have lived together in Northern India at least for some centuries. And lastly, came the Aryans not as conquerors but as teachers of religion and philosophy to the semi-civilized Dravidians, mostly on the invitation of their kings.

DISTRIBUTION OF PRINCIPAL TAMIL CASTES.
(IN THOUSANDS).
Tamil population—16, 647.

Castes.	Pallava.			Chola.		Pandya.			Kongu.		Total.	Percentage.
	Chingleput.	N. Arcot.	S. Arcot.	Tanjore.	Trichinopoly.	Madura.	Ramnad.	Tinnevelly.	Salem.	Coimbatore		
I. *Aryan.*												
1. Brahmans*	26	26	26	135	44	24	34	49	12	22	480	3
II. *Dravidian.*												
2. Vellalas	93	217	125	223	331	234	166	168	269	640	2,535	15
III. *Naga* (mixed)												
3. Valaiyan †	5	7	17	125	2	89	62	...	7	22	423	3
4. Pallan ⎫	...	...	...	160	145	137	144	193	20	37	866	5
5. Shanan ⎬ Mallar.	22	16	14	38	13	32	106	271	43	77	612	4
6. Idaiyan ⎭	69	102	92	75	48	58	110	97	21	17	735	5
7. Maravan. ⎫ Maravan.	...	...	...	...	...	37	135	177	...	...	365	2
8. Agam- badiyan ⎭	...	...	17	126	...	59	88	...	11	29	250	2
9. Paraiyan ⎫	351	303	591	336	169	100	59	98	150	70	2,364	14
10. Kaikolan ⎬ Eyina.	34	52	38	22	40	12	9	22	41	61	368	2
11. Kamma- lan ⎭	26	36	46	64	51	71	66	79	30	55	559	3
12. Palli or Vanniyan ⎫	292	482	758	257	189	25	7	...	48	6	2820	17
13. Kallan ⎬ Pallava or Kurumba.	...	...	...	202	28	192	57	...	...	...	535	3
14. Amba- laka- ran § ⎭	27	...	13	35	215	14	...	...	...	...	334	2
IV. *Naga* (Pure).												
15. Kuravan **	35	38	29	...	38	18	...	...	34	53	317	2
												82

* Includes 36 Tamil Brahmans in Malabar.
† Includes Sembadavan.
§ Includes Muttiriyan and Urali.
** Includes Vedan, Vettuvan, Irulen and other hill and forest tribes.

IV
THE TAMIL CASTES

An examination of the South Indian inscriptions shows that, from time to time, small bands of Brahmans from Northern India were invited by the Tamil kings and made to settle in their countries. Even at that remote period the Dravidians were sufficiently civilized and the Brahmans felt no necessity to bring with them either the Kshatriyas or the Vaisyas. We have neither heard nor read of any extensive immigrations, within historic times, of other races from outside the Tamil country. Of course, we leave out of consideration the handful of 'Skilled artisans from Magadha, mechanics from Maratam, smiths from Avanti and carpenters from Yavana (Ionia or Europe)'[1] who were found in the city

[1] "The name 'Yavana' was derived from the Ionians or descendants of Javan, the first Greeks with whom the Hindus became acquainted, and in the ancient Tamil and Sanskrit period denoted the Greeks in general. In subsequent times, when the Greeks were succeeded by the Arabs, it was the Arabs that were denoted by this name; so that in the later Sanskrit of the Vishnu Purana we are to understand by the *Yavanas* not the Greeks but the Arabs or more widely the inhabitants of both shores of the Persian Gulf, as that work speaks of the national custom of the *Yavanas* shaving their heads entirely without leaving a lock. The name *Sonagan* by which these Muhammadans of Arab descent are sometimes called in Tamil, is merely a corruption of the Skt. Yavana or Yavanaka "—See *Ind. Ant.* for 1875, p. 110

of Kaveripatam before its destruction which occurred in the early part of the second century A. D.

மகதவிீன ஒரு மராட்டக் கம்மரு
யவநதிக் கொல்லரும் யவனத தச்சரும்.— *Manu.*

We do not include in this all later immigrants of comparatively recent times such as the Telugu castes and Sourashtra weavers who followed the Vijayanagar Governors, the stray Kshatriyas and Vaisyas who hailed from the North during the Mogul rule, and the Mahratta Sudras who came in the train of the Mahratta leaders. We are concerned here only with the Tamil speaking castes and tribes of an earlier period. It is therefore certain that even those Tamil castes who trace their ancestry straight to the Vedic and Pauranic gods, calling themselves 'Viswa-Brahmans,' 'Dravida Kshatriyas' and 'Arya Vaisyas,' must have grown out of the Tamil tribes and castes which are described in ancient Tamil literature and inscriptions.

Broadly speaking, the Brahmans and the Sudras of the Tamil country belong each to a distinct race. In a way each had its own system of thought, religion, and ethical and social rules, so that an attempt to engraft the one on the other must look strange and preposterous. This fact has rightly been grasped by the English educated portion of the non-Brahman castes, who, as already pointed out, have been endeavouring to assert an indigenous Dravidian civilisation. This is only natural; and they merit the

THE TAMIL CASTES   61

sympathy and support of scholars if they confine themselves to a rational scientific enquiry.

It has been said in the last essay that there were at least three distinct types of pre-Aryans in the Tamil country, namely, (1) the Hill and Forest tribes, (2) the Nagas and (3) the Velir or the Vellala tribes. For want of a better name these are called collectively Dravidians, though, strictly speaking, 'Dravidian' should be applied only to the Vellalas, who were the latest of the pre-Aryan immigrants in Southern India. Sometimes the more significant compound 'Naga Dravidians' has also been used.

Before the arrival of the Aryans there was no caste system in the Tamil country. The earliest Brahman settlers tried, however, to introduce their four-fold division of people, and before they could succeed in it they met with much opposition. No Dravidian was considered worthy of being classed as Brahmans. The Tamil kings alone were elevated to the rank of Kshatriyas in spite of their marriage connections with the ancient Velir or Vellala tribes. These Velirs were on that account called Ilangôkkal or the 'minor kings'. The Brahmans got up for them very decent geneologies which traced their ancestry to the sun, the moon or the fire. This rendered the position of the Vellalas who had to oscillate between the Vaisya and the Sudra castes dubious and unsettled. Their greatest difficulty, however, was with the hill and forest tribes and the Nagas, who constituted the bulk of the South Indian population. They could not put these earlier Naga inhabitants in the Sudra division along with the Dravidian Vellalas for fear of injuring the feelings of the Tamil kings and the Velir nobility. To get over this difficulty they had to devise a new scheme of classification on an altogether different principle, which depended on the nature of the soil or region [1] in which the tribes happened to live.

REGION.	TRIBE.
1. *Neytal* or maritime.	Paravas, Nulayas and Valaiyas.
2. *Marutam* or fertile.	Mallar (Pallar) & Kadaignar.
3. *Mullai* or pasture.	Idaiyar and Toduvar.
4. *Palai* or desert.	Maravar and Eyinar.
5. *Kurinji* or hilly.	Kuravar, Irular, Savarai, Vedar and Villiyar.

This regional classification of the non-Aryan Tamil tribes is conspicuous by the absence of the Velir or the Vellala caste. It must, therefore, refer only to the pre-Dravidian tribes mentioned in Groups I and II given above. *Palai* is sometimes omitted or amalgamated with *Kurinji*; and the tribes of these two regions consequently interchange.

The earliest Tamil works inform us that there were two sections among the Velirs or pure Dravidians, namely the cultivating and the non-cultivating. As a rule the latter section furnished statesmen and

[1] The Tamil grammarians and lexicographers have classified the soil as five *tinais*,—Neytal, Marutam, Mullai, Palai and Kurinji, or as four *nilams* making Palai common to the other four.

generals to the Tamil kings. Its members were generally recipients of high titles like Kizhan, Udaiyan, Rayan or Arayan, Vel or Velan and Kaviti; and such Tamil names as Kudal-udai. Arisil kizhan and Kalinga-rayan appear now as the *gotric* names of the Karkatta Vellalas. They have ninety-six *gotras* or exogamous septs, thirteen of which end in Thirai, or Thiraiyan, fourteen in Rayan and sixty-nine in Udai or Udaiyan. The first designates the clan or tribe to which that section of the Vellalas originally belonged; the second is the title conferred on them by the Chola or Pandya kings; while the third appears to have been the names of villages of which they were the chieftains. Kaviti was a special distinction bestowed upon the ministers of state. Most of these *gotric* names may be found in the ancient Tamil inscriptions. No traces of the Tamil kings are to be found at present in this country, and it is highly probable that they should have merged in the pure Vellala caste. We say pure because the Vellala caste as a whole appears to have been receiving additions from time to time from other tribes as the following extract will show: வெட்வெரில் வெளான் கரியாஞன மருதங்கவேளான்.[1] Most of the Konga Vellalas were formerly Vettuvans. The preceding statement will show that the Coimbatore District contains an unusually large number of Vellalas—a fact which casts a serious doubt on their pure Dravidian or Vellala origin.

1. South Indian Inscriptions, Vol III, p. 45.

The occupations of the cultivating section were as given below,—

உழுது பயன்கொண டொலிநிரை யோம்பிப்
பழுதிலாப் பணடம் பகர்ந்து—முழுதுணர
வோதி யழல் வழிப்பட்டோம் பாதவீகையா
ஜ்தி வணிகாக் கரசு.—*P. V. M.*

(1) tilling, (2) cow-breeding, (3) trade, (4) studying the Vedas, (5) worship of sacrificial fire, and (6) giving alms. Here the Vellalas are spoken of as Bhu-Vaisyas. These occupations were, however, never confined to particular castes. Tilling was and has been done by the Mallars (Pallars), Maravas and others; cow-breeding by the Idaiyas and Kurumbas; trade in grains was formerly followed by a class of Vellalas called Kula-Vanikar or Vellan-Chettis and now by any caste; and giving alms by all the non-polluting castes. Vedic study and worship of sacrificial fire do not appear to have at any time been practised by the non-Brahman Tamils, except probably by an extinct section of the Vellalas known as the 'Vaidyas.' This name which occurs in a Vatteluttu inscription dated 770 A.D. should not be confounded with the Boidya caste of Bengal or with the class of native physicians called 'Vaidyan' as is sometimes done. 'Pre-eminently charming in manners, a resident of Karavandapura, the son of Maran, and a learned and illustrious member of the Vaidya family, Madhurakavi made this stone temple of Vishnu'. The Vaidyas were minis-

Anai Malai Inscription. **A.D 770.**
(VATTELUTTU)

ters under the Chola and Pandya kings and were good Sanskrit scholars well versed in the Vedas. Their royal title as ministers was 'Per-Arayan,' while that of a Brahman minister was 'Brahma-Arayan.' It will be interesting to observe that the great Vaishnava Saint Nammalvar and probably the Saiva ascetic Tayumanswami also belonged to this section of the Vellala caste.

In the Sendan-Divakaram, a work probably of the eleventh or twelfth century, the occupations of the Vellalas[1] are given, as (1) tilling, (2) cow-breeding, (3) trade, (4) playing on drums and musical instruments, (5) weaving, &c., and (6) service to Brahmans. Obviously, many inferior castes like the Kaikolas and Pallis are included here in the great Vellala tribe. And agreeably to it the word 'Kaikolan' makes its first appearance in this work as a caste name, and 'Pallava' is expunged therefrom, taking in the word 'Kavandan' to denote a man of the servile class. The Brahmans depended upon the Idaiyans for the supply of milk, ghee and butter, which were necessary for their subsistance and sacrificial oblations, and they were consequently elevated to the rank of Vaisyas, though they were never granted the privilege of wearing the sacred thread, to perform the Vedic rituals and to live within their villages. They had to live in a *Cheri* far removed from the village like the Paraiyas, Izhavas and

---

1. About the end of the eleventh century the occupations of the Vellalas were,—giving alms, tilling, cow-breeding, trade, music and service to Brahmans.—*Virasoliyam*, 85.

Kammalas. What a strange fitting of these non-Aryan tribes to the procrustean bed of the Brahmanical caste system!

Turning once more to the early Tamil literature and inscriptions, we find the following names of occupational castes mentioned:—Ambattan, Izhavan, Kammalan or the five artizans, Kani or Kaniyan, Kaviti, Kusavan, Marayan, Navisan, Panan, Panikkan, Pidaran, Sekkan, Sakkai (*Mal.* Chakkian), Uvaichan, Vannan, Vannattan, Valluvan, Variyan and Velan. All these castes now exist in Malabar though their occupations have since undergone slight change; while in the Tamil districts Kani, Kaviti, Marayan, Sakkai, Vannattan, Variyan and Velan have altogether disappeared. Most of these occur in the Tanjore inscriptions of Rajaraja Chola (A. D. 985—1013). Kani or Kaniyan was an astrologer; Kaviti, an accountant (but formerly a minister); Marayan, a title conferred on the royal musician of a temple, Pidaran is the reciter of the Devara-hymns, and it corresponds to the present day O'duvan; Sakkai is a temple actor; Vannattan is a high class washerman; Variyan an overseer in temples, and Velan a dancer in honour of Subrahmanya the hill deity; Ambattan was a medicine man and now a barber; Panan was a low caste minstrel and now a tailor; Panikkan was a teacher or instructor in gymnastics and now the name of a more advanced section of the Izhava or Shanan caste to which also belonged Enâdi Nâyanar the famous Saiva saint and athletic

THE TAMIL CASTES

teacher of a Chola king. Shanan has taken the place of Izhavan in the Tamil districts, for reasons which have not yet been ascertained.

Many of our readers must no doubt be familiar with the tribes enumerated in the regional classification given above. For a better understanding of the process of formation and growth of the numerically strongest Tamil castes which account for more than 80 per cent. of the Tamil population, we shall exhibit them in the subjoined table.

Original tribes.	*Modern castes.*
(1) Paravan and Valaiyan.	Paravan, Valaiyan, Sembadavan, Pattanavan, Karaiyan &c.
(2) Mallar (Pallar).	Pallan, Shanan, Panikkan.
(3) Idaiyan.	Idaiyan.
(4) Maravan and Eyinan.	Maravan, Agambadiyan, Paraiyan, Kaikolan, Kammalan, Kurumban, Palli or Vanniyan, Kallan, Muttiriyan and Ambalakaran.
(5) Kuravan, Irulan, Vedan and Villiyan.	Kuravan, Irulan, Vedan, Villiyan, Kadar, Malasar and minor hill tribes.

The other important castes like Ambattan, Vaniyan and Vannan were originally occupational guilds, consisting of peoples from various tribes, which have in course of time hardened into distinct castes. Even now in Malabar the Brahmans have their own barbers and washermen, while the Nayars and Tiyars have each their own. 'Vaniyan' is another form of 'Vanijyan' which means a 'merchant.'

All the hill and forest tribes of the present day, do not belong to the Negrito race alluded to in Group I. Some of them like the Kurumbas, the Malaiyalans and the Malayamans are emigrants from the plains. During the dynastic convulsions and terrible civil wars of the early Tamil period, several bands of the Naga tribes who were driven from the low lands took shelter on high mountains and in inaccessible forests, which had from the earliest times been under the rule of petty refractory chieftains called Kuru-nila-Mannar. Early Tamil literature tells us that there were feudatory chiefs on the Vengadam (Tirupati) hill, Kollimalais, Malainad, Tonnimalai, Kudirai-malai and Mudiram. Some of them are eulogized by ancient Tamil poets as the most benevolent of rulers; while of the seven third-rate[1] Vallals (வள்ளல்) or grantors of *doceur* some were hill chiefs. They had always been the allies of one or another of the three Tamil kings, like their remote monkey ancestors who had helped Sri Rama in his war with Ravana.

A study of the various sub castes returned during the Census of 1891 supplemented by the latest ethnological researches should lead one to the irresistible

---

[1] Three grades of donors are mentioned in Tamil literature. Those who give any present unasked belong to the first class; those who offer what is asked belong to the second class; and those who give grudgingly after much importunity belong to the third class.

inference that Ambalakkaran, Muttiriyan, Kallan, Kurumban and Vanniyan belonged to the race of Nagas who inhabited the Northern Tamil districts, which constituted the ancient Pallava country or Tondaimandalam. When the power of the Pallavas was in its zenith, that is about the sixth and seventh centuries A. D., their conquests extended to the south as far as Trichinopoly, and it must have been then that the Kallan and the Muttiriyan sections of the great Pallava, Palli or Malla tribe migrated to the Chola country—Tanjore and Trichinopoly. As a caste name neither Palli nor Kallan[1] occurs in early Tamil literature or inscriptions, but this extensive tribe was known as Pallava, and Mallava (பல்லவர் சோன், *P. T.*). The Pallava army was recruited from this martial tribe of Pallis or Kurumbas, and some of them were also feudal governors under the Pallava kings. Like the Paraiyas some of them claim their descent from Sambu or Siva, while all Pallis style themselves Vahni Kshatriyas. One section of the Palli or Pallava tribe, called the Muttarasar (Tel. Mutracha) ruled in the Chola country, first as feudatories of the Pallava and then of the Pandya kings during the eighth century A.D. It was during this period that *Naladiyar* was composed under the auspices of the Muttarasa governors. The Pallavas were the hereditary enemies of the three Tamil kings—Chera, Chola and Pandya—and their subjects

1. There is a doubtful reference to the *kalvars* or *kallar* in the Agananuru, and it corresponds to the 'Dasyus' of the Indo-Aryans.

were regarded as intruders in the southern districts. Hence, the term Pallava has come to mean a 'rogue' in the Tamil language, while a section of the Pallava subjects who settled in the Chola and Pandya countries received the undesirable appellation of Kallar or thieves. All these doubtless belonged to the Naga race, as one subdivision of the Palli caste called the agavadam, Nagapasam or Nagavamsam and the occurrence of such names as Mugali-Nagan, Oli-Nagan and Sanka-Nagan in the Mamallapuram (the Seven Pagodas) inscriptions will show; and they must have migrated from the Telugu and Canarese districts as soldiers of the early Pallava kings during the second or third century A. D. For this reason the Pallavas were always considered as strangers to Tamil districts and were never mentioned favourably in ancient Tamil works. As regards their connection with the Kurumbas and Pallars enough has been said by Mr. (now Sir) H. A. Stuart in the Madras Census Report of 1891.

Maravan and Eyinan occur very often in ancient Tamil works, and they are said to have been skilful bowmen and soldiers. The Maravas were and even now are very numerous in the Pandya country, and the habitat of the Eyinas appears from time immemorial to have been the Pallava and Chola countries. Prior to the tenth century, the Kaikolas and Agambadiyas did not come into existence as distinct castes, and the origin of the former will be given presently.

'Idaiyan' literally means a 'Middleman,' because in the regional grouping he came to occupy the middle or the pasture land. He had to live next to the Eyinas on whom he depended for the supply of cows and buffaloes.[1] As late as the tenth century A D. a man of any other tribe might become an Idaiyan or cowherd by following that profession. The Kalla and Samban sub-divisions of this caste connect them with the Kallans and Paraiyans. The latter sub-division which is by far the most numerous not only bears out their origin from Sambu or Siva, but also justifies the proximity of their residence to the *Cheri* of the Eyinas or Paraiyas in ancient Dravidian villages. The following description of a typical Idaiyan of old is very suggestive:—

பாசிலெடுதாடித்த வுவலேக்கண்ணி
மாசுணுடுகசுக மடிவாயிடையன்.—*Pur*.

(The shepherd with his thick (turned down) lips, dirty cloth and garland of green leaves.)

There was no such caste as Pallan, but in its stead we find in early Tamil literature Mallan and Kadaignan, the latter appearing as a sub-division of the Pallan caste. They are found chiefly in the Pandya country and correspond in their traditional occupation to the Palli or Vanniya caste of the Tondainadu. These people were agricultural labourers and soldiers

The origin of the term Shanan is much disputed and it is found nowhere in Tamil literature in that form.

---

1. In this connection lines 130-180 of the *Perumpanarruppadai* might be read with advantage

As late as the 13th century the Shanans were known as Izhavans, and a tax called the *Izha-putchi* was levied by Tamil kings on all toddy-drawers. They were surely a polluting caste in those days as now, and it would therefore be absurd to derive it from *Sauron*, the sun, as the educated section of the Shanar caste is attempting to do. According to a tradition current in Malabar, the toddy-drawers are considered immigrants from Izham or Ceylon. If this theory be correct, they may be regarded as a more civilised section of the Veddahs. And if Izham is taken to mean ' toddy,' the Shanars must be a class of Pallars, allied to the Vedar or Vettuvar, leading the settled life of palm cultivators, while the other continues a nomadic hunting tribe. In either case, it is to be observed that the Pallar and the Shanar castes are most numerous in the Tamil districts which are adjacent to Ceylon—the abode of the Veddah, Yaksha or Naga tribes.

The caste names Valaiyan (net-man), Sembadavan, Pattanavan and Karaiyan do not occur in early Tamil books. Sembadavan is a boatman, Pattanavan is an inhabitant of a sea-coast village, and Karaiyan is a man of the beach. The absence of any of these fishing castes from the maritime district of Tinnevelly is noteworthy. Probably they must have returned their caste name as 'Native Christian' in the census of 1911. All these fishing castes form part of the great Naga race who lived on the South Indian sea-board.

About the middle of the fourteenth century there were, it seems, only eighteen principal castes or tribes among the non-Aryan Tamils as might be inferred from the saying பன்னுப்பதற பதிெனட்டு ஜாதியும் (the 18 castes inclusive of the Pallas and Paraiyas). Within the last five hundred years they have increased tenfold, on account of various causes which will be explained below.

The elements which contributed to the break up of the few Dravidian tribes into innumerable castes were, (1) food, (2) occupation, (3) religion, and (4) locality. The Dravidians of antiquity like the Vedic Aryans used to eat beef, pork, venison, mutton and fish, and as late as 250 A. D. even Brahmans of South India appear to have been meat-eaters. But under the humane influence of Jainism, the Brahmans had ceased long before the Pauranic period to eat any animal food, and some of their Dravidian neighbours followed suit. This, by the way, may be observed as a remarkable case, quite unique in the sociology of a whole people—the Brahmans—changing its habit from meat eating to vegetarianism. Killing of animals was condemned as a sin, the gravity of which increased according to their usefulness to the Brahman's personal comforts and religious offerings. Thus, the cow became the most sacred animal, because of her five products, *panchagaryam*, which were necessary for their food and sacrifice, and the killing of such an animal was and is still being considered one of the greatest of sins. It has given rise to an imprecatory saying usually appended to all grants, *viz.* கங்கைக்கரையில் காராம்பசுவைக் கொன்றபாவத்தில் போவ ராகவும் (may he incur the sin of having slaughtered a black cow on the banks of the Ganges). The Dravidians, chiefly the fighting classes, indulged very freely in intoxicating drinks and the manufacture and sale of liquor was not considered a mean occupation by the ancient Tamils. The simple fact that the word 'toddy' has at least eighty equivalent words in the Tamil language proves the extensive use of that beverage throughout the Tamil land. It was only after the advent of the Jains and Brahmans that drinking was condemned, and its sellers and producers came to be shunned as polluting castes

The five artizans, potters and weavers were much requisitioned by all castes high and low, and these industries consequently tended to bring them in closer contact with the Brahmans. And with the rise of temples and other religious institutions, the social status of these classes began to improve. The Brahmans conferred on them flattering distinctions, high titles, and fabricated for them divine origins, which, besides elevating their social status, humoured them and made them willing workers in the new social organisation Thus, the seeds of all subsequent quarrels and dissensions were sown. All these Dravidian castes were granted the privilege of wearing the sacred thread.

The power of a religion to rend asunder large tribes and races is too well known. The want of easy and quick communication of any kind in the Tamil country at the time, and the geographical conditions of the country accelerated this splitting up of larger castes and favoured the crystallisation of the smaller communities.

The introduction of the Indo-Aryan caste system in the Dravidian country produced severe social troubles for many centuries. If the Brahmans of olden time were responsible for the superimposition of their own social organization, the measure was one of doubtful expediency. As already pointed out it had been the cause of serious and unceasing disputes, particularly among the artizan classes, which those Brahmans had to decide with reference to their Dharmasastras An inscription[1] of Kulottunga Chola, dated 1118 A. D., records the decision of a curious question whether the Kammalas are entitled to wear the sacred thread. In support of their decision allowing the Rathakaras (Kammalas) to perform 'only the *Upanayana* (thread wearing ceremony) without quoting the *mantras*', the Brahmans had first to grant that they were the sons of Mahishyas by Karani women. A Mahishya is the offspring of a Kshatriya male and a Vaisya female, and Karani of a Vaisya male and a Sudra female In the Dravidian country whence did the Brahmans get so many Kshatriyas and Vaisyas as to bring forth by illicit unions about 650,000 Kammalas ?

1 The Madras Government Epigraphist's Report, dated the 28th July 1909, p. 95.

It will be a huge task to attempt to trace the origin and development of every Tamil caste. We shall therefore take only the Eyinas or Paraiyas, which is perhaps the third largest of Tamil castes, and examine what other castes have evolved from them and how they managed to secure their present social-position. But, by way of introduction, it is highly desirable to present before the reader a description of the constitution of an ancient town or village, in which the regional classification of tribes explained above is clearly discernible.

We shall first take the city of Kanchipuram as described in the *Perum-panarruppadai*, a Tamil work of the third or fourth century A. D. In the heart of the town were the Brahman 'quarters where neither the dog nor the fowl could be seen'; they were flanked on the one side by the fishermen's (வலைஞர்) streets and on the other by those of traders (வணிகர்), and these were surrounded by the *cheris* of the Mallas or Pallas (உழவர்) and toddy-drawers (கள்ளமெழாளர்). Then, far removed from them were situated at one extremity of the city the *pallis* of the Idaiyans; and beyond these lay the isolated *pura-cheris* of the Eyinas and their chiefs. Next to the Malla (உழவர்) streets were the temple of Tiruvehka and the royal palace of king Ilam-Tiraiyan.

By the end of the tenth century the social position of certain tribes was somewhat changed. The Idaiyans had come to occupy a higher rank on account.

of the diffusion of the Krishna cult, while the toddy-drawers and the five artizan castes were still regarded as polluting castes and assigned separate sites by the side of the Paraiyas And these may be illustrated by a few extracts from the Tanjore inscriptions of the great Rajaraja Chola (1004 A.D.):—

' The village site, the pond, the sacred temples, the burning ground, the Vannaracheri, the pool of the Paraiyas (*S.I.I.*, II. 44). The village site, the ponds, the sacred temples, the burning ground, the Kammalacheri, the Izhacheri, Paraicheri (*Ib.* 50). The temple of Pidari and its Court, the village pond and its banks, the temple of Aiyanar and its court, the village granary, the burning ground of the Vellalas, the burning ground of the Paraiyas, the Paraicheri, the Izhacheri ......' (*Ib.* 55). What relative social rank each of these castes held we cannot now definitely say. But it is tolerably certain that the Paraiyas, Kammalas, Izhavas and Vannans were all considered polluting castes as these are at present in Malabar and Travancore. Thus, the above arrangement in the constitution of a Dravidian village is specially noteworthy, as it combined with the circumstances described below to degrade the social position of the Paraiya descendants of the Eyina tribe.

Of the six servile tribes—Paraiya, Pulaiya or Cheruma, Mala, Holaya, Palla and Madiga—which constitute nearly one-sixth of the population of the Madras Presidency, the Paraiya is by far the most important and interesting. They are found chiefly in the districts of Arcot, Chingleput and Tanjore where the Eyina tribe had formerly lived and where numberless cromlechs and kistvaens abound to this very day. The term Paraiyan as a caste, or more correctly an occupational, name first occurs in a poem of Mangudi Kilar, second century A. D.

துடியன் பாணன் பறையன் கடம்பனென்
நிகான் கல்வது குடியுமில்லை.—*Pur.*

Here ' Tudiyan ' means one who plays on the Tudi or a kind of drum peculiar to the hill or jungle tribe ; 'Panan' is a minstrel ; ' Paraiyan' is a drummer ; and 'Kadamban' is a hill man. All these are occupational names and seem to refer to four sections of the Kurinji (hill) or Palai (jungle) tribes Besides this casual reference, we do not find the name Paraiyan mentioned either in early Tamil literature or in the inscriptions, until we come down to the time of the great Rajaraja Chola (A. D. 1013), from which period it evidently obtained currency as a caste denomination. It is commonly derived from *parai,* a drum by Dr. Caldwell and native writers. This etymology though plausible and tempting seems unsatisfactory, as it is inconceivable that the beating of drums could be the occupation of nearly two and a half millions of labourers, while the Murasu or the drum-beating section of that comprehensive caste forms only $\frac{1}{120}$th part of it. The more accurate derivation seems to be that of Col. Cunningham, M. Letourneau and Dr. Oppert from the Sanskrit *pahariya,* a hill man, or from Tamil *Poraian,* which is more in keeping with the regional division assigned to the Eyinas by the ancient Tamil grammarians.

According to the inscription already referred to, the Paraiyas were divided in ancient times into at least two sub-divisions the *Ulavu* (ploughing) and *Nesavu* (weaving) ; and there probably existed many more occupational groups among them, like Panan &c. Some of the most significant of the sub-divisions returned by them in the Census of 1891 were,—Valluva, Kottai, Kottakara, Jambu, Virabahu, Panikka, Koliya, Saliya, Kurava and Ambu. The Valluvas are the priests to the Paraiyas, and were formerly superintendents of religious ceremonies (more probably conductors of funeral obsequies) in a king's household :

வள்ளுவன் சாகைக யெனும பெயர் மன்னன்
குள்படி கருமத்த%லவற கொன்றும்.

This may not look strange if we only remember that the Marayans, (a barber caste) officiate as *purohits* at the funeral rites of the Nambudri or 'Vedic' Brahmans of Malabar. The Valluvas were also heralds under the Tamil kings.

என்புழி வள்ளுவர் யானேமீ மிசை
நன்பறை யறைந்தனா —*Kam*

(The Valluvan proclaimed the news beat of drum from the back of an elephant.)

Kottai is a fort ; *Kottakaram* is a granary, for in ancient days the land-tax was levied in kind as well as in money ; *Sambu* is Siva and *Virabahu* is one of the mythical commanders of Siva ; *Panikkan* is a teacher ; *Koliyan* and *Saliyan* are weavers ; *Kuravan* is a hill man ; and *Ambu* is an arrow. The Eyinas were considered good archers.

All these point to their former greatness, the vestiges thereof still survive in the form of rights and privileges which cling to them in the village organization. The settlement of a land dispute by one Vesali Paraiyan and his councillors regarding the ownership of a field belonging to a temple at the village of Mudepakavar is mentioned in an inscription of the eleventh century; and the Paraiyar's decision was deemed final and absolute.[1]

The Eyinas or hunters of the above districts were the earliest of the Naga-Dravidian tribes to clear the forests of Dandakaranya and Shadaranya for purposes of cultivation and to build small forts therein for their safety. Such of them as had been employed in the clearing of jungles came to be called the Vettiyan (hewers), while others engaged in the sinking of wells and the digging of tanks for irrigation grew up into the *tôti* (*tondu*, to dig) or digger caste. As early as the third or fourth century A. D. they had their chieftains reigning at Ambur, Vellore and other places. The Eyinas had well supplied granaries (*kottakaram*) and strong forts (*eyil*) with deep ditches and lofty walls ; they had musicians and dancers (Panans) to amuse them when out of work; they had priests (Valluvans), carpenters, masons, weavers (Kohyans), gymnastic instructors

1. The Madras Government Epigraphist's Report, dated the 25th July 1910, p. 94.

(Panikkans), shoe-makers (Semman), barbers, washermen and what not. The Paraiyas, or the modern representatives of the ancient Eynias, as Dr. Caldwell rightly observes, thus constituted 'a well defined, distinct ancient caste independent of every other'. The high honour of founding villages in the south during the remote period belonged to the sylvan ancestors of the despised Paraiyas. They were the mayors and aldermen of the villages they had established, and this is even now recognized by all other castes in the old custom of referring any boundary dispute to a Paraiya, Toti or a Holeya Kulavadi. And in almost all the ancient village ceremonies of a communal nature, the Paraiyas play an important part. For example, on the occasion of any festival of Siva at Tiruvalur in the Tanjore district, a Paraiyan has an hereditary right to precede the god's procession holding a white umbrella. A detailed account of the existing customs observed in various places cannot, however, conveniently be given here.

So much for their forgotten greatness. But with the advent of the Indo-Aryans about the second century A.D. there came a change in the constitution of the Paraiya tribe, their food and occupation contributing largely to their self-degradation. It has been said above that there were amongst them people following all sorts of pursuits. The social standing of those men who had been following occupations indispensible to the well-being of the Brahmans rose high in the long run and they now pass for high caste Hindus. Of course, learned Brahmans discovered decent Hindu pedigrees for the low but highly serviceable tribes and stamped them with the seal of sanctity in the name of *puranas*

The Kaikolas, who trace their descent from Virabahu, one of the nine commanders of god Subrahmanya, seem to have been originally (before the tenth century A.D.) Eyina weavers like the Koliya Paraiyas, though some of them have very recently caught the infection of wearing the sacred thread to claim an equal position with the high caste Hindus. Five reasons may be adduced in favour of this origin:

(1) They are chiefly found in the districts where the Paraiyas and Brahmans are most numerous—S. Arcot, Tanjore, and Trichinopoly.

(2) The word Kaikolan is simply the Tamil equivalent of the Sanskrit 'Virabahu', a mythological hero from whom both the Kaikolas and a section of the Paraiyas claim descent.

(3) It is said that they were formerly soldiers like the Eyinas and Paraiyas, under a monkey-faced king named Muchukundan; and that the art of weaving was taught to them by Tiru-Valluvar at the command of Subrahmanya, the patron deity of the Kaikolas and other Naga tribes. Two of the Tillaistanam (Neyttanam) inscriptions of Gandaraditya (A. D. 960) record the gifts made by 'Samara Kesari-terinja Kaikolar, Vikrama-Singa-terinja Kaikolar and Virachola terinja-Kaikolar'.[1] They were natives of Tanjore and

[1] The Madras Government Epigraphist's Report dated the 29th July 1912.

served as soldiers under the Chola king Parantaka I.
(A. D. 906-949). Other inscriptions of a later date
speak of the Rajaraja-terinja-Kaikolar and the Kaikola-
Perumpadai. All these clearly prove that the word
'Kaikolar,' like 'Velakkarar' and 'Viliyar' (archers),
which occur in the inscriptions of Rajaraja Chola I,
was the name of the regiment enlisted or selected
(*terinja*) by Parantaka, whose titles were Samara Kesari
(the war-lion), Vikrama-Singa and Vira Chola and by
Rajaraja I. One of the soldiers of the above regiment
was a Kadikavan *Kallan*. They were known also as
Sengundar or the 'Red Lancers.'

(4) In the inscriptions of Rajaraja Chola, (A. D.
1013) the loom (*tari*) of the Kaikolas does not occur
though the Parai-tari, Tusa-tari (washerman) and
Saliya-tari are given.

(5) In ancient Tamil literature the weavers were
called Kamiriyan, a term which also included the
present Kammalas.

கம்மியர் யவன ரோவியர் விதத்கர்
கம்மாளர் தபதியர் பொதப்பெயர் கட்டுரை.—*Ping.*, 788.

It will be interesting to learn that the early
Tamils were never good weavers. They had to
depend upon their Telugu neighbours for cloths of
finer texture. Thus superior cloths have come to be
called in Tamil *kalingam*. In the Tamil country
coarse weaving was done by a section of the Paraiyas
or Eyinas. Dissatisfied with the quality of the work
turned out by the Tamils, probably Rajaraja Chola

brought the Saliya-weavers from Kalingam, the modern Telugu districts of Vizagapatam, Godavari and Kistna. From them probably the Eyina weavers or Kammiyans learnt during the eleventh century A. D. how to weave finer cloths. Since the earliest mention of Kaikolan as a caste name is found in a Conjeevaram inscription of the fourteenth century, it is highly probable that this class of weavers began to be recognised as a distinct Hindu caste of some standing, between the eleventh and fourteenth centuries, when the greatest Kaikola poet, Ottaikuttan, commanded a great influence at the court of Kulottunga Chola (1150 A. D.). And it happened probably a few years after the Kammalas were granted the privilege of wearing the sacred thread.

Again, to take another instance, the Panans were minstrels under the ancient Tamil kings, and with the extinction of the latter in South India their profession as bards ceased to exist, most of them finding their way into Kerala, the Land of Charity, for a livelihood. The descendants of these emigrants are now found in Malabar and Canara as devil-dancers and basket-makers. On the other hand, the Panans of the Tamil country, especially those living in Madura and Tinnevelly style themselves Pandya Vellalas and earn their bread as tailors. They are also called Mestris, which is a Portuguese word introduced by the early Roman Catholic Missionaries, under whom the Paraiya Panans served as workmen. The low origin of the

Panans is, however, betrayed by about 5 per cent. of that caste who live in out-of-the-way villages of the Madura district returning Paraiya as the name of their main caste.

The Semman is another important sub-division of the Paraiyas, whose existence is almost unknown outside the districts of Madura and Tinnevelly. It was once a numerous caste of Tamil leather-workers, (புகன்றேதாற்றுன்னர் செம்மார்.—*Nig.*). Since the immigration of the Telugu and Canarese Madigas or Chakkiliyans. sometime after the fifteenth or sixteenth century, the Semmans have almost entirely given up their traditional occupation, and adopted, like the Panans, menial services in villages and tailoring and lime selling in towns.

We shall content ourselves with one more instance furnished to us by the artizan castes, whose social status has undergone within the past nine centuries a thorough change which never could have been dreamt of by their humble ancestors.

The Kammalas assert that they are the descendants of Visvakarma the architect of the gods, and in many parts of the country they wear the sacred thread calling themselves Visva-, Deva-, or Devagna-Brahmans and deliberately refuse to give precedence to the Brahmans. Without going into the details of their origin we shall simply indicate a few reasons to prove that they are one of the undoubted Naga tribes,[1] forming an advanced section of, or closely allied to, the Eyinas of the Tamil country.

(1) The Dharma Sastras, a social code common to all Hindus, assign no place to the Kammalas in the Hindu caste system, purely because they stood out of the Aryan pale; and this fact has been clearly brought out by the author of the Ramayana Further, it is said that the artisans were supplied by the mixed classes—a theory strongly confirmed by the ancient decision already quoted.

(2) It is generally supposed, even in Upper India, that all the artisan castes and weavers were begotten of a Sudra woman by the celestial architect Visvakarma, from whom also the Kolis of the United-Provinces, a weaver caste allied to the Koliya Paraiyans of Madras, trace their descent. 'They worship Sakti and village deities and are, as a rule, considered undesirable neighbours in a village.'

(3) Tamil inscriptions prove that as late as A. D. 1013 the Kammalas were regarded as a polluting caste like the Izhuvans and Paraiyans and were not allowed to live within the villages, or to blow conches and beat drums on the marriage and funeral occasions, or to plaster their houses with mud or chunam, or even to wear shoes. And it appears that

[1] With this compare what Mr. Charles Johnston, I. C. S. says on the subject: 'It is probable that among them [black Dravidians] first grew up the system of trade guilds which gradually developed into hereditary caste of artisans and craftsmen, the chief of which are the workers in gold, brass, iron, stone and wood'. The black Dravidians' are our Nagas.

they were regarded as slaves and given from time to time certain privileges since the twelfth century A. D.[1]

(4) In Kerala (Malabar and Travancore), a country first colonized largely by the Tamils, a country where caste rules and observances have been scrupulously maintained for several centuries, the Kammalas occupy a low position in the social scale and are regarded by the other people of that district (probably on the authority of the Vaikhanasa Dharmasura) as a polluting caste like the Tamil Kammalas of the eleventh century They are allowed neither to wear the sacred thread as in the other parts of the Presidency, nor to enter the houses of castemen, except during construction, which when completed undergo purification, a custom still followed in the Tamil districts. As late as the fourteenth century the Kammalas and the Vaniyans (oil-pressers) were considered as slaves in Malabar. This we learn from the Kottayam plates of Viraraghava Chakravarti wherein it is stated thus :—

வாணியரும் ஐங்கம்மாளரையு மடிமை கொடுத்தோம்.

(We have given the Vaniyas and the five Kammalas as slaves.)

The Kammalas of Malabar and of the Tamil districts must have descended from the same stock of the Naga-Dravidian artisans mentioned in the early Tamil literature and inscriptions already referred to, though, on account of difference in circumstances which will be explained hereafter, the former have

[1] South Indian Inscriptions, Vol. III, p 47.

retained their original 'distance pollution,' while the latter have risen so far in social scale as to claim equality with the Brahmans.

(5) The custom of burying their dead, partiality to the worship of Kali and other village deities, and the entire absence of Vishnu worship seem to connect them with the pre-Dravidian or aboriginal Naga tribes.

Thus it will be seen that the claims of the Kammalas for Brahmanhood are not based upon any recognised Veda, Sastra, Itihasa or Purana, and that their arguments in its favour are opposed *toto cœlo* to customs and usages prevalent at any period of Indian history.

Now with regard to the food of the Eyina tribe of hunters, the 'Ten Tamil Idylls' and the Puranânuru say that they ate pork and the flesh of the wild cow and freely indulged in spirituous liquors.

எயினர் தந்த வெய்மானெறிதகைப
பைஞ்ஞிணம்பெருத்த பசுவெள் எமஜே.—*Pur.*

(The new white rice boiled with the flesh of the swine just killed by the Eyinas.)

எயிற்றியரட்ட வினபுளிவெஞ்சோறு
ஆமான் குட்டின மைவரப்பெறுகுவிர்.—*Sir.*

(Thou shall get the hot rice cooked by the Eyina women with sweet tamarind and roasted beef.) Even after a lapse of nearly fifteen centuries we see no change in the food of their Paraiya descendants. Some of them are said to eat frogs, a strange habit which connects them with the Yanadis of Nellore.

To the Hindus the cow is a sacred animal as well as the bull, the Vahana of Siva, the killing and eating of which are abominable. Not less hateful is the use of intoxicating drinks. It was therefore natural that the people who ate beef and drank liquors should be treated by Brahmans as a filthy polluting caste. From the Brahmanical standpoint the best recommendation for a non-Aryan tribe to rise higher in the social scale was the giving up of the above practice. The Kaikolans, Panans, Semmans and Kammalas did so, and we can see the good relation between them and the Brahmans.

But above all, the primary cause of the revolution in the organisation of the Paraiya tribes seems to have been the Brahman exclusiveness. They did not allow the Paraiyas and the polluting castes generally even to enter their *agraharams* and villages. A careful perusal of 'Nandan's Life' will give our readers some idea as to how these Paraiya labourers were treated by the Tamil Brahmans. The influence of the Brahmans is now gone; and their power is crippled by the stronger Anglo-Saxon race, who have assumed, as Leyden naively remarked, the character of Kshatriyas in the estimation of the subdued Brahmans, while the beef-eating Paraiyas are still looked down as being outside the Hindu social system though admitted to be Hindus in religion.

Among the Paraiyas the sub-division that first suffered from the Brahman domination was the Ulavu

Paraiyans, who now form about 50 per cent. of that labouring class. They had to work in the fields all day long without having any access to the Brahman lord. They, toiling and moiling on the fields, which were once their own but were wrested from them by the Tamil kings to encourage and support the Brahman advisers and their religious institutions, became as it were, a part and parcel of their rice fields Their masters changed with the change of ownership of land. Thus arose the predial slavery which, however, was put down when the country passed luckily into the hands of the British.

With the exception of the dog-eating Nâyâdis of Malabar, the Paraiyas are supposed to carry with them a high degree of pollution, so that even the Pulaiyas and Holayas of the West Coast and the Khonds of Vizagapatam think they will be defiled by the mere touch of a Paraiya. What is pollution then according to the Hindu notion ? It is something imaginary, flowing out of the social gravitation which exists between an Aryan and a non-Aryan Hindu. The degree of the pollution varies inversely with the degree of adoption of the Brahmanical customs and manners. The Paraiyas were stubborn and the least inclined to adopt them, and consequently their approach within a radius of thirty yards has been considered polluting to a high caste Hindu. The hatred which existed between the early Dravidians and Aryans is best preserved in the Kuricchan's (a hill tribe in Malabar, corresponding to the Kuravas of the Tamil country) custom of plastering their huts with cow-dung to remove the pollution caused by the entrance of a Brahman. During the past three centuries the Jesuit and other Missionaries on the one hand, and the Siddhar School of Tamil philosophers on the other, we are glad to observe, have been working to elevate these classes and alleviate the evils arising out of their social degradation, which has rendered their position anything but happy.

V

THE TAMIL CASTES—(*continued*).

In the last chapter it has been shown that among the ancient Tamils there was no caste system similar to that of the Aryans; that most of the Tamil castes of modern times, probably with the exception of the Vellalas, could be traced to the ancient Nagas and to some of the hill and forest tribes; that it took at least five centuries for these castes to attain their present position in the social economy of the country; that the present diversity of castes was caused by the differences in food, occupation, religious beliefs and the physical condition of the countries inhabited by them; and that the Brahmans were instrumental in bringing about this result, though the precise extent to which their influence prevailed is a matter not easily determinable. This applies to all the non-Aryan castes and tribes of Southern India.

The introduction and expansion of the caste system among the Dravidian Tamils had in course of time bred discontent, jealousy and mutual hatred in their social life, which in the end culminated in the disputes of the 'right and left hand factions,' into which the whole Dravidian society was divided. And this division has been the cause of endless feuds and mischief from the time of its inception.

About the middle of the fifteenth century (1449 A. D.) the inhabitants of the kingdom of Padaividu in the North Arcot District appear to have been divided into three factions irrespective of their nationality, creed or occupation—வலங்கை யும் இடங்கையும் மகாஜனமும்—(the right-hand, the left-hand and the *mahajanam*, *i. e.*, the Brahmans). Again, on the 5th November 1652, that is within fifteen years after the foundation of Fort St. George, the inhabitants of Madras were fighting for certain privileges and disturbing the public peace and safety to such an extent that the authorities of the East India Company were obliged to call on the heads of the respective factions to draw up an agreement settling all the differences between the right-hand and left-hand castes. Some sixty years after this, the same tragedy was enacted once more at Chintadripetta, a suburban colony of artizans and merchants, the dispute arising out of the right claimed by certain Chetties or traders to recite Sanskrit *Mantras* before the idol of Vignesvara. Now coming to the last century, the contest was fought with renewed vigour among the impoverished inhabitants of Seringapatam. This town, shortly after it had fallen into the hands of the English, was found divided into two portions, one occupied mainly by the adherents of the right-hand faction and the other by the upholders of the left. And it is also said that the faction feuds were so rampant there, that the British Government was driven to the necessity of prohibiting for a time marriage and other processions within the Fort in order to preserve public peace and tranquillity. About thirty years ago another quarrel ensued at Dummagudam in the Godavari district, which, however was immediately put down. It was on the occasion of a marriage in the Kamsali caste, the ring-leader being a Madras Paraiyan. Moreover, this jealousy in guarding the rights underlying the factious feud has very often led to painful litigation and prosecutions in the Civil and Criminal Courts of Chittur, Salem and Chingleput. Unlike other segregating forces it extended its evil influences even among members of the same families while the caste system has only divided the people into ethnic, territorial, professional or sectarian classes. It is no wonder then that it has attracted the attention of ethnologists ; but none has yet been able to throw sufficient light on its origin or subsequent history.

An enquiry regarding the probable date of the genesis of the faction and its subsequent growth will not, it is hoped, be uninteresting to the reader ; and it is not without some confidence that the following explanation based on a rather prolonged and careful study of the subject is offered, in the belief that it carries with it at least the merit of historic probability. And in order to get a correct idea of the minute details of this curious distinction, an accurate historical account of each and every caste comprised within the division is highly desirable.[1] But the lists

---

1. Brief historical notices of some of the most important castes which are given in the statement will be found in Chapter X of the Madras Census Report for 1891, and in the Caste Glossary appended to the Report on the Census of 1901.

THE TAMIL CASTES 95

ve have examined give conflicting accounts of the everal castes, which will be noticed later on. Nevertheless, we subjoin a tolerably correct statenent which exhibits the names of important caste nd the traditional occupations followed by the nembers thereof prior to their division into these ocial factions :—

Occupation :	Right-hand.	Left-hand.
Traders.	Balija, Banajiga, Komati, Vellan Chetti.	Beri Chetti, Vaniyans (who yoke two bullocks).
Weavers.	Jandra, Saliyan, Seniyan.	Devanga and Kaikolan.
Artizans.	Nil.	Kammalan, Kamsali, Panchalas.
Leather-workers	Madiga or Chakkilian. (females)	(Males.)
Field labourers and soldiers.	Malaiman, Nattaman, Palli (females), Vedan or Vettuvan, Paraiyan, Mala and Holeya.	Bedar, Palli (Males) Pallan.

Of these the Mala, Holeya and Paraiyan were mostfield labourers ; and the Kaikolans were soldiers. ; a rule, most of the labouring classes and hunters ere enlisted as sepoys by the Tamil kings. All the other South Indian castes not mentioned in the above table belong either to the right-hand faction or to the left, or hold with the Brahmans a neutral attitude in the dispute. It will be curious to note that later immigrants in South India such as the Musalmans, Guzaratis, Marwaris and Patnulkars are classed with right-hand castes. This strange dissension, which is confined only to South India, exists in no other part of the country. Similar distinctions may still be found among the Sakti worshippers of Bengal ; but this religious sect does not seem to have any connection whatever with the social division of the non-Brahmanical castes of the Madras Presidency. The members of the two divisions struggle for certain honorary distinctions, such as the use of twelve pillars in the marriage *pandal*, the beating of five big drums on certain ceremonial occasions, the ride on horse-back or the carrying of a monkey flag. These privileges are claimed by the right-hand castes on all public and festive occasions, and whenever any of these privileges are exercised by a member of the left-hand faction, fights usually occur.

The Pancham Banajigas of the Canarese province, the Paraiyas of the Tamil districts and the Malas of the Andhra country are the strenuous supporters of the right-hand division. They are assisted by the Holeyas in Mysore and Canara, and by the weavers in the Tamil and Telugu districts. The left-hand division is commanded throughout the presidency by the Kammalas, Kamsalis or Panchalas with the indefatigable assistance of the Madigas or Chakkilians. But for the zealous support of these degraded classes, this enemy of public peace would have disappeared from the land several centuries ago.

Yet such a distinction, notwithstanding Dr. Macleane's statement to the contrary, is not maintained with so much zeal and pertinacity in the Tamil districts as in the Canarese and the Telugu parts of Southern India. The Pallis or Vanniyas have, in their fond hope of becoming Kshatriyas, forgotten all about the feuds; many Kaikolas have, in order to wipe off the so-called tribal or rather the social indignity still clinging to the left-hand faction, become within the last six centuries dancers and singers in Hindu temples as the following Kanchipuram inscription will show :—

முசண்மையும் அடைபடும் தேவர் அடிமையும் கைக்கோளமை யும் தாங்கள நின்ற அடைவுகளிலே விற்றும் ஒற்றிவைத்தும் கொள்ளக கடவர் ஆகவும்.—(S. I. I. I. 122.)

[May sell or mortgage the head-ship, the right of lease, service to god (dancing, &c.), and weaving.]

Again the Kammalas in asserting that they are the Deva- or Visva-Brahmans not only try to conceal their Naga origin but also take shelter in a tradition that all the above privileges were granted to them by Kali, and that 'they are of the highest rank having been placed by that goddess on her left-hand side which in India is the place of honour.' Further, before the introduction of this distinction in Malabar by the later settlers from the surrounding Tamil and

Canarese districts, this inter-caste dispute was a thing quite unknown to the Malaiyalis, and even now it exists only among the weavers and Canarese immigrants. Thus as a matter of fact the dispute is practically confined only to the lowest castes—Paraiyas, Holeyas and Madigas—occasionally encouraged by the Kammalas.

The origin of this distinction is involved in obscurity; but it is clear that it is purely a Dravidian schism, though countenanced, and even sometimes fomented covertly, by the later Aryan immigrants in the south. Many traditions, however, have been manufactured either by the Brahmans to elevate the status of the low but serviceable tribes of the Dravidian race, or by the busy and ingenious artizans, who scarcely let slip an opportunity to elevate their low position. And in proof of it we give below a story current among the Kammalans. The tradition, perverted and mutilated though it be, so as to support their chimerical claims for a higher social status, is not altogether devoid of an historical interest, as it seems to suggest the probable age and origin of this endless dispute. ' The Panchalas (artizans) say they were the hereditary priests for the royal family of the Cholas. During the reign of Parimalan, Vedavyasan waxed jealous of their influence in the kingdom and devised a scheme to oust them from their spiritual office. Accordingly he murdered the king while out hunting and raised his illegitimate son to the throne. This event was followed by unpleasant results. The people refused to cultivate, and tumult and disorder ruled everywhere. The king therefore declared that all people who supported him should be called the right-hand people. A neighbouring Rajah hearing of this, invaded Kalingam and carried off its king as captive, for dismissing the Panchalas and appointing Vyasan, and for dividing the people into the right-hand and left-hand castes.' Another old tradition of equally historical value says that the division into the right-hand and left-hand castes took its origin from the command of the goddess Kali at Kanchipuram (the seat of so many religious and political changes) where, it is said, exists to this day special halls for the two parties called the வலங்கைமண்டபம் and இடங்கைமண்டபம். It is further stated that the pagoda at Conjeevaram has a copper-plate bearing inscriptions which give the origin of this queer distinction of castes. Though both parties referred to it, neither of them, it appears, could produce this important document before the Zillah Court of Salem or Chittur in the course of litigation between the two irreconcilable factions. It appears, however, that the Kammalas have forged a series of copper plates (dated 1098 SS.) in favour of the left-hand faction to justify its preference over the right-hand in matters social.[1]

All that we can infer at present from the above stories is, that some Dravidian castes such as the Valluvas, were priests or *purohits* to the Tamil kings

[1]. The Madras Govt. Epigraphist's Report dated July 1910.

before the arrival of Brahmans, and that the arrangement of the Dravidian castes into two grand divisions (the right and left hands) took place at Kanchipuram under the royal command of a Chola king. In this connection it would be well to remember the origin and former social position of the Valluvas which have already been explained.

Various suggestions have been made concerning the probable origin of the dispute between the right-hand and left-hand factions. One writer in the *Indian Antiquary* (Vol. V) says 'it does appear to have been caused by some person or persons who were strangers to South India'. But who that person or persons could have been he does not say. Another writer tells us that it is a dispute between the principal artificers and the agricultural, mercantile and other classes ; while a third observes that the ' distinction arises primarily from the land-owners and their serfs being the heads of one class, and the Brahmans, the artisans and other interlopers, form the other '. The last view is maintained by the Superintendent of Census in Mysore (1891) who goes on to say that the origin of this irreconcilable faction is due to the professional jealousy that existed between the indigenous mercantile community and the larger and more powerful traders. This is, no doubt, borne out by the alternative names of the factions, *Desa* (foreign) and *Peta* or *Nadu* (native) which are current only in the Mysore State. But the quarrel is found throughout the presidency and is not confined to the circumscribed limits of that province; and there are no grounds to assign to it a western origin. Since co-operation and combined effort are necessary to the wellbeing of a nation why should the cultivating classes be always at enmity with the Kammalas? We learn from the inscriptions already referred to that the Brahmans adhered to neither side, though some lists erroneously mention them as partizans. The serfs of the cultivating castes, namely, the Pallis, Pallars &c., were included in the left while their masters, the Vellalas, espoused the right-hand division. The very fact of the inclusion of the Telugu and Canarese Madigas and Bedars and the Tamil Pallars and Pallis in the left-hand faction goes to confirm the origin of this dispute from outside the Kalinga, Karnataka, Pallava and Pandya countries; and the exclusion from it of the corresponding Tamil castes—Malaiman, Vedan and Paraiya—seems to point out the Chola kingdom as the land of its origin.

To call into existence such a powerful and wide-spread social division, a single cause of small magnitude would never suffice. It has, therefore, been suggested by Rao Bahadur M Ranga Charyar that this division originated from the Dravidian family organization during its passage 'from the matriarchal to the patriarchal state'. He says that 'in their families …the mother seems to have been the head thereof and property seems to have descended from the mother to the daughter'. And in proof of the universal existence of this matriarchal system among the early Dravidians he adduces two facts : (1) In the Dravidian languages 'the name for the father-in-law and the maternal uncle is the same ; for the mother-in-law and the paternal aunt is the same '. (2) 'The division is unknown in Malabar, because its people never passed from the matriarchal to the patriarchal condition'. 'The eighteen communities of the right-hand side seem to have approved of the change, while the nine communities of the left-hand side seem to have opposed it'. Mr. Rice also observes that there is a 'doubtful passage in the Mahawanso which may be supposed to refer to it, and if so, the institution would seem to be of great antiquity '; and in support of it he quotes a tradition that ' when the Pandya princess was sent from Madura to Ceylon, in response to an embassy from Vijaya soliciting her hand in marriage, she is said (according to one version) to have been accompanied by a thousand members of the eighteen castes and five different clans of workmen '.

With due deference to the two high authorities quoted above, I doubt very much the tenability of their arguments in support of the origin and antiquity of the dispute for the following reasons :—

It has been shown in the last essay that there was no caste system among the ancient Dravidians like that which we find amongst them in modern times. Then how did the 18 *panas* or castes of the right-hand and the 9 *panas* of the left come into existence so early as the sixth century B. C.? The above tradition, therefore, seems to us a *post facto* concoction of the Canarese people; and in the whole range of Tamil literature, especially of the early period, there is no reference to this 'ancient' social division, though it was of such vital importance. Further, there is not the slightest vestige of the matriarchal system in South India except in Kerala and in the *Pendukku Meykki* sub-caste of the Idaiyans of the Madura District.

In the Dravida country, as everywhere else, the lowest castes and the hill and forest tribes are the least affected by, or are very slow to adopt, the Aryan civilisation, and even amongst them the matriarchal system was unknown. Malabar and Travancore are no exceptions to this principle. Here the transition from the patriarchal to the matriarchal state is in various stages. Most of the polluting castes and all the aboriginal tribes follow the Makkatayam system as in the other parts of India, while the Ambalavasis, Saliyans, Tiyans and others, who may be said to be in a state of transition, follow both the Makkatayam and the Marumakkatayam system of inheritance. This is doubtless due to the influence of the Nayars and to a desire to imitate the custom of higher castes. Among the non-polluting (by distance) castes it is only the so-called Kshatriyas and the Nayars, whose females had and still have *Sambandam* or marital relationship with the Nambudri Brahmans, that have adopted completely the

Marumakkatayam system. It is thus clear that the matriarchal system of Malabar should have come into existence only after the arrival of the Brahmans into the Kerala country, and that the patriarchal system alone has been in vogue for ages everywhere in South India since the earliest historic times. Whether the matriarchal system was entirely due to the influence of the Nambudri Brahmans or whether there had been other causes at work in that direction, it is beyond the scope of this essay to determine.

As for the absence of this division from Kerala, it may be said that this disaffection did not find its way amongst the non-Brahman castes of that country on account of the iron-hand of the Nambudris, which kept them down under its strong grip. Further, the people of Kerala led a comparatively simple life, as at present; there was no building of large temples; and there was no such demand for skilful labour of the artizans and weavers as in the Tamil districts. The Kammalas, therefore, never aspired for Brahmanhood, nor did the Nambudris invest them with the sacred thread as the Brahmans in the other parts of India did.

The forms of marriage prevalent among the ancient Dravidians were *gandharvam* (Tam. களவு) and *rakshasam* or marriage by capture as we have shown in a previous essay. And the marriage tie was so loose that it could be broken at the will of either party as we now see among the lowest castes.

In this state of connubial relationship there was no need for terms to express the idea of a 'father-in-law' or a 'mother-in-law.' The early Dravidians had no words for father's sister, mother's brother, &c., their relationship being confined only to father, mother, brother and sister. Thus the term *mama* (Tam. மாமா) was borrowed from Sanskrit, and the meaning of *attai* (Tamil. அத்தை), which is also not a Dravidian word, is so vague and indefinite that it meant in Tamil mother, elder sister, mother-in-law, father's sister and the teacher's wife. Similarly *akka* and *ammai* are both mother and elder sister ; *aiyan*, father-in-law, mother's brother, etc. Then, these words do not help us in the least to infer one way or the other regarding the matriarchal or the patriarchal theory, except that the Dravidians were in a very primitive state destitute of terms to express any relationship other than father, mother and children.

Turning now to the origin of the dispute, we find from a careful study of the Tamil inscriptions and the history of the South Indian castes that there are three obvious causes. The first and the most important is the political dissension which led to the final overthrow of the powerful kingdoms of the Pallavas (which besides other provinces then embraced the modern state of Mysore) and the Pandyas. They were the hereditary enemies of the Cholas ; the very name Pallava was hateful to them ; and the Pallava gods of Kanchipuram shared the miserable fate of the Pallava kings and their subjects. As the Kanchipuram inscriptions of Kampana Udaiyar will show, the Pallava temples were closed for a long period of nearly three centuries, and their lands alienated by a Choliyan edict. About the ninth century A. D. the Pallavas were defeated by the Chola and Chalukyan kings in a series of battles, after which the vast empire was broken up into small principalities such as Gangaipadi, Nulambapadi, Tadigaipadai, &c.

Again, in the first quarter of the eleventh century Rajaraja Chola, the richest and one of the mightiest of the Chola sovereigns, invaded and conquered Vengi Nadu, Rettaipadi, Gangaipadi, Kollam, Kalingam, Ilam (Ceylon), Madura and other countries. Towards the close of his prosperous reign he seemed to have marshalled his extensive armies, which he had posted at different quarters to defend his newly conquered dominions, into two grand divisions—the one consisting of those men who had won for him victories in all his foreign campaigns, and the other composed of new soldiers from the Pandya, the Telugu and Canarese countries, who had formerly fought against him from his enemies' camps. The former, recruited chiefly from the Vedan, Nattaman, Malayaman and Paraiya castes, he called the right-hand army (வலங்கை வேளைக்காரர்—the right-hand infantry), while the latter made up of the Pallans, Pallis, Madigas and Bedars was called the left-hand army. This alone, we think, could account for the anamolous grouping of the Bedars (Canarese hunters) in the left, while their Tamil brethren, the Vedans, were placed in the right-hand division. The Pallans, correctly Mallar, formed the Pandiyan army, the Pallis constituted the Pallava army, while the troops of Kalingam and other countries were recruited chiefly from the Bedars and Madigas or Chakkiliyans The male members of these military classes were put in the lefthand, but their females who could not have naturally taken up arms against Rajaraja were treated as belonging to the right-hand faction. The inscriptions of Rajendra Chola prove that this distinction was observed by his army though not so strictly as in his father's time. The expression வலங்கைப்பழம்படைகள் which occurs therein means the 'old troops of the right-hand' as opposed to the new soldiers of the conquered dominions. And by the time of Adhirajendra Chola (A. D. 1065) a poll-tax [1] was levied on all the male members of both factions who were in a position to use the implements of war. All these clearly prove that the origin of the division was purely of a military or political nature.

Again, the tradition already referred to informs us that the distinction originated in the reign of a Chola king of the Kalinga country, and we know of no earlier Chola kings than Rajaraja and Rajendra Chola, who invaded and temporarily subjugated Kalingam. For these reasons the present writer is strongly inclined to assign to this social distinction a date not earlier than A. D. 1010.

The second agent, also in the order of time, which

1. South Indian Inscriptions, Vol. III, p. 115.

tended to swell the ranks of the two factions, was the aspiration of certain castes to rise higher in the social scale. One of the six principal duties of the ancient Hindu kings being the preservation of caste rules and observances as dictated by the Sastras, it is very likely that any violation of the established custom by any member of a caste or tribe would have met with the severest punishment. The Kammalas were, as stated above, a guild of Dravidian or Naga origin, holding a place outside the pale of the Aryan caste system. They were, however, skilful artificers and as such their services were in constant demand by the Brahmans and other classes. During the great temple-building epoch—the tenth and eleventh centuries—the Hindu kings not only patronized these people, but also appointed them permanently for the extension and repair of the temples they had built. In this way their connection with the religious institutions and consequently their closer contact with the Brahmans contributed largely to elevate their social position. And as Sir W. W. Hunter observes, ' the Brahmanical element here finds itself so weak, and so accustomed to compromise with the original population, that the priests have invented a legend, to give a semi-Aryan descent to five castes, which everywhere else rank as Sudras'. But without being content with the concessions and privileges granted to them, they began to clamour for a still higher status, nay, even claimed an equal rank with the Brahmans. This offended the Chola king, probably Rajendra, the reputed conqueror of Kalingam and other northern countries; many were persecuted, many were ordered to be destroyed, and the rest were classed along with other hostile tribes in the left-hand division.

The other castes which strive for a higher social position are the Kaikolas and the Devangas, the former of whom claim direct descent from Virabahu, one of the nine commanders of god Subrahmanya, and the latter, wearing the sacred thread, fight for Brahmanhood. This kind of struggle for Brahmanical rank is strongest in Mysore and South Canara, but it is almost unknown in the neighbouring district of Malabar. For example, the potters of South Canara returned their caste name at the Census of 1891 as *Gunda* (pot) Brahmana; the artisans as *Visva-*, *Deva-*, *Surya-*, and *Subrahmanya* Brahmana; the *Kshatriya* and *Vaisya* Brahmana; and the Madigas (leather-workers) as *Matanga* Brahmana. Encouraged by the novel and anti-Brahmanical doctrines of Basava, which did away with all the caste distinctions, the servile classes styled themselves Brahmans; and in so doing have adopted uncouth nomenclature from the Sanskrit and Canarese vocabularies. The names of the Lingayat septs are legion, but some may be given here :—Chikkamane Sampradaya Brahmana, Dhuli Pavada Brahmana, Gaudalike Jangama Brahmana, Hirihasube Banajiga Brahmana, Sthavara Jangama Brahmana, &c. It is this, we believe, that has misled Sir W. W.

Hunter when he speaks of the non-Brahmanical ryot class of Mysore as "the peasant Brahmans." Thus, the high aspirations of certain low castes had provoked the Aryan Brahmans, who out of jealousy and anger managed with the assistance of their kings, to class such men in the left-hand division, so that there might crop up unceasing quarrels, in almost all of which they were requested by the heads of respective factions to sit as judges for settling disputes. It is significant that this feud is very strong in the districts where there is a large number of Lingayats.

In addition to the two sources already explained, Dr. Oppert suggests a third one. He says 'the imminent decay of the Jaina power opened a fair prospect to the Brahmans of which they were not slow to take advantage. They gathered round them their followers, while their opponents, who represented in certain respects the national party did the same . . . The influence of Jains was perhaps strongest in towns, where the artizan classes form an important portion of the population, while the Brahmana appealed to the land owning and agricultural classes'. This is a cause, but not *the* cause of the dispute. Because firstly, the struggle for Brahman supremacy had almost been over in the south before the tenth century A D. ; and had this been the only cause for the division into rival hands, it would have taken place prior to that period. But it is not mentioned in any work or inscription of that date. Secondly, granting that the struggle between Brahmanism and Jainism was the essential cause of this curious division, the logical inference would be that most of the artizans would have adopted the Jaina faith, and the Brahmans and Jains would have respectively espoused the right and left hand factions. But the census statistics of 1891 clearly showed that only 40 artizans were Jains, and even these belonged to the right-hand faction, while the Brahmans occupied, as already stated, a neutral position. Jainism was on the decline in the south during the eighth and ninth centuries, but it had not lost its strong-hold in the Pallava and Kadamba kingdoms. The Periyapuranam and the Tiruvilayadalpuranam give graphic descriptions of constant struggles between the Brahmans and Jains, and of the zeal and enthusiasm evinced by the Chola and Pandya sovereigns in putting down Jainism in their countries. And we know how long Sri Ramanuja had to struggle with the Jains before he succeeded in converting Bitti Deva (Vishnu Vardhana), the Jain king of Mysore (A. D. 1138). It is therefore possible that Jainism, an anti-Brahmanical religion professed by the enemies of the Chola kings, might have acted as a third cause for the division into the right-hand and left-hand factions. The supposition, therefore, of Mr Nelson that religious difference has little or no connection with this remarkable feud cannot be accepted, though he is very near the mark in suggesting that the obstinacy of the Panchalas in disputing the supremacy of the Brahmans and their adoption of the Brahmanical customs must have laid the foundation for this social distinction.

We have said above that the Jains belong to the right-hand division, although one would, on the contrary, expect to find them in the left-hand. The reason for the change is, says a Mysore inscription of A. D. 1368, that the Brahmans and Jains were fighting for the use of the five big drums and the *Kalasa*, a privilege usually exercised by the right-hand castes, when in the same year the then king of Mysore, Vira Bukka Raya, effected a compromise between the Jains and the Brahmans, and ever since that time the Jains have been admitted as belonging to the right-hand party.

To summarise, the distinction into right-hand and left-hand castes, now maintained by the agricultural classes on the one side and by the artizans on the other, originated in the Chola country about 1010 A. D., the cause which led to it being,(1) the enmity that had existed between the Cholas and the neighbouring kings,(2) the aspirations of certain low castes to attain a higher social status, stimulated by the newly inculcated anti-Brahmanical doctrines of Basava, and (3) the struggle between the Jaina and the Hindu religions for existence in the Pallava and the Kadamba countries. Or, to put it more briefly, this faction dispute is the outcome of the political, social and religious jealousies amongst the Hindus of South India during the eleventh and twelfth centuries of the Christian era.

VI

THE TAMIL ALPHABET

In that classic of Tamil literature—the Kural—Tiruvalluvar describes "Numbers" and "writing" as the two eyes of humanity.

எணெண்ணென்ப வேனே யெழுத்தென்ப விவ்விரண்டேக்
கணெண்ணென்ப வாழு முயிர்க்கு.—*Kur.*

So high was the importance attached to these two "Rs." In Tamil 'ezhuttu' includes letters as well as picture, and as a mark of distinction writing or alphabetic letters have been called கண்ணெழுத்து or signs for the eye. It is also called நெடிங்கணக்கு or the 'long account' in contra-distinction to numbers, எண் or கணக்கு. *Kanakku* is a vague term meaning account, letters or knowledge, as in 'Samaya-kanakkan', a thelogian.

Pavanandi, the popular grammarian of the thirteenth century treats the subject of Tamil letters or orthography under twelve-heads, namely,—number, name, order, origin, form, quantity, initial, middle and final letters (in words), similarity in sound, wordbuilding and combination.[1] Including his famous Nannul there are about half-a-dozen authoritative treatises on grammar which were written at different times; but in every one of these the history of the Tamil alphabet has been studiedly avoided. The fact seems to be that the native grammarians knew little of it, and their ignorance has led some of their commentators to bungle as regards certain points of historical import. It is therefore proposed to deal at the outset with the historical side of the Tamil alphabet at some length, touching very briefly on the other points connected therewith in the concluding part of the present essay.

The Tamil alphabet now in use is not what it was a thousand years ago. Its form appears to have undergone changes from century to century until about the fourteenth, when it reached the present stereotyped condition. There were, however, two different kinds of writing in use in the Tamil country —the one introduced by the Brahmans and the other indigenous to the Tamil race. The former is known as the Grantha-Tamil alphabet, and it was the parent stock from which some of the modern Tamil characters have sprung, while the latter is called by palæographists as the Vatteluttu or the Chera-Pandya alphabet The Tamil districts including Malabar and Travancore abound in inscriptions of both varieties.

---

[1]. The classification of letters by some early Tamil Scholars into (1) graphic (உரு), (2) Nominal (பெயர்), (3) phonetic (ஒலி) and (4) conceptual (கருத்து) seems to me unpsychological.

Very recently writings in the Asoka or Brahmi characters also have been discovered in the districts of Madura and Tinnevelly.

But the introduction of all these did not take place at one and the same period. The Vatteluttu or the original Tamil alphabet was supplanted by the Grantha-Tamil or the modern Tamil characters in the Tamil kingdoms at different periods, which were perhaps conterminous with the migration and settlement of the Brahmans in these countries. In the Pallava province (Tondaimandalam), where they settled first before proceeding to the southern districts, the Pallava characters—an off-shoot of the Brahmi or the North Indian script—were in use prior to A.D. 650. We have no documentary evidence to prove at what period the Vatteluttu was in use there. The earliest Chola inscriptions belong only to the tenth century, and all of them are in the Grantha-Tamil characters, which appear to be a later development of the Pallava-Tamil used in the Kuram and Kasakudi copper-plates of the seventh and eighth centuries. Occasionally, Vatteluttu inscriptions may also be met with in the Chola country, but most of these belong to the Pandya kings. It is not therefore possible in the absence of the earlier Chola records to state when the Vatteluttu was ousted by the Grantha-Tamil characters in the Tanjore District. In the Pandya country, on the other hand, we have inscriptions in both scripts going up to the eighth century A.,D., and from these it will appear that Vatteluttu came nto desuetude sometime after the conquest of that country by the Chola king Parantaka I during the first quarter of the tenth century. In Travancore and Malabar the Vatteluttu survived some centuries longer.

The two main questions we have now to consider in connection with the earlier Tamil alphabet or Vatteluttu are,—(1) the date of its introduction into the Tamil country; and (2) whether it was borrowed by the Tamils direct from the north-western Semitics, or was only an earlier modification of the Asoka or Brahmi characters as some scholars seem to think.

The earliest Vatteluttu inscriptions known to us belong to the eighth century A. D. and do not go further back ; and the earliest description of that alphabet is what we find in the grammar of Tolkapyar. It is said that Agastya was the first Tamil grammarian ; but we know nothing about his date or the existence of his grammar, except that Tolkapyar was his student, even which seems extremely questionable. The date of the introduction of the Vetteluttu alphabet cannot for the present be carried earlier than the age of Tolkapyar. In his monograph 'On the Aindra School of Sanskrit Grammarians', Dr. Burnell assigns the eighth century A.D. as the probable date of Tolkapyar, assuming that there was no Tamil literature before that period and that Tolkapyar professed Jainism or Buddhism, the predominant religions at the time, according to this writer, in Southern India. Both these premises have since

THE TAMIL ALPHABET

been proved to be false. Tolkapyar was a Brahman *Rishi* and belonged to the Jamadagni tribe ; and the contemporary scholar, Athangottasan who passed his work at the royal court of the Pandya king was also a Brahman deeply versed in the four Vedas.

In the Colophon to the Tolkapyam the author says that he has mastered the Sanskrit grammar of Indra.

ஐந்திரம் நிறைந்த தொல்காபியன்.

When the epoch-making work of Panini had long been considered the highest authority on the subject in Sanskrit, why Tolkapyar should study and follow Indra's work in his grammar of the Tamil language is inexplicable, unless it be that Panini was not known to the Southern Hindus of Tolkapyar's time. One of the sixty-four predecessors quoted by Panini in the field of grammatical science was Indra, and he should therefore have flourished before him. Thus, Tolkapyar must have lived anterior to B.C 350 which is the date assigned to Panini by the best authorities.

Again, it will be seen from the following *sutras* that, at the time of Tolkapyar, there were in use some Tamil words in the middle of which letter combinations like (ல்ய) lya, (ளய) lya, (ஞய) jnya, (ஞய) nya, (ம்ய) mya, (வ்ய) vya and (ம்வ) mva, could occur.

லளஃகான் முன்னர் யவவுஞ தோன்றும். I, 24.
ஞநமவ வென்னும் புள்ளி முன்னர்
யஃகானிற்றன் மெய்பெறன்றே. I, 27.
மஃகான் புள்ளி முன்வவ்வுஞ் தோன்றும. I, 28.

Commenting on these *sutras* Nacchinarkiniyar writes thus,—இங்ஙனம் ஆசிரியர் சூத்திரம் செய்தலின் அக்காலத்து ஒருமொழியாக வழங்கிய சொற்கள் உளவென்பது பெற்றும் ; அவை இக்காலத்து இறந்தன

Not a single word of the kind referred to in the *sutras* is to be found in the whole range of the existing Tamil literature. The earliest work of any magnitude—that is the Kural of Tiruvalluvar—goes back to the first century A.D., and the period when such words were current should have been at least three or four centuries before the age of that work. For these reasons, it would not be too much to suppose that Tolkapyar flourished before B.C. 350, that is five centuries earlier than Apollonius, the Stoic philosopher and the first grammarian of the Latin language. *A fortiori* Tolkapyar's teacher and first Tamil grammarian and divine *rishi*, Agastya must have lived before the fourth century B. C. When these two Indo-Aryan scholars began to write their grammars, Tamil had already become a written language

It is said by Prof. Macdonell of Oxford that the Katantra of Sarvavarman, the famous minister of the Andhra king Satavahana, served as a model for the native grammar of the Dravidians. As this is a work of the second century A.D., Tolkapyar could not have

---

1. This view has, however, been questioned by the authors of தொல்காப்பியச் சூத்திரவிருத்தி and திராவிடப்பிரகாசிகைfollowing the commentaries ofஇளம்பூரணர் and சேனாவரையர். But we are inclined to follow நச்சினார்க்கினியர்.

followed it, and if he had done so he would have plainly said காதந்திரநிறைநத instead of ஐந்திரநிறைந்த. It is, however, believed by Tamil scholars that Sarvavarman's work was imitated by Buddha-Mitra (A D 1075) in his Virasoliyam. And the difference in the treatment of the subject adopted by the authors of Tolkapyam and Virasoliyam, appears to favour the view that Katantra was not imitated in the former work.

Thus then the introduction of the Vatteluttu alphabet must have taken place long before the fourth or fifth century B. C., and this approximates the earliest date assigned by European scholars to the introduction of writing in India, which was the seventh or eighth century before the Christian era

As to who first brought the alphabet from the western Semitics—whether the Southern Dravidians or the Northern Aryans—it is not quite easy to settle. On this point western scholars hold contrary opinions, Dr. Rhys Davids, the learned Bhuddhist scholar, thinks ' that all the present available evidence tends to show that the Indian alphabet is not Aryan at all ; that it was introduced into India by Dravidian (Tamil) merchants in the eighth or seventh century'. And the same writer goes on to say that 'after the merchants brought the script to India, it gradually became enlarged and adapted to the special requirements of the Indian learned and colloquial dialects.' This is also the view taken by that pioneer orientalist and antiquary, Mr. E. Thomas. Dr. Burnell seems to think that Vatteluttu had an independent source and had nothing to do with the Brahmi alphabet of Northern India. This alphabet, he says, 'was formed and settled' before the Indo-Aryan grammarians of the Tamil language came to Southern India.

In opposition to this view Drs. Caldwell, Buhler and Grierson maintain (and on insufficent ground as will be shown later on) that the Vatteluttu alphabet was borrowed or rather adapted from the Brahmi or Asoka alphabet of Upper India. 'The older Mauryan alphabet', says Dr. Buhler, 'was used over the whole of India.' He says further 'from a palæographical point of view, the Vatteluttu may be described as a cursive script which bears the same relation to the Tamil as the modern alphabets of the clerks and merchants to their originals ... Perhaps it may be assumed that the " round hand " arose already before the seventh century, but was modified in the course of time by the further development of the Tamil and the Grantha scripts. Owing to the small number of the accessible inscriptions, this conjecture is, however, by no means certain.' Dr. Caldwell asserts 'that the Tamil characters were borrowed from the earliest Sanskrit, and the language of the Tamilians was committed to writing on or soon after the arrival of the first colony of Brahmans.' He even goes to the length of confirming this hypothesis by saying that the 'oldest known Dravidian alphabet (he means the Vatteluttu) makes no difference between long

THE TAMIL ALPHABET 121

and short *e,* எ and *o,* ஒ which is one of the arguments that may be adduced in favour of the theory of the derivation of that alphabet from the Sanskritic alphabet of Asoka' All these are mere theories. So far as we are aware, neither Dr. Caldwell, nor Dr. Buhler, nor even Dr. Grierson has disproved the other hypothesis by any crucial instances.

In support of the theory advocated by Mr. E. Thomas, Drs. Rhys Davids and Burnell—on whose side the balance of authority seems to rest—that the Tamilians had introduced the Vatteluttu and developed it independently of the Asoka or the Brahmi alphabet, the following arguments may be adduced:—

It has been shown in a previous essay that the Tamil people or rather the early Dravidians were a civilized race allied to the 'ancient Accadians, with whom they lived in Babylonia and Assyria before their migration to Hindustan. They were acquainted with the Phœnicians and Egyptians as early as the 14th or 15th century B C. It would, therefore, be highly probable that these early Dravidians might have brought with them the alphabet when they migrated to India And it is also probable that the Indo-Aryans borrowed it from their Dravidian neighbours.

Long before the settlement of the Aryans in South India, the Tamils had commercial intercourse with the Egyptians and other Western nations, as will be inferred from the existence of Tamil words like *tokai* (peacock) and *agil* (a fragrant wood) in the Hebrew Bible, and *arisi* (rice) in Greek. Like the Banyas or the Aryan merchant caste of Upper India, the Tamils had no caste scruples prohibiting them from sea-voyage In fact, among the Dravidians of the remote past there was no caste system, and they were expert seamen.

Although the Tamilians owed their grammar to Agastya and to Tolkapyar, it should not be inferred that they were indebted to them for the art of writing also. The existence of pure Tamil words like *ezhuttu* (letters), *suvadi* (book) &c. before they came to the south disproves the theory that Agastya brought the alphabet with him from Upper India. The gratuitous assertion of Dr. Caldwell that ' the language of the Tamilians was committed to writing on or soon after the arrival of the first colony of Brahmans', therefore, falls to the ground.

Again, his statement that the Dravidian alphabet makes no difference between the long and short *e*, எ and *o*, ஒ is a mere specious argument, if by Dravidian he meant Tamil, because the Vatteluttu alphabet of the early Tamils did make the distinction, as the author of the Tolkapyam has distinctly ruled that,—எகரஒகர மெய்ப்புள்ளி பெறும் ; and this *sutram* will have no meaning if no such distinction was observed in his days.

While writing about the formation of the letter *m*, ம the grammarian, Tolkapyar clearly defines that, உட்பெறுபுள்ளியுருவாகும்மே. What he meant by this rule was that the form of *p*, ப (Vatteluttu ౮) should be

THE TAMIL ALPHABET

carefully distinguished from that of *m*, ம (Vatteluttu ꢀ) which received an inner dot. Here the right hand tail of உ was joined in later times with the inner dot, which was quite natural in cursive writing on palm leaves with an iron stylus, as Nacchinarkiniyar has rightly observed—மகரம் உட்பெறு புள்ளியை வளைத்து எழுதி னர். In the Brahmi, Asoka or Mauryan alphabet உ and ம were written as ␣ and ␣. There was a letter in the Asoka script which in form approached the Vatteluttu ம, but that was *ph.* and not *m*. It will thus be seen that there is not the least resemblance between the Vatteluttu and the Asoka *p* and *m*, nor can we perceive any appreciable similarity in the other letters of both alphabets except in the case of *k, p, r, l, t,* and *ch,* which may after all be only accidental, both being borrowed from the same Semitic source, as will be seen from the comparative table of the ancient alphabets given below:—

English	k	p	r	l	t	ch	th
Asoka	ㇾ	ᄂ	]	↲	ᄃ	d	..
Vatteluttu	ㇾ	ಲ	]	∾	ᴗ	ச	ᴈ
Phœnician	⊣	⌐	ᛐ	ѕ	-	.	?
Hebrew	]	-	]	և	-	-	..
Arabic	-	.	⁾	ل	؎	-	-
Tamil	க	ப	ர	ல	ட	ச	த

If Tamil borrowed and developed its alphabet from Brahmi of North India like the other cultivated languages of the Dravidian family, it should have taken place before its grammar was written And in that case, the tendency should have shown itself in an efficient and complete alphabetic system as in the sister languages, Telugu and Kanarese On the other hand, the simplicity of the alphabetic and the deficiency of its phonetic systems, and their stationary character for nearly 2,000 years point to a different source for its origin. We are glad to observe that this is also the view taken by Mr. R. Sewell, I.C.S. He writes thus : ' The meagre character and simple forms of the Tamil alphabets almost certainly derived from a Semitic source, perhaps, Aramic or Himayaritic, point to its having been adopted and having become fixed before the Kharoshti was known'.

Among the Dravidian races of South India the Tamils alone made use of the Vatteluttu alphabet from time immemorial, whilst their Telugu and Kanarese neighbours have, so far as epigraphical researches reveal, been using some alphabet or other which had its origin from the Brahmi of Upper India. The principle of adding a dot for consonants is peculiar only to Tamil, and is found in no other alphabetic systems adopted from Brahmi. It is possible that the Tamils might have borrowed it from the Semitics of Western Asia and used it for consonants instead of for vowel signs, as in the Hebrew and other Semitic alphabets.

The vast difference that exists between Tamil and the Aryan languages in their vocabulary, between the Tamils and the Indo-Aryans, the contempt which the one had for the other, and the great antiquity and the divine origin which the Tamils claim for their 'sweet' language and its grammar—all these seem to favour the indigenous origin of the Tamil Vatteluttu alphabet.

The latest epigraphical researches have brought to light the existence in the Pandya country of the Brahmi or Asoka inscriptions. Rai Bahadur V. Venkayya, Epigraphist to the Government of India, believes that this discovery 'in the Madura and Tinnevelly districts proves beyond doubt that the Mauryan alphabet was in use all over India', and that this seems to him ' to militate against the theory of the indigenous origin' of the Vatteluttu alphabet. We do not for a moment question Dr Buhler's statement ' that the older Mauryan alphabet was used over the whole of India'; but it is extremely doubtful whether this alphabet was used in the Tamil country by the literates of all castes and creeds—Buddhists, Jains, Hindus and Animists alike. As a matter of fact we know that the English alphabet is at present in use from the Himalayas to Cape Comorin among the educated classes, and even English inscriptions are found almost everywhere in India. And yet, do we not see side by side with it scores of Indian alphabets? The ubiquity of an alien alphabet in a particular country cannot, therefore, be a proof for the non-existence of other alphabetic systems and of its necessity for the aboriginal inhabitants of that soil.

History informs us that Emperor Asoka sent Buddhist Missionaries to the three Tamil countries about B.C. 250, and there is very little evidence to show that there were Buddhists in these lands prior to that date. The Brahmi inscriptions alluded to above are believed to belong to the Asoka or post-Asoka period. It has been shown above that Tolkapyar flourished anterior to B. C. 350, that is, at least a century before Asoka. As it has been proved that the description of the alphabet given by Tolkapyar in his grammar is applicable only to the Vatteluttu characters, but not to the Brahmi or Asoka alphabet, it is evident beyond any shadow of doubt that Vatteluttu alone was in use among the Tamils before the introduction of Buddhism in their country. The Brahmi was evidently used only by the Buddhist monks and missionaries, and perhaps by Brahmans also This theory should hold its own against any others, until it could be established from inscriptional sources, that the Brahmi alphabet was universally used by all classes in the Tamil country before the days of Tolkapyar (B.C. 350).

The mere fact that the Brahmi alphabet was in use all over India proves nothing concerning the origin of Vatteluttu, any more than the use of the English alphabet regarding the source of the Indian alphabets. The Moplahs of the West Coast use the Vatteluttu (Koleluttu) characters to this very day, while the

Hindus there gave it up three or four centuries ago. That is to say, the Vatteluttu and the Grantha-Malayalam alphabets have been in existence side by side for at least the last three or four centuries in a particular part of the ancient Tamil land, the former being used by the pure Tamilians (Malayalis) and the latter by the Aryanized Dravidians. Again, we observe in the Vatteluttu copper plate grants of Jatila Varman, Ravi Varman, Sri Valluvan Kodai and others, that Grantha characters were used freely to express pure Sanskrit words and Vatteluttu for the Tamil ones. All the South Indian alphabets, not excepting the modern Grantha-Tamil, may be traced to the Brahmi script of Upper India. Had Vatteluttu been borrowed and developed from the Brahmi, like the Grantha and other alphabets of India from the earliest times, it would be difficult to account for the Tamils alone using both the characters simultaneously in their inscriptions. This anamoly is nowhere to be found outside the Tamil country. And this one fact, combined with the other considerations set forth in the previous paragraphs, must lead one to conclude that Vatteluttu had an indigenous origin, and that the Brahmi characters might have been understood and even largely used by the Brahmans, Buddhists and Jains, while the rest of the people in the Chera and Pandya countries made use of the Vatteluttu alphabet. And, notwithstanding the divergence of opinion among high authorities, the above arguments compel us to accept the theory that the Tamil alphabet

(Vatteluttu) was not borrowed from the Brahmi or any other Upper Indian alphabet, but had been introduced directly from Western Asia by Tamil merchants during the eighth or seventh century B.C., who developed it independently of the northern alphabets until it was partially supplanted by the Grantha characters in or about the tenth century.

But for the mighty influence of the Aryan Brahmans, such an ancient and original alphabet might have survived among the Tamils as amongst the Musalman Moplahs of Malabar. Before the introduction of the Grantha-Tamil characters, the influx of Sanskrit words in the Tamil language was extremely limited ; and even those words appeared in the Tamil garb or in the form of *tadbhavas*. Thus, we find in the *Tiruvoymoli* of Nammalvar tamilized Sanskrit words like பற்பநாபன், சிற்தான், இருடீகசன், விகிருதம், இராக்கதன், விடமம், ஆணை, மனிசர், சிட்டன், உருத்திரன், &c. But with the large influx of Sanskrit words and phrases—*tadbhavas* and *tatsamas*—in consequence of the importation of the Aryan religion and philosophy among the Tamils, the introduction of the Grantha-Tamil characters in the Pandya and Kerala countries became a matter of necessity. And new rules for the adoption and naturalisation of Sanskrit words in Tamil, not given by Tolkapyar, were added in the grammars of Buddha Mitra and Pavanandi, the former of whom flourished in the eleventh and the latter at the beginning of the thirteenth century.

Of the thirty-one Tamil letters of the Grantha-

Tamil alphabet, the consonants ண,ச,ந and ய only appear to have been adopted or borrowed from the Pallava characters, the rest being modified survivals of the defunct Vatteluttu. In the Yanaimalai inscriptions of the Pandya king Jatavarman (A. D. 770), we find some of the Pallava-Grantha characters mixed up with the Vatteluttu. For example, in the Tamil word மாறன் the Vatteluttu மா, *m*, is used, and in the Sanskrit word மந்திரி the Pallava or the Brahmi ४; and the *y*, ய of the earlier Vatteluttu appears like the Telugu ల, while in the Museum plates of Jatavarman like the modern tripartite letter ய, ய. Minor differences in the forms of the Vatteluttu themselves may be noticeable in inscriptions from different quarters.

The tacking of vowel signs to the consonants was regular in Vatteluttu, but not so in the Grantha-Tamil which is doubtless due to the mixture of the two alphabets. The vowel-consonants of Grantha-Tamil are exactly after the formation of the Nagari characters, excepting that most of the vowel signs, as for ஆ, எ, ஏ, ஐ, ஒ, ஓ and ஔ stand detached from the Tamil consonants. This may be 'made intelligible by commenting on the following note of Nacchinarkiniyar :—

உருவுதிரிந்து உயிர்த்தலாவது மேலுங் கீழும் விலங்கு பெற்றும் கோடு பெற்றும் புள்ளி பெற்றும் புள்ளியுங் கோடும் உடன பெற்றும் உயிர்த்தலாம். இ, ஈ முதலியன மேல்விலங்கு பெற்றன. கு, கூ முதலியன கீழ்விலங்கு பெற்றன. கெ, கே முதலியன கோடு பெற்றன. கா, நா முதலியன புள்ளி பெற்றன.

அருகே பெறற புள்ளியை இக்காலத்தார் காலாக எழுதிஞர். மகரம் உட்பெறு புள்ளியை வளாத்து எழுதிஞர். கொ,கோ, வொ, கோ முதலியன புள்ளிபுங் கோடும் உடன்பெற்றன.—*Tol.* I., 17. Here, விலங்கு means a curve, கோடு is a loop or curl, புள்ளி is a dot, and கால is a vertical stroke. Thus in இ the consonant க் has received the upper curve and in கு a nether one. The letter கெ is formed by prefixing a loop or coil to it. In the early stage the loop which was only the first half of the vowel எ was attached to the consonant, though now separated from it. The case of கோ and கை is peculiar, and it clearly proves that the Grantha-Tamil system of forming vowel-consonant has been adopted instead of the old Vatteluttu system. The letter கெ is formed by the addition of a loop and a vertical stroke (originally the sign of long ஆ), the one preceding and the other succeeding the consonant. But the dot or புள்ளி was never used for this purpose, either in the Grantha-Tamil or in the Vatteluttu characters. The statement of Nacchinarkiniyar that அருகே பெறற புள்ளியை இக்காலத்தார் காலாக எழுதிஞர் seems, therefore, purely unauthorized. In the Vatteluttu the stroke was horizontal, and it always stood for a long vowel ; but in the Grantha-Tamil it is vertical and does not always indicate a long vowel, except in the case of ஆ. The long vowel ஆ and the vowel-consonants ணை, று, and ளை have received a nether curve, while a perpendicular stroke is put after the other consonants. This is surely unsymmetrical, though not more anomalous than the joining of such parts of உ to consonants (as in கு, சு, and து) as fit in with their form. All these afford unmistakable evidence for the mixed character of the modern Grantha-Tamil alphabet. Long ன and ள were originally written with a vertical stroke added to உ and ஒ thus உ], ஒ] which in the course of a few centuries assumed the shape of a ள. The short or the long ஒ was formerly distinguished by means of a dot over it. As late as A. D. 1740, no distinction was made between the short and long vowel-consonantal signs of எ and ஒ, ஒ, ஒா. Beschi seems to have been the first to make this reform by rounding the upper end of the loop for the long sound. The sign for ஊ in கூ is a double loop or curl as in the Grantha but joined together in later Tamil; and the two loops were originally placed sometimes one above the other and sometimes side by side. The letter ஆய்தம் is written with three dots like the English symbol for 'therefore' and it is neither a vowel nor a consonant.

The Vatteluttu or the Tamil archaic alphabet is so called on account of its round or circular form like the modern Telugu alphabet, while its modern development has assumed the angular or, as some would say, square shape. This angularity was due to the facility in writing on palm leaves with an iron stylus, or in cutting on stones or copper plates with a chisel. Further, the left-hand vertical line or stroke which goes to form an angle with the top horizontal stroke in letters like க, ச, த, ங and ர is a later meaningless addition not found in the Tamil inscription prior to A. D. 1050. The letters ட, ப, ம, ய, வ and ழ had no angles on either side, because each of them had only a curve at the bottom like ८, ౮, ౨, ധ, ౨ and ஐ. In the Vatteluttu the vowel உ, ౨ was half a வ, and ம was a ப with an inner dot ; ப is simply another form of வ. Hence உ, ப, வ, and ம are almost alike both in form and sound.

So much for the form of Tamil letters. Let us now take their number, order, and pronunciation. There are thirty-one letters ; twelve vowels and eighteen consonants and one semi-vowel Tolkapyar adds to these the shortened இ and உ making them thirty-three. As there are no separate signs to express these two sounds, the number of Tamil letters should be taken as only thirty-one. Of the twelve vowels, அ, இ, உ, எ, ஒ, are short (குறில்) and ஆ, ஈ, ஊ, ஏ, ஓ, ஐ and ஔ are long (நெடில்) ; strictly speaking ஐ and ஔ are not long vowels but only diphthongs or சந்தியக்கரம் ; and they may be represented by அ+இ or அ+ய் and அ+உ or +அவ். The letters அ, இ and உ are called primary vowels, hence they are placed first with their cognate long sounds எ, ஏ and ஐ, ஒ, ஓ and ஔ are considered in Sanskrit secondary or compound vowels formed by the union of அ and இ and அ and உ respectively. With this compare the example, நர + இந்திரன் = நரேந்திரன் ; நர + உத்தமன் = நரோத்தமன். It will thus be seen that there are no short எ and ஒ in Sanskrit. The arrangement of Vowels in Tamil is, therefore, exactly after the Sanskrit model. There are eighteen consonants in Tamil. Of these

THE TAMIL ALPHABET 133

க், ச், ட், த், ப் and ற் are surds ; ங், ஞ், ண், ந், ம and ன are nasals ; and ய், ர், ல், வ், ழ் and ள் are liquids. The order followed in their arrangement is also that of Sanskrit. To shew that ழ், ள். ற் and ன are letters peculiar to Tamil they are placed last.

Quantity or மாத்திரை is different from pronunciation ; the one relates to music in poetry, and the other to the enunciation of letters and words in speech. We are not, therefore, concerned here with அளபெடை, prolation or the increase in quantity, which is applicable only to poetry. However, among Tamil vowels இ and உ have sometimes a lesser quantity even in ordinary speech. Sivagnana Swami, the uncompromising critic of இலக்கணவிளக்கம் says, the shortened இ and உ are indicated by a dot ; but the truth of his statement is questionable. The dot was never used either in the Tamil inscriptions or in the ordinary writing. Now-a-days a dot is used in Malayalam to denote a final short உ which in this language approaches a sound mid-way between அ and உ as in செய்து ஐ and ஒள being diphthongs, their quantity is shortened at times, the first in all the three places and the second only at the beginning of words. But this does not satisfactorily account for their existence. The semi-vowel ஆய்தம் gets decreased in quantity when words beginning with த combine with words ending in ல் and ள். All these are called சார்பெழுத்து or dependant letters as the changes in quantity occur only in words, but never in isolated letters themselves.

Coming to consonants, we find the Tamil alphabet very defective, and in some cases redundant also. Surds coming after nasals lose their hard sounds as in செங்கு, இஞ்சி, நுண்டு, கந்தகம் and செம்பியன்; and in Malayalam they are changed' into nasals as in மாங்கா for மாங்காய், குஞ்ஞி for குஞ்சி, இருந்து for இருந்து and so on. Sometimes க and ச even when not preceded by nasals get the soft sound similar to the Arabic *ghayn* and the Sanskrit ஹ as in செகுத்த and பசித்த respectively. Thus for the thirty-one letters we have fifteen vowel and twenty-five consonant sounds, or forty in all. This is certainly a defect. But some might say that when the alphabet was first introduced, the Tamil language had only thirty-one sounds, and that the remaining nine explained above crept in during later times owing to the influence of the Indo-Aryans. This may be accepted as partly correct, as we find to this day, if one is careful enough to observe, slight variations in the pronunciation of the Jaffna Tamils and the Tamil Brahmans.

The letters peculiar to Tamil are ஃ, ழ, ற and ன. The sound of ஃ is midway between the Arabic *ghayn* and the Sanskrit ஹ. It is found in no other Indian or European languages, and it seems to suggest some connection of the Tamil race with the Semitic or Western Asiatic nations. The letter ழ is equally a private property of Tamil and a terrible bugbear for Europeans to pronounce. It has been variously transliterated in some of the European languages by li, zi, zh, rl, l, zy, &c., Dr. Pope's rule for its pronunciation is to 'apply the tip of the tongue as far back as you can to the palate and pronounce a rough r in which a sound of z will mingle.' This is only an English rendering of the Nannul sutra,—

அண்ண நுனிநா வருடசழவரும்.

Even the Tamils cannot pronounce this letter correctly, and in some districts they substitute ர, ய, and ல for it or omit it altogether. In Madras ய and ல are used by the lower classes, while in Madura and Tinnevelly ர is preferred. I presume that it was this letter which frightened Mr. J. C Molony and led to his remark on the Tamil language, which any Tamilian would resent, notwithstanding his indirect compliment to the people that speak it. 'Few would call Tamil beautiful ; yet its great harsh words, that one can almost bite as they pass the teeth, the stubborn inelasticities of its construction, suggest a certain doggedness in the people who have subdued such an untractable organ to their daily use.' (C.R p.7) The letter ற has the sound of a rough r and ன்ற that of tr. The sounds of ந and ன are almost identical and it may be supposed that the second ன is redundant But their origin shows a slight variation and justifies the necessity for the existence of both, because ந is a dental while ன is a palatal letter.

In Tamil no distinction is made between an accent, and an emphasis or intonation There is only one word in the Tamil language which changes its meaning by the accent or intonation, that is தபு, *tapu.*

When the accent falls on the first it means to 'die' and if it falls on the second it means to 'kill'. Intonation is of three kinds,—rising tone or எடுத்தல், falling tone or படுத்தல் and level tone or நவிழல். Of these, only the first two are in use. In கடு when the accent falls on டு, that is when it is uttered in a rising tone, it denotes a command, and when the accent falls on க or pronounced in a falling tone it becomes a simple root. In phrases and sentences, emphasis on particular words alters their meanings. Thus, the phrase அறிவிலாதவன் may mean either 'a stupid man' or 'a man as intelligent as the sun'.

Concerning the origin of Tamil letters enough has been said in the Tolkapyam and Nannul. The Panniru-pattiyal — பன்னிருபாட்டியல்—a grammatical compilation, assigns a divine origin to all the letters except ஃ. It says the twelve vowels were created by Brahma and the eighteen consonants by Siva, Vishnu, Muruga, Indra, the Sun, the Moon, Kubera, Yama and Varuna at the rate of two each. This is a curious piece of information to a modern philologist. It shows that these were the only important deities known and worshipped by the Tamil Hindus of Poigaiyar's time *i. e.* about A. D. 500.

In Tamil the interchange of letters which have almost similar sounds is allowed. This is, perhaps, due to wrong pronunciation and defective hearing. It occurs mostly at the end of words, sometimes at the beginning and middle also. These letters are,— அ for இ as in அரயன் for அரையன் ; ஒ for ந as in ஞெண்டு for நண்டு, ஞான் for நான்; ச for த as in பிச்ச for பித்து; ய for ச as in சேயம் for நேசம்; ன், ல் for ம், ர் and ள் as in கலன்-கலம், திறல்-திறம், மதில்-மதிள் &c. The Malayalam language which may be taken as a highly differentiated dialect of Tamil affords plenty of instances of this sort of interchange in letters, technically called போலி But the reader must be warned against confounding it with the ungrammatical or vulgar usages pointed out by Buddha-Mitra as prevalent in different parts of the Tamil country even in his days :— நாளி கோளி மூளா உளக்கு வாளா வளி எனவும், விழக்கு பழிங்கு தழிகை இழமை எனவும்...கருநிலஞ்சுறறின தேசததுச் சிலா வழஙகுவர். வெச்சிலே முச்சம் கசசை எனவும், உற்றியமபோது எனவும், மற்றியம் பிற்றைவாங்கிவிற்றுன் எனவும்...காவிரிபாய்ந்த நிலத்துச் சிலர் வழஙகுவர். நெல்லுக்கா நின்றது வீட்டெக்கா நின்றது என்று பாலாறு பாய்ந்த நிலத்துச சிலர் வழஙகுவர் மற்றும இவனேப்பாக்க இங்காக்க அங்காக்க எனவும், இப்படிகொற்ற அபபடிக்கொற்ற எனவும், சேத்துநிலம ஆத்துக்கால் எனவும், வாயைபபயம கோயிமுட்டை எனவும், உயிர் மயிர் எனவும், பிற வாற்றுனும் அறிவிலலாதார் தமிழைப பிழைக்க வழங்குவர்.— *Vir.* p. 64.

Rules are given in Tamil grammar books to determine what 'words are of pure Tamil origin and what are borrowed. They are highly important to a Dravidian philologist. There are 247 letters, both single and compound; but all are not used in the building up of Tamil words. Some letters may come at the beginning, while some others at the end of words. The grammarian [1] Tolkapyar took only the Tamil words and framed his rules accordingly, while other grammarians have included in them such of the Sanskrit words as have been adopted in the Tamil vocabulary. The differences between the Tamil and Sanskrit words will be pointed out as we go on.

INITIAL LETTERS: In the Tamil language there are forty-two one-letter words, and they are either long vowels or long vowel-consonants. Short vowels cannot form single letter words except with consonants. Among words of two or more letters, any word may begin with any one of the twelve vowels or the twelve vowel-consonants க், த், ந், ப and ம. The letters ச, ஞ்ச and ஞ்ஞ will not come at the beginning except in words of Sanskrit origin. According to Tolkapyar ஞா, ஜே and ஜோ may commence a word; but to this Bhavanandi adds ஞ். The letters ஔ, ஓ, ஙெ and ஙோ are not allowed at the beginning. யா is the only letter in the ய series that can come at the commencement of pure Tamil words. The first three short

---

1. Mr. A H. Keane writes about Tolkapyar as follows:—'The first in Tamil, known as the Tolkapyam, dates from about the eighth century of our era, and is, perhaps, the very oldest Tamil work extant...The Tolkapyam, itself, however, is rather a treatise on grammar composed in Tamil, than a Tamil grammar in the strict sense; and though not written in Sanskrit must still be considered as an Aindra work, that is the work of a disciple of the Aindra School of Sanskrit grammarians'. This is clearly derived from a wrong source

THE TAMIL ALPHABET

vowels அ, இ and உ are called சுட்டெழுத்து or demonstrative prefixes; and ங is the only letter in the series which may begin a word with them as அங்ஙனம் இங்ஙனம் and உங்ஙனம்; but these words have no independent existence without this combination. Thus, there are in all 94 letters with any one of which a pure Tamil word may begin.

FINAL LETTERS: Any vowel except எ, ஒ and ஔ either by itself or combined with consonants will come at the end of a Tamil word; usually உ and ஊ will not unite with ந and வ, எ and ஒ with ஞ; and ஔ will join only with க and வ. There are, however, exceptions to these rules. According to Virasoliyam, Tamil words may end with the following letters, ண, ம், ய், ர், ல், ழ், ள, and ன், and all vowels except எ and ஒ. To these may be added ஞ, ந் and வ். There is only one word in ஞ் (உரிஞ்), two words in ந (பொருந் and வெரிந்) and four words in வ் (அவ், இவ், உவ and தெவ்). These words are all now obsolete. Among the words which end in ன் there are only nine in the neuter gender, but are not modifications or போலி of ம் They are எகின், செகின், விழன், குயின், மயின், அழன், புழன், கடான், and வயான். In the ஞ series all except ஒஞு, சேஞு, ஞொஜா, சேஞா, and ஒஞௌ may be at the end of words. Generally, து, தூ, வ and ஆ may not be final letters. There are only two words ending in சு, namely, உசு (உரு) and முசு (குரங்கு), and only one word ending in ப which is தப் (to kill or to die); the உ in the other words ending in ப is the shortened உ or குற்றியலுகரம். Thus according to Tolkapyar there are 161 letters that may come at the end of Tamil words. But as Nacchinarkiniyar has observed the examples for eighteen of these (namely, கே, கோ, ணே, ணை, சே, மே, வீ, வீ, யு, யே, ரோ, வே, ழே, ழோ, னே, னா, றே, and றே) are not to be found in any Tamil dictionary.

MIDDLE LETTERS: In the middle of Tamil words the letters க, ச, த, ப, வ, ங, ந and ம coming after the consonants ம், ந் and ழ் must double. Of these ர and ழ் will not come after short vowels or consonants, nor can they double in any position. In poetry ன and ம் may join together as in போன்ம். The letters க, ச and ப will follow ட், ற், ல் and ள்; and ய and வ may come after ல் and ள். After nasal consonants will come their corresponding surds. The seven letters க, ச, ஞ, ம, ய and வ may join with ண் and ன். Combinations of letters like ஞய, நய, மய, லய, ளய, வய and மவ were tolerated in Tamil words, but are now obsolete. And the consonants ம், ந் and ழ் may precede க, ங, ச, ஞ, த, ந, ப, ம, ய and வ.

The remaining two subjects, namely, the word-building and word-combination (இளவியாக்கம் and புணர்ச்சி) will be dealt with in the next essay.

VII

PLACE OF TAMIL IN PHILOLOGY

Tamil is the language of a section of the Dravidian race inhabiting the extreme south of the Indian Peninsula. The area within which it is now spoken has been given in a previous essay. Owing to its antiquity and its high culture at a very early date, this language long ago assumed two forms, the one called the *kodun* or colloquial, and the other the *sem* or good literary Tamil.

The locality in which the Sen-Tamil was spoken is not described by Tolkapyar; and his commentators are not unanimous on this point. Senavaraiyar and Nacchinarkiniyar give its boundaries thus,—செந்தமிழ் நிலமாவது, வையையாற்றின் வடக்கும் மருதயாற்றின்றெற்கும் கருவூரின் கிழக்கும் மருவூரின்மேற்குமாம் (The "pure Tamil" was spoken in the tract bounded by the Maruta-yar on the north, the Vaiga on the south, Maruvur on the east and Karuvur on the west).

According to Tamil saints and poets the Sen-Tamil land seems to have been the modern district of Madura; this seems to me to be more accurate in as.

much as the Punal Nadu or the Tanjore district and Ten-Pandi Nadu or the Tinnevelly district have been included in the twelve Kodum-Tamil *nadus* or districts which are enumerated in the following stanza :—

தென்பாண்டி குட்டங் குடங்கறகா வேணபூழி
பன்றி யருவா வதன்வடக்கு—நன்றுய
சீதம் மலாடுபுனனுடு செந்தமிழ்சே
சேதமில் பன்னிருநாட் டெண.

An earlier list gives Podunga-Nadu and Oli-Nadu instead of Venadu and Punal-Nadu. It must be remembered that the ancient districts of Kuttam, Kudam, Karka, Ven and Puzhi were in the Travancore State and in the modern district of Malabar; Aruva and Aruva-vadatalai were in the Chingleput and North Arcot districts; Sitam was the Nilgiris; Maladu or Malai-Nadu was in South Arcot; Panri was on the north-west of Madura; and Podunga and Oli were probably somewhere in the ancient Ramnad country. It cannot therefore be said that either the Chera country, or the Tondaimandalam, or even the Chola Desam was the land of pure or Sem-Tamil, in spite of the claims put forward by some patriotic scholars for that honour.

The mediæval Tamils were entirely ignorant of the Indian Geography, and their ignorance is betrayed in the description of the countries which surrounded the Tamil Nadu. Nacchinarkiniyar mentions twelve, namely, Singalam, Pazham-divu (the Laccadives), Kollam, Kupam, Konkanam, Tulu, Kudagam, Karunatam, Kudam, Vaduku, Telugu and Kalingam. According to

Keralolpatti, Kupam was the Malayalam speaking country lying between Kunnatri and Cape Comorin. Kollam (Quilon) and Kupam, which formerly constituted the modern State of Travancore, must have separated from the Kodum-Tamil Nadus, before the time of our commentator ; and yet, without knowing the geography of the West Coast, he has given Kuttam, Kudam, Ven and other Nadus which formed part of that province in the list of Kodum-Tamil Nadus, following the division of *nadus* or districts that existed in Tolkapyar's days. But his ignorance of geography is not so great as that of later Tamil scholars who have included in the list, countries like Arabia, Bengal, Burma, China, Java, Orissa, etc. as described in the following stanza :—

சிங்களஞ் சோனகஞ் சாவகஞ் சீனந் துளுக்குடகம்
கொங்கணங் கன்னடங் கொல்லந் தெலுங்கம் கலிங்கம் வங்கங்
கங்கமகதங் கடாரங் கவடங் கடுகுசலஞ்
தங்கும் புகழ்த்தமிழ்சூழ் பதினேழ் புவிதா மிவையே.

Philology is mainly an historical science, because language which is its subject matter is the work of man, and it implies change and progress. It is the property of a society and not of an individual ; and its object is to trace the development of human thought as expressed in the speech of that society. It cannot therefore be the creation of any individual It has life, growth and death, co-extensive with the state of the society or race that uses it. A living language like Tamil is in a condition of constant change, which cannot be arrested by a scholar, poet or grammarian by means of his writings. The condition of Tamil (or any other living language) one thousand years ago was not what it had been a thousand years still earlier. And its grammar, which is essentially an empirical or inductive science, necessarily varies with the conditions of that language. In any language, literature always precedes grammar; and this fundamental principle was not unknown to the early Tamil grammarians, who have explained it in unmistakable terms thus:—

இலக்கி யத்தினின் றெடுபடு விலக்கணம—*Agat.*
இலக்கியங் கணடதற கிலக்கண மியம்பல்—*Nan.*

(Literature yields the grammar; grammar follows the literature.)

They have also recognised the principle of change in a living language, and provided for popular acceptation of innovations.—

கடிசொ வில்லூக் காலத்துப்படினே.—*Tol.*

(Usage sanctifies any new word.)

பழையன கழிதலும் புதியன புகுதலும்
வழுவல கால வகையி னென.—*Nan.*

(The order of things is for the old to give place to the new.)

Thus the statement of Sivagnanaswami that, தொல்லா சிரியா வழக்கே வழக்கு. பிற்காலத்து வேறு படவழங்கப்படுமொ யின் அவ்வழக்கு இலக்கணத்தோடு பொருந்தாதென விலக்குக, is not only unscientific, but also an obstinate clinging to that old superstition which believed the ancients to have discovered all wisdom.

PLACE OF TAMIL IN PHILOLOGY

According to Prof. Whitney changes in the growth of a language may take the following forms :—

I. Alteration of the old materials of language, which may be either change in form, or change in meaning. A word may change its form to any extent without change of meaning; in Tamil கற்பு and கல்வி mean learning; துண்டு and துணடம, a piece; நா and நாக்கு, the tongue, &c. It may take on an entirely new meaning without the change of form, as in அடுப்பு which formerly meant 'withering' as well as the 'hearth', but now only the latter; ஆடு was 'sheep' and 'victory' in old Tamil, but now only the 'sheep', தொடை was the body and now the 'thigh', கிழக்கு was a 'pit' and now the 'east', &c.

II. Loss of the old materials of language. It may be a loss of complete words or a loss of grammatical forms and distinctions. There are many Tamil words which are not used by modern authors, so freely as the ancients did, though they have co down to us in poetical dictionaries These words may therefore be said to be practically dead to the present Tamilians. But yet, there are other kinds of words such as the revenue terms like சில்வரி, இறைவரி, சினனம், முள்ளடி, கார்த்திகைபபச்சை, &c., words signifying certain social customs, such as முதுமககட்டாழி, குமமாயம், கறிதமிதத்தல்,&c. the exact meanings of which are now lost. Thus with the change of customs and political institutions, those words went out of the people's memory and were for a practical purposes lost. As for the loss of grammatical forms, we may find some occurring in early Tamil, but which have now become obsolete ; for example, past tense in உ as in நக்குபு, future in கு as in இரக்கு, instrumental case in இன் as in நின்னினிற்றந்த, &c.

III. Production of new materials—new words and new forms. Civilization brings with it new thoughts and new ideas which require new words to express them. Such words are either borrowed or coined for the nonce out of the existing words in the language, or by metaphorically extending the meanings of old words. Most words relating to religion and philosophy are borrowed from Sanskrit; revenue terms are adopted from Persian and Arabic; administrative terms are borrowed from English; besides some colloquial words like 'gate', 'compound', 'coat', 'tiffin', 'clean', etc., used in daily life. There are not very many grammatical forms newly introduced as we find in English (if we compare modern English with that of Bede or Chaucer), because the grammar of the Tamil language was written so early as the third or fourth century B. C., and the conservative instinct of the Tamils has been so strong, that new grammatical forms either by coinage or by loan have been jealously guarded against. It is a settled principle that when a language borrows, it borrows mostly nouns and adjectives ; verbs are rarely taken from other languages ; and particles never.

All the above changes were due to the operations of the principles of phonetic decay and emphasis, and analogy, aided, doubtless, by climate, food and education of the society but not of the individual. These will be explained fully with reference to Tamil in the following pages.

According to M. Hovelacque, Tamil is one of the five hundred principal languages spoken on the face of the globe at the present day. Morphologically, the existing languages are divided into four groups, *viz.* isolating, agglutinative, polysynthetic and inflectional. The morphological classification is based entirely on the form or manner in which the roots or the final elements of a language are put together to form words and sentences. In the isolating languages, like Chinese, the roots are used as words, each root preserving its full independence, unrestricted by any idea of person, gender, number, time or mood ; and, in fact, languages of this kind do not require any grammar. This is called the radical stage. In Chinese, *nan*, male ; *niu*, female ; whence *nan tse*=son, *niu tse*=daughter, *niu jin*=woman. In the agglutinative languages when two roots join together to form a word, one of them loses its independence subjecting itself to phonetic corruption. This is called the terminational stage. In Tamil *maga*, issue, becomes by the addition of *n* and *l* (corruptions of *avan* and *aval*) *magan*=son and *magal*=daughter. When words blend together in a sentence by syncope and ellipsis, it is called polysynthesis. This is a feature peculiar to American languages. Thus in the Algonquin, the sentence *Nadholineen*=bring us the canoe, is made up of *naten*=bring, *amochol*=

canoe, *i* = euphonic, and *neen* = to us. Languages in which relations between words are expressed not only by suffixes and prefixes, but also by a modification of the form of roots, are called inflectional languages. For example, in Sanskrit *Vinsati*, twenty, is composed of two roots *dvi*, two, and *dasati*, ten ; and the Sanskrit *cti*, he goes, is composed of two roots, *i*, to go and *ta*, the demonstrative pronoun.

Some philologists do not make much distinction between agglutination and polysynthesis, thus counting only three forms of speech in preference to four, which is the view accepted by recent writers on the subject. The theory that languages must pass through the monosyllabic and the agglutinating phases successively before reaching the inflectional stage—a theory current when Dr. Caldwell wrote his *Comparative Grammar of the Dravidian Languages*—has now been given up. An isolating dialect does not become agglutinative, or an agglutinative one inflectional. The radical feature of a language explained in this fourfold classification, besides being innate to that tongue, is expressive of the racial character of the people that speak it ; it cannot change from one class to another though it can be modified or altered by external circumstances.

To the agglutinative group belongs Tamil, while Sanskrit is the most ancient cultivated member of the inflectional family Morphologically, the one has no connection whatever with the other. Some Tamil scholars seem to expect that their language will, in the ordinary course, one day or other, reach the inflectional stage and claim sisterhood with Sanskrit. Their expectation will, indeed, prove a baseless dream ; and similarly, the attempt of some Malayalam scholars to elevate their Dravidian home-speech to the dignity of the classic inflectional Sanskrit, by purging it of its native element in order to import therein *en bloc* the grammar and vocabulary of that sacred language, may remind one of the 'Jackal miracle' of saint Manikka Vachakar.

Relying on the traditions narrated in the Tamil *puranas*, the non-Brahman Saiva *pandits* of the orthodox school hold that Sanskrit and Tamil were created by god Siva as his twin children, and in proof of their divine origin they cite the Vedas and the Devara hymns. The 'Kanchipurana' and the 'Tiruvilayadalpurana' assert that Siva taught the Tamil grammar to Agastya, as he had in former days taught the Sanskrit grammar to Panini.

வடமொழியைப் பாணினிக்கு வகுத்தருளி யதற்கிணையாத தொடர்புடைய தென்மொழியை யுலகமெலாந் தொழுதேத்தக் குடமுனிக்கு வற்புறுத்தா கொல்லேற்றுப்பாகா.

According to a third tradition Subrahmanya was the teacher of Tamil to that sage. Sivagnanasvami, a conceited Saiva monk and scholar of the eighteenth century, writes in his 'Tolkapya-sutra-vritti' that the Tamil grammar of Agastya was the only Tamil work that had come into existence on the day of the creation of the Tamil language.—செந்தமிழ் நிலத்து மொழிதோன்றுவ காலத்து உடன் தோன்றியநூல்

அகத்தியமொன்றே யாகலான். On the other hand, the Jains believe that Agastya learnt his Tamil from Avalokita. Following the traditions current in their days, the poets Kamban and Villipputturar have said that the language itself was created by Agastya :

தமிழெழுனுமளப்பரிய சலதிதந்தவன்.—*Kam.*
அகத்தியனபயந்த செஞ்சொலாரணங்கு.—*Vil.*

All these would only amuse the school children of modern days.

But Sanskrit and Tamil, though they may have been the oldest, were not the only two languages prevalent in the Bharata Varsha. In the extreme south we have now Telugu, Kanarese and Malayalam besides minor dialects, each being considered by its speakers as valuable as, and even more than, Tamil. The Telugus call Tamil *aravam* or 'soundless', and the Kanarese speak of it as the 'stammerer's language' (*tigalu*). These vernaculars which are, however, closely allied to one another are collectively known as the 'Dravidian family'.

No definite laws for the permutation of vowels and consonants in the allied words of these languages, like those of Grimm or Vernor, could be framed as they had been influenced to a very considerable extent by Sanskrit before their grammars were written. Tamil is the only solitary exception. Though Malayalam has been the most unfortunate of the family, having been affected most by Sanskrit, the consonantal interchanges in Dravidian words between it and Tamil are almost trifling, except such as we find between the refined Tamil and its vulgar form. This proves the lateness of its separation from Tamil. We give below a table to show some of the striking changes which the words undergo in Tamil, Malayalam, Kanarese, and Telugu.

Tamil.	Malayalam.	Kanarese.	Telugu.
(1) k. *kai*.	k. *kai*.	g. *gei*.	ch. *chey*.
(2) ch. *sevi*.	ch. *chevi*.	k. *kevi*.	ch. *chevi*.
(3) p. *pattu, pampu*.	p *patta, pampu*.	h, v. *hattu, havu*.	m. *padi, pawu*.
(4) v, zh. *vazhai*.	v, zh. *vazha*.	b, l. *bale*.	...
(5) r. *periya, valiya, teri*.	l. *valiya*.	...	d, l. *pedda, telisi*.
(6) zh. *ezhu*.	zh. *ezhu*.	l. *elu*.	d. *edu*.

The degree of relationship between Tamil and Sanskrit, which are the only two important language known to the Tamils, has been variously estimated. During the early centuries of the Christian era, the Tamils, who were not much acquainted with Sanskrit, seem to have always held that Tamil was an independent language and that it had nothing to do with Sanskrit. They did not attribute its origin to Siva, Subramanya or Agastya, as the imaginative and sectarian scholars of a later date have done. But when they came under the influence of Sanskrit culture, that was subsequent to the seventh or eighth century A. D., and when Sanskrit *puranas* and other Sanskrit religious literature were introduced, the views of Tamil scholars began to change. Most of them were acquainted with both Tamil and Sanskrit ; yet they had greater love and reverence for the latter, as their Vedas and Puranas and Agamas were written in that language ; and this partiality or rather a sentiment verging on *odium theologicum* induced them to trace Tamil from Sanskrit just as the early European divines tried to trace the Western languages from the Hebrew. The authors of ' Nemmadam ' and ' Virasoliam' and the commentators of the Tolkapyam and the Kural countenanced the above view. Again, in the eighteenth century the authors of 'Ilakkanakkottu' and 'Prayoga Vivekam', both of whom were good Sanskritists, boldly asserted that Tamil was a dialect of Sanskrit with a grammar common to both. Swaminatha Desika writes.—

அன்றியுந் தமிழ்நூற் களவிலே யவறது
ளொன்றே யாயினுந் தனித்தமி மூண்டோ
வன்றியு மைந்தெழுத தாலொரு பாடையென்
றைறையே நாணுவ ரறிவுடை யோரே;
ஆகையால், யானு மதுவே யறிக
வடமொழி தமிழ்மொழி யெனுமிரு மொழியினு
நிலக்கண மொனறே யென்றே யெண்ணுக.

He thinks that *savants* will be ashamed to say that a language can exist, whose distinguishing feature is the possession of only five letters, namely, ஃ, ழ, ள, ற and ன, or எ, ஒ, ழ, ற and ன, and wants us therefore

PLACE OF TAMIL IN PHILOLOGY 153

to accept that the grammar is one and the same both for Tamil and Sanskrit. This is the logic and the philological acumen of a divine and the head of a non-Brahman Saiva monastery. While another scholar and a Brahmnan contemporary of the above has almost upet the Tamil grammar by his indiscreet substitution of Sanskrit terminology. His book, after all, is a logomachy and is no improvement on its predecessors. He says,—வடமொழிக்குந் தமிழ்மொழிக்கும இலக்கண மொன்றென்பதறியாது சமஸ்ருபேதத்தாலும் பாடை வேற்றுமையாலும் இகழ்ந்து வேறென்பாரை நோக்கி யென்க.

In determining the affinity of any two languages the points that must be considered are,—(a) the similarity of general structure, grammar (both in form and meaning) and signification; and (b) regular and uniform interchange of phonetic sounds between the languages compared. Of these, the first two relate to grammar, and the rest to the vocabulary of a language. We shall at the outset deal with the vocabulary which is less important.

The vocabulary of modern Tamil is composed essentially of two elements only, the Tamilic or southern and the Sanskritic or northern. There are, indeed, a few dozens of foreign words chiefly relating to commerce and adminstration, introduced into the Tamil language during the past two or three centuries. Eliminating all the Sanskrit words from the Tamil dictionary, there will be a large residue of native words, which must have been the vocabulary of the original Tamils. They had been a tolerably civilized race before they came in contact with the Aryans. They had and still have their own terms pertaining to agriculture, anatomy, architecture, astronomy, commerce, domestic economy, family relations, fauna and flora, language and literature, medicine, minerals, politics, religion, war, weights and measures, &c., all of course in their primitive stage நாறு and செய், ஞாயிறு and திங்கள, கை and கால், மாறு and கொள், நெல் and பால், முற்றம் and மச்சு, தாய் and அப்பன், தெங்கு and தாழை, புலி and பூசை, எழுத்து and சொல், பா and திண, நோ and வலி, வெள்ளி and பொன், இறை, ஊர் and கோ, ஆவி and கடவுள், அம்பு and வில், மா and கழஞ்சு are all pure Tamil words, and they are not to be found in the Sanskrit language. In fact, every word of daily usage is Tamil. To establish any linguistic affinity, at least words denoting the simplest and the most ordinary family relationship must be identical. For example, the words 'father' and 'mother' in English are represented by *pitri* and *matri* in Sanskrit, *pater* and *meter* in Greek, *pater* and *mater* in Latin, *vater* and *mutter* in German, *pitar* and *mater* in Zend, and so on. On the other hand, the corresponding relations are expressed in Tamil by *appan* and *tay*. This in itself is sufficient to prove that Tamil has no philological affinity with either Sanskrit or any Indo-European tongue.

There are, however, certain words apparently of Tamil origin which may be found in Sanskrit. Dr. Caldwell gives a list of some thirty words which, he thinks, Sanskrit has borrowed from Tamil. They are,— அக்கா, அத்தை, அடவி, அம்மா, ஆணி, கடுகு, கலா, குடி, கோட்டை, நீர், பட்டணம், பாகம், பலம், மீன், வள்ளி &c. Some are common to both languages and a more rational view is to believe them to have come from a common source. They are,—அடி, ஊா, கட, கிழி, குறி, (short), ஒகி, தீ, நட, ஒகய், பல, பாடி, பால், பொறு, பேசு, டி, வல், &c. The following canons will be of some help to detect such words.

(1) When a word is an isolated one in Sanskrit without a root and without derivatives, but is surrounded in Tamil with collateral derivative words, that word is of Tamil origin.

(2) When a word is not to be found in any of the Indo-European languages allied to Sanskrit, but is found only in Tamil, that word does not belong to Sanskrit.

Words of this kind are very few and form too slender a basis to prove the linguistic affinity or othrwise between Sanskrit and Tamil.

Let us now pass on to grammar

ORTHOGRAPHY : Sanskrit has 46 letters or *Varnas*— 13 vowels or *Svaras* and 33 consonants or *Vyanjanas*, or 47 including ள which occurs in the Vedas. Besides these there are *anuswara* and *anunasika*, represented by a dot, and a crescent and a dot respectively. Thus there are in all 49 letters. Whereas we have in Tamil only 12 vowels, 18 consonants and a semi-vowel. Of these, two vowels and four consonants (including ஃ) are peculiar to Tamil and are not to be found in the

Sanskrit language; deducting these six we have 25 letters which are common to both; and Sanskrit has 24 letters the sounds of which are not represented by any letter in Tamil. The possession of peculiar sounds like ழ, ற, ன and ஃ exhibits the physiological characteristics of the Tamil people, differentiating their language from the Aryan tongues ; and the very fact that Tamil possesses and largely employs the short sounds எ and ஒ points to an origin, quite independent of Sanskrit. The short எ and ஒ are not peculiar to Tamil, which every language except Sanskrit posesses although Swaminatha Desikar and other native scholars, blindly following Sanskrit grammarians, seem to think otherwise. In Tamil *sel* is to go, and *sêl* is a kind of fish; *mel* is to chew and *mêl* is above; *kol* is to kill and *kôl* is a stick, *tol* is old and *tôl* is the skin, *noy* is softness and *nôy* is sickness; and so on.

Dr. Caldwell states that the diphthongs ஐ and ஔ had no place in the Dravidian languages and that they were placed in their alphabets solely in imitation of Sanskrit. He further asserts that ஐ in Tamil is a compound of எ and இ but not of அ and இ as in Sanskrit, and that it is an equivalent of ா in Malayalam and of எ in Kanarese. As for ஔ he believes that it has no place in the Tamil alphabet except for pronouncing Sanskrit derivatives only. As against these observe what Tolkapyar says.—

 அகர இகர ஐமகாரமாகும்.—1. 54.
 அகர உகர ஒளகாரமாகும்—1. 55.
 பனனீருயிரு மொழி முதலாகும—1. 59.

It is thus unsafe to accept Dr Caldwell's view in violation of the above rules, as there are pure Tami word in ஐ and ஔ, as ஐவனம, ஔவியம், தையல், தௌவை, பைதல், பௌவம், &c. The Tamil ஐ becomes அ but not எ in Malayalam; compare தீலை and தல, கரை and கர, நீலை and நில, &c.

WORD FORMATION:—The peculiarities of structure of Tamil words may be briefly noticed here. In the last essay something has been said of the initial, middle and final letters in words. That will doubtless help the reader to settle for himself which words are native, and which foreign. The following additional rules are worth his careful consideration.

(1). Double consonants at the beginning, and triple consonants of different *Vargas* or classes in any position are not allowed in a Tamil word. Compare Sanskrit *trayi, vaktram* and *vastram.*

(2) In the middle of a word double consonants of different classes are not, as a rule, allowed; words with ல்ய, வ்ய, ண்ய, ன்வ, ந்ய, ம்ய, ம்வ, &c., do not occur.

(3). The doubling of the same consonant is very common in Tamil, but not so in Sanskrit. In Tamil we have *akka, attai, annan, attan, appan, ammai,* &c.

(4) No Tamil word can begin with ச, சை, and சௌ; but Sanskrit allows these initial letters as in சம்பு, சைனயம் and சௌர்யம். The Tamil words சட்டி and சமழ்தல் are a later introduction.

(5) Only the long யா can come at the beginning of a Tamil word, while others do not. In Sanskrit we have யவனர், யுக்தி, யூபம், யோகம் and யௌனம்.

(6) No Tamil words will end in க், ச், ட், த், and ப். But in Sanskrit there are words like *pritak, vach, rat, pat,* and *yup.*

As in Sanskrit, Tamil words are either simple or compound. Simple words are formed from roots, which are either nominal or verbal, by the addition of formative particles, like கு, ச, இ, து, டி and று, அ, அம், அர், அல், அன், ஆ, ஆல், ஆன், இ, இல், உ, ஊ, உம், ஐ, கை, சி, தி, ப, மை, வி, வை and றி, and காடு, பாடு, அரவு and ஆணை. Nouns, verbs, adjectives and adverbs, might be formed in this way. To prevent hiatus அ, ம் or ன is sometimes added. From the verbal root நில், to stand, the following words are formed,—நிலை, நிலம், நிலவு &c ; from √ அட், to kill, we have அடி, ஆடி, அடவி, அடிப்பு, அட்டு, அடம, அடல், அடங்கு, &c; from √ அற், to cut, we get அறு, அறை, அறுவை, அறம், அறப்பு, அற்றம், அறுதி, அறல், &c ; and from √ நட், to walk or dance, are derived நட, நடத்தல், நடப்பு, நடை, நடகை, நட்டம், &c. The nominal root கண் (the eye) becomes காண், to see, by lengthening the vowel.

In Tamil, roots are always monosyllabic, ending in long vowels, or in a short vowel and a consonant. There are 42 single-letter words, which must essentially be monosyllabic, and these are either verbs or nouns. There are other monosyllabic nouns like சொல், கல், மண், மான், &c. Compound words are made up of simple words; for example, பரி-மா (horse) is a compound of பரி=to run, and மா=a beast, கடு-வாய்(tiger) from கடு=rough or cruel, and வாய்=mouth. Mostly such compounds are epithets or metaphors.

PLACE OF TAMIL IN PHILOLOGY

It will be seen from the examples given above that the formative elements or terminations are all post-positions, and that the roots rarely change their forms, barring the shortening or lenthening of verbs as in கண்-காண், விடு-வீடு, and the slight consonantal changes peculiar to Tamil euphony.

On the other hand, the terminations used to form derivative bases in Sanskrit are of two classes:—

(1) *Krt* or primary affixes which are added to verbs to form nouns, adjectives, &c For example, *karah* (the hand) is the noun form of *kri*, to do; *chur* (to steal) becomes *chorayat*, stealing; *ukta* is the adjectival form of *vach*, to speak; and *ishta* from *yaj*, to sacrifice, &c., Prepositions are prefixed to roots to form nouns, &c., as in *a-kash, nis-chitya, vij-kri*, &c.

(2) The *taddhita* or secondary affixes are added to substantives to form secondary nominal bases. One studying *vyakarana* is a *vaiyakarani*; that which is made by a *kulala* is *kaulalakam*; father of *pita* is *pitamaha*; son of *Dakshi* is *Dakshayanah*; son of *Agni* is *Agneyah*; a herd of *hastin* is *hastikam*; belonging to *Panini* is *Panineya*; one possessing *vak* is *vachalah*, &c.

A comparison of the terminations or affixes used to form words, and of the methods of forming them, in Tamil and Sanskrit will convince the reader that they differ in both languages. The *taddhita* class, especially, is characteristic of Sanskrit, and it was only the lack of the historic sense, so common among the Tamil grammarians, that led the author of *Prayoka vivekam* to say 'விணக்குறிப்புபபெயரெல்லாம் தத்திதன்.'

In consequence of the differences in the structure and formation of words their coalescence or *sandhi* (T. புணர்ச்சி) must also differ in the two languages This difference is observable chiefly in vowel changes. The Tamil rule of *sandhi* is,

இ. ஈ. ஐ வழி யவ்வும் ஏணயுயிாவழி வவ்வும்.—*Nan*. The short உ has the nature of a consonant According to this rule, மணி+அழகு=மணியழகு ; இரா+அன்று=இராவன்று ; பலா + இலை =பலாவிலே; மா + உரல்= மாவுரல் ; நாகு+அரிது=நாகரிது ; சிறு + அன்=சிறுவன். Whereas according to *svara-sandhi* they should become மண்யழகு, இரான்று, பலாலே and மரோரல். There are many other peculiarities in the combination of Tamil words not found in Sanskrit, which it is in possible to explain in this essay.

Simple words join together to form compounds. In Sanskrit there are six classes, namely, (1) Dvandva or உம்மைத்தொகை,(2) Tatpurusha or வேற்றுமைத்தொகை (3) Karmadharaya or பண்புத்தொகை, (4) Dvigu or எண்ணுத்தொகை, (5) Bahuvrihi or அன்மொழித்தொகை and (6) Avyayıbhava or the adverbial compounds. Corresponding to these we have in Tamil a set of six compounds known as,

வேற்றுமை விணபண் புவமை யும்மை
அன்மொழி யெனவத் தொகை யாறுகும்.—*Nan*.
உவமைத்தொகை is included in the Karmadharaya ; and எண்ணுத்தொகை or Dvigu of Sanskrit (Ex : அழுகால், பன்னிருபடலவம்) is contained in உம்மைததொகை, பண்புத்தொகை and அன்மொழிதததொகை of Tamil. Thus

விணத்தொகை alone remains to be accounted for and that is peculiar only to Tamil.

The peculiarities of structure and formation of words in Sanskrit have compelled the Tamils to modify them, when borrowed, so as to suit the morphological features of the Tamil tongue. The words thus borrowed are of two classes—the *tatsamas* and the *tatbhavas*. It is only the second class that undergoes change in Tamil At the time of Tolkappyar the Sanskrit words in Tamil were very few, and he felt no necessity to frame rules for their adoption. He was content by saying,—சிதைந்தன உரிது மிசைந்தன வரையார. The later Tamil grammarians, however, observing the large influx of Sanskrit words and their use in a variety of forms, were constrained to give fixity to them by providing authoritative rules; and they are to be found explained in the தத்திதப்படலம் of Virasoliyam and in the பதவியல் of Nannul. Their main object was to evade or soften difficulties in pronouncing two consecutive consonants in a word, or a word beginning with a consonant not allowed by the Tamil usage, by introducing vowels. Thus Sanskrit *ratna* is changed into *aratanam* or *irattinam*, *sakshi* into *sakki* or *satchi*; *yaksha* into *iyakkan*, *lakshana* into *ilakkana*, &c. This is evidently a stage more advanced than the monosyllabic Chinese which converts 'Christ' into 'Ki-li-su-tu' and 'Maharashtra' into 'Mo-la-cha,' but far below the inflectional Sanskrit, which evinces 'the strength and directness of character and scorn of difficulties' in the Ind

ETYMOLOGY: There are four parts of speech or சொல் in Tamil, namely பெயர் (noun), வினை (verb), இடை (particles) and உரி (attributives). It is an accepted principle with Tamil grammarians that all parts of speech are ultimately reducible to only two—substantives and verbs, and this is also the view of modern philologists. Says Tolkapyar,

சொல்லெனப் படுப பெயரே வினையென்
றாயிரண் டென்ப வறிந்திசி னோரே.—II, 160.

Of these the noun and the verb require no explanation. இடைச்சொல் means the *middle* word—that is a part of speech common to both nouns and verbs. It consists of all particles, terminations or postpositions which go to change or modify the meaning of nouns and verbs with reference to time, place, subject, action, &c. Thus it embraces the particles of tense, personal terminations, case endings, demonstrative letters, conjunctions, interjections, euphonic expletive particles, and in fact every particle that has no meaning by itself, independent of the noun or verb to which it is attached. உரிச்சொல் treats of the various qualities of nouns and verbs, and it therefore includes adjectives and adverbs. The metaphysical explanation of உரிச்சொல் given by Sivagnanamuni is, —குணபபண்பும் தொழிற்பண்புமாகிய பொருட்பண்பையுணாத் துஞ்சொல உரிச்சொல் Elsewhere, he goes on to say that நட, வா, முதலிய முதநிலைகளுக் தொழிற்பண்பை யுணர்த்தஞ் சொற்களாகவின உரிசசொல் லேயாம். This explana is the merit of his commentary to make it more abstruse and unintelligible than the text itself. It will thus be seen that the classification of words, other than பெயர் and வினை, into இடைச்சொல் and உரிச்சொல் was neither definite nor philosophical. These words have been variously classified and often in a conflicting manner by later grammarians. For instance, the author of Prayoga-Vivekam has said that சொல்லெல் லாம் உரிச் சொல்லேயா மெனத் துணிக.

The differences between the Tamil and Sanskrit parts of speech may be briefly stated as follows :—

(1) Like all other classical languages Sanskrit has three numbers, while Tamil has only two. The dual number or இருமை must have existed in early Tamil. It evidently became mixed up with பன்மை or the plural number and so vanished out of Tamil grammar. இர் or ர which means 'two' was the dual termination, and கள் for the plural. Now ர is reserved as an honorific termination for pluralising 'high caste' nouns and verbs, and கள் for all.

(2) All nouns denoting inanimate objects and irrational animals are of the neuter gender (அஃறிணை), and those denoting rational beings (like man, God, and Nagas) are of the high-caste or superior gender உயர்திணை. Whereas in Sanskrit no such philosophic and sexual distinctions are made ; here the grammatical gender is only ' a secondary accident of speech ornamental, perhaps from an æsthetic point of view, but practically highly detrimental.' No definite rules could, therefore, be laid down for determination

of gender in Sanskrit; *soma*, the 'moon' is masculine, *ruchi*, ' taste ' is feminine, and *putran*, ' son' is neuter. It will thus be seen that gender in Sanskrit depends on the peculiar structure of words, but not on the sex or the intelligence of the objects expressed by them.

(3) Tamil nouns are inflected not by means of case terminations, but by means of suffixed postpositions and separate particles. The inflectional base in the oblique cases is the root in Sanskrit, while in Tamil it is the nominative, except the first and second personal pronouns நான், நீ, நீர் and நீவிர் which alone change their forms. For example, in Sanskrit the roots *vach* (speech) and *raj* (king) become *vak* and *rat* in the first or nominative case, while in Tamil the roots சொல் (word) and கல் (stone) remain the same. In declining nouns the same case terminations are added to the root for the singular and to the plural terminations for the plural (*e. g.*, கல்லை, கற்கள்). But in Sanskrit and other Indo-Germanic languages, the case endings of the plural differ from those of the singular. As Dr. Caldwell rightly observes,—'the imitation of Sanskrit was certainly an error, for whilst in Sanskrit there are eight cases only, the number of cases in Tamil, Telugu, &c., is almost indefinite,' being limited only by the number of postpositions that may be attached to the noun. And it is this indefiniteness that has given an endless trouble to the Tamil grammarian Tolkapyar, who has devoted three complete chapters for cases only ; and these have been supplemented by another by the auth

(4) Tamil has no relative pronouns. The existence of two pronouns of the 1st person plural, one of which includes and the other excludes the person addressed, is a peculiarity of Tamil, affiliating it to Turkic and other agglutinating tongues and differentiating it from Sanskrit.

(5) There are six tenses and four moods in Sanskrit, while Tamil has only three tenses and three moods. The existence of a negative and a passive voice in the verbal system is peculiar to Tamil, the latter being expressed by auxiliary verbs signifying to 'suffer'. The subjunctive and the optative moods are expressed by means of suffixed particles, and the other three tenses by means of auxiliary verbs. There is no benedictive mood in Tamil. The structure of the verb is strictly agglutinative, the second person singular of the imperative being an exception. The view of Senavaraiyar and Sivagnana-muni that— ஆ யென்னும விகுதிகுன்மி நடவா உண தின் என நின்றன வல்லது முதனிலேகளே போகைசவேறு பாட்டானவ்வாறு நின்றன ஒவனபது படாது—does not seem to be acceptable.

(6) In Sanskrit, adjectives are declined like nouns, which they qualify in gender, number, and case. In Tamil, adjectives which are only nouns of quality (உரிச்சொல்), have none. In Sanskrit the adjectives have degrees of comparison, while those of Tamil have none at all. The Sanskrit adjective *priya* is positive, and its comparative and superlative are *priyas* and *preshta*.

(7) There are no prepositions or conjunctions in Tamil except உம் which is only a continuative particle. It is the peculiarity of Tamil derivatives that none of them are formed by prefixed particles. But some might say that in அவன், இவன், &c., the letters அ, இ are prefixes. But they are pronominal words or roots, but not particles.

RHETORIC: The Tamil rules of prosody relating to the structure and division of syllable, foot, stanza, rhyme, &c., are different from those of Sanskrit. Venba, Asiriyappa, Kalippa and Vanjippa are all peculiar only to Tamil. The treatment of Porul matter) into *agam* (subjective or *amatory*) and *puram* (objective, chiefly warlike), and the division of conduct into five திணை &c., are not to be found in Sanskrit.

The foregoing arguments, to show the independence of Tamil from Sanskrit, may be summed up in the words of Sivagnanamuni as follows: தமிழ் மொழிப்புணர்ச்சிக்கட்படும் செய்கைகளும, குறியீடுகளும, வினைக் குறிபபு, வினைத்தொகை முதலிய சொல்விலக்கணங்களும், உயர் திணை உஃறிணை முதலிய சொற்பாகுபாடுகளும், அஃமபுறமென் னும் பொருட்பாகுபாடுசளும், குறிஞ்சிநெய்தி முதலிய திணைப் பாகுபாடுகளும், வெண்பா அவற்றின் பகுதிகளும் முதலிய செய்யுளிலக்கணமும் இனதேரன்ன பிறவும் வடமொழியிற் பெறபபடா. Even the author of Prayoga Vivekam who has attempted in the early chapters of that work to prove the identity of Tamil and Sanskrit grammars is obliged to admit with candour the essential differences between the two languages thus: திணையுணர்த்தும் வினை விகு ஃபுர், ஆண்பால் பெண்பால உணர்த்தும் வினைவி

குதியுப்படமொழிக்கில்லை. தமிழ்மொழிக்குப் பிரதமாவிபத்தியும் இலிங்கத் திரயமுமில்லை.

With such authoritative admissions before us, the complete independence of Tamil from Sanskrit must be accepted, in spite of the futile attempts of later Tamil grammarians to trace one from the other. All that we can say at present is that Tamil occupies the same position in the Dravidian family that Sanskrit does in the Aryan—that is, Tamil is the oldest and the most cultivated of the Dravidian or South Indian family of languages.

But it cannot altogether be denied that Tamil or at any rate its Dravidian parent and the Aryan languages, though they do not possess the least morphological features in common, did not influence one another before their separation. Dr Caldwell gives the following Indo-Europeanisms as discoverable in the Dravidian languages :—

(1) The use of n, ன், as in Sanskrit and Greek to prevent hiatus. Ex : Skt. $a + adi = anadi$; Tam. $ni + a = ninā$.

(2) The existence of gender in the pronouns of the third person and in verbs, and in particular the existence of neuter gender. Ex : அவன், அவள் and அது.

(3) The existence of a neuter plural, as in Latin, in short அ. Ex: T. வநதன, Lat. templa (temples).

(4) The use of d or t (த) as the sign of the neuter singular of demonstrative pronouns, or pronouns of the third person. Ex : Skt. *tat* ; Tam அது, &c.

(5) The formation of a remote demonstrative from a base in அ, the proximate from a base in இ. Ex : Skt. *adah, idam* ; Tam. அது, இது.

(6) The formation of preterites by *d*. Ex : Skt. *ji, jita*. Tam. வா, வந்த, &c.

(7) The formation of some preterites by reduplication. Ex : Skt. *pash, papacha* ; Tam புகு, புக்கு, &c

(8) The formation of verbal nouns by lengthening the vowel of the verbal root. Ex: Skt. *nat-nâtya, guh-gûdam*, &c ; Tam. மீன்-மீன், நக்கு-நாக்கு, &c.

It is said that the Dravidian languages in their turn exerted an equal, if not greater, influence on Sanskrit and her North Indian dialects. This is what everybody might naturally expect, considering that the Prakrit dialects came into existence during historic times and that the peoples whose mother tongue they are, have, from remote antiquity, been living in the midst of the Dravidian races. Moreover, all those who speak them are not Aryans.

The Dravidian influence on the grammar of the Indo-Aryan languages has been detailed by Dr Caldwell as follows :—The inflection of nouns by means of separate post-fixed particles added to the oblique form of the noun ; the inflection of the plural by annexing the same sign as for the singular; the use of two pronouns for the first person plural—the one including and the other excluding the party addressed; the use of post-positions instead of prepositions ; the formation of verbal tenses by means of particles ;

the situation of the relative sentence before the indicative; the situation of the governing word after the governed; the use of *l*, ள; and the preference of cerebrals to dentals

AFFILIATION OF TAMIL : It is superfluous to mention here that Tamil is the oldest member of the Dravidian group of languages. No scholar has yet attempted to construct the primitive Dravidian language from which the modern Tamil, Telugu, Kanarese and other dialects have sprung. A comparison of this hypothetical language with the other groups of the agglutinative family might yield satisfactory facts for establishing its affiliation. But in the absence of such data we must take the aid of ethnology and such linguistic resources as may at present be available.

In the chapter on the origin of the Tamil people we have said that the original Dravidians came to India from Western Asia through the North-Western passes on the Himalayas, and that they mingled with the aboriginal races of Nagas and the Negrito people after they had settled in the extreme south of the Indian Peninsula. Hence the language of the Dravidians must have undergone changes as a result of the influence of the crude Australian dialects spoken by the Naga and Negrito autochthones. As however, the modern Dravidian languages have not yet been completely analysed, it is not possible at present to separate the Dravidian from the aboriginal linguistic elements. But this much seems to be certain, that the primitive Dravidian language was influenced by Semitic and the Aryan languages on the one side, and by the Finno-Hungarian idioms on the other. And, but for some broad morphological peculiarities, there is no trace of the Australian influence to be found in the Dravidian languages. From what has been said in the first essay and from what follows, it will be plain that the Dravidian languages must be allied to the Uralo-Altaic group, though they cannot be geneologically classed with it. No other theory can satisfactorily account for the presence of Greek, Keltic, Hebrew and Finno-Hungarian words in Tamil.

The following grammatical features are common to the languages of the Dravidian family and the Uralo-Altaic group :—

(1) Words are never formed by prefixes but always by suffixes so that the principal root may invariably stand first. Ex : நட, நடந்த, நடந்தது, &c.

(2) Declension is effected by agglutinating secondary or relational particles to the principal root Suffixes are added to the root or to the plural element, that is the plural sign is always intercalated between the noun and the post-position. Ex: கல், கல்லே; கறகள், கற்களே.

(3) Consonantal system is simple, and letters approaching in sound the Tamil ழ will be found in some languages of the Uralo-Altaic group.

(4) The adjective which is a mere qualifying noun comes always before the word it qualifies except in

Basque, and the degrees of comparison are expressed by words meaning 'more', 'less', &c.

(5) Tenses and moods are formed by the insertion of certain elements between the root and the personal ending. Ex : செல்+ற்+ஆன்=சென்றான்.

(6) There are no relative pronouns in Basque as in Tamil.

(7) The existence of two pronouns of the first person plural, one of which includes and the other excludes the person addressed, is a peculiarity of the Dravidian languages.

(8) Use of continuative particles in the place of conjunctions. Ex: சேரனும் சோழனும்.

(9) The crude root verb is capable of being used in the imperative of the second person singular. Ex: கட, வா, etc.

(10) There are only two numbers in Turkish.

In all these languages the so-called cases are formed by agglutination, their number being limited only by the number of post-positions that may be attached to the noun.

Till very recently it was usual with comparative philologists to classify all languages which are neither Aryan, Semitic nor Hamitic under the Turanian or Scythian or Allophylian family. But it has now been proved that there cannot be such a family as the Turanian or Scythian, as no two languages which are brought under it bear the same geneological relationship to each other as Sanskrit bears to Latin or Greek in the Aryan family except that they are morphologically connected. The roots of each are different; so are their grammatical elements. The explanation for this difference lies in the fact that the Aryan languages—Sanskrit, Greek, Latin, Keltic, &c—separated at an epoch when their structure was already perfect. On the other hand, the so called Turanian or Scythian languages seem to have parted when their structure was in an imperfect condition ; and so each of them was obliged to depend on its own resources or on borrowed elements available at hand to complete its inner structure. It has also been observed that in the course of formation and growth some of the languages of the Uralo-Altaic group made use of incorporation—a feature peculiar to the American languages. In the case of the Dravidian languages, their development and approach towards the incorporating stage must have been arrested at a very early period by their literary culture, which was no doubt due to the Aryan influence. The position assigned to the Dravidian languages by M. Hovelacque in the linguistic systems seems to us quite appropriate. He says,—' they must be comprised among the first in the ascending order, that is among those immediately following the isolating system, and anterior to Turkish, Magyar, Basque and the American languages.'

So much for the origin of Tamil and its place in the linguistic systems of the world. Coming now to the history of the Tamil language, it may conveniently be divided into three periods, namely, (1) the early Tamil comprising the period between the sixth century before and after Christ ; (2) the mediæval Tamil, occupying the interval between the sixth century and the twelfth century, and (3) the modern Tamil, extending from the twelfth down to the present day. It is not proposed here to deal with it as completely as the importance of the subject demands. We shall, however, briefly indicate the characteristics of each period to justify the rationale of the above classification

EARLY TAMIL: During the first half of this period the prevailing religion was animism or the worship of the spirit of departed heroes and ancestors. It was afterwards supplemented by Buddhism and lastly by Jainism. Brahmanism, though it had already been transplanted into the Tamil country, was very weak. The conflict of these religions for supremacy had not yet commenced. All the four religions existed side by side and were tolerated.

Early Tamil was the language used by the writers of the academic and the classic periods. And the peculiarities of this Tamil may be observed in the literature of those times, the important of which being the Agananuru, the Purananuru, the Pattuppattu, the Padirruppattu, the Silappadikaram and the Manimekalai. The standard grammars of the epoch were the Tolkapyam, Pannirupadalam, Usimuri, &c. In our review of Padirrupattu, the special characteristics of the early Tamil will be described at some length. We shall ۱   few words here concerning them under the four-heads of vocabulary, grammar style and matter.

According to the late Mr. P. Sundaram Pillai's calculation the percentage of Sanskrit words in three of the Ten Poems (Pattuppattu) is between one and two. In the Nedunalvaḻai there are altogether but twenty Sanskrit words, and in the Madurai-Kanchi, a poem of 782 lines, the number does not exceed fifty-five. And in fact the introduction of Sanskrit words is strongly condemned by the best writers of the academic period. It was considered by them as the mark of an imperfect education. Two of the earliest Kanarese poets have characterized it as 'an unnatural union...' or as the 'stringing of pearls along with pepper-corns.'

Words of foreign origin were never introduced, notwithstanding the commercial intercourse of the Tamils with the Greeks, Romans, and Arabs, whom they indiscriminately called the Yavanas. Sanskrit words were very sparingly used and even these were mutilated in their form as will be seen in the following examples: முழுத்தம், பாசம், ஆணை, அவை, தசசன், திரயம், அமிழ்து, உளசி, பாசி, &c. Some Tamil roots were used in sentences without formative particles as காவ for காற்று, வெவன் for வெற்றி, அவ், இவ், உவ் and யா for அவை, இவை, உவை and யாவை. Some words were used in senses which have now become obsolete. For example, சேவல் meant a 'horse', கணடி meant a 'he-buffalo,' களிறு meant 'a pig' and பொன் was 'iron' &c. Re̅ sister,

என்ஊன=my lord, எகைத=our lord or father, துநதை= your father, and தமர், நமர், நுமா, have all become obsolete. Some classical words like ஒழிய, to 'die', முகதி, to 'eat', அககட்டி, 'there', பைய, 'slowly', &c. have now become slang.

Sometimes post-positions were added directly to the roots without the euphonic particles or சாரியை. For example, புளிங்காய for புளியங்காய், ஆஊன for ஆவிஊன, 'இல்லாகுக for இல்லையாகுக, கேளவம் for கேட் டறியோம், தம்மென for தாருமென, தட்ப for தடபப, மேயல் for மேயச்சல், மாடி for மாட்டி, &c. The plural termination ர் is very sparingly used and கள் never, the abstract terms வேந்து, அரசு, &c., being perferred to concrete terms to avoid number. The use of distinctive terminations for the seven cases is not strictly adhered to, one or two post-positional particles like இன் or இல் being used for all the seven cases. In fact, no finality concerning the uses of case terminations was attained in practice. This இன or இல் is a peculiar particle and it was used to express comparison also; the expression பண்டையிற் பெரிது meant, 'greater than it was before.' The present tense did not come into existence. The indefinite past and the indefinite future were the only tenses in use as in Hebrew and other languages. And some of the tense particles like ஈ, ஊ, கு, பு, கம், மின which were then in use have become obsolete, together with உகது for உம் (as in தருஉகது for தரும். The post-position ஐ was added to nouns to form verbs in the second person singular. The phrase தானகநாடஊன meant 'you who are the lord of the forest country.' The formation of some causative verbs like ஒழுகு-ஒழுக்கு, தெளி-தெளித்து (to cause to become clear). Some verbal nouns were formed by adding to roots the suffixes which are used in modern Tamil to produce different senses,— கிழக்கு (pit), முன்பு (strength), பறை (flying), இலம் (poverty), புகல் (abode), பொயப்பு (lying), நமபு (noun), கதிர்பபு (brightness), and so on.

Some of the adverbial and other particles which were freely in use during this period have become obsolete. They are தில், கொன்றே, எற்று, மற்று, மனற, தருசம, குறை, மோ, மதி, இகும், இசின், உநது, etc

The literature of this period is all poetry—simple blank verse in chaste classic style devoid of rhetorical flourishes, figures of speech, hyperbolic descriptions, and intricacies of later prosody which mar the excellence of modern Tamil poems; Asiriyappa, Kalippa, Venba, and Kuratpa are the metres mostly used. The descriptions of events and scenery are all faithful and true to nature.

The subject matter of most of these works is the panegyric of reigning kings, descriptive of their military prowess, their liberality, and their administration. Some of them depict poverty, chiefly of bards, in a very pathetic manner. Some are on morality, while only a few relate to religion. We subjoin a few specimen of early Tamil.

(1) இல்லுணைத் துறத்தலி னின்மறநதுறையும்
புலவுனாக குடிமிப புதல்வன் பண்மாண்
பாவில வறுமுலே சுவைத்தனன் பெறஅன்

னுள்ளில் வறங்கலந் திறந்தழக கண்டு
மறபபுலி யுரைத்து மதியங் காட்டியு
நொநதன னாகி நுந்தையை யுள்ளிப்
பொடிந்தநின் செவ்வி காட்டென.—*Pur.* 160.

(No food in the house: the soft-haired babies sucked in vain the dried-up breast of their mother. Disappointed, they turned up the empty pots, and cried. The mother hushed them with tales of the cruel tiger, and pointed to them the moon. Wearied and troubled she told the starving ones to let their father see their misery.)

(2) கார்மழை முன்பிற கைபரிக் தெழுதரும்
வான்பறைக் குருகி னெடுவரி பொற்பக
கொல்களியு மிடைந்த பஃறேழ்ற் றெழுஇியாடு
டெடநெடேர் நுடங்கு கொடியவிர் வரபபொலிநது
செலவுபெரி தினிதநிற் காணு மோர்க்கே.—*Pad* 83.

(Like the white paddy birds flying beneath the canopy of dark winter clouds was the march of your army—the white banners streaming from above the herd of deadly elephants, thick shielded-men and chariots. So pleasing was the sight.)

MEDIÆVAL TAMIL : It embraces the Brahmanic and the sectarian periods of Tamil literature. The early part of it was one of struggle for predominence between Brahmanism on the one hand and Buddhism and Jainism on the other, in which the former came out triumphant, Buddhism being deprived of following in this land and Jainism crippled. From this time forward the Brahman's influence became supreme; temples were erected for their gods; and they themselves secured fertile villages for subsistence. Sanskrit puranas, local as well as general, were written and translated for the benefit of the Tamils. Then came into prominence a split among the Brahmans, which led to the formation of the Vishnu and Siva cults. The latter with all its attendant horrors of death and destruction became popular among the warlike Tamils. The literature of this epoch consists of hymns to Siva and Vishnu and of the accounts of the life and adventures of Siva and Subrahmanya, Rama and Krishna, and Jina. The standard works on Tamil grammar during this period were Tolkapyam, Virasoliyam, Nambi's Agapperul, Neminadam, &c.

Sanskrit words, chiefly relating to religion, were largely introduced, and some of the Tamil words and forms current in the preceding epoch gave way to new ones. Plurals in கள், double plurals in நகள் and னகள், present tense particles இன்று and இறு and the use of distinctive case terminations came into existence. Some adverbial particles like கொன்னே, தஞ்சம், இல், தெய்யு, &c., completely went out of use.

For poetry or metrical composition, which was still the only form of literary production, Asiriyam and Venba metres were not so much in favour as the Vrittam, Tandakam and others of Sanskrit prosody. These were introduced with their *alankaras* or embellishments. Rhyme and *antadi* form were introduced to render the recital of sacred songs easier. As for their style, the pure simplicity and the natural beauty of the academic period were gone. Affectation and artificiality even in excess were considered a literary excellence. As it was a period of struggle for religious supremacy every one of the four sects attempted to excel the rest by extolling and exaggerating its own doctrines, and by fabricating miracles to support them. Truth was thrown in the back ground and its place was taken up by mythological accounts of preter-natural events, such as one might find in the *puranas* and *itihasas*. Thus Chintamani, the Ramayana, the Skandapurana, the Tiruvilayadalpurana, the Periyapurana and the Mahabharata came to be replete with stories of this kind. However, a true spirit of devotion and piety, though blind or fanatical it might appear to us, pervaded the writings of this very troublous period. We give below some extracts :—

(1) ஓவுநா ஞுணர் வழியுநா ஞுயிரா ேஜாசுநா ஞுயர் பாடைமேற் காவுநா ளிவை யென்றலாற் கருதேதன் கிளர் புனற் காவிரிப் பாவு சண்புனல் வநதிழி பாஞ் சோதிபாண்டிக் கொடுமுடி நாவலா வுனே நான்மறககிலுஞ் சொலலுநா நமச்சிவாயவே.

(2) வாருகிமண்ணுகி வளியாகி ெவாளியாகி ஊருகி யுயிராகி யுணமையுமாய் யினமையுமாய் கோருகி யாெனன தென்றவரவரைக் கூததாட்டு வாருகி நின்றுணப என சொல்லி வாழ்த்துவனே.—T.V.

(3) ெவன்றி யாககலு மேதக வாககலுங் குன்றி ளுர்கீனக குனெறன வாககலு மன்றியுங கலவி யோடழு காககலும் ெபானனுஞ் சாகததி ளுய்ப்பாருள் செயயுமே.

(4) பொன்னி லுகும பொருபடை யப்படை
	தன்னி லுகுந் தாணி தாணியிற்
	பின்ன யாகும் பெரும்பொரு எ படபொருள்
	துன லுங் கா‍லச தன் லுதன வில்‍லயே.—*Chin.*

(5) தண்_‍ல மயிலகளாடத் தாமரை விளக்கந்தாங்கக் [கத்‍-
	கொண்டல்கண முழுவிணேங்கக் குவணகண்விழித்துநோக்‍-
	தெண்டிரை பெழினிகாட்டத் தேம்பிழி மகரயாழின
	வணடக ளிளிதுபாட மருதம்வீற்றி ருக்குமாதோ.

(6) சிலமபுகள் அலபபிடை செரித்தகழலோடு
	நிலபபுக மிதிதசன ணெரிததகுழி வேலேச்
	சலம்புக வனற்றறு கணந்தகனு மஞ்சிப
	பிலமபுக நிலகிரிகள் பினறொடா வநதாள்.—*Kam.*

MODERN TAMIL: To the Tamils the modern period which begins from the thirteenth century is important in every respect. The ancient kingdoms of the Cholas and the Pandyas were subverted. A powerful Telugu empire was coming into existence on the banks of the Tungabhadra, which before the close of the fifteenth century absorbed all the Tamil kingdoms. Then came the Mahratta and the Musalman hordes from the north, and lastly the Europeans from beyond the sea. Though the Telugus and the Mahrattas had come into the Tamil countries as fortune seekers, they settled there permanently being members of the same creed and nationality. The Musalmans were not so; they plundered the country, forcibly converted some of its people, and returned with booty leaving behind their deputies at certain centres of strategic importance like Arcot and Trichinopoly. They farmed out the desolate country to renters, who oppressed and tortured the ryots. Many had to sell their lands for nominal prices to escape persecution. In this way the people had suffered till the country passed into the hands of the British, whose advent was a god-send to the poverty-stricken and down-trodden Tamils. I cannot better express the happiness and prosperity of the Tamils which resulted from this change of sovereignty than in the words of Pugazhendi,

கார்பெறற தோகையோ கண்பெற்ற வாண்முகமோ
நீபெற் றுயர்ந்த நிறைபுலமோ — பார்பெற்று
மாதோடி மன்னன வரக்கண்டமாநகர்க்கு
ஏதோ வுரைப்ப னெனீர்.

(The king regaining his dominions enters the city with his consort. With what shall I compare the universal joy of the people? Is it like the joy of the peacock at the sight of the gathering clouds, or of the face that has got back its eyes, or of the withering crop that quickens into life when the rain falls?)

Till about the end of the seventeenth century the Tamil countries were ruled by Hindu governors. Brahmanical influence was in the ascendent. The learning of Sanskrit, Tamil and Telugu was encouraged. Several original works in all these languages were written, besides innumerable commentaries in Tamil as well as in Sanskrit on ancient works, especially on the Nalayira Prabhandam,—all tending to harden and aggravate the sectarian and the tribal animosities, until a reaction set in during the succeeding period of Musalman despotism. Then for about half-a-century there was a lull, which was followed by the production of anti-Brahmanical, Christian and Islamic literatures. And it was only during the first half of the last century that the vernacular literature began to revive under the fostering care of the British administration.

With the change in government, religion and social customs many Tamil words had gone out of use giving way to new ones—நாடு, கூற்றம் and கோட்டம் as the administrative divisions of a country, நெல்லாயம், கார்த்திகைப்பச்சை, சின்னம், தறியிறை, செக்கிறை, மகன்மை, &c., as names of public taxes, அமாத்தியம், வாரியம், காவிதிமை, சம்பிரிதி, &c., as official terms, குழணி, பதக்கு, தூணி, முநதிரி, காணி, கழஞ்சு, and other words of native weights and measures are fast dying out except in out of the way villages, along with காசு, பணம், துட்டு, வராகன், and other denominations of old coinage. Most of the revenue and judicial terms, names relating to office furniture and stationery, and generally most words relating to the administrative machinary are Arabic, Persian or English The religious terms, of course, are all Sanskrit.

There is nothing new in the gammar of this period, perhaps with the exception of a leaning towards a greater use of Sanskrit and foreign words by the educated classes, and the unconscious creeping in of several English words in the home-speech of the English educated Tamilians.

Poetry was the only medium of literary expression of thought in Tamil till about the begin-

PLACE OF TAMIL IN PHILOLOGY

ning of the last century, excepting of course, the extensive commentaries and copious notes on ancient poems. However, the natural ease and beauty of the writings of the academic and the hymnal periods were gone. The கலம்பகம், மாலே, அந்தாதி, பிள்ளைத்தமிழ், பரணி and உலா were the different kinds of poesy adopted for shorter literary compositions, and the Kavya (காப்பியம்) form for longer and more descriptive works like the puranas. For these quasi-religious compositions all kinds of metres enumerated in the grammar books on prosody were freely made use of. Learning was then confined to a class of indolent men or religious fanatics, who had no other work than this sort of exercise in prosodial gymnastics and who depended for their precarious subsistence on the bounties of kings and noblemen. Their object was to display their skill in versifying and to scare the ordinary readers by making their stanzas obscure by the use of obsolete and ambiguous words as the following examples will show:—

(1) பிரமபுரத்துறை பெம்மா னெம்மான்
பிரமபுரத்துறை பெம்மா னெம்மான்
பிரமபுரத்துறை பெம்மா னெமமான்
பிரமபுரத்துறை பெம்மா னெம்மான்.—*T. T.*

(2) தத்தித்தா தூதுதி தாதூதித தத்துதி
தித்தித் திதைதிதுதைத்ததா தூதுதி
நித்தித்த நித்தித்த தாதெது நித்தித்த
தெத்தாதோ நித்தித்த தாது —*D. A.*

. A word before closing this chapter. The evils of competition are overtaking even the Indian people. Modern industrialism and city life are taking away the taste for healthy reading, while forcing him to work all day for the day's meal for himself and his family. Let it not be said that the scholars of this country were responsible in any way for creating a literature which, by being unsuited to the needs and taste of the people, has weakened the people's appreciation of good literature and the capacity to live a healthy life, and to find a joy in it. The Tamilian of to-day can hardly find any time to rack his brains in wading through the moth-eaten pages of the rigmarole *puranas* of a Kachiyappa or a Minakshisundram. We have already had enough and more poetry—sonnets, idylls, dramas, ballads and epics; nay, even works on philosophy, religion, ethics, history, grammar, dictionary, medicine and on every imaginable subject are all poetry. Poetry and versification had their value in the past, and they may still be of use in some cases. For our literary models let us go to the writings of Sattanar or Ilango-adigal whose beauty, simplicity, smoothness and grace it is a pride and glory to approach in our efforts. But communication of knowledge in these days is best done in prose not poetry. We want therefore plenty of prose, but not Asiatic prose, and little of poetical literature. The prose should be simple and idiomatic, free alike from pedantry and baldness.

VIII

PERIODS OF TAMIL LITERATURE

Among the Dravidian tribes of South India, the Tamils were the first to cultivate a literature. Their earliest poems, which are now extant, the Aga-nanuru, the Pura-nanuru and the anthologies of that kind show that they were, like the ancient Assyrians and the early Germanic tribes, a warlike race. Here is a type of the ancient Dravidian woman who in response to an enquiry about her son answered thus:—'I know not where my son is; but he will any-how suddenly appear on the battle-field, for (pointing to her belly) this is the cave that gave birth to that tiger.'

என்மகன்
யாண்டுள ஞப்பினு மதியே ஞேரும
புலிசேர்ந்து போகிய கல்லளைபோல
வீன்ற வயிற்றே விதுவே
தோன்றுவன் மாதோ போர்க்களத்தானே.—*Pur*. 86.

The dignity they attached to military pursuits, the chivalrous attitude towards their women, their scorn for an uneventful life and natural death, and their spirit of independence and adventure are patent in every song of the above collections. All these, however, grew weaker under the influence of the Buddhist and Jaina teachings, and were eventually stamped out by the peace-loving Brahmans, who in those days wielded such a mighty influence on the Tamil nation as to leave an indelible mark of Aryanism on everything non-Aryan.

Yet in every department of Tamil literature we can still perceive a slender vein of Dravidian thought running through. Its ground-work is purely non-Aryan and its super-structure necessarily Aryan; because, it was not as conquerors that the Aryan Brahmans entered the Tamil country, but as teachers of Vedic religion and philosophy. Unlike Islamism which carried fire and sword with it, wherever it went, the Indo-Aryans established their spiritual supremacy by gentleness, refinement and persuasive manners. Musalmans were dreaded by the conquered, whereas the Aryans were honoured and respected as the 'andanar' or the possessors of tender qualities, and 'parpar' or the seers of the Vedas. The early Musalman could not find a place for anything foreign to his less cultivated taste and intolerant militant religion, while the Aryan assimilated and absorbed whatever was good outside his racial culture and exalted it by associating it with his higher civilization. It is the characteristic of a conquering and victorious army which is not held in check by elevated national traditional culture and refined sense of honour to disregard, and even to destroy the literary and artistic treasures of the conquered people. Such was the attitude of the Muhammadan invaders when they first came to South India. So we find in the early part of the fourteenth century, when the Musalman hordes poured down into South India, the Tamils had to lament the loss of almost all their literature. All the libraries were ransacked in the country, and all that the Tamil genius had reared for ages were committed to flames. On the contrary the Brahmans, the Jains and the Buddhists actively worked to found universities, literary academies and libraries, and added refinement and stability to the Tamil language and literature. And it was through the deep interest and tender care of those people that Tamilians were inspired with new thoughts and ideas, and their literature enriched with new forms of expressions. Again, during modern times, the Musalmans who had learnt to live on friendly terms with the Hindus, and the Christian Missionaries who had come into South India as harbingers of western civilization have also in a way affected, though in an imperceptible degree, the Dravidian life and thought. Thus, the influence of the Aryans—both Indian and European—was essentially religious and philosophical. All these will be explained later on in their proper places.

Indian grammarians have divided Tamil literature into three classes, namely—Iyal (belles letters), Isai (Music) and Nataka (Drama). As this essay is concerned mainly with the literature of the

Iyal Tamil, it will not be inopportune to first briefly say something about the *Isai* and the *Nāṭakam* or *kuttu*, before we proceed to our subject.

Tradition says that Agastya was the only grammarian who wrote complete treatises on the grammar of all the three classes of Tamil, but none of them are now extant. During the early centuries of the Christian era attention seems to have been paid by the Tamils to all the three. They had their own dances and music—vocal and instrumental. They, of course, with the help of Brahmans, developed the art of dancing to a high degree of perfection and many treatises were written on this fine art; even their gods had their characteristic favourite dances. Music too, was in a state of perfection, and their *pans* or tunes were *sui generis* to the Tamil race. The only ancient Tamil work of the nature of the drama that has come down to us is the Silappadikaram (third century). It gives a vivid description of the stage, the actor, the singer, the drummer, the flute-player, the yazh-player and others of the troupe; and contain beautiful specimens of *vari* (வரி), *pattu* (பாட்டு), *kuravai* (குரவை), *ammanai* (அம்மானை), *usal* (ஊசல்), *kandukam* (கந்துகம்), *vallai* (வள்ளை), and other classes of musical songs.

A brief description of the *yāzh*—a stringed musical instrument, similar to the guitar, peculiar only to the ancient Tamils may not be uninteresting. It was of four kinds, *viz*—பேரியாழ், மகரயாழ், சகோடயாழ் and செங்கோட்டியாழ். The Per-yazh had 21 strings; aMakrayazh, 17 ; Chakota-yazh, 16 ; and Sengottu-yazh, 7. Perhaps these were the instruments in use during the days of Ilango-adigal. And the Per or big 'yazh' which is supposed to have been in use in the days of Agastya had become extinct even before the third century A. D. It is said to have had one thousand strings,

ஆயிர நாமிற்றுகி யாழாகு
மேனையுதபபு மொபபன கொளளே.

But with the growing influence of the Jains and Brahmans, spirituality received more attention, much to the detriment of the physical side of his development, which was neglected and even condemned. Self-mortification and abstinence from pleasure were advocated and recommended as the high road to salvation. And the works on music, dancing and the drama written by ancient Tamils, such as பெருநாரை, பெருங்குருகு, பஞ்சபாரதீயம், தாளவகையாதது, பஞ்சமரபு, இந்திரகாளியம், இசை நுணுக்கம், &c., (on music) and பரதம், முறுவல், சயந்தம் குண நூல், செயிற்றியம், கூத்தநூல், பரதசேறுபதீயம், மதி வாணநாடகத்தமிழ்நூல், &c. (on dramaturgy) were neglected and left to shift for themselves; and by the time of Adiyarkunallar about (1200 A.D) most of them were lost. With them the Dravidian music and dances became extinct. No one can now say what those *pans* and dances were like. Their places were gradually taken up by the Indo-Aryan *ragams* and *natyams*.

However, these æsthetic arts were given a religious tone and allowed in that condition to prolong their feeble existence for upwards of ten centuries from about the seventh. Their sphere of exercise was transferred from the house to the temple.[1] The Saiva and Vaishnava hymns forming the Devaram and the Nalayira Prabandam, were collected and set to Dravidian music and sung in Hindu temples. During festivals and processions of gods, dancing was encouraged and plays were acted to draw large crowds of devotees. Hundreds of dancing girls or *gandharvis* were attached to every important temple. This was the origin of the institution of singing by *Odhvans* and *Araiyans*, and the public representation of *natakas*, *pallus* and *kuravanjis* in Hindu temples. Of these the first alone now survives. The same institution was carried to the West Coast, and it now survives in the Chakkiyar *kuttu*. The persons concerned in this institution were, as given in the inscriptions of Raja-raja Chola, நாடகமும் யன, சாக்கை, கானபாடி, பிடாரன், காமரபீபைரயன், வாததி யமாராயன, ஆரியம்பாடுவார், காந்தர்வி, &c. It was only during the eighteenth century that drama and music began to revive; and Arunachala Kavi (A.D. 1712-1779) the famous author of Rama Natakam may be justly called the father of modern dramatic literature, and under the Mahratta Rajahs of Tanjore

---

1 It is said that the Hindu drama, like that of the Greeks, was derived from, and formed part of, their religious ceremonies. Lassen considers the Indian drama to be of native growth, while Weber thinks it was influenced by the Greek dramas performed at he court of Greek (Bactrian) kings.

a fresh impetus was given to music. We might say that both these arts flourished in highly developed forms about the time of Surfoji Raja of Tanjore (1780-1830). Subsequently, plays in imitation of Shakespeare's dramas, *Kirtans* and *Harikatas* were written for public performances and music came to be appreciated and patronized by the middle and lower classes, who under the British rule were rising in importance, and the arts themselves were being affected by democratic influences. This is a subject which the writer does not feel competent to treat adequately. The reader is referred to the interesting book of Mr. Day and the illuminating contributions of Dr. Coomaraswamy.

From the existing Tamil literature it is not possible to determine its exact range, as it was subject to vicissitudes, one of which we have already mentioned. Several works by Jains and Buddhists, who were among the earliest to encourage the growth of Tamil literature, are not now forthcoming ; and it is believed that most of them were destroyed when Buddhists and Jains were persecuted during the seventh and eighth centuries. As we have said elsewhere 'a good portion of its extensive literature preserved for ages on palm leaves had long ago been consumed by fire and white ants... And such as had escaped these destructive agencies remained locked up in the dingy cellars of the lascivious Mathadhipatis and in the thatched houses of penniless *pandits*' Even if all the writings of the early and mediæval

Tamil authors had come down to us in full preservation it is extremely doubtful whether Tamil literature would be as extensive as its Sanskrit compeer. And this has been confirmed by Dr. Caldwell who very truly observes that 'Tamil literature as a whole will not bear a comparison with Sanskrit literature as a whole.'

Of the different branches of knowledge the early Tamils appear to have cultivated only the polite literature. They knew only so much of elementary arithmetic as was absolutely required for trading purposes, and higher mathematics, science, philosophy and theology in which the Indo-Aryans excelled all other civilized nations of antiquity were unknown to the Dravidians. Some Tamil scholars might say that astronomy was not unknown to their ancients and quote,—

செஞ் ஞாயிறறுச் செலவுஞ் ஞாயிற்றுப
பரிபபும் பரிபபுசூழ்ந்த மண்டிலமும்
வளிதிரிதருதிசையும்
வறிது நிலை இயகாயமும் மென்னிலை
செனறளநதநிங்தோர் போல வெனறு
மீனதடதன் போரு முளரே.—*Pur.* 30.

One or two of them went even to the length of asserting that 'Saiva philosophy and religion in its original elements was purely Tamilian'. Mr. Kanakasabhai believes that ' in the ancient Tamil classical works, the terms relating to music, grammar, astronomy and even abstract philosophy are of pure Tamil origin', and that 'they indicate most clearly that those sciences were cultivated by the Tamils long before the arrival of the Brahmans or other Aryan immigrants'. This is not good logic, as these terms might be later Tamil translations or adaptations from Sanskrit. It would be more reasonable to ask,—Did the Tamils possess any literature on these subjects before the arrival of the Brahmans? So far as we know they had none. We need not attempt to refute these statements seriatim, but shall content ourselves for the present with quoting the views of Dr. Caldwell on the pre-Aryan civilization of the Tamils. 'They were without hereditary priests and idols and appear to have had no idea of ' heaven ' or ' hell ' or the 'soul' or 'sin'...They had numerals up to 100 ; ...but no acquaintance with sculpture, architecture, astronomy, astrology, grammar or philosophy'.

The existing Tamil works, most of them, are either translations or adaptations of Sanskrit originals. There are, however, certain compositions which are not so. The five major and the five minor epics, the eight anthologies, the ten major and the eighteen minor poems belong to this class. Dr. Caldwell thinks that 'in one department at least, that of ethical apothegms it is generally maintained that Sanskrit has been outdone by Tamil.' But, on the other hand, we are inclined to think that the existence of so many works on the ethics of daily life is an indication of the low state of morality among the early Tamils. Because it was the Dravidian whose teeth were blunted by the eating of flesh,

கொல்லையுழு கொழு வேய்ப்பபபல்லே,
யெல்லேயு மிரவு மூன்றின்று மழுஙகி.—*Pal, II.,*117.

that required the advice,

அருளல்லதி யாதெனிற் கொல்லாமை கோறல்
பொருளல்ல தவ்வூன்றினல.—*Kur.*

And the following extracts will show that most of the Tamil kings were tyrannizing over their subjects:—

1. நடுவிகந் தோரீஇயனில்லான் விணவாங்கக்
    கொடிதோராத்த மன்னவன் கோல்போல.
2. செறுமிக சினவேந்தன் சிவந்திறுத்த புலமபோல.—*Kal.*

The early Tamilians considered it an honour and virtue in a military man to carry off other men's wives, to devastate the enemy's fields, to destroy their houses and to lift the cattle of neighbouring tribes. A people with such principles of conduct really needed books on practical morality.[1]

The ethical code of the Tamils is contained chiefly in the eighteen minor poems already referred to. None of the works on morals which our learned bishop makes so much of, appear to have been written by the Tamils before they had come under the civilizing influence of the Indo-Aryans, be they Brahmans, Buddhists or Jains. It is even supposed that the Kural of Tiruvalluvar and the Acharakkovai of Peruvayil-Mulliyar are adaptations from Sanskrit

1. The fact that Brahmans were called மெய்யர் or 'truth speakers' proves that lying was common among the early Tamil speaking tribes.

Mahabharata, Dharmasastras, &c., as will be seen from the following extract :—

திருவள்ளுவனுர்தம் பெருநூலே வடநூலார் மதமபற்றி தமிழா னேதகின்று ராயினும் தமிழ்நூலகளோடும் பொருந்த வைத்துக் கூறினரென்பது பரிமேலழகர் கொள்கை. இவர் பொருட் பாகுபாட்டினே அறம்பொருளின்பமென வடநூலார் வழக்குப்பற்றி யோதுதலான்...அறத்துப்பால் விஷயங்களே மது முதலிய நூல்களோடும், பொருட்பாலேச் சாணகியம், காமந்தகம என்னும் நூல்களோடுமே, காமத்துப்பாலே வாத்ஸ்யாயன முதலிய வற்றேடும் பொருநதவைத்து வள்ளுவனுர் கூறினரென்பது.

Thus it is evident that the whole of Tamil literature is permeated with Aryan influence and that practically there was no literature worth the name among the Tamils before the migration of Brahmans to South India, and it has been boldly asserted by M. Hovelacque that 'all the works of which it is composed, down to the smallest fragment are long posterior to their first contact with the Aryans.'

The science of history is foreign to the Hindus; and a history of literature is much more. They made no distinction between mythology, tradition and history. Periods of time were of no consequence ; to them past and present in the growth of a language or literature were an eternal now and meaningless. The Tamil scholars, ancient as well as modern, have had no idea of the exact range of their literature. The average Tamil scholars were mostly poets or versifiers, and their acquaintance with literature was limited to some standard works on grammar, vocabulary and of one or two epic poems Kamban's Ramayanam, Ativiraramapandya's Naishadam, Tolkapyam,. Pavanandi's Nannul, Amritasagarar's Karigai, Dandi Alankaram, Divakaram and Chudamani Nigandu together with one or two *antadis* and *kalambakams* met all the requirements of these versifiers. This easily earned scholarship and consequent self-complacency, blinded them to the merits of many important Tamil works written by Buddhists and Jains, which were disliked on account of their authorship. These were left in the sun and rain to decay or to be eaten up in course of time by white-ants; while many more were consigned to the floods of the 18th of Adi (August)

But such a charge cannot be laid at the feet of Nacchinarkiniyar, or Adiyarkunallar and generally of all the erudite commentators of the middle ages. Their study was extensive and their exposition thoroughly logical ; and yet the critical methods of research and investigation which characterize the inquisitive scholar of modern times were absolutely unknown to them ; for, as Dr Caldwell, pertinently remarks, the critical spirit even in the west is of modern growth. The ancient Hindus did not cultivate it, because they had the greatest, perhaps blind, regard and veneration for their ancestors and their works ; and implicitly believed as sacred truths whatever their elders said, absurd though they might be. Further, the Science of Philology or the historical and scientific study of languages did not come into existence then. Literary forgeries passed for genuine productions ; and the native scholars who have been duped by them owing to their credulity are miserably incapable of detecting them. Even the so-called Tamil scholars of the present day who profess to follow the critical and historical methods in their researches cannot discriminate the famous Brahman author of Kurinjippattu from the saintly composer of the Siva-Peruman Tiruvantadi, or even from that recent Dravidian writer of an anti-Brahmanical song; or the author of Gnanâ Vettiyan from the immortal writer of the Kural. We give below specimens from three different poems wrongly attributed to one and the same Kapilar by Tamil scholars of the old orthodox school :—

(1) அறங்கரைந்து வயங்கிய காவிற்பிறங்கிய
வுரைசால் வெள்வி முடித்த கேள்வி
யந்தண ரருங்கல மேற்ப நீர்பட்
டிருஞ்சே ருடிய மண்ணன்மலி முற்றத்துக்
களிறுநிலே மூன்றிய தாரருந தகைப்பிற்
புறஞ்சிறை வயிரியம் காணின் வல஦ே
யெஃகுபடை யறுத்த கொயசுவம் புரவி
யலங்கும் பாண்டி விழையணிக் தீமென
வாருக் கொள்கையை.—*Pad* VII. 64.

(2) போகபந்தத் தந்தமின்றி நிறபீர் புணத்தார்முடிமே ஙக
பந்தத் தந்தநாளம் பிறையிறையான்பயந்த மாகமந்தத்
தந்தமா மழைபோன்ற மதத்துக்கதப்போ ரேகதந்தத்
தெங்கைதசெந் தாளிண பணிந்தேத்துமினே.—*Mut*, 10.

(3) தென்றிசைப் புலையன் வடதிசைக் கேகிற்
பழுதற வோதிப் பார்ப்பா னுவான்
வடதிசைப் பார்ப்பான் றென்றிசைக் கேகின்
நடையது கோணிப் புலைய னுவான்.—*Agaval.*

No doubt this must partly be attributed to prejudice, racial feelings, and mistaken faith. With the spread of Western culture and the study of scientific methods they seem to be gradually disappearing.

Mr. Damodaram Pillai's Classification :— Among the *pandits* of the old type we must undoubtedly include Mr. Damodaram Pillai, the learned editor of Tolkapyam, Virasoliyam, Kalittogai and other works. Though a lawyer and judge by profession, his zeal and admiration for his native literature and his Tamil race have not only blurred his judgment but also carried him away from the sacred precincts of historic truth. In a lengthy introduction to his edition of Virasoliyam he has attempted to give a brief history of Tamil literature, besides making some uncalled for remarks on the non-Saivites in his violent Jaffnese style. His reputation as a good Tamil scholar and the valuable service he has rendered to the Tamil nation by his publications make it necessary to notice his views along with those of Dr. Caldwell and others. According to him there were eight periods in the history of Tamil literature namely :—

1. அபோதகாலம் (Pre-historic).   Before Agastya. There was then no alphabet.

II.	அஃகரகாலம் (Alphabetic).	From the date of the invention of the alphabet by Agastya to the period of completion of his grammar.
III.	இலக்கணகாலம் (Grammatic).	The period of composition of Tamil grammar by his twelve disciples.
IV.	சமுதாயகாலம் (Academic).	Period of the three Tamil academies (B.C. 10,150 to 150).
V.	அநாதாரகாலம் (Lethargic).	200 years. After the destruction of the third Sangam when the Tamil literature, was not patronised (B. C. 150—A. D. 50).
VI.	சமணகாலம் (Jain).	300 years. When Chintamani, Nannul, Virasoliyam and other Jain works were written (A. D. 50— 350).
VII.	இதிகாசகாலம் (Puranic).	800 years. In this period Puranas, Naishada, Ramayana and other works of that kind were written (A. D. 350 —1150).
VIII.	ஆதீனகாலம (Monastic).	700 years. When the Saiva monks of Tiruvaduturai and other places encouraged, the study of Tamil literature (A. D. 1150—1850).

The above classification appears to us on the face of it unscientific and historically monstrous. It is marked by a total want of a sense of proportion and historical acumen. Coming as it does from the pen of a lawyer of English training it is really pitiable. In his opinion the age of Tamil literature must be at least 12,000 years which is 4 or 5 millenniums older than the earliest known civilisation. The history of Egypt commences from not more than 3,000 years before Christ; that of the Greeks ascends scarcely to 2,700 years from to-day. It serves no good to enter into the details of his classification; its improbabilites and fanciful dates assigned to different works will be brought out in the sequel.

Mr. Suryanarayana's classification :—To pass on from the dubious field of blind faith and tradition to the domain of reason and history, we find in Mr. Suryanarayana Sastri saner views. His little book on the history of Tamil language is a useful attempt worth imitating on a larger scale by Tamil scholars trained in the occidental methods. He devotes a chapter to an outline history of Tamil literature which he divides into the following periods :—

I. Early.   B C. 8000 to A. D. 100. This includes the age of the three academies or Sangams.

II. Mediæval.   (*a*) First half: 100—600 A D. The five major and the five minor epics, Tiruvachakam, Divakaram, Muttollayiram and other works were written during this period

(*b*) Second half : 600—1400 A.D Tevaram, Kalladam, Tiruvoymozhi, Agapporul, Purapporul, Ramayanam, Nala Venba and other works were written.

III. Modern. From A.D. 1400. Ativirarama Pandiyan, Villiputturar, Arunagiri, Paranjoti, Sivaprakasar, Tatvarayar, Tayumanavar, Viramamuni and other poets flourished.

The above classification, though not open to serious objections like the preceding one, seems to us somewhat unsatisfactory in that it is wanting in historical perspective ; nor is each period sufficiently explanatory of the spirit and influence of the time which it professes to deal with. It is a strange mixture of conflicting traditions with historical facts. His early period, which covers a long interval of 8100 years, no historian of any existing literature would make up his mind to believe. He seems to accept unreservedly the traditional account of the Tamil academies which no scholar acquainted with the modern critical method would do. His mediæval period extends over a pretty long period of 1300 years, while his third occupies only 500. It is not understood on what established data he has based his classification, no distinguishing land-marks being assigned to it.

Dr. Caldwell's Classification :—In his introduction to 'A Comparative Grammar of the Dravidian Languages', Dr. Caldwell aims at giving a brief history of Tamil literature. He divides it into seven cycles or periods citing some authors or works as representative of each cycle. They are,

I. The Jaina cycle or the cycle of the Madura

Sangam or College, from the eighth or ninth century A. D. to the twelfth or thirteenth century. The important works of this period were Kural, Naladiyar, Chintamani, Divakaram and Nannul.

II. The Tamil Ramayana cycle—the thirteenth century. Kamban, Pugazhendi, Ottaikkuttar and Auvaiyar were the poets of this age.

III. The Saiva Revival cycle—the thirteenth and fourteenth centuries. The Tevaram and the Tiruvachakam were composed during this period.

IV. The Vaishnava cycle—about the same period. To this period he assigns the composition of the Nalayiraprabandam.

V. The cycle of the Literary Revival—the fifteenth and sixteenth centuries. The works and authors were Vasishtam, the Saiva Siddhantam, Ativirarama-Pandyan and Villiputturar.

VI. The anti-Brahmanical cycle in which the compositions of the Siddhar School came into existence—seventeenth century. Agastya, Siva Vakkiyar, Tirumular, Bhadragiriyar, and all the eighteen Siddhas flourished at this period.

VII. The modern school—the eighteenth and nineteenth centuries in which Pattanattar, Tayumanavar and the authors of Prabhulingalilai and Tembavani lived.

It will be seen from the above classification that there was no literature in Tamil before the eighth century A. D. Elsewhere, the same writer goes on to say that ' the Tamil literature now extant enables us to ascend, in studying the history of the language only to the ninth or tenth century A. D.' And in a third place he assigns the eighth century A. D. as the age of Tolkapyam with the following remark:—'Whatever antiquity may be attributed to the Tolkapyam it must have been preceded by many centuries of literary culture. It lays down rules for different kinds of poetical compositions, which must have been deduced from examples furnished by the best authors whose works were then in existence. A rule is simply an observed custom'. Don't we observe in these statements apparent contradictions ? Whatever may be the date of the Tolkapyam, did he endeavour to learn the names of the best authors who had furnished examples for that grammar? The truth seems to be that, when his great work was published nearly half-a-century ago, some of the earliest Tamil classics like the Silappadikaram, Manimekalai, Pattuppattu, Purananuru and several others were unknown even to many Tamil pandits of those days. Moreover, his division of Tamil literature into cycles and his determination of the dates of certain important Tamil works were based upon some doubtful inscriptions of a Rajendra Chola or a Sundara Pandya Deva and upon a misconception that the Alvars were the disciples of the great Vaishnava reformer, Sri Ramanuja Charya. But within the last thirty years epigraphy has progressed so far and has brought to light so many important facts, literary, social, and historical, as to necessitate a complete modification of almost every one of his statements concerning the dates of Tamil authors. The learned Bishop has devoted several pages of his invaluable grammar to a vain discussion of the age of Sundara or Kun Pandya of Trignanasambandar's time, wrongly identifying him with the Sunder Bendi of the Muhammadan historians, in order to bring the authors of the Devara hymns down to the 13th century A. D. His statement that 'the poetical compositions of seven of the twelve *Alvars* or Vaishnava devotees, followers of Ramanuja, which are included in the Nalayiraprabandam are still more numerous than those of Manikkavachakar, Trignanasambandar and other Saiva devotees,' might be a clear proof of his total ignorance of the magnitude of any of these sacred hymns. And it might be said with greater confidence that he had not seen or even heard of several works in the Tamil language. I do not propose to enter into any detailed examination of his views, as they have already been sufficiently criticised by the late Mr. Sundaram Pillai of Trivandram.

Classification of Sir W. Hunter and others :—The most prominent among the later writers on Tamil literature is Sir W. W. Hunter. He writes thus. 'The Saivite and Vaishnavite revival of the Brahman apostles in Southern India from the 8th century onwards stirred up a counter movement on the part of the Jains. The Dravidian Buddhists and Jains created a cycle of Tamil literature anti-Brahmanical in tone, stretching from the 9th to the 13th century. Its first great composition, the Kural of Tiruvalluvar, not later than the 10th century A. D. is said to have been the work of a poet sprung from the Pariah or lowest caste. The Jain period of Tamil literature includes works on ethics and language; among them the Divakaram literally the 'Day-making Dictionary'. The period culminated in the Chintamani, a romantic epic of 15,000 lines by an unknown Jain author ..Contemporaneous with the Jain cycle of Tamil literature the great adaptation of the Ramayana was composed by Kambar for the Dravidian races ... Between that period and the 16th century two encyclopædic collections of Tamil hymns in praise of Siva were gradually formed... During the same centuries the Vaishnavite apostles were equally prolific in Tamil religious songs... After a period of literary inactivity the Tamil genius again blossomed forth in the 16th and 17th centuries with a poet-king as the leader of the literary revival. In the 17th century arose an anti-Brahmanical Tamil literature known as the Sittar school ... The Tamil writers of the 18th and 19th centuries are classified as modern. The honours of this period are divided between a pious Sivaite and the Italian Jesuit, Beschi.' The above extracts from Dr. W. W. Hunter's Gazetteer will clearly show that he has simply followed Dr. Cadwell's classification, paraphrasing it in his usual racy style. It might be said here once for all that all other English writers on Tamil literature, including

Dr. Grierson, Dr. Rost and Professor Frazer[1], have wittingly or unwittingly followed the learned Bishop's statements and propagated the obvious errors he had committed, and did not take the least trouble to correct them, on account of his high authority and of their total ignorance of the extent and importance of Tamil language and literature. To these may be added their instinctive slight for a non Aryan race and culture.

Notwithstanding the able and trenchant criticism of some of Dr. Caldwell's theories by the late Mr. Sundaram Pillai in his 'Some Mile-stones in the History of Tamil Literature', some European scholars, still draw their statements largely from the works of Drs. Burnell and Caldwell. No doubt, European scholars have done excellent service in the cause of Comparative Philology and the Indians are deeply indebted to them for the study of their languages on critical and historical methods. But so far as a thorough and intimate knowledge of the Vernaculars and their idioms are concerned, we cannot expect them all to be Beschis or Popes. In the days of Drs. Caldwell and Burnell the science of epigraphy was in its infancy and they were not justified in being dogmatic in their assertions relating to historical questions.

---

1. I am glad to find that Mr. Frazer has corrected most of his views (in 1912) agreeably to the latest researches in South Indian Epigraphy and early Tamil literature; and I believe he is the only European scholar who is up to date in his Tamil studies. See his article on 'Dravida' in the *Encyclopedia of Religion and Ethics*.

Within the past quarter of a century epigraphy has progressed by leaps and bounds, and the facts and theories of these writers require considerable revision. To quote from these writers would, therefore, be exceedingly unsafe. One example from the Imperial Gazetteer (New Edition) will suffice. In Volume II of this monumental work, Mr. R. Sewell, while speaking of the literature of the Tamils, writes thus:— 'Several Tamil poets of this age, *i e.*, about A. D 600—50 are greatly renowned, among whom may be mentioned the Saiva devotees of Tirunavukkaraiyar, Tirgnanasambandar and Sundaram irthi Nayanar ; Manikka Vasagar also belongs to this period' (p. 330). And Dr. Grierson who has devoted three precious paragraphs in the same volume for this ancient literature, says—' The worship of Siva in the Tamil country found its earliest literary expression in the Tiruvasagam or 'Holy word' of Manikka-vasagar who lived in the *eleventh century* (p. 425)... A later and larger collection of hymns addressed to Siva is the Tevaram of Sambanda, Sundara and Appa (p. 426)... After the Jain period we have the great Saiva movement of the thirteenth and fourteenth centuries to which we owe the hymnologies already described (p. 435).' It is not our object to decry the labours of these European scholars; but it is to be regretted that such paragraphs have found their way into the pages of the Imperial Gazetteer published under the authority of the Government of India.

Mr. Vinson's Classification .—The only other Western student of Tamil literature whom we should not pass over unnoticed is M. Julien Vinson of Paris. 'I can hardly admit', he writes, 'that Tamil literary age began before the seventh century A. D'. He further thinks that there were five periods in it, which for the sake of brevity and distinctness we subjoin in a tabular form:—

I. 6th and 7th centuries.	Period of essays, pamphlets and short poems.
II. 8th century.	Period in which the Jains predominated.
III. 9th century.	Period which saw at the same time the struggle between Saivas and Jains, and in which Buddhists came from Ceylon.
IV. 10th century.	Period in which the Saivas were the undisputed masters.
V. 15th and 16th centuries.	Period in which appear the Vaishnavas.

This classification, though it is a marked improvement on the previous one, is still open to the following objections:—

(1) For the first period of essays and pamphlets M. Vinson should have had in view Aingurunuru, Padirrupattu, Purananuru and other anthologies which were collected and arranged by the third academy. He must have either overlooked Tolkapyam, (fourth or third century B. C.), Kural (first century A. D.), Silappadikaram and Manimekalai (third century), or

discredited the dates assigned to them by Indian scholars. But I now see no sufficient reason to doubt the chronology of these ancient classical works on grammar and ethics, some of which in scientific accuracy, in originality of design, in beauty of expression and thought, and in faithfulness to nature would stand comparison with the best works of similar kind in other languages.

(2) The second and third periods, namely, the eighth and ninth centuries, are characterised by a bitter struggle between Jainism and Brahmanism. As will be seen from the lives and works of Tirumalisai and Tirumangai Alvars, the Vaishnava Saints had an equal share with the Saivas in the suppression of Jainism. It is not, therefore, correct to call it a struggle between Jainism and Sivaism. It may be that very few Buddhists came from Ceylon to Chidambaram, and had religious disputations with Manikkavachagar about the middle of the ninth century. But this was only a minor incident which left no permanent impress on either the literature or the religion of the Tamil people. Moreover, it was Brahmanism—not Sivaism—that had attained its supremacy so early as the ninth century, though Jainism had still a lingering existence. And it was during these two centuries that a great number of the Saiva *Nayanmars* and Vaishnava *Alvars* flourished and did their proselytizing work.

(3) During the fourth period (tenth century) not only the Saivas but also the Vaishnavas were left undisput-

ed masters in the religious field. It also witnessed the collection and arrangement of the sacred hymns of Appar, Sambandar, Sundarar, Manikkavachakar and other Saiva saints into eleven *Tirumurais* by Nambiyandar Nambi, and of the twelve Vaishanava Alvars into Nalayira Prabandam (Book of 4,000 Psalms) by Sri Nathamuni.

(4) M. Vinson assigns to the fifth period—fifteenth and sixteenth centuries—the appearance of the Vaishnavas. It is here, we think, that his ignorance of the history of Tamil literature, especially of the Vaishnava religion, is most marked. He has not studied or rightly understood the origin and growth of the Vaishnava sect in South India. Perhaps he was misled by the incorrect statement of Dr. Caldwell, that the twelve Vaishnava saints were the disciples of Sri Ramanuja Charya, the great reformer of the twelfth century. We may mention that the fifth period of M. Vinson is distinguished for the best controversial literature on the Vaishnava religion and for the scholarly commentaries thereon, in the *Manipravala* or composite style peculiar only to the Jains and the Vaishnava Brahmans.

Proposed Classification: None of the Tamil works bear a certain date; yet they are not wanting in criteria to enable the reader to assign to them a definite period in the literary development. For first there exists a difference in language demarcating the most ancient periods, and secondly the development of the literature has been upon such lines (mainly religious) that it is easy to say from content and method of treatment to which of its epochs a particular work might belong.

We shall now come to our classification. The following table gives a tolerably accurate outline of the important stages in the progress of Tamil literature. As has already been explained religion pervades almost the whole of every literature in India, and the table therefore exhibits the several periods of the religious history also.

Period.	Religion.	Literature.	Language
B. C. 600-200. B. C. 200-A. D. 150.	I. Animistic. II. Buddhist.	I. Academic (Tolkappyam, Kural &c.)	I. Early *Grammar*: Agastyam, Tolkapyam.
A. D. 150-500.	III. Jaina.	II. Classic (Silappadikaram, Manimekalai, Pattupattu &c.)	
A. D. 500-950.	IV. Brahmanic.	III. Hymnal (Tevaram, Tiruvachakam, Tiruvoymoli, &c.)	II. Mediaeval *Grammar*: Tolkapyam, Kalladam, Virasoliyam.
A. D. 950-1200.	V. Sectarian.	IV. Translations (Kamban's Ramayana, Kachiyappa's Skantham, &c.)	
A.D. 1200-1450.	VI. Reformatory.	V. Exegetical (Commentaries by Nacchi-narkiniyar, Adiyarkunallar, &c.	III. Modern *Grammar*: Virasoliyam and Nannul.
A.D. 1450-1850.	VII. Modern.	VI. Miscellaneous	

I do not claim any logical exactitude for the above division. But it is the best I could think of, and it represents the different stages in the growth of Tamil literature clearly and succinctly. No doubt one period overlaps the other, and it would be impossible to draw a hard-and-fast line between any two periods.

Tamil literature of course did not begin only with the founding of Academies as indicated in the table. This was preceded by what may be called the pre-academic period. But to attempt any account of it will be a groping in the dark, as all literary evidence we now possess relates either to the academic or to the post-academic period. Some Tamil scholars still believe that Agastya invented the Tamil alphabet. This is certainly erroneous. The use of pure Tamil words like எழுத்து and சுவடி by Agastya proves unmistakably the existence of the Tamil alphabet and the use of books among the Tamils long before his days. And even the compilation of the first grammar for this language by this Aryan sage, after the Sanskrit model, is an argument in favour of the pre-existence of literature among the Tamils of antiquity. That literature always precedes grammar is a stern philological fact recognized by Agastya and later grammarians.

எள்ளினின் றெண்ணெ யெடுப்பதுபோல
இலக்கியத்தினின் றெடுபடு மிலக்கணம —*Agat.*
இலக்கிய கண்டதற் கிலக்கணமியம்பல்.—*Nan.*

It is therefore almost certain that some sort of literature and also good poets must have existed before the academic era ; but nothing can at present be asserted about it in the absence of any literary or other records.

THE ACADEMIC PERIOD : The real history of Tamil literature begins with the Tamil academies which lasted from B. C. 500 to A D. 500. This millennium might perhaps appear to be a very long period ; but during the first half of it none of the extant Tamil works, probably with the exception of Tolkapyam and one or two others, were written. Further, when we consider the abnormally long period of 12,000 years allotted by native traditions to the three academies, the above is almost a trifle. Of the three academies the second was more or less continuous with the first, and both probably existed sometime between the fifth century B. C. and second century A. D. ; while the third, and the most important of them all seems to have lasted till A. D. 500. Whether the three academies really existed whether they did any useful work in the cause of Tamil literature, how long they lasted, and what poets flourished during this period—all these are questions which we have reserved for consideration in a subsequent essay.

To understand aright the general spirit of the literary productions of this period it is desirable that there should be some previous acquaintance with the political, social, and religious condition of the early Tamil people. Till about the second or third century A. D. there were only three principal Tamil kingdoms, namely, Chera, Chola and Pandya each of which had, of course, three or four protectorates under it governed by feudal chieftains. They were constantly at war with one another losing or annexing villages and districts on every occasion, till at last there came on the scene a foreign race, called the Pallavas, from the north-west, and usurped the northern Tamil districts then belonging to an illegitimate branch of the Cholas. Being intruders and people of foreign extraction, the Pallavas were never recognized as Dravidians by the Tamil nation, and consequently they are not even mentioned in the Tamil literature of those times. Nay, the word 'Pallava' had even acquired a bad sense,

பல்லவர் கயவர் பதகர் நீசர்.—*Ping.*

Caste system was unknown to them. The Tamils were, however, divided into tribes according to the nature of the soil in which they happened to live. A shepherd of the pasture land might become a tiller of the rice field or a fisherman of the beach. Of the eight kinds of marriages mentioned by Manu, marriage by capture (Gandharvan), Asuram and Rakshasam, seem to have been adopted by them ; and yet their women-kind had much freedom. They ate beef and all sorts of animal food and drank fermented liquor. They used to bury or burn the dead ; and while burying them the weapons of the deceased were put into big jars along with the corpse.

(1) முதுமாப போத்தின் கதுமென வியமபுங்
கூகை கோழி யாளுத்
தாழிய பெருங்கா டெய்திய ஞான்றே.—*Pur.* 364.
(2) சுட்டுக குவியெனச செத்தோர்ப் பயிருங்
கள்ளியம் பறநதீல.—*Ibid.* 240.

The early Tamils, like the ancient Egyptians and Romans, worshipped the manes of their ancestors, who were also propitiated with offerings of meat and liquor. After the advent of the Aryans from Upper India this animism had to contend against Brahmanism, then against Buddhism and lastly against Jainism. Until Brahmanism came out triumphant all these four religions—animism, Brahmanism Buddhism, and Jainism—had been struggling for existence in the Tamil country ; and in the course of this long struggle the first was merged in the second, which from that time forward began to expand absorbing every thing that was good and unobjectionable in the other two. An effective check was also given to the indiscriminate eating of meat and habitual drinking of liquor. We may find all these described in the literature of this epoch.

We know nothing about the works of the first and second academies except what is contained in the brief accounts given in Iraiyanar's Agapporul. The names of works which passed through the third academy will be found given in the following oft-quoted verses :—

(1) நற்றிணை நல்ல குறுந்தொகை யைங்குறுநூ
    றெழுத்த பதிற்றுப்பத் தோங்குப ரிபாடல்
    கற்றறிந்தார் பேசுங் கலியோ டகம்புறமென்
    றித்தனைத்த வெட்டுத் தொகை.

(2) முருகுபொரு நாறு பாணிரண்டு மூல்லை
    பெருகுவள மதுரைக் காஞ்சி—மருவினிய
    கோலநெடு நல்வாடை கோல்குறிஞ்சி பட்டினப
    பாலை கடாதடோடும் பத்து.

(3) நாலடி நான்மணி நாநூறப தைநதிணேழுப்
    பால்கடுகங் கோவை பழமொழி மாமூலம
    மெய்ந்நிலைய காஞ்சியோ டேலாதி யென்பவே
    கைந்நிலைய வாங்கீழ்க் கணக்கு.

Besides the eight anthologies or collected works, the ten major and the eighteen minor poems mentioned in the above stanzas, at least two of the five major epics—Silappadikaram and Manimekalai—were written during this period. These two most important works were left out of account, as they were the productions of Buddhist and Jaina authors. The famous poets of this age together with their principal works are given below :—

(1) Tiruvalluvar (Kural) ; (2) Sittalai Sattanar (Manimekalai) ; (3) Ilango-Adigal (Silappadikaram) ; (4) Kapilar (Kurinjippattu, Inna Narpatu, &c.), (5) Paranar (5th Ten in Padirruppattu) ; (6) Nallanduvanar (Kalittogai) ; (7) Nakkirar (Tirumurukarruppadai, Nedunalvadai) ; (8) Mangudi Marudanar (Maduraikkanji) ; (9) Kalladanar; (10) Nallur Nattattanar (Siru Panarruppadai) ; (11) Kadiyalur Rudran

Kannanar (Perumpanarruppadai) ; (12) Napputanar (Mullaippattu) ; (13) Perumkausikanar (Malaipadukadam); (14) Gotamanar (3rd Ten in Paddirruppattu); (15) Mudattamakanniyar (Porunararruppadai) ; (16) Peyanar (Mullai Tinai in Ainkurunûru) &c.

To these should be added Pannirupadalam, Markandeyanar Kanchi, Purapporul Venbamalai, Usimuri of Idaikkadar, Muttollayiram, Nakkiiar's Naladi-nul, Desikamalai, and the works on prosody by Maheswara, Avinayanar, Kaiyanar, Palkayanar, Kakkaipatiniyar and Narrattanar. Most of these works were lost except a few quotations from them.

THE HYMNAL PERIOD: During this period Brahmanism came into conflict with Buddhism and Jainism. The Brahmans were reinforced by bands of Sanskrit theologians from Upper India, and the battle spread like wild-fire all over the peninsula and raged very hot. The Brahmans and Dravidians made common cause against them, and religious disputations took place at all the important Brahman centres, especially Conjeeveram, Chidambaram and Madura. Tirunavukkarasu, Tirugnanasambandar and Manikkavachakar fought for Sivaism, while Tiru-Malisai Piran, Tirumangai Mannan and Vishnu Chittan defended Vishnuism. The combined attack of the sectarian leaders did not go in vain. Buddhism and Jainism were routed; and Brahmanism was left in entire mastery of the field. And to ensure its stability in the Tamil country and elsewhere, the Brahmans caused hundreds of temples to Siva and

Vishnu to be erected all over the land. Small bands of Brahmans from Upper India were induced by Tamil kings to settle here. Endowments of tax-free lands were made for their maintenance and worship in temples.

During this period which lasted for nearly four centuries and a half (from A. D. 500 to A. D 950) the sixty-three Nayanmars of the Siva sect and the twelve Alvars of the Vaishnavas flourished. Some of these devotees who were also fine Tamil poets visited many of these temples, composed and sang extempore hymns before the deities. Each hymn consists of ten or eleven verses and is supposed to instil piety in the mind of its reader. The prominent poet-saints of the two sects, who have left behind them such hymns, are Tirunavukkarasu, Trignanasambandar and Sundarar, Tirumangaimannan and Nammalvar. Other poetical compositions of a secular and sectarian nature were not wanting. The best of its kind was written by Manikka Vachakar; the other writers were Karaikal Ammai, Kapila Deva, Parana Deva, Nakkira Deva, Cheraman Perumal, Kalladanâr, and Nambiyandar Nambi. It may be remarked here that the sacred literature of the Saivas in Tamil poetry was nearly thrice that of the Vaishnavas, the hymns of Sambandar alone being nearly as voluminous as all the works of the twelve *Alvars* put together. All these prove the greater popularity of Sivaism among the Tamil people of South India.

In the above struggle the Buddhists and Jains were not quiet; they tried in their own way to popularize their religion by appealing to the hearts of the old as well as of the young. The most useful works on theology, ethics, grammar and language were written by them. Three of the major (Kundalakesi, Valaiyapati and Chintamani) and five of the minor (Yesodarakavyam, Udayanakavyam, Nagakumarakavyam, Nilakesi and Chulamani[1]) epics, Naladiyar, Pazhamoli, Neminadam, Karigai (Prosody) and Chudamani Nigandu belong to this period. The Saivas compiled the Divakaram and Pingalandai lexicons.

TRANSLATIONS FROM SANSKRIT : Now that the Jains and Buddhists were cleared off the field, the Brahmans began to attend to their own religion. Finding more leisure and greater support from the Tamil kings, they set about separating the various sects which lay embedded in Brahmanism in a crude form. The Sanskrit *puranas* and *itihasas* furnished them with mighty weapons to develop and strengthen the different sects And in order to popularize each sect among the Dravidians, the Tamil scholars and theologians found it necessary to translate some of the most important works, as the Jains and Buddhists had done before them to popularize their own. The Mahabharata had already been translated by Perundevanar; Kamban and Ottaikuttan took up the

[1] This Jain work was composed by Tolamoli Devar probably in the reign of the Pandya king Jayantan (A. D 650) and named after his father Maravarman Avani Chulamani

translation of Ramayana ; Kacchiyappa translated the Skandapurana ; and Puliyur Nambi and Paranjoti Muni turned into beautiful Tamil verse the Halasya Mahatmya. Besides the translations of quasi-sectarian works Tamil versions or adaptations of other Sanskrit poems were also undertaken. Pugazhendi rendered Naishadam into excellent Tamil Venba metre ; Dandi wrote for Tamil the Alankara Sastra, while Buddha-Mitra composed his Virasoliyam on Sanskrit model and Pavanandi wrote the celebrated Nannul as an epitome of Tolkapyam.

Again it was during this period which lasted from A. D. 50 to A. D. 1200 that the sacred hymns and poems of Saivas and Vaishnavas, which had till then remained scattered, were collected and arranged. The Saivas assisted by Nambiyandar Nambi (A. D. 1025) compiled the Devaram hymns, the Tiruvachakam and other poems into eleven *tirumurais*, while the Vaishnavas assisted by Sri Nathamuni (A.D. 1025) gathered their hymns into a single volume and called it the 'Nalayira Prabandam' or the great 'Book of 4000 Psalms'. Sekkilar (A.D. 1135) wrote the lives of the Saiva saints and called it Tiruttondar Puranam ; while the Vaishnavas wrote their Divyasuri Charitai and Guru paramparai about that time. All temples dedicated to Siva or Vishnu were being regularly visited by the respective sectarians, and festivals were instituted and celebrated with scrupulous regularity The apotheosis of pious votaries was made complete and their images were set up in temples ; and to enhance their religious importance *Stala-puranas* in Sanskrit were written by learned Brahmans, some of which were deftly interpolated in one or the other of the Eighteen Puranas.

It was also the period of the Chola ascendancy From about the seventh to the beginning of the tenth century the Pandyas and the Pallavas were powerful in Southern India. With the decline of these dynasties the Chola kings from Aditya I (A. D. 895) downwards not only regained their strength, but also became aggressive and carried on wars with the neighbouring sovereigns. These formed the subject matter of a class of war-chants called *parani* and *ula*. 'Parani' is a poem descriptive of a campaign the hero whereof being supposed to have killed at least one thousand elephants on the battle-field. 'Ula' is a poem depicting the procession of a royal personage, his country, flag, war-drum, &c. The finest poem of the former class is the Kalingattupparani. It was written by Jayamkondan in honour of one Karunakara Tondaiman, who was probably the general of Kulottunga Chola I (1069-1118) that waged war successfully with the Kalingas towards the close of his long reign. The rhythm of the poem is rapid and stirring and best suited to the subject. We subjoin a stanza from that work as a specimen :—

எடெமெடெ மெடெ மென ெவடெத்தடெதா
ரிகெலாலி கடெலாலி மிகக்கெவே,
விடெவிடெ விடெ பரி கரிக்குழாம்
விடெம்விடெ ெமனு ெமாலி மிகைக்கெவே.

And the best 'ulas' are those composed by the famous poet Ottaikkuttan on Vikrama Chola (1118-1143) and Kulottunga Chola II (1143-1146). These together with the one on Rajaraja Chola (1146-1163) are known as the Muvar-Ula. The following oft-quoted stanza confirms what we have said above :—

வெண்பாவிற் புகழேந்தி பரணிக்கோ
செயங் கொண்டான விருத்தமென்னு
மொண்பாவி துயர்கம்பன கோவையுலா
வந்தாதிக கொட்டக் கூத்தன
கண்பாய கலம்பகததிற் இரட்டையாகள்
வசைபாடக் காளமேகம
பண்பாகய பகர்சநதம் படிக்காச
லாதொருவா பகொாணுதே.

THE EXEGETICAL PERIOD : From the table it will be seen that this period of Tamil literature was co-extensive with the era of sectarian reformation and that it lasted from A. D. 1200 to A. D. 1450. The cleavage between the Saivas and Vaishnavas had become permanent and each of them crystallised into a distinct sect Sri Ramanuja Charya rose and laboured hard to strengthen the foundation of Vishnuism. Sri Vedanta Desika and Sri Manavala Mahamuni constructed two enduring edifices of different designs on the foundation laid by Sri Ramanuja. For Sivaism similar work was undertaken by Meykanda Deva, Arunandi Siva Charya, Maraignana Sambanda and Umapati Siva Charya. The Vaishnava Acharyas wrote mostly in Sanskrit and their works are now being studied only by Brahmans; while the Saiva *Guravas* mentioned above wrote only in Tamil as their writings were chiefly intended for non-Brahmans.

Further the same table will show that we have already crossed the mediæval and entered the threshold of modern Tamil. From the close of the academic to the beginning of the exegetical period there was an interval of nearly seven hundred years. In the course of such a long period, it is almost impossible for a living language, cultivated though it be, to remain unchanged either in its grammar or vocabulary. Moreover, there had occurred immense changes in the customs and manners of the Tamils on account of Brahmanical influence. The classical works of the academic period, especially the collected writings, could not be easily understood even by scholars without the help of commentaries. And this want was supplied by Perasiriyar, Ilampuranar, Senavaraiyar, Parimelazhagar, Nacchinarkiniyar, Adiyarku Nallar and other annotators. Similar difficulties were experienced by the Brahman Vaishnavas in understanding the Tamil of the Nalayira Prabandam. The Vaishnava Acharyas from Nam Jiyar down to Periya Jiyar wrote elaborate commentaries on them, which to a lay student of Tamil would be more difficult than the original itself. These commentaries were not intended for ordinary Tamil people, but only for the orthodox Vaishnavas thoroughly conversant with the

Sanskrit Upanishads Itihasas and Puranas. Any one can at a glance perceive the immense difference between the easy flowing chaste Tamil of Nachchinarkiniyar or Parimelazhagar and the mixed style of Periyavachan Pillai.

THE MODERN PERIOD : The latest stage in the history of Tamil literature has been called 'modern', and it covers the interval between A.D., 1450 and A.D. 1850. During this period the works produced were not confined to any one subject or department of literature. They embraced Hindu theology, philosophy, ethics, traditions and grammar. Islamism and Christianity also added their contributions to the Tamil literature. of this period.

Politically this was an important epoch, because it witnessed the downfall and total extinction of the ancient dynasties of Tamil kings and the occupation of the Tamil *nads* successively by the Telugu speaking Nayaks, the Mahratta chiefs, and the Musalman generals. Naturally these people had no sympathy for Tamil literature.

Though Tamil had thus lost state patronage, it did not want supporters. The Saiva monasteries richly endowed and managed by Tambirans and Pandarams, learned in the Saiva Agamas and Siddhantas, were coming into existence ; and they served as seats of Tamil learning and centres for the propogation of the Saiva cult among the Tamil Dravidians. Ilakkana-kottu, Ilakkana Vilakkam and Suravali Tolkapya-sutra-Vritti, Nanneri, Nitineri-Vilakkam,

Prabhulingalilai and Dravida Mahabhashyam were all written during this period. And the famous ascetic Tayumanaswami composed his sweet religious and philosophical songs ; Ativira Rama Pandyan published his Naishadam and Vetriverkai and translated the Linga and Kurma Puranas, while his brother wrote Kasikandam and other works. Among the Vaishnavas, Villiputturar translated the Mahabharata and Pillaiperumal Aiyangar wrote his eight Prabhandas. Among the Muhamadans, Umaru Pulavar wrote the Sira Puranam, and Javvadu Pulavar composed Muhiud-din Andavar Pillai-Tamil; while the celebrated Italian Missionary Constantius Beschi (Tam. *Viramamunm*) rendered the biography of Jesus Christ into a Tamil epic (Tembavani), after the fashion of Kamban's Ramayanam, and published it in A. D. 1769, together with a work on Tamil grammar entitled Tonnul Vilakkam. In 1895 Mr. H. Krishna Pillai, a native Christian poet of Palamcotta, translated Bunyan's Pilgrim's Progress in fine Tamil verse.

This period is marked by the cultivation of Sanskrit learning by the Vaishnavas as well as the Smartas. Settling on the fertile banks of the sacred rivers and streams, and congregating in *agraharas* around a Vishnu or Siva shrine hidden beneath shady groves and surrounded by extensive rice fields, the Brahmans formed themselves into exclusive communities, sometimes venerated, sometimes disliked, but always administered to by their Dravidian neighbours. Tutored and encouraged by the Tambirans, Pandarams and such Tamil castes as the Kammalas and Lingayats, who claimed equality with the priestly class, some of the non-Brahmans began openly to question the superiority of the Brahmans and their authority in all social and religious matters. And the advent of Musalmans and the appearance of European Missionaries in the Tamil land during the 16th and 17th centuries, whose habits and social opinions were opposed to the social ideal and organisation of the Brahmans, only tended to aggravate this animosity. Such was the spirit and tendency of the people in South India during the early years of the latter half of this eventful epoch.

THE ANTI-BRAHMANICAL SCHOOL: The Brahman supremacy and vigorous exercise of the powers, which their aggressive culture had won for them in earlier years had their reaction; and the circumstances described above led to the rise of an anti-Brahmanical or the Siddhar school of philosophical rhymists. They were Yogis as well as medical men. The number of Siddhas or men who attained *siddhi* or the 'conquest of nature' is ordinarily reckoned as eighteen. Most of them were plagiarists and impostors, while some assumed the names of the great men of antiquity like Agastyar, Kapilar, and Tiruvalluvar. Being eaters of opium and dwellers in the land of dreams, their conceit knew no bounds. On the supernatural powers of the Siddhas one of them writes thus :—

எட்டுமலைகளைப் பந்தாயெடுத்தறிவோம், எழு கடலையும்

குடித்தேப்பமிடுவோம், மட்டுப்படாமாணலேயும் திரித்திடுவோம்,
... மண்டலமுமற்றுஙகையான் மறைத்திடுவோம், வானத்தை
யும் வில்லாய் வளேத்திடுவோம், ... மூண்டெரியுமககினிக்குள்
மூழ்கிவருவோம், முன்னீருள்ளிருப்பினு மூச்சடக்குவோம்,
தாண்டிவரும் வெம்புலியைத் தாக்கிவிடுவோம், செப்பரிய மூன்
றுலகுஞ் செம்பொன்னுக்குவோம், செங்கதிரைத் தன்கதிராச்
செய்துவிடுவோம், இப்பெரிய வுலகத்தை யிலலாமற்செய்வோம்,
வேதன்செய்த சிருஷ்டிகள்போல் வேறு செய்குவோம், ... நாத
னுடன் சமமாக நாளும் வாழ்குவோம், நாங்கள் செய்கையிது
வென்றுடாய் பாமபே.

The Siddhas did not like the Brahmans; and they ridiculed in their writings the Brahmans' social institutions, religious observances and Sanskrit Vedas.

(1) நட்டகல்லே தெய்வமென்று நாலுபுட்பஞ் சாத்தியே
சுற்றிவந்து மொணுமொணென்று சொல்லுமந்திரமேதடா?
இருக்குநாலு வேதமு மெழுத்தையற வோதிலும்
பெருக்கநீறு பூசிலும் பிதற்றிலும் பிராணிரான்.
வாயிலேகுடித்தநீரை யெச்சிலென்றுசொல்லுநீர்
வாயிலே குதப்புவேத மெனபபடக கடவதோ?
ஆட்டிறைச்சி தினறதில்லே யண்றுமின்றும் வேதியர்
ஆட்டிறைச்சி யல்லவோ யாகங்கள் பண்ணுநீர்?—*Siv.*

(2) ஒட்டியர் மிலேசசளுணர் சிங்களர்
இட்டிடைச் சோனகர் யவனர்சினத்தார்
பற்பலர் நாட்டினும் பாரப்பாரிலேயால்.—*Kap.*

Their religion was theism; sometimes the stress they laid on the *siddhis* or the powers a man can acquire over nature gave it a secularistic colour which occasionlly comes very near atheism and may be mistaken for it. The *summum bonum,* the highest bliss 'or the *paramananda* of their existence was to apprehend and approach that eternal light which they termed 'paranjoti', 'peroli', 'pazh-veli' or 'vetta-veli.' It will be seen from the above extracts that their language is quite modern and their style simple and at times slang.

PROSE LITERATURE: If we omit the commentaries on abstruse early poems, the whole Tamil literature including theology, philosophy, grammar and dictionary, is all poetry. In the whole range of Tamil literature prose had no distinct place. For a long time the Tamils made no distinction between prose and poetry, the former being regarded as a form of poetry. It might be said that the early Tamils did not recognize prose. The earliest form of prose composition is what we find in the Silappadikaram, an heroic drama of the third century A. D. The same style was adopted later in the Tamil version of the Mahabharata by Perundevanar and in the Tagadur Yattirai. Both of them are known as உரையிடை இட்டபாட்டு or poems interspersed with explanatory prose. To these may be added the commentary on Iraiyanar's Agapporul written by some unknown author (not by Nakkirar as hitherto believed) during the early part of the eighth century. And from the excerpts subjoined below it will be seen that they are a sort of poetic prose in pure Tamil, sweet and rhythmic like the English of Hooker's 'Ecclesiastical Polity' or Ruskins' 'Modern Painters':—

(1) குடத்துப்பா லுறையாமையுங் குவியிமிலேற்றின்மடக் கண்ணீர் சோராதலு முறியில் வெண்ணெயுருகாமையு மறிமுடங்கி யாடாமையு மான்மணி நிலத்தற்று வீழ்தலும் வருவதோர்

தன்பழமுண்டென மகளோ நோக்கி மனமயங்காதே மண்ணின்
மாதர்க்கணியாகிய கண்ணகியுந்தான் காண வாயர்பாடியிலெருமன்
றத்து மாயவனுடன் றன்மூளுடிய பாலசரிதை நாடகங்களில்
வேனெடுங்கட்பிஞ்ஞகு யோடாடியருரவை யாடுதும்யா மென்
றுள் கறவைகன்று தயா நீஙகுகவெனவே.—*Sil.*

(2) இவ்வூர் உபபூரிகுடி கிழார் மகளுவான் உருத்திர சன்ம
னென்பான், பைங்கண்ணன் புன்மயிரன் ஐயாட்டைப்பிராயத்
தான் ஒரு மூனக்கைப்பிள்ளேயுளான ; அவனே யன்னனென்றிக
ழாது கொடுபோந்து ஆசனமேலிரீக் கீழிருந்து சூததிரப்
பொருளுரைத்தாற் கண்ணீர் வார்நது மெய்ம்மயிர் சிலிர்க்கும்
மெய்யாயின உரைகேட்டவிடத்து.—*Agap.*

Till we come to the exegetic period we can scarcely hear of any prose work. The Jains and the Brahman Vaishnavas had some of their *Puranas* and religious works translated or written in prose ; but they were purely sectarian and in a composite or Sanskrit-Tamil style. And in strange contrast to it the commentaries of Gunasagara, Nachchinarkiniyar or Adiyarkunallar were written in chaste Tamil. We give below two extracts from these works :—

(1) கங்காயோகயளுகிய பர்த்தா ஸஹஸ்ர கூடஜின பவ
னத்தை யடைதலும் சம்பகவிகாசமும் கோகில கோலாஹலமும்
தடாகபூரணமும் தத்கதகுமுதவிகாசமும் மதுகரசஞ்சாரமும்
கோபுரகவாடவிகடனமு மாகிய அதிசயங்களளவாகுமென்று
ஆதேசித்தனர்.—*Chin* p. 27.

(2) பும்ஸபர்ஃக்லேச ஸம்பாவநுகந்தவிதிரமாய் பரத்ய க்ஷாதி
ப்ரமாண விலக்ஷணமாயிருந்துள்ள நிகில வேத ஜாதத்திக்கும்
வேதோப ப்ரம்மணங்களான ஸ்ம்ருதீதிஹாஸபுராணங்களுககும்
க்ருத்யம் ஸகல ஸம்சாரி சேதனர்க்கும் தத்வஞானத்தை
ஜனிப்பிக்கை.—*Tat. Sekh.*

Coming to modern times works written wholly and deliberately in prose, not reckoning commentaries as such, commence with Beschi's Vediyar Ozhukkam. And we may even say that a new impetus was given to prose composition only during the early part of the last century by the Tamil pandits of the early Madras University, of whom Tandavaraya Mudaliyar, Viraswami Chettiyar, and Saravanapperumal Aiyar deserve special mention. In the latter part of the nineteenth century a number of Tamil prose works, translations as well as original productions, were published by learned Tamil scholars. The labours of the late T. E. Srinivasa Raghava Chariyar and Arumuga Navalar may still be in the memory of every lover of Tamil literature. And the foremost among the living writers of Tamil prose and scholarly commentaries is undoubtedly Mahamahopadhyaya V Swaminatha Aiyar Avargal of the Madras Presidency College, who may be styled the Nachchinarkiniyar of the present day.

A prose literature worth the name is only a recent growth, which is sufficient to account for the absence of prose classics in Tamil. The influence of English literature, the great increase in the Tamil reading public, and the conditions of life in this age with its forms of popular government, its commercialism and industrial activities favour the rapid expansion of prose literature ; and a prose style also has begun to form.

IX

THE TAMIL ACADEMICS

One of the chief features of progressive civilisation is the institution of literary and scientific societies. In Western countries they began to be established only after the Renaisance. Even so late as A. D. 1599 'modern science had not yet been born, mathematics were in their infancy, the literatures of the great modern languages were only beginning to be made'. The eastern nations, on the contrary, were in their own way so far advanced in civilisation as to found literary academies and to hold commercial intercourse with the highly civilized Greeks, Phœnicians and Romans. And the epigraphical discoveries in Southern India and the critical study of early Tamil works have disclosed many facts tending to confirm the very high antiquity of Tamil literature, and the tolerably advanced state of Tamil civilisation so early as the first or second century before the Christian era.

The ancient classics of the Tamil people frequently refer to *sangams* or societies of learned men.

Tirumangai Alvar, a Vaishnava saint who lived about the latter half of the eighth century, speaks of 'Sanga-muka-Tamil' and 'Sanga-mali-Tamil' in his Periya Tirumoli (III. v. 10). Manikka Vachakar, one of the four great Saiva Saints of the ninth century, refers indirectly in his Tirukkovai to a Tamil *sangam* at Madura. Allusions to the Tamil *sangams* may be quoted from the works of other poets. One of the most trustworthy references to the founding of a Tamil academy prior to the eighth century will be found in the copper plates discovered at Chinnamanur in the Madura district. And lately there are references to the Madura College in the Tiruvilayadal or Madura Stalapurana.

The Tamil *sangam* is known to some English scholars as the 'Madura College' and to others as the 'Madura University.' In Sanskrit the word *sangam* means an association (of learned men), and it seems to have been introduced into the Tamil language by early Buddhists from Northern India, no Tamil word having existed before to express that idea. Some Tamil scholars are, however, of opinion that *avai* which was in use in the days of Tolkapyar to denote such an association or assembly is a pure Tamil word. But *avai*, *savai* or *sabhai* is also a Sanskrit word. A college ordinarily means a teaching institution, and a university is also a body of examiners. The Madura *sangam* was an examining association, but it was never a teaching institute. To designate this sort of society another word now widely current is 'academy'. And as the chief function of the *sangam*, like that of the French Academy, was the promotion of Tamil literature, the name 'academy' seems to be appropriate to this institution and is therefore used in the following pages.

According to Tamil writers there were three *sangams* in the Pandya country at different periods. After the dissolution of the last of them spasmodic attempts were made at various times to establish new *Colleges*; but none of them were very successful. These later academies did not attain the high rank, distinction and influence of their predecessors, nor were they recognised by learned Tamil scholars as of such importance as to deserve mention.

A full account of the three academies, their dates, the places where they were founded, the Pandya kings who patronised them, the works that were approved and sanctioned by their *senatus academicus*, the number and names of the members and lastly the influence they exerted in moulding the Tamil language and literature will be given below; and of the rest only a passing notice.

Before entering upon the discussion of the ages of the academies severally, it would be convenient at the outset to determine approximately the earlier and the later limits of the period during which the three academies existed. It is admitted both by Indian and European scholars that the civilisation of the Tamil nation was, in the main, due to the Aryan colonists in the south, and that the first academy owed its origin to Agastya, the reputed leader of the first band of Brahman immigrants in South India. The date of Agastya is lost in myth, and the traditions, which are in themselves conflicting, represent him as still living on the Pothiya mountains in the Tinnevelly district.

Let us therefore turn our attention to other sources to discover his date. The introduction of the Tamil alphabet seems to afford us the best clue to get at this date, because prior to it no society of learned men or any seminary could have come into existence, and because it would almost be impossible for a race without a system of writing to possess a literature. Undoubtedly, the Sanskrit Vedas had been in existence long before they were committed to writing; but the case of the Vedas is altogether different from that of the Tamil poems, which in the opinion of J Vinson, were 'essays, pamphlets and short poems.' The Vedas were the sacred scriptures of the Aryans and were, therefore, handed down orally from generation to generation as a sacred trust and were preserved in their memory. Even after the introduction of writing in North India the conservative attitude of the Brahmans resisted all inducements to write down their Vedas for a long time which have been, for that reason, known as the 'unwritten word', or the எழுதாகிளவி. Whereas among the Dravidian Tamils there was no such priestly class, and none of their earlier poems belonging to the earliest or the pre-academic period was held in such veneration as to deserve handing down by rote like the Vedas. Amongst the ancient Tamilians there was, no doubt, a class of minstrels called the *panans* (பாணன்) more or less resembling the troubadours of mediæval France, whose duty it was to recite songs or lays of fighting and adventure before kings and nobles on festive and other occasions. But most of these men were illiterate mendicants and their poems and songs were in no sense religious. They had no interest in preserving in the memory of the people the heroic tales of temporal power and in transmitting them orally to their posterity. It is thus pretty clear that the earliest literary activity of the Tamilians could have shown itself only after the introduction of writing in South India, which must have taken place long before the fourth century B.C. We shall not therefore be wrong if we look for the foundation of the first Tamil academy or Sangam somewhere between the sixth and fourth centuries before the Christian era.

Having fixed approximately the upper limit of the age of the Tamil academies, we may now proceed to give a detailed history of each of them separately. In order to follow the arguments the reader is expected to possess some knowledge of the history of the early Pandya kings, a brief outline of which will be found in Appendix I.

Regarding the first academy the following particulars are mentioned in Nakkirar's commentary on Iraiyanar's Agapporul, which, though meagre, is we believe the only earliest source of information on the subject. According to this account the members of the first academy were Agastya (President), gods Siva and Subrahmanya, Mudinagaraya of Murinjiyur, Nitiyin Kizhavan and 544 other poets. The number of authors who obtained the *imprimatur* of the College for their works was 4449. Dakshina or Southern Madura was the seat of the University, and it is also stated that this city of Madura submerged in the Indian ocean. Its patrons were eighty-nine Pandya kings from Kaysina-valudi or Ugra Pandya to Kadum-Kon, seven of whom were also poets Some of the works which were approved by the academy were Paripadal, Mudunarai, Mudu-kuruku and Kalariyavirai. Their grammar was Agastyam. It lasted for 4,440 years.

If the above facts be submitted to strict historical criticism, most of them will have to be rejected as pure myths, there being nothing to corroborate them either in Tamil literature or in the contemporary annals of other countries. The number of members of the academy and of the kings who patronized it and the long period during which it is stated to have lasted, are all incredible and cannot be verified. The list of eighty-nine Pandya kings is not to be found either in the Puranas or in any other extant works Nor have any of the writings attributed to this academy come down to us in their entirety, excepting probably a few doubtful quotations from Agastyam and one or two others. Apparently all these had been lost long before the tenth or eleventh century.

The only authors of this period about whom any account, however scanty it might be, can be extracted from Tamil literature are Agastya and Murinjiyur Mudinagarayar. The rest of the members seem to be half mythical persons. The life of Agastya is clothed in myth ; but this much is certain that he was a Brahman of North India and that he led the first colony of Brahmans which settled in the Tamil districts. According to another tradition he was a member of the Sanskrit academy at Benares, which was presided over by Vyasa, the compiler of the Vedas, and, after quarrelling with his colleagues there, he wended his way down to the Tamil country and established the first Tamil Academy at Madura. It is said that the Tamil language is indebted to him for its grammar. He was the first to introduce the worship of Siva and the science of medicine among the South Indian Dravidians. Though most of the Tamil works now existing on chemistry, physiology and medicine which are commonly attributed to him are pure forgeries, he might have been acquainted with the art of medicine and the first Rishi to teach it to the Tamil nation.

He is said to have had twelve students, namely, Tolkapyan, Athangottasan, Duralingan, Semputchay, Vaiyapikan, Vayppiyan, Panambaran, Kalaramban, Avinayan, Kakkapatiniyan, Natrattan and Vamanan. It is believed that they specialized their studies and wrote works on music, dramaturgy and prosody, and that the lost work of Agastya embraced all the three. The twelve desciples wrote each a chapter on Purapporul which collectively was known as பன்னிருபடலம் or the 'Twelve Chapters'. Its existence is doubted, but in its place we have now the 'Venba-Malai' of Aiyanaridanar which is said to have been based on the above work. According to Adiyarkunallar Sikhandiyar was a student of Agastya; and he is said to have written Isainunukkam, a treatise on music, which is now lost. Quotations from the grammatical works of his students Kakkapatiniyan, Natrattanar and Avinayanar may be found in the ancient commentaries on Agapporul, Tolkapyam, Yapparunkalam and other standard books. Chief of them, Tolkapyar was also a member of the second academy like his renowned master. About the precise date of Agastyar's migration to the South nothing definite can be said, but as has been pointed out above, it cannot be earlier than the fifth or sixth century B. C

It is believed that in the first Sangam there was a poet by name Vanmikiyar His work, the name of which is not known, was considered by Nacchinarkiniyar as the best of its kind. From this dubious statement and similarity in names a writer of the Neo. Tamil school jumps to the conclusion that Valmiki, Gautama, Kapila and other famous sages and Sanskritists of Upper India were by birth Tamilians, and that after they had become famous they were admitted as members of the Tamil academies. It is not worth entering into any controversy with him as he claims to himself a 'sense of truth and critical acumen' which he may not be so charitable as to concede to his opponents.

In Purananuru, which is an anthology or a collection of 400 lyrics compiled by some poet of the third academy, there is a sang ascribed to Mudinagarayar who was a member of the first *sangam*. This poem is a sort of epistle addressed to a Chera monarch named Udiyan Cheraladan. The poet here extols the king as the commissary agent or supplier of provisions to the contending armies on the battle field of Kurukshetra :—

நீயோ பெரும,
வலங்குனப புரவி யையவரோடு சீனஇ
நிலந்தலைக் கொண்ட பொலம்பூந் தும்பை
மீசரம் பதினைமரும பொருது களத்தொழிய
பெருஞ்சோறறு மிகுபதம் வரையாது கொடெத்தோய.

This informs us that the Chera king Udiyan Cheraladan, lived at the time of the Mahabharata war, i.e. about the 10th or 11th century B. C. Among the nations and tribes who fought in the great war of the Pandavas against the Kauravas, the Cheras and the Cholas did not actually fight; but as allies helped them with armies or supervised other details of the company. Pandiya king Sarangadwaja, a friend of Sri Krishna and a devoted admirer of the Pandavas, drew only one contingent of troops from each of the other Tamil tribes. Another tradition says that Arjuna came to Madura and married the daughter of a Pandya king. Some Tamil scholars endeavour to prove the very high antiquity of the Tamil civilization in the Pandya country by quoting such references from Valmiki's Ramayana and Vyasa's Mahabharata. In his Maduraikkanji (40, 41) Marudanar of Mangudi says that the Pandya country was in existence at the time of Ravana, king of Lanka, and that the Pandyas checked his invasion with the help of their family priest, the divine Rishi Agastya.

ஒதன்னவற் பெயரிய துன்னருந் துப்பிற்
ஒரென்முது கடவுட் பின்னா மேய
வரைத்தாழருவிப் பொருபபிற் பொருந.

But it must be remembered that neither epic was wholly composed by any one person and at any one epoch. Both contain interpolations and accretions, judging from which the dates of their present edition have been fixed as the first century B.C. and 350 A.D. respectively. Moreover, the Ramayana refers only to the Greeks (Yavanas) while the Mahabharata mentions them as well as the Sakhas (Scythians). All that can be inferred is, that the three Tamil kingdoms in the South were in existence from very ancient times. No one doubts this fact, as these countries are mentioned in the edicts of Asoka (B. C. 250) and in the commentaries of Katyayana (fourth century B. C.).

The identification of Dakshina Madura, the seat of the first Academy has been a controversial point. Regarding the destruction of this place there are certain allusions both in the Madura Stalapurana and in the Silappadikaram. The learned commentator of the

THE TAMIL ACADEMIES

latter work writes as follows :—' Between the rivers Kumari and Pahruli there existed an extensive continent occupying an area of 700 *kavadams* (a Kavadam being equal to ten miles). This land consisting of forty-nine *nads* (inclusive of Kollam and Kumari), innumerable forests, mountains and rivers had been submerged in the Indian ocean as far as the peaks of Kumari,' by a terrific convulsion which resulted in the upheaval of the Himalayan range. Geological, ethnological and linguistic researches also seem to confirm the above theory. But who can say with any authority whether the submerged country had a town called Madura or Kudal, whether it was governed by precisely eighty-nine Pandya kings, or whether the Dravidian inhabitants of this *terra incognita* were so far civilized as to establish literary academies? What seems to be reasonable is that the Madura of Agastyar's days must have been destroyed by an unusual inundation of the Vaiga and the Kritamal rivers, before the modern town was built at the present locality. The old Madura must have situated five or six miles south or south-east of the later one, and about the same distance east of Tirupparamkunram hill which has been described to have situated exactly west of it;

மாடமலி மறுகிற் கூடற்குடவயின்.—*Nak.*

This hill is now four miles south-west of Madura. And it is for the above reason that the old city was called the south or Dakshina Madura.

About the second academy the same authority

furnishes the following information :—The members of the college were Agastya, Tolkapyar, Mosiyar, Sirupandarangan, Vellur Kappiyan, Tuvaraikkoman, Kirandaiyar and fifty-two other scholars ; and the works of about 3,700 poets were passed by this academy. The seat of it was another submerged town, called Kapatapuram. It was patronized by fifty-nine Pandya kings from Venderseliyan to Mudatirumaran, five of whom were also learned scholars. The standard works of this period were Kali, Kuruku, Vendali, Mapuranam, Vyalamalai, Bhutapuranam, Isainunukkam, &c. It lasted for 3,700 years.

It will be seen that the interval between the abolition of the first and the founding of the second academy could not have been long, as Agastya and some of his students were represented at the latter College-board also. Consequently the second must be considered a continuation of the first, but held at a different place after the destruction of the original Madura by the flood. This supposition is strengthened by the statement of Adiyarkunallar in his valuable commentary on the Silappadikaram, that one of the seven Pandya poet kings of the first academy by name ' Makirti' was also at Kapatapuram, as a patron or royal visitor of the second academy. Kapatapuram which in Sanskrit meant the ' gate city', must have been a village situated three or four miles east of Madura, occupied temporarily as the king's residence before the modern city of Madura was built. Out of the questionable mention of this Sanskrit name as well as of Manalur (which Sanskrit scholars think to be later interpolations) in the Ramayana and the Mahabharata, some Tamil pandits are endeavouring to make much capital about the great antiquity of Tamil culture and civilization. As for the other particulars, we may dismiss them at present as more fictions than facts.

To arrive at the date of the second academy the commentator of Silappadikaram gives us an indirect hint in his preface to that work. While speaking of the story of Udayana he says that it was composed in imitation of the classical works of the second academy, and refers to it elsewhere as Perum-Kathai (Skt. *Brihat-Katha*). Evidently it is a Tamil rendering of Gunadhya's Brihat-Katha. It is therefore obvious that the poets of the second Sangam must have flourished sometime before, or contemporarily with, Gunadhya. In the opinion of Dr. Buhler the age of Gunadhya goes back to the first or second century A. D. He served as minister under king Satavahana (A. D. 113) of the Andhrabhritya dynasty at Paithan on the banks of the Godavari. 'He received,' it is said, 'seven stories in the language of the Paisachas (probably ancient Telugu) from Kanabhuti and wrote them down in 100,000 slokas each with his own blood.'

One of the poets of this academy, Mosiyar, has contributed about fourteen lyrics to Purananuru. Neither the kings alluded to by him, nor the incidents described therein afford any clue to work out his date. He was a native of Uraiyur and lived in the reign of the Chola king Perunarkilli[1]. If Dittan the father of Perunarkilli was identical with Dathiya the Tamil usurper of the Singhalese annals (B.C. 90), it may be said that he flourished about B.C. 75. Again the present edition of the Ramayana which was recast about 100 B.C. mentions in its geography the Pandya country and its capital Kapatapuram. Nothing further is known about Tolkapyar, whose Tamil grammar is with us, than that he was a Brahman student of Agastya and that he lived in a village near Madura during the reign of the Pandya king Makirti. All the works of this academy have also been irretrievably lost, except the grammar of Tolkapyar and a few poems which luckily found their way into the anthologies compiled at the third academy.

From the foregoing it will be seen that the first and the second academies were more or less continuous, and that they existed occasionally sometime between the fifth century B. C. and the second century A. D. This conclusion seems to me irresistable as we find no references to the *Yavanas* or Romans in any of the works composed by the poets of these academies, especially when we know that in the heyday of the early Pandyas there was a colony of Roman merchants two or three miles east of Madura from the second to fifth century A.D.

So much for the first two academies. We shall

---

[1] The Killi line of Cholas appear to have reigned in Uraiyur during the first century before and after Christ

now pass on to the third, which was by far the most important, and about which we are particularly concerned. Almost all the best Tamil classics we now possess are the productions of this last Sangam. The history of this academy should therefore be fully gone into, as there are ample materials in the shape of innumerable literary traditions, puranas, and casual references. But the difficulties also proportionately increase, because unfortunately no two of them agree. An academy being an association of men of letters, its history cannot be separated from their biographies; and it would be our work in the following pages to collate such of the literary traditions as have any bearing on their lives and to construct a tolerably trustworthy account of this third Sangam.

We shall first give the traditional account mainly as preserved for us in the scholarly commentary on Iraiyanar's Agapporul, and then discuss in detail every point with reference to the latest researches in epigraphy.

The members of this academy were Nakkirar (President), Sittalai-Sattanar, Kalladar, Kapilar, Paranar, Ugra Pandya, Mangudi Maruthanar and forty-two other scholars. Including them 449 poets obtained the sanction of the senate for their writings. The seat of this Sangam was Uttara (northern) Madura. It was patronized by forty-nine kings from Mudattiru-maran to Ugra Pandya, three of whom were also poets. The classical works of this period were Nedumtokai, Kurumtokai, Natrinai, Ainkurunuru, Paditruppattu, Kurumkali, Paripadal, Kuttu, Vari, Perisai, Sitrisai, Muttollayiram, Akananuru and Purananuru, besides many minor poems. It lasted for 1850 years.

Concerning the foundation of the third Sangam nothing definite can be said. Tradition says that it took place in the reign of one Mudattirumaran, and this seems to have been tacitly accepted by the commentator of Iraiyanar's Agapporul and Adiyarkunallar. The name Mudattirumaran appears to be a synonym for Kun or Kubja Pandyan. If this identification be correct, the third academy must have been established in the reign of Sundara Pandya, that is about 670 A.D. But this is against all tradition and facts. The Tiruvilayadal Purana tells us that it was established in the reign of one Vamsa Sekhara Pandya, who is also credited with the founding of the Madura city after the 'deluge'. Neither of these Pandyas is mentioned in the literature or in the inscriptions which have been examined, and it is therefore impossible to ascertain the precise date of the establishment of the third academy.

It has been said that Kalladar [1] and Mangudi Marudanar were members of this academy These two poets have sung the military exploits of Nedum Seliyan of Talaiyalankanam fame If these poets were contemporaries of this king, they should have been

1. He was not that Kalladanar who wrote 'Kalladam' and 'Kannappar Tirumaram' (See Appendix).

THE TAMIL ACADEMIES 247

living in the latter half of the second century A.D. Again, Sittalai Sattanar another member of this academy and the author of Manimekalai also lived at about the same time. Had all these poets been really members of the third academy, it must have been founded during the first century A. D., or even long before that time. This tradition thus militates against our conclusion that the second academy existed till the second century, and it must, therefore, be rejected as a pure fiction.

Again according to the *Tiruvalluvamalai* one of the fortynine professors of the third Sangam was Perundevanar, the famous translator of the Mahabharata; as a member of this academy the compilation of the eight anthologies (எட்டுத்தொகை) is also attributed to him. If it was really so, a learned scholar and poet of this reputation must have been mentioned by Nakkirar (or whoever he might be) in the account of Sangams given in Iraiyanar's Agapporul. As his name is not in the list, it is evident that he was not a member of the third academy, and this inference is clinched by an allusion in his Bharatam to the Pallava king Nandivarman who won the battle at Tellar. The poet Perundevanar must have thus lived at the latter part of the eighth century. With it the general belief that the compiler of the eight anthologies was the self-same Perundevanar falls to the ground, unless it be that the third academy actually existed about that period and that its forty-nine professors together with Tiruvalluvar were his contemporaries—all which are absolutely incredible and contrary to the testimonies of epigraphy and literary history.

The list of the forty-nine Pandya kings under whose auspices the third academy thrived is not given anywhere ; but the name of the last (Ugra Pandya or Ugra Peruvaludi) alone occurs both in the *stalapurana* and in Tamil literature. It was in the reign of this king, according to one tradition, that the third Sangam or the famous seminary of learning at Madura came to an end, when its members were completely vanquished in a poetical contest with the low caste Tiruvalluvar. But Tiruvalluvar (A. D. 80) lived at the time of the second academy, and had therefore nothing to do with the third Sangam or its destruction. That he was instrumental in bringing about the downfall of the third Sangam, that all the forty-nine members of it eulogized the Kural before they were drowned in the "golden lily" tank, that the famous Kapilar of this academy was his brother, and that he was a Paraiya by caste—all these are figments of the Dravidian imagination. In the early years of the Christian era there was no Paraiya caste ; Kapilar was a Brhaman poet of Tiruvadavur in the Madura district, and was the author of Kurinchipattu, Innanarpatu and several other poems ; none of the forty-nine commendatory verses belong to the same period, nor were they composed by poets of the same *nadu*; and lastly it is not possible to believe that all these poets conferred with one another and agreed to extol the Kural in poems of the Venba metre and that in the first century A. D. The subjoined eulogistic verse usually attributed to Auvai, the renowned sister of Tiruvalluvar, is enough to discredit the truth and antiquity of the Tiruvalluvamalai:—

தேவர்குறளுந் திருநான்மறை முடிவு
மூவர் தமிழு முனிமொழியுங்—கோவை
திருவாசகமூட் திருமூலர் சொல்லு
மொருவா சகமென் றுணர்.

In the above quotation we find references to Appar, Sambandar, Sundarar, Manikkavachakar and Tirumular, the latest of whom lived in the second half of the ninth century. There are several other verses of this sort in praise of the Kural. This stanza makes Tiruvalluvar a contemporary of Manikkavachakar ! What we are inclined to think is that the Tiruvalluvamalai or the 'garland of Tiruvalluvar', like every other account relating to this famous moralist, is a strange mixture of doubtful traditions and absurd fictions written by some later Dravidian author of the ninth century to popularize the celebrated work of Tiruvalluvar. Thus, it will be seen that the tradition which attributes the destruction of the third academy to poet Tiruvalluvar and in the reign of the Pandva king Ugra Peruvaludi, is not only absolutely unfounded, but also contrary to the statement in the Madura Stalapurana which ascribes to the same king the foundation of the first Sangam or academy.

For the extinction of the third academy we must look elsewhere. If the compilation of Purananuru was made by this Sangam, the date of its abolition could be easily determined. In the above work we find a poem addressed to the Chola king Kocchengannan by poet Poigaiyar [1]. The exact age of this poet is not known ; but the Chola king has been referred to by the saints Trignanasambanda and Tirumangai Alvar (A. D. 650-750) as the builder of several temples to Siva and Vishnu. For this pious act he has been canonized as a saint and included in the hagiology of the Saivas. Granting that a period of about a century had elapsed between this Chola king and Sambandar, the probable date of Kocchenganan would be about A. D. 580. As there is no reference in Sambandar's work to the Tamil academy at Madura, where the Saiva saint must have stayed for some time before the Jains were impaled, and las a poem addressed to this king is found in Purananuru, there is every reason to believe that the third academy came to an end during the second half of the sixth century.

This was the time when the struggle between Jainism and Brahmanism was very vehement. The kings and scholars of this transition period in the south were completely absorbed in religious controversies, and they hardly had any time to devote to literary pursuits. And it was probably at this period that the Pandya country was conquered and temporarily held by the Kalabhras or Kalambras, till

1. This poet must not be confounded with the Vaishnava saint Poigai Alvar who lived about A. D. 650.

THE TAMIL ACADEMIES 251

they were expelled by Kadunkon about the beginning of the seventh century. All these religious and political disturbances contributed to the extinction of the third academy.

The religion of the members of the three academies it is not easy to determine, as all the accounts we now have are from the Saiva source, and none from Buddhists and Jains. However, so late as the third or fourth century A.D. there was no Sivaism or Vishnuism as understood now. But there was Brahmanism or the religion of the Vedas ; and side by side with it there were also Jainism and Buddhism. The members of the first and second Sangams, which continued up to the second century, must have belonged to different persuasions. Agastyar and Tolkapyar were Hindus, and presumably professed Brahamanism. The writings of Tiruvalluvar, Kapilar and Paranar do not show that they were Saivas, while those of Nallanduvanar and Nakkirar show that they were ; yet all these, except Tiruvalluvar are given in the Saivite accounts as Saivas, which is evidently unwarranted. One at least of the forty-nine professors, that is Sattanar, was a Buddhist.

At about the fourth or fifth century the religious struggle made its first appearance. Buddhist and Jaina scholars must have seceded from the Hindus and started Sangas or colleges of their own at Madura and other places for the advancement of Tamil literature. One was started by Vajra Nandi in A.D. 470 in opposition to a Hindu college, probably the third Sangam, which was then conducted mainly by the Saivas. The five minor and the five major Kavyas and some of the eighteen minor ethical poems must have been passed by these Buddhist and Jaina Sangams or institutions, which, with the downfall of these religions, must have come to an end. It might be noticed here that the word *sangam* (Sangha) was probably of Buddhistic origin.

It will be well at this stage of our enquiry to examine the importance and value of the earliest traditional account, which is attributed to Nakkirar and upon which all the others are based, so far as the facts revealed by epigraphy and early Tamil literature enlighten us on the subject. The entire period of existence of the three Sangams or academies is said to be 9990 years. This seems to us fabulous. They were patronised by,

First Sangam—89 kings from Kaysinavaludi (A.D. 100) to Kadunkon (A.D. 600);

Second do —59 kings from Vendercheliyan (A.D. 740) to Mudattirumaran (A.D. 650);

Third do —49 kings from Mudattirumaran to Ugra Peruvaludi (A. D. 100).

Of these Kaysinavaludi and Ugra Peruvaludi might be identified with Ugra Pandya of early Tamil literature. Mudattirumaran might be the same as Kun or Kubja Pandya, and identified with Nedumaran of Nelveli (A. D. 650). Kadunkon lived about A. D.

600 and Ter cheliyan was a title of Arikesari Parankusan (A. D. 735). Thus it will be seen that the traditional account, which must have originated sometime after the second half of the eighth century, not only gives conflicting details about the three academies, but also throws serious doubts as to their relative ages and their very existence.

Again, the illustrative *kovai* or garland of verses, quoted in the so called Nakkirar's commentary on Iraiyanar's Agapporul, frequently refers to the same Pandya king Arikesari Parankusan (Ter-cheliyan) and his military achievements. The commentator, or at any rate the author who committed it to writing, unconsciously betrays himself as Nilakantanar, the tenth in succession from Nakkirar the supposititious writer of the commentary. Allowing twenty years for each generation of studentship, we arrive at A. D. 750—160 or 590 as the age of Nakkirar or of the composition of Agapporul by Iraiyanar. But even this period seems to be too modern for Nakkirar, because the language and subject matter of Tirumurugarruppadai show that he could not have lived later than the fourth century A. D. In this connection it must be observed that none of the members of any of these academies, (excepting a certain writer by the name of Nakkirar) refers to his academy or Sangam. Thus we see that the above account of the academies is a clear fabrication, like all other *pauranic* tales, out of the names of some Pandya kings, poets and institutions vaguely known to the Tamilians of those times and foisted upon Nakkirar.

Several attempts in later times were made to establish Tamil Sangams. The one referred to in the Chinnamanur grant seems to have been the first and the earliest endeavour after the dissolution of the famous third academy. It was probably the fourth, and lasted for one century and a half from about A. D. 600 to A. D. 750. Though it was not so famous as the third, it appears to have done some useful work at least by way of collecting and preserving rare Tamil works which would otherwise have perished. Perundevanar, the author of Bharata Venba must have belonged to this academy[1], as his name, famous though it was, does not appear in Nakkirar's list of the members of the third academy. Naladiyar (A. D. 750) and some other poems included in the eighteen minor works (பதினென்கீழ்க்கணக்கு) should, I think, be attributed to this Sangam. From the expressions சங்கத்தமிழ் and சங்கமுகத்தமிழ் which occur in the works of Tirumangai Alvar, I am inclined to believe that the great Vaishnava apostle knew this fourth Sangam, though he was not probably its member.

1. According to the astronomical calculation made by Divan Bahadur Swamikkannu Pillai Avl. from a reference in the Silappadikaram, the poets Ilango-adigal and Sattanar must have flourished in the eighth century. If so, the latter author must have been a member of the above academy. We cannot now go deeper into this question or accept Mr Swamikkannu Pillai's theory, until stronger and more convincing evidences be forth-coming.

Another attempt in later times seems to have been made by Poyyamoli Pulavar the author, of an erotic poem known as the Tanjaivanan Kovai. He lived, it is said, in the reign of one Vanangamudi Pandyan whose date cannot be determined at present. From the brief account of this poet given in the Tamil Plutarch, it might be inferred that the poet's petition to the Pandya king to establish an academy did not meet with the royal approbation. But at the time of Tiruttakka Deva (about 900 A. D.) there was, it is said, a Sangam at Madura, and one Poyyamoli was an admirer of the reputed author of Chintamani. If this Poyyamoli was the poet alluded to above, we shall have every reason to think that he did partially succeed in founding an academy which was probably the fifth.

The Pandya and Chola kings, some of whom were lovers of Tamil literature, might have assembled societies of learned men at different times ; but no history of them has come down to us, probably because none of them attained the high rank of the first three academies. Yet, most of the Tamil kings from Parantaka Chola (A. D. 906) downwards appear to have encouraged the growth of Tamil learning by patronising eminent poets who adorned their courts and by showering on them munificent presents. A few of them like Gandaraditya (tenth century) and Ati Vira Rama Pandya (seventeenth century) were themselves poets, and gave an impetus in later times to the advancement of learning in the Tamil country.

Before proceeding to consider the work done by the Tamil academies which existed at various times, it is desirable to give a brief summary of their history. The early Pandya kings were the foremost to encourage Tamil learning by establishing academies at Madura. Vague and exaggerated accounts of some of them appear to have been handed down in traditions, until they were committed to writing, first by the commentator of Iraiyanar's Agapporul, and then by the writer of the Madura Stalapurana, some time after A. D. 750. Some of their members seem to be fictitious persons, while others, probably excepting a few, do not appear to be contemporaries. Their constitution, function and age, as described in these works are extremely unreliable. All what we can now say is that the Pandya kings maintained a Tamil academy or University at their metropolis from about B. C. 450 to about A. D 550, and that it was subject to varying fortunes. When the Pandya country was invaded and temporarily occupied by the Kalabhras during the sixth century and when the religious struggle had already commenced, the last Sangam or college ceased to exist as a corporate body. From this time, the Jains had their own Sangams, which were more or less like the Jesuit seminaries of the middle ages ; and the Hindus had their own academy which might have been in existence during the early part of the eighth century. It was at this last Sangam that Perundevanar translated the Mahabharata and wrote his invocatory stanzas to the eight anthologies, and it was also at this college that the eighteen minor poems were collected. In the face of the above references to the Tamil Sangams or academies throughout the ancient Tamil literature, it would be impossible to deny their existence in some form or other before the eighth century A. D.

Having said so much for the history of the various Tamil academies, we shall now proceed to consider the amount of influence they exerted in giving shape to the Tamil language and literature.

The object with which the three academies were founded was threefold, namely, (1) the purification of the Tamil language by the writing of a grammar for it and by enforcing strict adherence to its rules, (2) the gradual introduction of Aryan civilisation in the Tamil country, and (3) the regulation of literary patronage so as to promote these ends. This task was first taken up by the Brahman sage Agastya, of course, under the guidance and patronage of the Pandya kings. With a view to carry out these plans the preliminary measures adopted were, first the assembling of a large body of literary men from different parts of the Tamil land ; secondly, the formation of a literary academy with Agastya, the traditional priest of the Pandya family, as its president ; and thirdly, the promulgation of a royal mandate prohibiting the circulation of any literary production before it was approved by the academy.

Language has life and growth, and when left to itself sprouts out into divers dialects like the branches of a living tree. 'The bit and bridle of literature' says Max Muller, 'will arrest a natural flow of language in the countless rivulets of its dialects, and give a permanency to certain formations of speech which, without these external influences, could have enjoyed but an ephemeral existence.' This linguistic principle was clearly understood and fully recognised by the founders of the Tamil academies. To secure, therefore, permanency to the Tamil language the boundaries of the country where it was current were roughly described and the particular locality in which pure Tamil (செந்தமிழ்) was spoken was sharply defined; then the form and pronunciation of letters were settled; rules were laid down to distinguish pure Tamil words from those of foreign origin, and to determine the structure and combination of words in sentences. These and many other restrictions on the free growth of the language were dealt with in the first Tamil grammar. Treatises were written on prosody, rhetoric and *porul* (details of conduct in matters of love and warfare). Poetical dictionaries or *nikhandus* were compiled in order to give fixity to the form and meaning of words in the language, and to check the indiscriminate and unlicensed introduction of alien words in the Tamil vocabulary.

The canons of literary criticism were severe and were applied impartially. In this connection there is a tradition pertaining to Sittalai-Sattanar, a noted member of the so-called third academy and author of the unrivalled epic Manimekalai. When a new poem was recited by its author before the learned assembly, he used to strike his head with the butt-end of his iron stylus whenever he found a flaw in it. The wound thus caused by his constant blows grew into a purulent sore. (He was on this account called Sittalai or 'pus-head' Sattanar). This wound, it is said, defied all curative treatment, but healed of itself on hearing the Kural of Tiruvalluvar.

சிந்திநீர்க் கண்டங் தெறுசுக்குத் தேனளாய்
மோந்தபின் யாாக்குந தீலேக்குத்தில்—காநதி
மீலக்குத்து மால்யாீன வள்ளுவாமுப பாலாற்
நீலக்குத்துத் தீர்வுசாத தற்கு.

In this way the Tamil language, which passed through the crucible of the three academies, was refined and given to the Tamil land as a perfect instrument for the expression of the best thoughts and sentiments of its people. The influence of these academies is markedly seen in the Tamil writings which received their approval, their style and language and choice of words differing much from that of the Tamil works of the post-academic period. The reader may compare with advantage the Purananuru or Pattupattu with the Tevaram or the Tiruvoymoli.

For the advancement of literature and academies the Tamil kings did much. Liberal presents in the shape of money, elephants, palanquins, chariots with horses, lands and flowers of gold were bestowed upon deserving poets. Titles of distinction like ஆசிரியர் (doctor), புலவர் (pandit), கவிச்-

சக்கரவர்த்தி (emperor of poets), etc., were also conferred on them. Poets were honoured and respected to such a degree that even kings did not think it dishonourable to act as their palanquin bearers. To appease the wrath of a poet, a Pandya queen is said to have borne his palanquin one whole night in the disguise of a male carrier. Instances of the Tamil kings honouring poets, and of their indirectly encouraging learning are only too many. One point, however, might be noticed in this connection. The Tamil kings of Chera, Chola and Pandya were liberal patrons of Tamil literature. In the Tamil work entitled Padirruppattu, the poet Kannanar of Kunnattur is said to have received, for having composed ten poems, a grant of five hundred villages and the revenues of the southern districts for thirty-eight years; the poet Kappiyanar obtained from the Chera king a gift of forty lakhs of *pon* (a gold coin valued at Rs. 2-8-0 each) for his ten poems ; and the poetess Nacchellai was given by another Chera monarch nine *tulams* (Tulam=600 Rs. weight) of gold for making jewels and one lakh of gold coins, besides the honour of a seat by his side. Such was the munificient patronage of poets by the Tamil kings.

A comparison of these ancient institutions of the Tamil people with the modern Royal Academy of the French will be interesting, since both of them were alike in their constitution, work and influence. The French Academy was established in A. D. 1635, that is nearly two thousand years after the first Tamil academy, and its members were fixed at forty. Its object was to cleanse the language of the impurities, which had crept into it through the common people who spoke it and 'to render it pure, eloquent and capable of treating the arts and sciences....It has done much by its example for style and has raised the general standard of writing...though it has tended to hamper and crush originality.' It has been remarked by a Danish scholar that academies of the kind described above operate as a check to the liberty of speech and generally to national independence, and quotes as an example the absence of similar institutions among the liberty-loving British race. The same author continues as follows :—'In England every writer is and has been free to take his words where he chooses, whether from the ordinary stock of every day words, from native dialects, from old authors, or from other languages, dead or living. The consequence has been that English dictionaries comprise a larger number of words than those of any other nation.'

The above remarks of Dr. Jespersen apply with equal force to the Tamil people. In the Tamil language there are 34 synonyms for the word 'wind,' 50 for 'water,' 35 for 'cloud', 62 for ' earth,' 60 for ' mountains ' &c. The ancient Tamils were a war-like race ; they had their war songs and lyrics. Though the blazing fire of independence and patriotism was put out by the magic influence of the peace-loving Brahmans of South India, the native bellicose spirit of the ancient Tamils makes its appearance at times among the present day Maravar, Kallar and Shanar tribes of the southern districts, though they have lost the grace and dignity of the real warrior. The war-like Nayars of the west coast are also the descendants of ancient Tamil clans.

The Tamil dictionary is very copious and the number of pure Tamil words in it exceeds that of any other Indian vernaculars. Synonyms are plentiful. Even slang terms acquired classical merit and were made use of in literature. We may illustrate this usage by a concrete example. Kamban, the prince of Tamil poets, coined the word *tumi* (துமி) in his Ramayana to rhyme with *timi* (திமி). While reciting his work at the royal court, Ottaikuttar, another poet of almost equal ability and younger contemporary, took objection to its use and demanded his authority for its currency. Kamban replied that it was a cow-herd's slang; and Ottaikuthar required him to prove it. Thereupon, Kamban invoked Sarasvati, the goddess of learning, who in the disguise of an Idaiya woman uttered the word *tumi* in the sense of a 'drop' or 'spray' from an apartment in a shepherd's house, so loudly as to be heard by the two poets when passing along the street. This story clearly shows that the coining of new words was never tolerated, though the use of slang and obsolete terms was freely allowed.

So far as the Tamil language was concerned, the

influence of the academies was mainly conservative ; but it never arrested the growth of the imagination or fancy of the Tamil race. On the contrary, it afforded them unlicensed freedom to indulge even in what would appear to a moderner as hyperboles and anachronisms.

X
THE TEN TENS

'Padirruppattu' or the 'Ten tens' is the fourth of the eight poetical anthologies, the collection and arrangement of which are attributed to the third academy. As implied by the name it had originally ten books, of which the first and the last are now lost. The remaining eight books were composed by eight different authors in commemoration of the military exploits, the liberality and other noble qualities of eight Chera kings of ancient times. It is said that the authors of these books were given enormous presents by these kings. Parts of this work might have been written, so early as the end of the second or the beginning of the third century; and Chera was one of the Kodun-Tamil countries according to the early Tamil grammarians. The work under review is, therefore, a museum of obsolete words and expressions, archaic grammatical forms and terminations, and obscure customs and manners of the early western Tamil people who were the ancestors of the modern Malayalis.

The second book which was written by Kannanar of Kunnattur is addressed to the Chera king Imaya Varman Nedum Seraladan. In the epilogue to this book we are informed that this king was the nephew of Udiyan by Venmal Nallini and Veliyan, that he engraved the 'bow' on the Himalayas and that he conquered and subdued the far-famed Aryans and the hard-tongued Yavanas (Ionians). He was the uncle of Senguttuvan, a contemporary of Gajabahu I (169-191) of Ceylon. Regarding the Andhra king Viliyakura II (113-138 A. D.) Mr. V. A. Smith writes that 'he prided himself on his prowess in expelling the Sakas, Yavanas and Pahlavas from his dominions on the West-coast.' Further, it is said that 'the Scythians from the north raided southwards and there was war. In an inscription at Nasik the Andhra Gotamiputra is stated to have defeated the Sakas, Yavanas and Pahlavas, the Saka chief being the Kshatrapa Nahapana. This was about A. D. 125.' As Imaya Varman—a Chera king of the west coast and the uncle of Senguttuvan—also boasts of having fought with the Yavanas, there is every reason to believe that this king might have had a share in the expulsion of this Greek or Ionian people from Western India. These two kings were probably contemporaries, as Imaya Varman Nedum Seraladan is stated to have reigned for fifty-eight years. Thus it will be seen that this Chera king and the Brahman poet Kannanar must have flourished during the first half of the second century A. D.

The third book was composed by Palai Gautamanar (the தண்டமிழ் மறையோன் of Ilango-adigal) in honour of the Chera king Palyanai Chelkezhu Kuttuvan, a younger brother of Imaya Varman. He was a pious king and renounced the world after a reign of 25 years. He is stated to have performed ten Yagas or sacrifices for the sake of Gautamanar, directed his purohit Nedum-Bharatayanar to become an ascetic, and to have given away his kingdom to his relatives. He is further said to have decorated the temple of the family deity on the Ayirai[1] Hill. Gautamanar was a Brahman poet who is believed to have ascended the heaven with his consort after completing the tenth sacrifice. All these facts are also alluded to in the last book of Silappadikaram. The Chera king Palyanaichelkezhu-Kuttuvan and the poet Gautamanar must, therefore, have lived during the latter half of the second century.

Kappiyarru-Kappiyanar was the author of the fourth book, which is addressed to the Chera king Kalangkaykkanni Narmudi Cheral. He was born to Seraladan by the wife of Velavikkoman Padman. He conquered Puzhi-Nadu and defeated Nannan. He succeeded Cheral Adan and reigned for 25 years. The real name of the king is not known, and the one by which he is known is a nom-de-plume meaning

1. This hill, now known as Aivar-malai, is near Aiyampalayam in the Palani taluk of the Madura district. On the summit of this hill there are many Jaina images and a temple containing inscriptions of Varaguna Pandiya (A. D. 862).

'one who wears a garland of களங்காய் and a crown of plantain fibre'. Nothing further is known at present about this king and the poet.

The fifth book is a production of the famous poet Paranar ; and the hero of the poem is Senguttuvan, nephew of Nedum-Cheraladan by the Chola prince Manakkilli. This Chera king was a contemporary of Gajabahu I of Ceylon, of the Chola kings Uruva-Pahrer Ilamset Senni and Vel-Pahradakkai-Perunar-killi, and of the Pandya kings Nedu-Maran and Verri Vel-Seliyan. He was an ally of the Satakarnis of the Andhra dynasty, and with his assistance he defeated a confederacy of the Aryan chiefs—Kanaka, Vijaya and others—on the northern bank of the Ganges, and the nine rival princes of the Chola family at Nerivayil near Uraiyur and fought another at Viyalur with some unknown chief, and subdued Palayan of Mokur. He was the elder brother of Ilangko the reputed author of Silappadikaram and the hero of the third book of that famous work.

Paranar has contributed some 72 stanzas to the other collected works of this period. In Tamil literature his name is found invariably connected with Kapilar, another renowned poet and contemporary. The question of the age of these poets will be considered later on, and it is enough for the present to say that Senguttuvan, the Chera king flourished between 150 and 225 A.D. His reign extended to fifty-five years.

The sixth book consisting of over 210 lines was written by a woman named Kakkai-Patiniyar Nacchellaiyar in honour of the Chera king Adukot-pattu Cheral Adan. He was the nephew of Nedum Cheral Adan, by the wife of Velavikoman, and a liberal king who gave away cows and lands to Brahmans, and ruled his country justly from his capital at Tondi, the modern Kadalundi in the Malabar district. If he was a cousin brother of Senguttuvan noticed above he must have flourished during the first quarter of the third century A. D. He reigned for thirty-eight years.

The seventh book, addressed to Selvakkadungo-Azhi-Adan, was composed by Kapilar. This Chera king was the nephew of Anduvan Cheran by Porayan and his wife Perundevi, daughter of Orutandai. He was a valiant king and pious devotee of Vishnu, for whose worship he granted the village of Okandur as *devada-yam*. He fought several battles and performed many sacrifices. He is believed to have reigned 25 years. Nothing further is known about this king except that he was a predecessor of Senguttuvan, and that he must have flourished before A. D. 150.

Kapilar was a Brahman of Tiruvadavur in the Pandya country. It is not known why he has not composed even a stanza in praise of any Pandya sovereign in whose dominion he was born. Perhaps he had migrated while young to the hill country and settled there, as all his extant poems are descriptive of upland scenery (குறிஞ்சி) and of hill kings and chiefs. Other poems attributed to this author are, —one book in Ainguru-nuru, Kurinjippattu, Inna Narpatu, besides some poems in Narrinai, Kurungkali, Agananuru and Purananuru. He did not embrace any particular sect, as he worshipped all the *puranic* deities—Baladeva, Vishnu, Siva, Vinayaka, &c. It is not therefore safe to ascribe the authorship of certain sectarian poems on Siva or Mutta Nayanar to Kapilar. Further, there is much difference in the style and language of these two sets of poems (vide, p. 197). He has been extolled by his contemporaries and successors as one who never uttered a lie (பொயயாா விற்கபிலன்) and as one most upright in his conduct.

The eighth was sung by one Arisilkizhar in praise of the Chera king Perum-Cheral-Irum-Porai. This king was a nephew of Selva-Kadumko the hero of Kapilar's book by the wife of Velavikkoman. He boasts of having overthrown Adigaman of Takadur, and defeated the Pandya and Chola kings of his period near the Kollimalais. It is said that he was a contemporary of Ugra Pandya and that he reigned for seventeen years.

The ninth and last book is a production of Perungunrur Kizhar, and it eulogizes the military achievements of the Chera king Ilam-Cheral-Irum Porai. He was the nephew of Irum-Porai noticed above, by Maiyur Kizhan and his wife Venmal Anduvan Sellai. He boasts of having defeated the Chola king Uruvap Pahrer Ilamchet Senni (father of Karikala) and Palayan Maran, a Pandya chief, and destroyed the five hill fortresses of Vicchi. It is said that he was a descendant of Mandaram Cheral Irumporai (ix. 8, 10) and of the kings who had thrown lances to cross the ocean and decorated the patron deity at Ayirai. The author Perumgunrur Kizhar was a contemporary of Kapilar and praises him in the fifth agaval of this book as follows :—

உவலைக.ராக் கவலையினெருசி
னனவிற்பாடிய நல்விசைக் கபிலன்.

We shall now consider *en semble* the dates of the Chera kings and of the famous poets Kapilar, Paranar, Palai Gautamanar, Perumgunrur Kizhar and Arisil Kizhar. As may be gathered from the epilogues to this work the genealogies of the early Chera kings fall into two branches thus :—

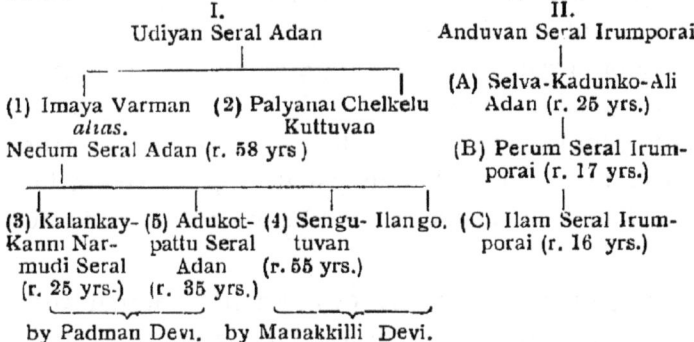

Of these the only king whose date has been definitely fixed is Senguttuvan[1] (No. 4 in Table I, A. D.

---

[1] It is not our purpose to enter into the controversy whether the Gajabahu alluded to in the Silappadikaram was the first or the second king of that name, as this question has been already settled by other scholars.

175-225); and the composition of Silappadikaram by his brother Ilango may, therefore, be placed between 200 and 225 A. D. In this work the exploits of the Chera kings Nos. 1, 2 and 3 in Table I, and of C in Table II are narratad (Book, xxviii, ll. 135-148). Consequently all the kings referred to in the two genealogies must have been the predecessors of Senguttuvan. The poet Paranar has sung Senguttuvan (No. 4) and his maternal uncle Nedum Cheral Adan (No. 1) besides Uruva Paher, Ilamchet Senni of Pukar, father of Karikala Chola of Kaveripatam and Vel-Pahradakkai Perunar-Killi of Uraiyur. Summing up the duration of the various reigns from No. 1 to No. 4, as given in Table I, the period comes to more than a century, and this could not surely be the age of Paranar. It is therefore clear that the length of the reign of each king includes the period of their viceroyalty in some part of the Chera country before their accession to the Chera throne, and that almost all kings given in the two tables must have reigned between A. D. 125 and 225.

This, I believe, is the period of Kapilar, Paranar and other poets mentioned above. It was the custom in these provinces as in the north, to appoint the sons of the reigning kings, especially the heirs apparent, as Viceroys of different provinces or Nadus under their sovereignty. As each of them styled himself a Chera, a Chola or a Pandya king, we have a number of such kings ruling at the same period; and there were as many as nine Chola princes at Uraiyur during the time of Senguttuvan ; and this is one of the stumbling blocks in fixing the genealogy of the Tamil kings. Further, this difficulty is enhanced in the case of the Chera kings on account of the Marumakkatayam law of inheritance, which had been then as now in vogue in the Malabar coast ; and it has become a hopeless task to determine their relationship on account of the temporary unions of the patriarchal and matriarchal royal families of the Pandyas, Cholas and Cheras. It was one of the causes for constant wars between them, and for the eventual separation of the Cheras from the other Tamil dynasties.

The genealogy of the Chera kings of this period given by Mr. Kanakasabhai in his *Tamils* 1800 *years ago* is as follows :—

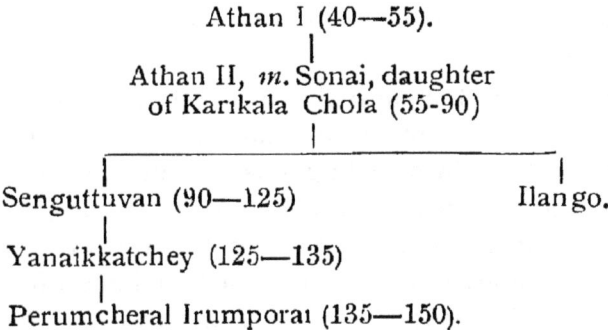

It will be seen that this table does not tally with our own, and it is not possible to say on what authority he has based it. But at any rate it is evident that he has forgotten the fact that succession in the Kerala

...ntry was according to Marumakkatayam law. ...his Senguttuvan was not the son of Athan II and the Chola princess Sonai as he has given; but he was the nephew of Athan as the following lines will show:—

குடவர் கோமா னெடுஞ்சேரலாதற்குச்
சோழன் மணககிள்ளி யீன்ற மகன்
* * * *
கடல் பிறக்கோட்டிய செங்குட்டுவன்

On the other hand, the Silappadikaram informs us that Senguttavan was the son of Seraladan by a Chola princess—சேரலாதற்குச சோழன் மகளீன்றணமகதன் செங் குட்டுவன். And elsewhere in the same work the Chola king Valavankilli is spoken of as the brother-in-law of Senguttuvan—நின்மைத்தனன்வளவன்கிள்ளி. I am inclined to believe that the word மகள் in the first quotation from Silappadikaram should be மகன், as otherwise the parentage given to some of the Chera kings in the Padirruppattu must all be false, which is improbable.

In the Tamil country the Aryan Brahmans had already settled in small numbers. They were patronized by kings with grants of land. Some of them were engaged as purohits or priests, while others occupied themselves in teaching the Aryan religion and philosophy to the Tamils. The Tamil poets Kapilar and Palai-Gautamanar were Brahmans. There were also poetesses like Nacchellaiyar; and education of women was not neglected in those days. Besides poets of both sexes among Brahmans and Vellalas, there was a low class of minstrels called

Panans (female Patini), who lived by begging, and whose duty it was to recite songs before kings and chiefs. They were rewarded with elephants, chariots and garlands of golden flowers. And they used to accompany kings to battles and visit camps in the hope of sharing with the victorious soldiers the booties taken in wars.

Rice, sugar and ginger, varagu, kollu and tinai, cocoanut and palmyra were largely cultivated. Meat was eaten by all classes, not excepting even Brahmans, and the drinking of liquor was very common. Soldiers used to wear garlands of ginger and flowers in order to eat that pungent root at intervals while quaffing liquor (v. 2). Rice cooked with flesh was the favourite viand of soldiers. They observed feasts when they returned after success in wars, or on the birthday of kings, and fasts on full-moon days (vi. 1). The Brahmans performed Yagas or sacrifices for the benefit of kings. The God Vishnu at Trivandrum was worshipped by all people of higher castes (iv. 1). Females, especially the class called விறலியர், were in the habit of tying their locks of hair divided into five knots like the Toda women of modern time (ii. 8). Compare with this the following extracts from Kalittogai which gives a graphic description of the coiffure in vogue among the Dravidian Tamil woman of antiquity.

(1) எஃகிடை தொட்ட கார்க்கவின் பெற்றவம்பால்.
(2) ஐதாக நெறித்தன்ன வறலவிர் நீளாம்பா
வணிநகை யிடையிட்ட வீகையங்கண்ணி.

Kalangu or the seeds of (guilandina bonduce) were used for counting (iv 2). They believed in omens and auguries, the withering of leaves in the silk-cotton tree being considered an evil foreboding (iv 10). They believed in astrology and in the appearance of eleven suns to dry up the universal deluge (vii.2). Chastity was considered the highest virtue and sign of 'learning' in women and they believed in the story of செம்மீன் or arundhati. Among the Tamils the ordinary custom was the burial of dead bodies (v. 4). They used to be kept in big pots and buried under Vahni (Prosopis spicigera) trees.

கழிந்தமன்னர் மறைத்ததாழி வனனிமன்றம்

Feudalism was prevalent. The Tamil kings and their governors of provinces were constantly at war. Each was bent upon subduing the other and becoming the overlord. Thus, at the battle of Nerivayil near Uraiyur as many as nine Chola princes were defeated by Senguttuvan, the Chera king. A part of the Chera country, called the Puzhi Nadu was conquered and lost alternately by the Cheras and Pandyas. These chiefs had small forts with deep ditches surrounded with forests, one tree among which—like the கடம்பு (Eugenia racemosa) of Nannan and the வேம்பு (Azadirachta indica) of Palayan—was considered sacred to the ruler. This was one of the vestiges of the Australian totemism. In war the first business of an enemy was to cut down such sacred trees and to make war drums out of the wood, to burn the villages, to plunder their cattle and to destroy their moats and ditches with élephants. When a fort was besieged by an enemy, the men in the fort used to fight even without taking food and write the number of days thus passed on the fort-walls (vii.8). The battlements were filled with bows and arrows, swords, anklets and wreaths of green leaves (vi. 3) ; the two last (worn by women) for distribution among the coward soldiers as marks of shame. It was also the custom to pour oil on the head of the vanquished leader and to drag him by both hands from behind. The victorious kings and soldiers used to dance with raised swords on the field of battle (vi. 6) and then give grand feasts to their men when the severed heads and bodies of the departed heroes lay strewn around them. This was களவேள்வி (camp feast) and துணங்கைக்கூத்து (war dance). They knew something of surgery and used to stitch the wounds received in battles with needles called Nettai or நெடு வெள்ளூசி (v. 2). They had their own military rules of discipline, and always preferred winter for military operations (ix. 2). Plunder was not their sole object, but a desire for power and authority actuated the Tamil kings to carry on wars with the neighbouring chiefs. Naval fights too were not unknown to them.

The standard authority on grammar for this period was Tolkapyam The following peculiarities may be found in the work under consideration. The plural of high caste nouns had, *ir*, while the neuter nouns had no plural at all. The termination, கள், was not in use then though Tolkapyar mentions it in his grammar. In the matter of gender, neuters like ஒக்கல், வேந்து, மன், சுற்றம், &c., were mostly in use, though masculine and feminine nouns like நெடியோன் and உரியள் are met with occasionally. The post-position for all the six cases was இன் or இல், but கு for the dative and அ for the genitive were also used. In பொன்னின்னன்ன, நின்னிற்றநத, மருபயின்யானே and சிலம்பிறறுஞ்சும் we find இன் stands for 2nd, 3rd, 6th and 7th cases; and in the phrase பிடியகுன்று the termination அ is a genitive particle. The formation of verbal-nouns as in தொடை from தொடு to attach, in தாவல் from தா to suffer, in பணிபு from பணி to bow, in மலர்பு from மலர் to blossom, in அடிப்பு from அடு to kill, in பொய்பு from பொய் to utter a lie, in அறுபு (separation) from அறு to cut, in எறு from எறி to beat or throw, in பறை from பற to fly, in இறை from இறு to tarry, and in பார்வல் from பார் to see. of personal nouns in ர் from verbs தா (தருநர்), பகர் (பகர்நர்), அற and அரி (அரிநர்); concrete nouns from verbs தின்—இற்றி, கொள்—கொண்டி (booty), அறுவை (piece of cloth), √ நீம் (powder) சீறு, தாறு); and of abstract nouns from verbs as வறம் (dryness), வறல், வெவ்வா, &c., are all now obsolete. Present tense was not in use at this period, the only tenses which were frequently used are the past and future. The particles or signs of past tense much in use were பு and இ; and those of the future were வும், க்கு, ப and பு—சேருகம் (we will go) இரக்கு, வருப, பாடு might be taken as examples. Causative verbs like ஒழுக்கு (to cause to behave); infinitives in சயர் as in தீஇயர் (to give), imperatives in மோ as in சென்மோ and மின as in உண்மின் have all gone out of use along with மன், கொன், பெஎ and மன்ற which were the adverbs of quality greatly used by the early Tamil poets.

As in most works of this period the metre used here is *agaval*.

Tolkapyar and Pavanandi have provided rules for the going out of the old and the coming in of new forms and words, so long as the language continues to have life and growth. Ignoring this important principle Tamil poets of all ages have slavishly adopted obsolete terms and expressions in their compositions. This is the chief cause for the great difference between the language of poetry and the colloquial dialect. We are not concerned here with the obsolete words and forms as they have been fully explained by the old commentators and in the glossaries appended to those classical works. We give below only such words as are current now but have undergone change in meaning by the influence of the psychological principles of contiguity, resemblance and contrast. ஆடு meant 'victory' from அடு to kill, now it means a 'sheep' or 'an animal that frisks'; முன்பு meant 'strength' and now it means 'front'; வைஞ்ஞியம் meant the 'people', now it means the 'green or fertile land;' அளத்தல் meant 'thinking', now restricted only to 'measuring'; அடுபு meant 'withering or dying,' now it means 'that in-which anything is cooked', hence an 'oven'; வாழ்க்கை meant 'property', now it means 'living'; பொன்[1] meant 'iron', hence any useful metal, but now restricted to 'gold'; களிறு meant also a 'pig', now only an 'elephant'; பகல் meant 'justice' நடுவுநிலைமை, now only 'mid-day'; கிழக்கு meant a 'pit' or a low ground from கீழ் 'below' and கு the particle of direction, now it means the 'east,' which was believed by the early Tamilians as the low-lying land in reference to the Western Ghats; கோடு meant 'cruelty' or 'that which was bent' and now, it means a 'branch' of a tree; கற்பு meant 'learning' (கல்வி) and it is now restricted to 'chastity'; இடம் in பகலிடம் meant *time*, as no distinction was made by the early Tamils between time (Skt. காலம்) and space (இடம்) or they had no term to express the notion of time; ஒடி meant to 'spoil or injure' generally, now it means 'to break or cut in twain' like a stick; பிழைப்பு meant 'death', now 'living' the opposite of it; வெறுகதை meant 'wealth,' or that which is 'liked', and now it means 'hatred'; அல்கல் meant 'staying or tarrying' now 'leaving'; அறுபு and அறுவை (from √ அற்- to cut) meant 'separation' and 'a piece of cloth', both of which are now obsolete, the latter word being ousted by another துணி of similar origin; இரவல் meant 'begging', and it is no longer used in that meaning; செப்பு is a very old word common to Tamil and Telugu, but it has become classical in Tamil and colloquial in Telugu.

[1] In Kanarese the name for 'iron' is 'Kabbonnu' or 'Karumponnu', which means the 'black gold.'

The authors of this collection have used Sanskrit derivatives (tadbhavas) very sparingly, and even these relate either to religion or mythology. They are ஆவுதி (sacrifice), பலி (offering), மந்திரம் (spell), காலன் (god of death), பாசம் or பசாசம் (devil), ஆரம் (garland), சாந்தி (purification), அவுணர் (Rakshas or demons), and ஆரியர் (Aryas). Thus in a work of about 1,800 lines only a dozen words of Sanskrit origin are to be found, and it speaks of the purity of the Tamil language. It can exist without the least help from foreign languages, as it had and even now has sufficient elementary words of native origin, out of which compounds can, with a little attention to phonetic principles, be formed to express modern thoughts and ideas.

XI

THE VISHNUVITE SAINTS

The study of the *azhvars* or Vishnuvite saints is beset with several difficulties. On the one hand, religious fanatics have gathered together a mass of legendary and superstitious accounts, often of a conflicting and sometimes of an incredible nature; on the other, the European critics, perhaps aided by the sectarian opponents from the fold of the Saivas who form the major portion of the Tamils, have done much to belittle the extent of their influence and the results of their work among the Tamil population. Foremost amongst them was Bishop Caldwell, whose opinion always carries that weight and authority which a life-long and sincere devotion to the study of South Indian problems has secured for him. But whatever claim to infallibility his conclusions on matters of language may carry with it, it is but natural that his inferences regarding social and religious movements should be biassed by his missionary leanings. In the following chapter an attempt will be made to study the religious activities of the Vishnuvite Alvars from a purely historical stand-point, and special care will be taken to substantiate statements from the literary, epigraphical and other evidences.

All over the continent of India Vishnu has been worshipped in some form or other; but mostly in his two latest incarnations as Rama and Krishna. He is an Aryan deity transplanted into the Dravidian soil by successive bands of Aryan settlers, and it would therefore be highly interesting to give at the beginning a brief outline of the origin and development of this cult in the land of its origin. The main reasons for prefacing this essay with such a resume are, (1) to compare its growth both in the Aryavarta and in the land of the Tamils, and (2) to guard ourselves in the course of the ensuing discussion against certain misapprehensions that might be raised by the orthodox traditions of the Tamil Vaishnavas.

History of religions in India tells us that the worship of Vishnu is as old as the Vedas, and that the doctrines of this sect had already passed through at least two stages—the Vedic and the Puranic—before they attained the present form. During the Vedic period the religion of the Indo-Aryans consisted in the adoration of the elemental gods like Indra, Varuna, Agni and Marut, and in the offering of sacrifices to Agni or the fire-god. Vishnu was then a solar deity 'and held an inferior position as a friend or comrade of Indra. This epoch

THE VISHNUVITE SAINTS 283

was immediately followed by the rise of Buddhism and Jainism, which greatly influenced or modified the succeeding period of Puranic Hinduism, when the elemental gods of the Vedic period had come to occupy an inferior position, the foremost rank having been taken up by Brahma, Vishnu and Siva, which were believed to be the triple forms of the Supreme Being. And to popularize this triad three classes of Puranas amounting to eighteen in all were written by the Brahman sages. They narrate all sorts of legends connected with each of the above three deities. Each Purana is devoted to the praise of one or another of these gods who is spoken of in that work as supreme, whilst other deities described in other Puranas are slighted and their worship even forbidden. They also prescribe rules for the worship of gods by means of prayers, offerings, festivals, and pilgrimages. The date of the oldest of these Puranas, probably Vayu-Purana, is believed to be from about 320 A D. and the latest to be of the eleventh century. It was during this period that idol-worship and the building of temples for images were substituted for the Vedic sacrifices, which latter, however continue to this day in a feeble form among the Brahmanical rites. This change is ordinarily attributed to the overwhelming influence of Buddhism and Jainism, which at this period were in a state of decline and their humane but heretical doctrines had ultimately degenerated into mere idol-worship.

In ancient times the Dravidian Tamils were a

fighting race. From Purananuru, Kalittogai, Padirruppattu and other collected works of the early *Sangams* (academies) we further learn that great honour was done to brave men as is shown by a number of memorial stones or *Virakkals* still to be seen in some Tamil villages erected to commemorate their heroic deaths. The expressions like காஞ்சி சான்ற வயவர், காஞ்சி சான்றஞெரு, etc. bear testimony to the martial spirit of the early Tamils. When a king died of sickness without losing his life in battle his body used to be laid on a bed of *kusa* grass and split up with a sword believing that men who died as warriors could go to heaven. Heroes who died in battle were buried on the road-side and tomb stones were set up with suitable inscriptions describing the names and the military achievements of these persons. Offerings of flower, cooked rice and liquor were also made by their relations and friends. Perhaps small temples were also erected over the sepulchres and worshipped. Irulan, Katteri, Nondi, Karuppan and other deities which now form the objects of worship by low caste Sudras and Paraiyas belong probably to this category. Thus, the religion of the ancient Tamils consisted mainly in spirit worship and in the drinking and offering of liquor. They ate all kinds of meat, including even beef, and indulged in alcoholic drinks.

According to Tolkapyar, the earliest Tamil grammarian, even gods were classified according to the nature of the soil. Thus, Indra was the god of fertile and, மருதம் ; Murugan of the hills, குறிஞ்சி ; Durga of the desert, பாலை ; Vasudeva of pasture land, முல்லை ; and Varuna of the sea-coast, நெய்தல். It must be remembered that all these deities belong to the Aryan pantheon, nay, the first and the last were purely Vedic gods. The only god who might be called Dravidian was Muruga, as he was almost unknown under that appellation to the people of North India. Traces of this traditional classification might still be found in some caste names like Devendra Pallan, Varunakulam (fishermen) and Vasudevakulam (shepherds). Such was in brief the condition of religion among the Dravidians when the early bands of Aryan immigrants settled in the Tamil country.

Having said something about the state of religion among the Tamilians in the remote period, we shall now proceed to notice the changes that were brought about by their contact with the Aryans. The materials for this section will be drawn chiefly from the Tamil works of the Sangam period, (A. D. 150—550) and from the inscriptions published up to date.

The earliest Tamil author whose date could be ascertained approximately was Tiruvalluvar. He flourished probably about the end of the first century A. D and in his Kural we find no traces of his predilection to any particular sect or religion. He was no doubt a monotheist and he is now claimed both by the Jains and the Saivas as their savant. He is even worshipped by the Saivas of to-day as one of their saints or Nayanars. We shall next take Kapilar. He was a Brahman of Tiruvadavur in the Madura district and lived probably during the early part of the second century. Among his writings we find poems in praise of Tirumal (Vishnu), Baladeva, Murugan (Subrahmanya) and Siva. With due difference to the profound scholarship of Mahamahopadhyaya Swaminatha Aiyar and of the older commentators we are of opinion that none of the Saiva poems included in the eleventh Tirumurai, with the single exception of Tirumurugarruppadi, were written by Kapilar, Paranar and Nakkirar of the academic period. Though a Vedic deity Indra was also worshipped at this time. From Silappadikaram and Manimekalai we learn that annual festivals were also celebrated in honour of this god.

(1) விண்ணவா தலைவனே விழுநீ ராட்டிப்
பிறவா யாக்கைப் பெரியோன் கோயிலு
மறுமுகச் செவ்வே ளணிதிகழ் கோயிலும்
வால்வளை மேனி வாலியோன் கோயிலு
நீல மேனி நெடியோன் கோயிலும்.—*Sil.*

(2) வச்சிரத் தடக்கை நெடியோன கோயிலுட்
போர்ப்புறு முரசங்கறங்க.—*Pur.*

Another celebrity of the later Sangam period, Nakkirar, informs us that during his time four gods of the Aryan pantheon were considered as holding the foremost rank among the South Indian deities.

எறுழ்வல னுயரிய வெறிமரு எவிர்ச்சடை
மாற்றருங் கணிச்சி மணிமிடற் றோனும
தோலா நல்விசை நால்வ ருள்ளும.—*Pur.* 56.

THE VISHNUVITE SAINTS 287

They were Siva, Vishnu, Balarama and Muruga. In his later life, however, this writer became a Saiva and composed a poem in praise of Murugan, for which he was canonized as one of the Saints of the Saiva sect.

This was probably a period of eclecticism, since the Vedic and the Puranic gods had not yet been subjected to the process of separation, but were in a nebulous form. Besides the four gods mentioned above the Vedic deities India, Yama, Varuna, Soma, Aditya, Rudra, Vasu and Marut had been adored or respected even at that time by the Aryan immigrants. Nakkirar tells us that the first four were 'great gods' (நாற்பெருந் தெய்வம்), while the rest were divided into thirty-three deities as follows—Aditya, 12; Rudra, 11; Vasu, 8 ; and Marut, 2. These were subsequently increased to thirty-three crores during the Puranic period.

நால்வே நியந்கைப் பதிெனாரு மூவர்.—*Nak.*
நால்வேறு தேவரு நலத்தகு சிறபபிற்
பால்வேறு தேவரு மப்பதி படர்ந்து.—*Mani.*

Greater attention was also paid to sacrifices both by the Brahmans and kings, the latter chiefly providing funds for their performance, as they had believed that the prosperity of the country depended mainly on such sacrifices. The following quotations will bear testimony to the prevalence of this belief:—

(1) அந்தி யாநதண ரருங்கட னிறுக்கு
முத்தீ விளக்கு.—*Pur.*

(2) வேள்வி முற்றிய வாய்வாள் வேந்த.—*Pur*.
(3) நீர்நாண் செய்வழங்கியு, மெண்ணுணப் பலவேட்டும்.—*Ib*.
(4) உரைசால் வேள்வி முடித்த கேள்வி.—*Pad*.
(5) யாதணர் கேள்விகேட்டுப் படிவ மொழியாத
வேள்வி வேட்டனே.—*Ib*.

The above is a brief account of Brahmanism in the Tamil country as it existed and was known to the authors of the Purananuru and other classics of the pre-Puranic period. And an outline of the Puranic Hinduism which follows will clearly show that none of the Saiva Nayanars or Vaishnava Alvars ever held the religious views explained in the above works. This one fact will in itself suffice to prove that both the Saiva and Vaishnava Saints, probably with the exception of one or two, flourished only during the Puranic period, viz., after A. D. 500.

The essential features of the early Puranic period were the setting up of idols and the construction of temples for them. The Tamil kings of this period—chiefly the Pallavas, the Cholas and the Pandyas—whose purohits or spiritual advisers were Brahmans, were imbued with devotion to Vishnu or Siva. It appears that Brahma had no votaries, as his name scarcely occurs in the academic works. Later on, however, he was united with Siva and Vishnu to make up the triad; and India and Baladeva were ousted from the Hindu pantheon. Still Brahma has been occasionally referred to in both the Saiva and Vaishnava hymns, though he had no temples to reside in like his friends Siva and Vishnu; and even now he has only

THE VISHNUVITE SAINTS 289

one temple in all India, and this is at Pushkaram in Ajmer. Vishnu and Siva alone were honoured with shrines, were regularly worshipped, and were given offerings three or four times a day. To propitiate them people observed fasts and held festivals Before the sixth century A. D. there were, however, only very few temples[1] dedicated to these deities and Muruga, as the following extracts from Pattuppattu, Padirrupattu, Purananuru, and Silappadikaram will show —

(1) புள்ளணி நீள்கொடிச் செல்வனும் வெள்ளேறு
    மூவெயின் முருக்கிய முரண்மிகு செல்வனு
    நூறுபபத் தடெக்கிய நாட்டத்து நூறுபல்
    வேள்வி மூற்றிய…திருக்கிளர் செல்வனு
    நாற்பெருந் தெயவத்து நன்னகர் நிலைஇய.—*Nak.*

(2) கண்பொரு திகிரிக் கமழ்குரா முழாஅ
    யலஙகற் செல்வன் சேவடி பரவி.—*Pad.*

(3) முககட் செல்வர் நகாவலஞ் செயற்கு.—*Pur.*

(4) விரிதிரைக் காவிரி வியன்பெருந் துருத்தி
    திருவமர் மார்பன் கிடந்த வணணமும்
    வீஙகுநீ ரருவி வேஙகட மென்னு
    மோங்குயர் மலையத தசசீமீ மிசை
    செங்கண் ணெடியோன நின்ற வண்ணமும்,
    திருமால் குன்றத்துச் செல்கு விராகில்
    *   *   * மலைமிசை நின்றோன்
    பொற்றுமரைத் தாளுளளம் பொருந்து மின்.—*Sil*

1. Srirangam, Tiruppati and Tirumal-kunram (Kalla Alagar) appear to have been the oldest and most famous of the Vaishnava temples in the Tamil country The famous temple of Varadaraja at Conjeevaram is not sung by any Vishnuvite Saint, as it is one of modern origin like those at Mannargudi and Melkota.

Temple building on a large scale was begun during the second half of the sixth and early part of the seventh centuries by Kocchengat Chola, Sundara Pandya Deva and Mahendra Varma Pallava. They tolerated all sects and religions—Saiva and Vaishnava, Jaina and Buddha—the last of which, however, was then on the decline at least in the extreme south. Though nominally worshipping any one of these gods, the kings were in the habit of invoking the triad in their grants. In the same family the father might be a Saiva whilst his son professed Vishnuism or very rarely even Jainism. Thus the Chera king Senguttuvan (about A. D. 250) was a worshipper of Siva and Vishnu, while his younger brother was a Jaina ascetic; the Saiva saint Tirunavukkarasu-Nayanar was a Jain in his early days while his sister Tilakavati was a Saiva devotee; and the Pallava king Simha Vishnu (A. D 590) was a staunch worshipper of Vishnu, whilst his son Mahendra Varman was first a Jaina and then an orthodox Saiva. It is no wonder, therefore, that when Hwen Tsang visited Conjeevaram in A. D. 640 there were in that city 100 Buddhist monasteries, with about 10,000 Brethren and about 80 temples the majority of which belonged to the Digambara Jains And he goes on to say that in Molokuta (probably the Pandya territory) the people were of mixed religions. There were many remains of old monasteries, very few being in preservation. 'There were hundreds of Deva temples and the professed adherents of various sects, especi-

THE VISHNUVITE SAINTS 291

ally the Digambaras, were numerous'[1] We see then, at the early half of the seventh century that Buddhism was in its decline, and the sects of Siva Vishnu and Jain were fighting with one another for ascendancy The later history of the Saiva and the Jaina cults will be dealt with in the second volume. As the subject matter for our immediate consideration is the development of Vishnuism we shall for the present part company with our Saiva and Jaina brethren.

For the separation of the Vaishnava cult and its development into a distinct sect in the Tamil country the Alvars were mainly instrumental. They were the first to hymn the praises of Vishnu and to propagate His worship. It might be gathered from their hymns that allusions and references to the miraculous deeds of Rama, Krishna and other incarnations of Vishnu were drawn largely from the two great epics— the Ramayana and the Mahabharata—and from the Bhagavata and Vishnu Puranas Their hymns were collected, arranged and compiled by Sri Nathamuni, probably under the editorship of Nammalvar into a single volume called the ' Nalayıra-Prabandam', or the ' Book of 4000 hymns ', about the middle of the tenth century A.D. Among the Tamil Vaishnavas (especially the Tengalais) this collection of Tamil poems is being regarded as sacred as the Sanskrit Vedas. Why this work has come to be esteemed so we cannot conceive. It is neither a translation of

1. Watters' Hwen Tsang, Vol. II, p. 228.

the holy Vedas of the Indo-Aryans, nor is it an exposition of their contents, rather than of the two great epics and the Puranas, and what is more surprising is that the four kinds of poetical compositions or *prabandas* of Nammalvar and the six varieties of Tirumangai-alvar's work are spoken of by the Vaishnava Acharyas as the counterparts of the four Sanskrit Vedas and their six Vedangas. This theory might appear false when it could be proved that Nammalvar lived two centuries after Kaliyan. The Devara hymns which constitute a more voluminous collection of the non-Brahman Saivas are not so much valued by the Smartha Brahmans of the Tamil districts.[1] This disparity in the estimation of the two Tamil works of exactly similar nature was probably due to the anxiety of the early Acharyas to make the religion of Vishnu more popular among the Dravidians, most of whom were followers of Siva.

The collection of hymns and religious poems by Appar, Sambandar, Sundarar, Manikka Vachakar and other Saiva devotees and their compilation into eleven *tirumurais* or series are usually ascribed to Nambiyandar Nambi In the ninth book entitled the Tiruvisaippa we find a hymn composed by Gandaraditya

1. Concerning this the Government Epigraphist writes as follows :—" The Saiva creed, does not appear to have paid much attention to Sastric karma, but taking unsullied devotion to Siva as its basis, it received into its fold all classes of people without any distinction of caste. This catholicity of the Saiva faith rendered it not very popular with the orthodox Brahmans".

Chola (A. D. 948-960) and another on the god of Raja Chola's shrine at Tanjore which was built towards the close of the tenth century, while a third by Karuvur Devar refers to a temple built by Gangaikonda Chola in or about 1015 A. D If the above tradition be trusted Nambiyandar Nambi should have lived about 1025. As it is said that the Periyapurana of Sekkilar is based upon one of the poems of Nambiyandar Nambi (திருத்தொண்டர் திருவந்தாதி), Sekkilar should have been either his contemporary or his successor. He was a minister under a Chola king and had the title of Uttama Chola Pallavarayan conferred on him as a personal mark of official distinction. Inscriptions inform us that the term Uttama was the name of Rajaraja's predecessor (A D. 970-985) and one of the *birudus* of his successor Rajendra I. (A. D. 1012). Several shrines are said to have been built by the first Uttama Chola and by his mother Sembiyan Mahadevi (queen of Gandaraditya) But it is said that the Periyapurana was written under the patronage of a Chola king named Anapaya, which, it is understood from an inscription in the Tiruvalur temple, was the title of Kulottunga Chola (A. D 1070—1118). Taking then the reign of Kulottunga Chola as the latest limit, it might be said with tolerable certainty that the Saiva poets Nambiyandar Nambi and Sekkilar1 flourished between

1. It will not be out of place to mention here that Chintamani, a Jaina work widely studied during the time of Sekkilar may have been written by Tiruttakka Deva about the middle of the tenth century A D.

A D. 1000 and A. D. 1150, a period which had immediately followed one of great Saiva activity (A.D. 950—990) Sri Natha Muni of the rival Vaishnava sect was also a contemporary of the Saiva poet and compiler, Nambiyandar Nambi, as will be shown in the sequel, and he should have been inspired by the Saiva revival of his time to render a similar service to his sect. And the above conclusions seem to receive support from the following statement of the Government epigraphist :—' We do not know of any epigraphic evidence earlier than the records of Rajaraja I where the recital of the sacred Saiva hymns of the Devaram are (sic) referred to for the first time as being instituted by him. Rajendra Chola I appears to have supported the cause of Saivaism by going a step further than his father and setting up the images of the famous Saiva Saints in the temple of Rajarajesvaram at Tanjore.'[1] It is therefore pretty clear that the practice of setting up images of the Vaishnava Saints in Vishnu temples might have come into existence some time after A. D. 1025.

The Alvars, who were elevated by the Vaishnava Acharyas to the rank of canonized Saints, are twelve in number; and they are being worshipped by them with greater devotion than they would adore their god Vishnu himself. Strictly speaking, the Alvars were only ten, Andal and Madhurakavi being left out of

1. Report dated 28th July 1909, page 103. Even before the 29th year of Rajarajachola images of Sundara, Sambandar, Rajarajachola and his queen Lokamahadevi were set up in the Tanjore temple.

account. From an inscription in the Vishnu temple at Kumaralingam (Madura district), it will be seen that all the ten Alvars were canonized and worshipped as early as A. D. 1230. And for making offerings to the images of these saints set up in the temple of Kalla Alagar at Tirumalirum Solai in Kil-Iraniya Mutta Nadu lands were granted by a certain devotee in the reign of Virarajendra Deva (S. S. 1153).[1] The word *alvar* means 'one deep in wisdom,' and any Alvar is, therefore, respected as a mediator to secure *Moksha* or salvation for the worshippers of Vishnu. The following table gives the names of the Alvars, the extent of their contributions to the Nalayira Prabandam, their birth place and the number of Vishnu shrines celebrated by them :—

Pallava	1 Poigaivar	100	Conjeeveram	7
	2 Pudattar	100	Mahabalipuram	14
	3 Peyar	100	Mylapore	13
	4 Tirumalisaiyar	216	Tirumalisai	20
Chola	5 Tiruppanalvar	10	Uraiyur	2
	6 Tondaradippodi	55	Tirumandangudi	1
	7 Tirumangaivar	1361	Tirukkurayalur	88
Chera	8 Kulasekhara	105	Quilon	8
Pandya	9 Periyalvar	473	Srivilliputtur	16
	10 Andal	173		8
	11 Nammalvar	1296	Tirunagari	30
	12 Madhurakavi	11	Tirukkolur	0

The arrangement of the names of Alvars adopted in the above table is not in accordance with the traditional chronology, which assigns to the earliest saint 4203

[1] Epigraphist's Report, No 665 dated 28th July 1910, p. 17.

and to the latest 2706 B. C., but with special reference to the four Tamil kingdoms in which they were born.

The orthodox Vaishnavas believe that the Alvars were the incarnations of the sacred weapons, the sacred ornaments and the sacred vehicles of Vishnu. Of these saints Tiruppan and Madhurakavi will not detain us long ; because, from a literary stand-point their contributions are almost trifling. The respective merits and the ages of the remaining Alvars will therefore be discussed in the following pages, leaving the miraculous incidents connected with their birth and life for the pious edification of the superstitiously orthodox Vaishnavas

No necessity for an essay of this kind should have occurred, had there been at least one reliable and faithful biography of the Vishnava Saints ; neither in Sanskrit nor in Tamil was there a single biographer of the type of a Boswell or a Lockhart. Legends of some kind or other are, however, not wanting among the Vaishnavas. One of these named the *Guruparamparai* or the 'Genealogy of the Gurus' professes to give the lives of the Vaishnava Saints and Acharyas ; and the accounts of the Alvars described in it appear to have been written after the fashion of the Periyapurana of the Saivas, the accuracy of the contents of both being highly questionable, as they are replete with miraculous incidents and anachronisms. We cannot expect more than these from the religious zealots of the combative

THE VISHNUVITE SAINTS 297

sects, who seem to have compiled them from distorted traditions and hyperbolic accounts which had come down to them several centuries after the death of these saints. Some of these were based on the casual utterances which are to be found in the writings of the Alvars themselves. The admissions of the saints which were made out of modesty and humility were, in certain cases, taken for real facts, and afterwards woven into long stories with embellishments drawn chiefly from their imaginative brains. Wherever traditions or autobiographical statements were wanting the biographers also were silent. Thus the lives of Poigayar, Peyar and Pudattar are almost blank, as there are no personal references in their *antadis*, while those of Tirumalisaiyar, Tirumangai-Mannan, Tondaradippodi, Periyalvar and Andal are comparatively full

And yet to impose upon the credulous disciples the Vaishnava Acharyas have cooked up even the horoscopes of their saints The asterisms in which Pudattalvar and Poigaiyalvar were born, as given in the Guruparamparai, do not agree with those assigned to them by the following inscription of Vikrama Chola (A. D. 1118) at Kanchipuram :—

திருவசதியூ ராழ்வாரைபபாடியருளின ஸ்ரீ பூதத்தாழ்வா ரும ஸ்ரீ பொய்கை யாழ்வாரும் பிறந்ததிருக கேட்டைநாள அரு ளாளப பெருமாள் புறபபட்டருளி ஏகாதசி திருமஞ்சனமூம் பெருந்திருவமுதுஞ் செய்தருள &c. But it is said in later works that Poigaiyar was born at Kacchi in Tiruvonam and Pudattar at Mamalla in Avittam.

The following lines which we here quote from the writings of the above saints seem to have furnished the data for their respective biographies:—

(1) *Tirumalisai Alvar*.—குலங்களாய வீரிரண்டிலொன் றிலும் பிறந்திலேன்; நாக்கொணடு மானிடம் பாடேன்.

(2) *Tirumangai Alvar*.—சேமமேவேண்டித தீவிஷைபெருக கித் தெரிவைமாருருவமே மருவி; கள்வனேனுனேன் படிறு செய்திருப்பேன் கண்டவாதிரி தந்தேனேலும் தெள்ளியேனுனேன

(3) *Tondaradippodi Alvar*.—சுதரும்க்கள்வருகித் தூர்த்த ரோடிசைந்தகாலம; மாதரார்கயற்கணனென்னும வலேயுள் பட்டழுநதுவேஷே, போதரே யென்று சொல்லிப் புநதி யிற் புகுநது தன்பால், ஆதரம் பெருகவைத்த வழகனுர ரங்கமன்றே; தொடையொதத துளவமும கூடையும் பொலிந்து தோன்றியதோள் தொண்டாடிப்பொடி.

(4) *Periyalvar*—வேதபபயன் கொளள வல்லவிட்டிசிததன; அணிகோட்டியா கோனபிமானதுங்கன்.

(5) *Andal*.—பொங்கிய பாற்கடற் பளளிக்கொள்வானேப் புணாவதோராசையினுல்; உன்னித்தெழுநத வெனதட முலைகள், மானிடவர்க்கென்று பேச்சுபபடில்வாழகில் லேன் கண்டாய் மன்மதனே; வாராணமாயிரம் &c

Quotations of this nature might be multiplied indefinitely. In our opinion some of the historical accounts given in the Periya-purana are comparatively more trustworthy, as the Saivas do not assign fabulous ages to their Nayanars. Most of the stories relating to the life of Tirumangai-Alvar,

THE VISHNUVITE SAINTS 299

especially the offer of treasure by Varadaraja and the making of arrangements by this Alvar for the recital of Nammalvar's Tiruvoymoli, are clear instances of gross anachronism.

The first Alvars.

It is a common belief among Tamil scholars that 'north' is the direction of prosperity (மங்கல திசை). We shall accordingly begin with the Pallava country, the northern-most kingdom of the Tamil people Another reason for this procedure is that it was from Tondai Nadu that social and religious reforms extended gradually to the other Tamil kingdoms.

In this country of the Pallavas were born the first three Alvars—Poigai, Pudam and Pey. Each of them was the author of an *antadi* or a centum of verses in the Venba metre in praise of Vishnu, the three poems forming a portion of that book of the Divya Prabandam entitled the Iyarpa. Their principal tenet was,

முதலாவார் மூவரம் மூவருள்ளும்
முதலாவாரமூ நீநீர் வண்ணன்.—*Poi.*

Hence the miraculous 'sports' and performances of Vishnu wrought during his incarnations as Vamana, Narasimha, Rama and Krishna form the main theme of their hymns.

The age of these Alvars is involved in hopeless obscurity. Traditions assert that all the three were contemporaries and that once upon a time they all met together at Tirukkovalur in the South Arcot district. But for this one incident the Guruparamparai gives no particulars regarding them. It is believed by some scholars that Poigai Alvar was no other than the author of Kalavazhi. If there was any truth in this supposition, the first three Saints must have lived during the reign of the Chola king Kocchengannan that is prior to the sixth century A.D. But the above hypothesis is not countenanced by other internal evidences. Of the two Poigaiyars one was a saint and the other a famous bard. The saint was no respecter of men as he has repeatedly said that,

(1) வாயவனே யல்லது வாழ்த்தாது ;
(2) பாடிலும்நின்புகழே பாடுவன் ;
(3) மாயவனே யல்லால், இறை யேறு மேத்தாதென்னா.

On the contrary the other Poigaiyar appears to have been a court poet under the Chera king Kodai Marpan and earned his livelihood by eulogizing the Tamil kings of the southern districts, in proof of which the reader may be referred to stanzas 48 and 49 in the Purananuru. Again the language of these two writers differs; and we have no faith in the vague statements of the old commentators regarding their identity. For these and the following reasons we are inclined to believe that the name Poigaiyar was borne by two different authors, who flourished at different periods.

The saints Poigai and Pey have celebrated the god of a place called Vinnagaram:

(1) வேங்கடமும் விண்ணகரும் வெஃகாவுமஃகா த
பூங்கிடங்கில் நீள்கோவல் பொன்னகரும்—நான்
இடத்தும் நின்றுனிருந்தான் இடந்தான் நடந்தான்
என்றுல்கெடுமாயிடர் —Poi. 77.

(2) விண்ணகரம வெஃகாவிரிதிரை நீர் வேங்கடம்
மண்ணகர மா மாடவேளுக்கை.—*Pey*. 62.

The word Vinnagaram is a corruption of Skt. *Vishnu Nagar* and it may mean any house of Vishnu. But from the manner in which it is used along with Vengadam, Vehka, Koval, Agaram and Velukkai in he above quotations, it must refer to a particular shrine in the Pallava country or Tondai Nadu. There is only one Vinnagaram in the whole of that country and that is in Conjeeveram. Further, Poigaiyar and Peyalvar were more or less local saints and their peregrinations were confined to Tondai-Nadu and to some of the most renowned shrines in the further south, namely, Srirangam and Kumbakonam in the Choladesam and Tirumalirum-solai and Tirukkottiyur in the Pandyamandalam. For these reasons we are disposed to identify the Vinnagar referred to by these Alvars with the Paramesvara Vinnagar of Tirumangaiyar's hymns. As it is explicitly staetd that the god of this place is in the sitting posture, it cannot refer to Tiru-Vinnagai (Uppiliyappan) another important shrine of the same name in the Tanjore district. According to Dr. Hultzsch the Paramesvara Vinnagaram[1] was built by the Pallava king Para-

1. Mr. S. Krishnasamy Aiyangar finds fault with Dr. Hultzsch for

mesvara Varma II (A D. 690). These three Alvars should, therefore, have flourished in the latter half of the seventh century A. D. It would be interesting to note here that the god on the Tirupati Hills (Tiruvengadam) had the appearance of both Siva and Vishnu in the days of Peyalvar.

Tirumalisai Alvar.

One of saints who is stated in the Guruparamparai to have lived in the Dvapara Yuga and to have had some acquaintance with the first three Alvars was Tirumalisaiyar. He was a native of the Pallava country; and his Tiru-chanda-viruttam and Nanmugan Tiruvandadi are admired for their harmonious versification He was a poet, philosopher and ascetic (yogi). His real name is said to have been Bhaktisara

the above statement He says that "this is not a necessary inference, as any other Pallava paramount sovereign might have had the title Pallava Paramesvara and the foundation when contracted might have become Paramesvara Vinnagaram, *c. g.*, Vidya Vinita Pallava Paramesvaram." *Ind Ant* for 1906, p. 229. We cannot quite understand what he means, as it is not explanatory of the point at issue. As a *title* the term Paramesvara like Maharaja is so vague that none of the Indian kings seem to have had it except as a proper name. There were Brahman settlements known by special titles of kings like Manabharana-chaturvedi-mangalam, Gangaikondan, Gunabharesvaram and Madhurantakam. In these cases we could say with certainty what kings had these titles, while it would be next to impossibility to hit upon a particular sovereign who had the title of 'Paramesvara' or 'Maharaja.' Compare the names of the following villages· Varaguna-mangai, Gandaradityam, Nandipuram Kulottunga Cholanallur, &c. In all these instances the villages were called after the names, not titles, of kings which we think was only a title and he is believed to have been the son of a Rishi named Bhargava, but brought up by a man of the hunting tribe. This latter statement is borne out by his own admission which occurs in the Tiru-chanda-viruttam:—

குலங்களாய வீரிரண்டி லொன்றிலும் பிறந்திலேன
நலங்களாய நற்கலைகள் நாலிலும் நவின்றிலேன்.

His writings, however, show that he should have acquired equal proficiency both in Sanskrit and Tamil and a competent knowledge of the sacred books of the other sects and religions. His mastery of the Ramayana, the Mahabharata and the Vishnupurana is displayed in both his poems. He was throughout his life a rancorous opponent to the Saivas, Jains and Buddhists, and a devout worshipper of Vishnu :—

(1) அறியார் சமணரயர்த்தார் பவுத்தர்
    இறியார் சிவப் பட்டார்.

(2) பேணிலும வரநதர மிடேக்கிலாத தேவரை
    ஆணமென்றடைந்து வாழு மாதர்காள்.

Tirumalisai Alvar was a monotheist as he himself admits that தேருங்கால் தேவதெருவனென்றுரைபபார், and preached that that one god was Vishnu while the other two of the triad—Brahma and Siva—were created by him :—

நான்முகனே நாராயணன் படைத்தான் நான்முகனும
தானமுகமாய்ச் சககரனேத்தான படைத்தான !

Further he was a pantheist and held that Vishnu is omnipresent and pervades the whole universe, as taught by the etymological signification of His name. He invokes Vishnu thus :—

(1) ஊனினமேயவாவினீ உறக்கமொடுணாச்சினீ
ஆனில்மேய வைந்துநீ அவற்றுணின்ற தாய்மைநீ
வானிடேறுடு மண்ணுநீ வளங்கடற் பயனுநீ
யானும்நீயதனநீ யெமபிரானுமநீ யிராமனே.

(2) நீயேயுலடுகல்லாம் நின்னருளே நிற்பனவம்
நீயேதவத்தேவ தேவனும்—நீயே
எரிசுடரும்மால் வரையுமெண்டிசையு மண்டத்
திருசுடருமாய விவை.

And yet this all powerful omnipresent Vishnu is neither visible to, nor cognisable by, man.

(1) ஒருத்தருமே நிஹுது தன்மை யின்னதென்ன வல்லரே !
(2) எங்கள் செங்கண்மாலே யாவர்காண வல்லரே ?

Then to whom is this God knowable and how are we to perceive Him ? Our Alvar says in reply :—

புன்புல வழியடைத்தரக்கிலச்சினே செய்து
நன்புலவழி திறந்து ஞானநற் சுடற்கொளீடு
என்பிலெள்கிடுநஞ் சுருகியுள்கனிந் தெழுந்ததோர
அன்பிலன்றியாழியானே யாவர்காண வல்லரே.

(Vishnu who wields the sacred disc will be cognisable only by those who, after having closed the narrow paths of the five senses and sealed their doors, opened the broadway of intelligence litting the lamp of wisdom and mellowing their bones with a heart melted by the intense heat of piety.)

As regards the date of this Alvar, there is no internal evidence in his writings to proceed upon with any degree of certainty. But from their general tenor it might be inferred that he should have lived at a period when the Jains, Buddhists and Saivas were fighting with one another for religious supremacy. This age, so far as it could be ascertained was the seventh century A D., when the great champions of the Saiva faith, Tirunavukkarasu and Sambandar, were busily engaged in the work of religious disput- ations. Moreover, there is a tradition, which as we have pointed above, connects him with the first three Alvars. It is said that during his pilgri- mage to Kumbakonam he stayed for some time at Chidambaram or Perumpuliyur. As he has not celebrated the Vishnu god of that famous stronghold of Sivaism, it is almost certain that in his days the shrine of Govinda Raja did not come into existence. Tirumangai Alvar informs us that this god was set up and worshipped by a Pallava king who may have, in all probability, been Nandivarma I or Peramesvara Varma II, A. D. 690. Tirumalisai Alvar should, there- fore, have lived at least half a century before Tiru- mangai Alvar, that is in the latter half of the seventh century. Again in the 93rd stanza of this *antadi* our Alvâr addresses Vishnu thus,

. . . . . ஆக்கை
கொடுத்தளித்த கோனே குணப்பரனே.

The expression 'குணப்பரன்' reminds us of the Pallava king Mahendra Varma I whose *birudu* or title was 'Gunabhara', and whose inscriptions are still to be seen on the rock at Trichinopoly. He was also the builder of the Siva temple called Gunabharesvaram. His date is said to be the early part of the seventh century A. D.[1] Being a stanch Vishnuvite, our Alvar it appears was also persecuted by a Pallava king, very likely the above Mahendra Varma I or Narasimha Varma II (A. D. 675) both of whom were devout followers of Siva and builders of several temples to that deity. Taking all these circumstances into our careful consideration we shall not be unreasonable if we assign the middle of the seventh century A. D. to our Alwar's active work. He should, therefore, have been a contemporary of the Saiva saints Tirunavukkarasu Nayanar and Sambandamurti Nayanar.

It is said in the Guruparamparai that he had entered into all the religions of his times before he became a Vishnuvite, and that when he was a Saivite he assumed the name of Sivavakkiyar. There is such a close resemblance in the metre and the harmonic flow of the poems of Sivavakkiyar and the Tiruchchanda Viruttam of our Alvar, as to make one believe that both the poems were composed by one and the same author. Further, some of the stanzas occurring in both are almost identical, and had the present Copyright Act been in force then, either of them should have been prosecuted under it.

---

1. This was the date of the Saiva saint Tirunavukkarasu Nayanar. It was during the reign of this Pallava that he, formerly a Jain, was converted to Sivaism by his beloved sister Tilakavati who was a Saiva devotee.

(Compare verses 1, 2, 3, 4, 17, 79 &c. in Tiruchchanda Viruttam with 308, 237, 266, 265, 264, 268 &c. in the poem of Sivavakkiyar). But Sivavakkiyar was a theist belonging to the Siddhar School and lived at least eight or nine centuries posterior to our saint. The style of Tirumalisaiyar is sublime and philosophic, while that of Sivavakkiyar is insipid and at times vulgar. The story given in the Guruparamparai connecting the saintly Tirumalisai Piran with the iconoclastic Sivavakkiyar must, therefore, be a later interpolation.

Tiruppanalvar.

We shall now take Tiruppanalvar and Tondaradippodi Alvar for consideration. First of them was born of a Panan family at Uraiyur, while the second was a Soliya Brahman of Tirumandangudi in the Tanjore district. The Panans were an inferior caste of minstrels frequently alluded to in the Purananuru, Padirruppattu and other works of the academic period. In the Census of 1891 Panan was returned as a sub-caste of Paraiya and was always considered very low in social scale. Like Nandan of the Saivites, Tiruppan Alvar was a devout worshipper of Vishnu Yet he was not permitted to enter the Vishnu temple at Srirangam, as he belonged to the lowest out-caste. There is a tradition to the effect that Ranganatha commanded one Lokasaranga, a sage, to bring him to his shrine on his shoulders. In consequence of this story our Alvar is known also as 'Muni Vahana.'

The above tradition proves the superiority of Bhakti, and emphasizes the fact that a Vishnu *bhakta* to whatever caste he might belong was worthy of greater honour and veneration than a Brahman well-versed in the four Vedas. The same idea is conveyed in the following lines of the Brahman saint Tondaradippodi Alvar :—

பழுதிலா வொழுகலாற்றுப் பலசதுப் பேதிமார்கள்
இழிகுலத் தவர்களேலு மெம்மடி யார்களாகில்
தொழுமினீர் கொடுமின் கொண்மின்.

His faith in the god Vishnu had taken so deep a root on his mind that he became intolerant of other sects. He expresses his hatred against other religions especially Buddhism and Jainism, thus :—

(1) புலையற மாகின்ற புதெதாடி சமணமெல்லாம்
கலையறக் கற்றமாநதர் காண்பரோ கேட்பரோ தான்
தலையறப புணடெஞ்சாவேன் சத்தியங் காண்மினேயா
சிலையிஞ விலஙகைகசெற்ற தேவனே தேவளுவான்.

(2) வெறுப்பொடு சமணர்முண்டர்விதியில சாககியர்கணின்பால்
பொறுபபரிய னகள்பேசில் போவதே கோவதாகி
குறிபடெனச கடையுமாகில் கூடுமேல் தலையையாஙகே
அறபபடதே கருமங்கண்டா யரஙகமா நகருளானே.

There is no data in the songs of these Alvars to determine their age. But we shall not be far from the mark if we put them towards the close of the eighth or the beginning of the ninth century A. D. It is, however, said that there are references to these Alvars in the Mukunda Mala of Kulasekhara Perumal.

The real name of Tondaradippodi was Vipra Narayana and he does not seem to have worshipped or ever uttered the name of any Vishnu deity other than Ranganatha of Srirangam. His Tirumalai and Tiruppalli Ezhucchi form part of the Nalayiraprabandam to which Tiruppan has contributed the decad named Amalan Adippiran

Kulasekhara Alvar.

The next Alvar in our list is Kulasekhara Perumal. He calls himself king of Kolli, Kudal (Madura), Kozhi (Uraiyur) and Kongu (கொல்லி காவலன், கூடல நாயகன், கோழிக்கோன்). It is not known at what period the four Tamil kingdoms Chera, Chola, Pandya and Kongu were under the sway of a single sovereign. But this much is certain according to the Kongu chronicle and inscriptions the Cholas became powerful once more in A. D. 890, when Vijayalaya and Aditya I not only regained their lost kingdom but also annexed to it the Kongu country (Salem and Coimbatore districts) Kulasekhara has celebrated the Vishnu god of Chidambaram and refers to the shrine at Tiruvali (ஆவினகாகத்திபதிே, viii. 7). We have stated before that the Vishnu shrine at Chidambaram should have come into existence in the latter half of the seventh century; and the temple at Tiruvali was probably one of those built by Tirumangai Alvar in his own Nadu. From Keralolpatti, a work of extremely doubtful authority, we learn that

Kulasekhara was one of the successors of Cheraman Perumal who died about A. D. 825.

Again the same traditional history of the Kerala country says that Kulasekhara Perumal organized the kingdom into small chieftainships to protect it against the Mappillas and that after a reign of eighteen years he went to heaven with his body. Kulasekhara Alvar must, therefore, have lived between A. D. 780 and 890. But in accepting this date there arises one difficulty, that is, our Alvar calls himself Kudal Nayakan or the Lord of Madura. At this period the Pandyas were powerful as will be seen from the Chinnamanur grants. The only reconciliation for this discrepancy would be that Kulasekhara was a scion of the Pandya family who inherited the Kerala throne under the *marumakkatayam* system He was known in the Chera country as Pandya Kulasekhara Perumal.

Kulasekhara had equal proficiency in Tamil and Sanskrit. He was the author of Mukunda Malai in Sanskrit and 105 stanzas in Tamil which form part of the Nalayiraprabandam. His Tamil hymns on Tirupati and Srirangam are exceedingly pathetic like the Tiruvachakam of Manikkavachagar and can melt even sceptic minds ; while his Mukunda Malai is equally so. The similes employed by him in the Vittuvakkodu hymn are quite appropriate and convincing. Like the previous saints he was also an uncompromising opponent to other sects. We give below three stanzas from his poems as specimen :—

(1) மெய்யில் வாழ்க்கையை மெய்யெனக் கொள்ளுகிவ்
வையந்தனே ஏடும கூடுவ தில்லையான்
ஐயனே யாங்கேவா வென்றழைக் கின்றேன்
மையல்கொண் டொழிந்தே னென்றன் மாலுக்கே

(2) பிறையேறு சடையானும பிரமனு மிந்திரனும்
முறையாய பெருவேள்விக் குறைமுடிப்பான மறையா
வெறியாாதண் சோலைத்திருவேங் கடமேலமேல் [னென்
நெறியாய்க் கிடக்கும் நிலபுடையேளுவேனே

(3) வாளா லறுத்துச சுடினு மருத்துவன்பால்
மாளாத காதல் நோயாளன்போல் மாயத்தால்
மீளாத் தயாதரிலும் வித்துவக்கோட் டம்மாநீ
ஆளா வனதருேே பார்ப்ப னடியேனே.

Tirumangai Alvar.

The third Alvar of the Chola country was Kaliyan or Tirumangai Mannan. He was the foremost of all the Vaishnava saints and has left behind the greatest number of hymns on Vishnu shrines. Further, there are sufficient materials in his writings to work out his date with greater certainty, and to arrive at the conclusion that he was one of the most learned of all Alvars. His life and work should, therefore, be given here with fuller details.

Tirumangai Alvar was born of a Kalla family at Tirukkurayalur in the Tanjore district. His parents named him Kaliyan or Kalikanri. It appears that he held the office of generalissimo under the Chola kings and that he was the feudal chieftain of a small district or a group of villages called Ali Nadu in the north-eastern part of the Chola country. His headquarters appear to have been Tirumangai, and from the way in which he speaks of this place (நிண்ணூர் மாடங்கள் சூழ்திருமங்கை) it must have been an important town in his days, though it could not be identified with any of the existing villages in the Shiyali taluk. He married the daughter of a certain Vishnu *bhakta* who belonged to the Vaidya class, a caste much superior to his own. By her initiation and preaching Kaliyan became a stanch worshipper of Vishnu.

Excepting Tirumalisaiyar and Satagopan he was undoubtedly the most learned of all the Vaishnava saints. His contributions to the Nalayiraprabandam amount to 1361 stanzas and consist of six separate poems, namely, (1) பெரியதிருமொழி, (2) திருக்குறுந்தாண்டகம், (3) திருநெடுந் தாண்டகம், (4) சிறியதிருமடல், (5) பெரிய திருமடல் and (6) திருவெழுகூற்றிருக்கை. Even in his own life time he should have been admitted as a famous poet, successful controversialist and great donor of charities, as will be seen from the following quotation —

அங்கமலத்தடவயல் சூழாவிநாடன
  அருண்மாரியரட்டமுக்கியடையார் சீயம
கொங்குமலர்க்குழலியர் வேள்மங்கைவேந்தன்
  கொற்றவேற்பாரகாலன் கலியன் சொனன
சங்கமுகத்தமிழ்மாலே . . .

At a poetical contest he was given the title of நாற் கவிப்பெருமாள் or the 'Master of the four kinds of poetry', and as to the excellence of his works Kurattalvar speaks thus : தமிழ் நன்னூல் துறைகள் அஞ்சுக் கிலக்கியம் பாகாலன் பணுவலகளே

In his later days he resigned his office, perhaps on account of some misunderstanding between him and the Chola king, and set out on a tour of pilgrimage from the Himalayas to Cape Comorin. For the diffusion of Vishnuism he toiled much and he is even said to have had religious disputations at Shiyali with Trignansambandar, the greatest of the Saiva Nayanars. Some sort of similarity which we observe in the style and composition of Tirumangai Alvar and his Saiva rival seems to countenance the above supposition. Being a man of considerable wealth and influence, Kaliyan visited all the Vishnu temples of his time and sang hymns in praise of the Vishnu gods. Thus out of the 108 Vishnu temples approved as holy by Acharyas he left only twenty unvisited ; and these twenty shrines—including Srivilliputtur and Alvar Tirunagari (Kurugur)—were visited, a century or two afterwards, by one or the other of the two later Alvars Vishnu Chittan and Satagopan. We shall revert to this question when we come to speak of these saints.

The above fact proves beyond dispute that these twenty temples, with the exception of Padma nabha at Trivandram, did not come into existence at the time of Tirumangai Alvar. Nevertheless, Mr. S. Krishnaswamy Aiyangar considers the celebration by Kaliyan of most of the Vaishnava temples, as a proof of the comparative lateness of this saint's existence. In spite of our regard to his sagacity, we must say with greater assurance that he is far from being correct in this view. The paucity of temples celebrated by these Alvars does not prove the antiquity of the one or the modernity of the other. According to his theory Tondaradippodi Alvar should have been the earliest, because he visited only one temple; and the order of precedence would be like this: Tondaradippodi, Tiruppan, Poigai, Kulasekhara, Andal, Putam, Pey, Periyalvar, Tirumalisai, Nammalvar and Tirumangai Alvar; surely it is neither the traditional nor chronological order.

In those days of difficult communication, of constant wars between the Tamil kings and their feudatories, and of the fear of robbers and dacoits on the forest-clad highways and foot-paths, the circumstances which could have afforded facilities to a pilgrim in visiting a larger number of temples, were wealth, retinue and chiefly one's religious proclivities. Tirumangai Alvar had all these, as he was the ruler of a small but fertile province or *nadu* besides being a robber chieftain; he had plenty of money and a good many followers to cater for him in his peregrinations. The other Alvars, probably with the exception of Kulasekhara, had none of these accessories, and they were more or less local saints. Tirumalisai and Nammalvar were *yogis* and did not care to visit all the Vishnu temples of their days. The former did not mention at all

Tirumalirumsolai, when his contemporaries and predecessors have praised it ; Tirumangai Alvar did not visit Trivandram the god of which place is alluded to in Padirruppattu ; and Nammalvar has not sung Tirrukkottiyur, Tirukkovalur, and Tiruvehka which were celebrated by the earliest Alvars. Are we then to infer from this that the above shrines were not in existence at the time of these saints? Certainly not. The theory of Mr. S. Krishnaswamy Aiyangar that 'he (Tirumangai Alvar) was the latest of the saints is amply borne out by the fact that he celebrates most, if not all, of the well-known temples to Vishnu in India while others celebrate only a few,'[1] is therefore evidently absurd as it is not supported by actual facts.

Tirumangai Alvar expended large sums in building the third *prakara* or wall at Srirangam, which has been known to this day as Tirumangai Mannan Tirumadil or 'the sacred wall of Tirumangai Alvar', while the inner two are those erected by Dharmavarma and Mahendra Varma, the latter of whom was a Pallava king who is believed to have ruled over the Chola country also. To secure funds for this sacred work our Alvar is said to have demolished a golden image of Buddha at Negapatam which was in his days a deserted seat of Buddhism. Like his predecessor Tirumalisai Piran our Alvar was a bitter opponent to the Saivas, Jains and Buddhists as the following quotations will show :—

1. *Ind. Ant.* for 1906, p. 229.

(1) பிண்டியாா மண்டையேந்தி பிறாமணே திரிதந்துண்ணும் உண்டியான் சாபந்தீர்த்த வொருவனூர்; (2) வெளளியார் பிண்டியார் போதியாரென்றிவரோதகினற, கள்ளநூல்; (3) புந்தி யில சமணர் புததா;

He taught that Vishnu alone was God, that He created Brahma, Siva and all other gods, that He is self-existent, that He assumed three different forms of Brahma, Vishnu and Siva, and that He pervades the whole Universe :—

(1) இநதுவார் சடையீசனேப்பயந்த நான்முகனேத் தன்னெழி
[லாரும்
உந்திமாமலர் மீமிசைபபடைத்தவன...

(2) தன்னுளே தன்னுருவம் பயந்த தாளுயத்
தயங்கொளிசோ மூவுலகுந்தாளுய் வாளுய்
தன்னுளே தன்னுருவில் மூர்த்திமூன்றுய்த்
தாளுயளுயிளுன்சரணென்றுய்வீர்.

And to realize this God one should be righteous, should subdue his five senses and fix his mind on Him with love and devotion. *Bhakti* is the only indispensable passport to attain salvation; and one need not waste his energy in austere penances and self-mortification. Thus, as a commentator has rightly observed, Tirumangai Alvar was one of those devotees who suffered their souls to endure the heat of the sun and their bodies to enjoy the coolness of shade.

To understand aright the spirit and teaching of his poems, a thorough knowledge of the adventures of Krishna and Rama and of the stories concerning the earlier incarnations of Vishnu as narrated in the

Puranas and the two great epics, is expected of every reader.

Now coming to the age of this Alvar, we have ample references to the Pallava and the Chola kings and to the political events of their times. In his hymn on the god of Paramesvara Vinnagaram our Alvar mentions that one Pallava king, Pallava Mallan, defeated the Pandyas, தென்னவனை, fought a battle at Mannai and another at Nenmeli, நென்மெலி We have said above that the Vishnu shrine called Paramesvara Vinnagaram was built by Parameswara Varma II (A. D 690). Further we gather from the Udayendram and Kasakudi copper plates published in the *South Indian Inscriptions*, Vol. II, part 3, that the battles at Nenmeli and Mannaikudi were fought by the Pallava king Nandivarman (A. D. 720—760). One of them informs us that he was a devout worshipper of Vishnu. ' Nandivarman who worships the feet of Hari, who split (the head of) the opposing Sabara king, called Udayana in the terrible battle of Nelveli, who destroyed Kalidurga which was protected by the goddess Kali, and defeated the Pandya army at the village of Mannaikudi.' Again in another hymn on the god of Ashtabujam at Conjeevaram our Alvar refers to a king named Vajra Meghan to whom the Pallava king did homage—தொண்டையர் கோன் வணங்கு நீண்முடிமாலேவயிர மேகன். This was one of the titles (*birudu*) of Dantidurga or Dantivarma II, a Rashtrakuta king of Malkhed A.D. 755[1]; and

[1] *Ind Ant* xii, p. 17

he is said to have 'completed the acquisition of sovereignty by subjugating the Lord of Kanchi.'[1]

Again our Alvar has a hymn on the god of Nandipura Vinnagaram. This temple must have been built by the same Nandi Varma, as among the South Indian kings hitherto brought to light there appears to have been before the time of Kaliyan only one sovereign of that name. Other references to Pallava and Chola kings are :—

(1) பைம்பொன்னும் முத்ததும் மணியுங்கொணாநது
படைமன்னவன் பல்லவா கோன்பண்ந்த ...
தில்லேததிருச்சித்திரகூடம்.

(2) தளங்கு நீண்முடியரசர் தவகுரிசில்
தொாண்டை மன்னவன திண்டிற லொருவற்கு
உளங் கொளன் பிஜேடினனருள் சுரங
தங்கொடி நாழிகை எழுடனிருப்ப
வளங்கொள் மங்கிரம மற்றவர்க்கருளி...

(3) இருககிலங்கு திருமொழிவாயெண தோளீசறகு
எழில்மாடமெழுபது செய்துலகமாண்ட ...
செங்கணுன் கோசசோழன் சேர்ந்தகோயில.

It has been said in a previous section that at the time of Tirumalisai Alvar there was no shrine to Vishnu at Chidambaram. The Pallava king referred to in (1) should, therefore, have been either Mahendra Varma II or Paramesvara Varma II both of whom were worshippers of Vishnu and donors of great charities; the first of them, Mahendra Varma II, is said to have done meritorious acts for the benefit of

1 *Bombay Gaz.* Vol I, part 2, p. 389

temples and Brahmans, and the second was the builder of Vinnagaram at Conjeevaram. And the king alluded to in (2) should have been Mahendra Varma II (A. D. 650) as he is stated to have built the second *prakara* or wall at Srirangam Lastly, the Chola king referred to in (3) was Ko-Chengannan who has been canonized as a Saint by the Saivites, and described as Kocchengatchola Nayanar in the Periyapuranam. The Saiva saint Tirugnanasambanda also refers to this king. Like his distant successor Parantaka 1 (Vira Narayana Chola of the Kongu chronicle) he may have been an ardent worshipper of Vishnu in his early days and afterwards changed his faith to Sivaism, as the apostles of both sects praise him in their works. In a previous chapter (*Vide*, p. 250) the date of this Kocchengannan has been tentatively fixed as 580 A. D.

In his Siriya Tirumadal our Alvar speaks of one Vasavadatta. This suggests that he may have been acquainted with the Sanskrit play of that name written by Subandhu about the beginning of the seventh century, which must be taken as the earliest limit of his date. Again, he has a hymn on the god of Tirumokur in the Madura district. Two miles near it and at the foot of the Yanaimalai there is another Vishnu temple, which as the following inscription will show, was built by a Pandya minister in A. D. 770 and endowed with a rich *agrahara* for its maintenance. 'Pre-eminently charming in manners a resident of Karavandapuram the son of Maran and a learned and illustrious member of the Vaidya family, Madhurakavi made this stone temple of Vishnu. The same Madhurakavi the wise minister of the Pandya named Parantaka also gave away to the first born (Brahmans) this immensely rich *agraharam*. When 3871 years of Kali had passed on the day of the sun in the month of Kartigai this image of the god was duly set up there'. Had this temple been in existence in our Alvar's time he must surely have visited it. As there are no hymns on this god when he has sung the deity at Tirumokur, it is almost certain that our Alvar must have visited this part of the Pandya country sometime before A D. 770.

Taking all these facts into our careful consideration we cannot help concluding that Tirumangai Alvar must have flourished between A. D. 680 and 760.

Periyalvar.

Let us now pass on to the Vaishnava Saints of the Pandya country. Periyalvar or Vishnu Chittan was a Brahman of Srivilliputtur. He calls himself புதுவை மன் and புத்தூர்க்கோன்; here மன் and கோன் mean simply an influential man; and in our Alvar's time Srivilliputtur was a newly created Brahman settlement. At the instance of Selva Nambi of Tirukkottiyur (a Purohit of the Pandya king), a conference of theologians was held at Madura And in the religious controversy which took place there, Periyalvar is said to have come out successful and established Vishnuism in his part of the Tamil country. His contributions, mostly descriptive of the life of Sri Krishna, numbering about 416 stanzas form part of the Nalayira-prabandam. His style is modern and contains a large admixture of colloquial and provincial words and many Sanskrit *tadbavas*. He has not said one word against the Jains or Buddhists, probably because by that time these two religions had almost died out in the Pandya country. Nor did he use any unpleasant words against the Saivas, a fact which proves that it had already established itself firmly in the Tamil country and that the two rival sectarians had been reconciled. The only harsh sentiments he gives vent to against the Saivas and which also explain his religious views are :—

(1) நீறேறு செஞ்சடை நீலகண்டனும் நான்முகனு முறையால், சீறேறு வாசகஞ்செய்ய நின்ற திருமால்; (2) எருத்துக்கொடி யுடையானும் பிரமனும்இந்திரனு மற்றும், ஒருத்தரு மிப்பிறவி யென்னும் நோய்க்கு மருந்தறிவாருமில்லே.

To determine the age of this Saint there are no clear references in his works. But the following extracts combined with the tradition that he lived at the time of the Pandya king Sri Vallabhadeva must throw some light on his date :—

  (1) கொங்குங் குடந்தையும்—II, vi, 2.
  (2) நெடுமாறன கூடற்கோன்.—IV, ii, 7.
  (3) கோட்டியர்கோன் அபிமானதுங்கன்.—IV, iv, 8.
  (4) பருப்பதத்துக் கயல்பொறித்த பாண்டியர்.—IV, iv, 7.

The Vaishnava commentator Periyavacchan Pillai explains கொகுகுங்குடகுடகதை as Kudandai (Kumbakonam) which belonged to or was in the Kongu country. In a former section we have said that Aditya I conquered and annexed Kongu in or about 890 A. D. We learn further from other sources that Kumbakonam was a temporary capital of that newly conquered country from which the Chola prince or the Yuva Raja ruled the new province. The second quotation informs us that the Pandya king was Nedu Maran, while the third tells us that his *purohit* or spiritual teacher was a pious Vaishnava Brahman who bore the title of Abhimana Tungan. (It was one of the customs of those days to give the titles of a king to his favourite ministers and *purohits*. Manikka Vachagar had the title of தென்னவன் பிரம்மராயன், Sekkilar was called உத்தம சோழப்பல்லவராயன்.) The word Maravarman is no doubt a title borne by all kings of the Pandya dynasty; but this when combined with the name Sri Vallabhadeva and the eponym Abhimana Meru, does certainly refer to a particular Pandya king. From the Chinnamanur plates referred to above we are given to understand that Raja Simha II had the title of Abhimana Meru Mara Varman, that he was a grandson of Maravarman Sri Vallabha Deva, and that he was killed by Parantaka Chola in A. D. 910. Among the well-known temples of the Pandya country Srivilliputtur is one that was not visited by Tirumangai Alvar ; and when the god of Tiruttangal, a village some eight or nine miles distant from our Alvar's birth-place, has been celebrated by Kaliyan, he has omitted this important shrine. Taking into account all these facts we are inclined to believe that Srivilliputtur or the 'new village of Villi' should have come into existence only after A. D. 750, and that our Vishnu Chittan or Periyalvar should have flourished between A. D. 840 and 915 ; that is, he might have been a younger contemporary of Kulasekhara Perumal. It is worthy of note that this Alvar who is said to have carried the prize (இழி) in a religious contest held at Madura, has not celebrated Kudal Alagar of that city, though it has been referred to in one of the hymns of Tirumangai Alvar. We know that Madura has always been a stronghold of Sivaism, and it is quite possible that this Vaishnava temple was closed temporarily by the bigotted Saivites of that city.

On the authority of certain expressions like பரமவைஷ்ணவனாகுளகி &c. which occur in the Madras Museum plates of Jatila Varman, the Editor of 'Sen Tamil' is inclined to put the date of Vishnu Chittan before A.D. 770, making him a contemporary of Jatila Varman or Parantaka I of the Yanamalai inscriptions. If this was so our Alvar should have been as well a contemporary of Tirumangai Mannan and a predecessor of Kulasekara and Nammalvar. But this was not the case for the reasons that are given in the sections dealing with the above saints.

One of the Vaishnava saints was a lady named Kodai. She is also called Andal, and believed to have been the daughter of Periyalvar, பெரியாழ்வார்

பெற்றெடுத்த பெண்பிள்ளை, while others think that she was a foundling, but brought up by the saint Vishnu Chittan. Her contributions to the Nalayiraprabandam consist of 173 stanzas ; of these the Tiruppavai has been considered to be her finest poem. She was no doubt an ardent worshipper of Vishnu and all her poems are an exposition of Sri Krishna's stories. It appears that she remained a virgin throughout her short life and spent her days in ministering to the deities at Srirangam and Tirumalirumsolai.

In her Varanamayiram she describes the dreams of her marriage with Vishnu, and this song is now being recited at all Vaishnava Brahman marriages. It must be remembered that her poems, which may have been largely influenced by the work of a contemporary—the *Tirukkovaiyar* of Manikka Vachakar—have an esoteric significance. The marriage described by her was the union of the *atman* with *Paramatman* or God and final absorption in the God-head. The devotion and attachment of the modern Vaishnavas to Andal is so great that the worship of the local deity adored by her at Srivilliputtur has been eclipsed. All the important festivals at this place are celebrated chiefly in honour of this lady Saint.

Nammalavar.

Conspicuous among the Vaishnava Saints was Nammalvar or Satagopan. He has been regarded as an incarnation of Senai Mudaliyar, the mythological commander and foremost devotee of Vishnu. His life and writings deserve, therefore, to be considered at some length

He was born of a Vellala family at Tirukkurukur or 'Alvar-Tirunagari in the district of Tinnevelly, to one Kari of that place and Udaiya Nangai of Tiruvanparisaram in the Chera country. His parents gave him the name of Maran ; and Satagopan was the Sanskrit title probably given to him by his spiritual *Guru*. Moreover, it was customary, as now, to have two names—one Tamil and the other Sanskrit. His Tiruvoymoli, Tiruvasiriam, Tiruviruttam and Tiruvandadi, all of which written with a definite purpose on a pre-conceived plan in the *antadi* form and amounting to 1296 stanzas, are included in the Nalayiraprabandam. His songs or hymns relate to the deities of some thirty places, of which twenty-four are in the Pandya and the Chera kingdoms. He was an ascetic or *yogi* and would seem to have retired from the world in his 35th year to perform Yoga or meditation under a tamarind tree, which exists to this day in Alvar-Tirunagari. Ultimately he is said to have attained eternal bliss or beatitude, about which he himself says :—

அவாவறச்சூழரியையையனாயானா யலற்றி
அவாவறது வீடுபெற்ற குருகூர்ச் சடகோபன.

He had two disciples—Sri Nathamuni and Madhurakavi—to whom he taught his Tiruvoymoli and other *prabandams*. The first heads the list of the Vaishnava Acharyas while the second has been elevated to the rank of a Saint.

Like all other *alvars* Satagopan was a Vishnuvite of the Visishtadvaitic School of Vedanta. He believed that Vishnu alone could offer *Moksha* to His worshippers, that He is uncreated, that He is omnipresent and that Brahma and Siva are only His other forms or manifestations assumed for the sake of conducting different offices. He proves the existence of God by means of arguments, teleological and metaphysical, in the fashion of Descartes and Spinoza, and gives us a clear description of His relationship with the world in his first two *padigams*, and of the means of approaching Him in the third. About the nature and attributes of God he says

(1) ஆணல்லன் பெண்ணல்லனல்லா வலியுமல்லன்
காணலுமாகாணு எனல்லனிவ உயல்லன
பேணுநகால் பேணுமுருவாகு மல்லனுமாம்
கோணே பெரிதடைத்த வெமபெருமானேக் கூடிதலே

(2) நீராய் நிலனுய்த் தீயாய்க் காலாய் நெடுவானுய்
சீரார் சுடாகளிரணடாய் ச்சிவனுயபணுய்

(3) யாவையும யவரும் தானே யவரவாசமையந்தோறம்மூர்த்தி
தோய்விலன புலனேந்துக்கும் சொலப்படானுணர்வில்
ஆவிச்செருயிச்னுள்ளா லாவது மோர்பற்றிலாத
பாவனேயதனேக்கூடி லவனேயும் கூடலாமே.

His idea of fruition or communion with God is explained in the following stanza :—

நன்றுப் ஞானங்கடந்துபோய் நல்லி நதிரியெமெல்லா மீர்த்து, ஒன்றுய்க் கிடந்த வரும் பெரும் மாமூலபடி லதனேயுணர்க் துணர்ந்து, சென்றுங்கின பதன்பங்கள் செறறுக்கனேந்து பசையறறுல், அனதே யப்போதே வீடதுவே வீடு வீடாமே.

THE VISHNUVITE SAINTS

He did not recognise caste distinctions and held that divine knowledge alone could make a man high or low in the social scale :—

குலந்தாங்கு சாதிகள் நாலிலும் கீழிழிந்து எத்த‌ணை
நலந்தா னிலாத சண்டாள சண்டாளர் களாகிலும்
வலந்தாங்கு சக்கர த்தண்ணல் மணிவண்ணற்கு ஆளென்றுள்
கலந்தார் அடியார் தமடியா ரெம்மடிகளே

The question of the age of this Saint is very much disputed. Diverse opinions are current. The Vaishnava *Acharyas* take him to the beginning of the Kaliyug or B. C. 3102 and attempt to bridge over the wide gulf of time between him and his disciple Nathamuni (tenth century A. D.) by asserting that the Alvar was his teacher in his *archavatar* or 'the *idolic* incarnation'; while some of the English, educated Vaishnavas would ascribe to him the opening years of the Christian era as his probable age. As we have in the writings of Tirumangai Alvar there are no allusions to any king or political events in the works of Nammalvar to determine his date. There are, however, several other indications to prove that he flourished about the beginning of the tenth century A. D, and that he was the last of the Vaishnava Saints. We shall briefly give them below and leave the reader to judge for himself whether the above conclusions are logical or otherwise

(1) The Tamil language of Nammalvar differs from the Tamil of the poets of the Sangam or academic period. Our *Alvar* makes a free use of Sanskrit words and phrases like திருமி, வாசகம், சன்மம், உப

காரம், கதி, மூடம், சோதி, வேதனே, சண்டாளன், அரவிந்த லோசனன், மாதா பிதவு, மதுரோடோகம், இந்திரஜாலம், மாக வைகுந்தம்; while none of these will be discovered in the early Tamil writings. The use of plurals in கள் and double plurals in னகள் as in காண்கின்றனகள் and of the present tense in கிறு as in கேட்கிறுன் is comparatively modern. With regard to the use of கிறு as a particle of present tense, the learned commentator Nacchinarkiniyar observes thus உண்கிறெனெனக்கிறு எனபது நிகழ்காவ முணர்த்தல இக்கால வழக்கு (*Tol.* II, 204). These were never used by the early Tamil authors anterior to the seventh century A. D.

Philological variations of the above nature in a living language like Tamil afford us the crucial test to determine the respective ages of literary works of different periods ; and yet, this test has often been completely ignored not only by Tamil *pandits*, but also by the early commentators of Tamil classics.

(2) At the time of our Alvar most of the Puranas had already come into existence and when he speaks of the Saivas, he refers to Linga-Purana by name (IV x. 5). It is only the Puranas that contain rules for the worship of gods by means of prayers, offerings, and festivals. Nammalvar refers to some of these observances in the following lines:—

ஞானவிதிபிழையாமே
பூவில் புகைபும் விளக்கும் சாநதமுயீரும்மலிந்து
மேவித்தொழு மடியாரும் பகவரு மிக்கதுலகே.

The above quotation distinctly proves that the observance of *puranic* rites had been in its full swing, and that a large number of temples to Vishnu and other deities had already come into existence before the days of Nammalvar.

(3) The chewing of betel-leaf [1] was almost unknown to the Hindu populace prior to A. D. 500 ; because, as one writer, observes its use is not mentioned by any author before the sixth century A. D. Our Alvar speaks of வெற்றிலை a more modern form of வெள் ளிலை [2] which we find in the inscriptions of the ninth and tenth centuries A. D. The author of Silappadikaram (second century A.D) does, however, refer to its use thus,—

அம்மென்நிறைய லோடடைக்காயீந்து.

But we doubt whether the custom had been so universal in the days of Ilango-adikal, as it was in our Alvar's time.

(4) It seems that at the time of our Alvar the struggle between the Vaishnava and Saiva sects on the one hand, and Jainism and Buddhism on the other had come to an end, that Brahmanism —Siva and Vishnu cults—had come out triumphant at least in the extreme south, and that a sort of reconciliation had been effected among the Saivas and Vaishnavas. While Tirumalisai, Tirumangai and Tondaradippodi Alvars speak very vehemently and pour forth their invectives against the non-Vaishnava

---

1. *F. R. A. S.* for 1908, p. 910.
2. இஃயமிஃது வெளளிஃஈரடுக்கு அடைக்காய்பத்து நாஃஒருசெவிட்டு.—*Epig. Ind.* Vol, IX, p. 90

sects and religions, Nammalvar only casually mentions in one place the Jains and Buddhists, besides Brahma and Siva as only other manifestations of Vishnu. A comparison of the following quotations from Nammalvar's works with those cited in the previous sections will clearly prove that Jainism and Buddhism had already died out in the Tamil country and that Saivas and Vaishnavas had come to regard each other as brethern :—

(1) இவ்விகைத்திட்ட புராணத்தீரும் சமணரும் சாக்கியரும் வலிந்து வாதுசெய்வீர்களும் மற்றுநுந் தெயவமு மாகி நின்றுன் ; (2) கடிகமழ் கொன்றைச் சடையனேயென்னும் நான்முகக் கடவுளேயென்னும், வடிவுடை வானேர் தலைவனேயென்னும் வண்திரு வரங்கனேயென்னும் ; (3) அங்குயர் முக்கட்பிரான் பிரமபெருமானவன் நீ ; (4) மாகத்திளமதியஞ் சேருஞ் சடையானைப், பாகத்து வைத்தான்தன் பாதம் பணிந்தேனே.

(5) It has been said before that Tirumangai Alvar visited all the Vaishnava temples of his time. Those shrines that are not sung by him are celebrated by Nammalvar, the most important of which being (a) Tirukkurugur, (b) Varaguna Mangai and (c) Sri varamangalam. If the traditional story of the orthodox Vaishnavas that Tirumangai Alvar made arrangements for the recital of Tiruvoymoli at Srirangam be true, he must surely have visited the birth-place of a great Saint honoured and worshipped by him, and sung hymns in praise of the god of that village. But we see nothing of this in his work. Again, Varaguna Mangai or Varaguna Mangalam is a village named after the Pandya king Varaguna. So far as

the epigraphical researches have disclosed, there were only two kings of that name, and the earlier of whom reigned about A.D. 820 Further, Srivaramangalam or Vanamamalai, wherein there have been from time immemorial an important Vishnu temple and a Vaishnava Mutt, came into existence in the reign of the Pandya king Ko-Maran-Sadaiyan (A.D. 880) under the circumstances set forth in the following extract from a copper plate grant of that king. ' While the seventeenth year of the reign of Nedum Sadaiyan,...the most devoted follower of Vishnu, was current...he gave with libations of water the village of Velangudi in Tenkalavalinadu, having cancelled its former name from old times and having bestowed on it the new name of Srivaramangalam to Sujjata Bhatta'... From the description of the boundaries given in the plates it is clear that the shrine and the famous Mutt should have been built towards the end of the ninth century A. D. This village is only a short distance from Tirukkurungudi another well-known shrine where Tirumangai Alvar spent the remaining years of his life. Yet, he has not said one word about this important temple anywhere in his hymns.

(6) Sri Villiputtur which is one of the famous shrines of modern times in the Tinnevelly district was not visited either by Tirumangai Alvar, because it was not in existence in his days, or by Nammalvar, as it did not come into prominence or was not known to the Vaishnavas outside the village. Peri-

yalvar should therefore have been an elder contemporary of Satagopan though unknown to each other.

(7) The Dravidian tune or *pan* (பண்) is invariably prefixed to all the *padigams* (decads) of Nammalvar while in the case of the works of other Saints, especially of Tirumangai Alvar, it has been found wanting. Probably the names of tunes assigned to these *padigams* must have been lost during the course of the long period that had elapsed before their collection and compilation by Sri Nathamuni. Had Tirumangai Alvar flourished three or four centuries later than Satagopan, as the Vaishnava biographers allege the *pans* of Tirumangai Alvar's hymns should have been preserved *a fortiori* with greater easiness. But the fact was otherwise. We cannot understand why these *pans* of Tirmangai Alvar were lost while those of his Saiva contemporaries and predecessors, Appar and Sambandar, were handed down to posterity. Perhaps the Aryan Vaishnavas had not cared so much for the preservation of the sacred writings of the Dravidian Saints before the days of Nammalvar and perhaps in imitation of the Saivas, the Vaishnava Acharyas may have got into their head the idea of collecting the works of Alvars and compiling them into one sacred volume, probably subsequent to the laborious undertaking of Nambiyandar Nambi of the Saiva sect.

(8) From the Elephant Rock inscriptions quoted above we see that the builder of the Vishnu temple was one Kari or Madhurakavi, a son of Maran and

a minister of the Pandya king. We learn further from the Guruparamparai that the name of Nammalvar was Maran, that he was a saint from his childhood, that he was the son of one Kari a Vellala by caste and that one of his disciples was Madhurakavi, a Brahman of Tirukkolur in the Tinnevelly district. Obviously, confounding the names Kari, Maran and Madhurakavi, which occur in the inscriptions as well as in the Vaishnava biography, a recent writer in the *Indian Antiquary* jumps, like Fluellen, to the conclusion that Kari or Madhurakavi was the son of Nammalvar or Maran and that both of them were contemporaries of Tirumangai Alvar. According to this perverted view Nammalvar should have lived prior to A.D. 770. We cannot understand how the Koil-olugu, on which the reviewer relies so much for his data, is more trustworthy than the Guruparamparai. The latter work unmistakably asserts that Madhurakavi Alvar was a Brahman and that Nammalvar was a celibate saint. Evidently this writer does not seem to have read either the Guruparamparai, or the works of Nammalvar, or even Mr. V. Venkayya's notes on the Triplicane Inscriptions of Dantivarman in the *Ep. Ind.* Vol. VIII. p. 290.

Nammalvar has one hymn on the god of Tirumokur and four or five on the famous shrine at Tirumalirum-Solai; but he has left none on the Vishnu deity at the foot of the Yanai Malai or the Elephant Rock which lies between these two places. Our Alwar must therefore have lived either before or long after A. D. 770 ; but the impossibility of the first has been proved in the previous pages.

The rich Agrahara referred to in the inscription should have been deserted and the shrine itself almost neglected at the time of Nammalvar, as it now is, owing to the ominous death of the builder of the temple before its completion and the unproductive rocky soil of the surrounding country. It is evident that a sufficiently long period, say at least one century and a half, should have elapsed between its creation and total abandonment; that is this shrine and *Agrahara* should have fallen into ruins only some time before A. D. 900 And this must have been the period of our Alvar's existence.

(9) The most important argument in favour of our theory that Satagopan was the last of all the Vaishnava Saints is furnished by the age of Nathamuni, one of his two esteemed disciples. Traditions relating to his life are conflicting and even scholars do not agree on this point. Mr. S. Krishnaswamy Aiyangar seems to believe the statement of the orthodox Vaishnavas that Nathamuni was born in A.D. 582 and died in A.D. 922. He goes on to say that ' it would certainly be in keeping with the most cherished tradition of the Vaishnavas that arrangement made by the Alvar (Tirumangai Alvar, A. D. 750) for the recital of Tiruvoymoli of Nammalvar had fallen into desuetude in the days of Nathamuni and he had to revive it at Srirangam after much ado' [1]. And, Mr. T. Rajagopa-

---

[1] *Ind. Ant.* 1906, p. 232

lachariar says 'that the sage was born somewhere in the first quarter of the ninth century and lived just over a hundred years' [1].

We shall now examine these statements. Guruparamparai or the lives of the Vaishnava Acharyas informs us (a) that Sri Nathamuni was born in the *agrahara* of Vira Narayanapuram in the district of South Arcot, and (b) died at Gangaikonda Cholapuram in Trichinopoly, and (c) that he was the grandfather of Alavandar, who died at Srirangam when Sri Ramanujacharya was about 25 or 30 years of age. Now, here are three points to be carefully sifted in arriving at the age of Nathamuni. There are also other traditions making him a contemporary of Kamban, but these are not trustworthy and may therefore be set aside for the present.

(a) As regards Viranarayanapurm the Kongu chronicle says that ' Viranarayana (Parantaka I, 906-946 A.D.) was a great devotee of Vishnu in the early part of his life and he created many tax-free Brahman settlements one of which was called after his own name Viranarayanapuram ' [2]. In other words this *agrahara* must have come into existence some time after 906 A. D.

(b) Sri Nathamuni is believed to have died at Gangaikonda Cholapuram which was made the capital of the Chola king Rajendra (A D. 1011-1044) about

---

[1] *The Ind Rev*, 1908, p 280

[2] *Salem Dt. Manual*, Vol. II. p. 375 and *Madras Journal of Sc. & Lit*, Vol. xiv

the year 1022. Admitting that our sage died about 1025 A. D, he should have been born about 915 A. D, and this gives him an age of 110 years. This is sufficiently a long age, and there is every reason to believe that he, being a Yogi, could have lived for such a long period.

(c) According to the inscriptions of Bitti Deva or Vishnuvardhana of Mysore, the great Vaishnava reformer Sri Ramanujacharya was living in 1134 A. D. Even if we allow him an unusually long age of 115 years, it is certain that he was about thirty years old in A. D. 1049, which must be assumed as the year of Alavandar's death ; that is, he may have survived his grand-father Nathamuni some 24 or 25 years Granting that Alavandar lived to an advanced age of eighty, he should have been born about A.D. 969 when Nathamuni was about 54 or 55 ; and it is not improbable for a man of this age to beget a grandson We are therefore inclined to believe that Nathamuni was a direct disciple of Nammalvar and studied Tiruvoymoli and Yoga philosophy when he was about 20 or 25 years of age under our most revered Saint. In other words Nammalvar must have been alive in A.D. 935. Moreover, it is said that about the writings of Nammalvar, Sri Nathamuni enquired one Parankusadasa, a disciple of Madhurakavi Alvar (afterwards his fellow student) who is believed to have been born in the Dvapura Yuga !

Further he should have also been the last of the Alvars, as one of our early Acharyas distinctly says in his வாழித்திருநாமம் that Nammalvar taught the 4000 hymns to Nathamuni—நாதனுக்கு நாலாயிரமளித்தான் வாழியே. It escapes our understanding how in the face of this clear statement Tirumangai Alvar could have lived after Nammalvar.

(10). In one of the inscriptions of Rajaraja Chola dated about 1004 A. D. Kurugur appears as the name of a dancing girl. From it we are to infer that this village had by that time become famous as the birth place of Nammalvar. This we suppose was due to the propogandist work of Nathamuni who used to visit the royal courts of Chola kings. Further it was the custom of those times to give the names of famous villages, of renowned Saints and of reigning sovereigns to men and women, out of reverence or gratitude as the following proper names will show: சீகுருகூர், திருநாவுக்கரசு, ராஜராஜ விழுப்பரையன், சுந்தர பாண்டிய ஆசாரியன் ; and this sort of naming first took place during the life time of these remarkable personages or when those noteworthy occurrences were quite fresh in their memories. An inscription of the same Chola king calls the name of the deity of the temple at Ukkal as Tiruvoymolidevar. From this Dr. Hultzsch seems to think that Nammalvar 'must have lived centuries before A. D. 1000.' But for the above reasons this was not really the case.

Some scholars might think that a considerably long time should have passed after the death of these pious reformers before their deification could have taken place. But this was not at all necessary, when we consider the spirit and the religious movements of this period of sectarian reforms (A.D. 950-1150), and the halo of divine glory which had shone even in their own life time. We are told in the biographies of the Vaishnava Acharyas that copper images of Sri Ramanuja were set up, in obedience to his orders, immediately after the termination of his earthly existence, and that Manavalamamuni gave away his copper water pot for the making of his image just on the eve of his departure to the other world. And it has been said above that the custom of setting up images for these canonized saints came into vogue only after 1000 A.D.

The above arguments must irresistably lead any unbiassed reader to conclude that our Nammalvar should have flourished in the first half of the tenth century A.D. which is full two hundred years posterior to Tirumangai Alvar. It is, therefore, clear that the traditional stories relating to these two Saints in which Mr. S. Krishnaswamy Aiyangar places so much faith and the fabulous difference of 3500 years between Nammalvar and his direct disciple Nathamuni, on which the *archavatar* theory of the Vaishnava Acharayas rests, must be rejected as pure concoctions of Manavalamamuni and his predecessors, devised in support of their absurdly cherished beliefs.

To summarise the results of our discussions regarding the Vaishnava Saints: (1) the reformation of the Vaishnava sect began in the Pallava country

THE VISHNUVITE SAINTS

and slowly but steadily travelled as far as the Pandya-desa in the South; (2) the 'First Alvars' and Tirumalisaiyar, all of Tondai Nadu, were the earliest, and Nammalvar of the Pandya country was the latest, (3) Tirumalisaiyar, Tirumangai Mannan and Tondaradippodi Alvar who were the bitterest opponents to the Saivas, Jains and Buddhists flourished when the two latter religions were struggling for existence in the Tamil country; (4) Nammalvar, the last of the Vaishnava Saints and the first of the Acharyas lived when the two atheistic religions—Jainism and Buddhism—had very nearly died out in the Tamil country and when the Saivas and Vaishnavas had been reconciled; (5) Tirumalisaiyar, Kaliyan and Nammalvar were the greatest of the Vaishnava Saints; (6) and lastly, all the Alvars flourished during the *pauranic* period, that is between A. D. 550 and 950, when temples in honour of the Brahmanic deities, Vishnu and Siva, were being built in all the Tamil districts.

XII

THE ORIGIN OF MALAYALAM

The home-speech of about seven millions of people in Southern India is Malayalam. It is at present an important language of the Dravidian family; and yet, the exact relationship which it bears to the other members of that family is a subject of some hot discussion among the Dravidian scholars. The solution of this problem is not an easy matter. Unless one has made an historical study of the Tamil and Malayalam languages his conclusion must remain for ever vague and indecisive Some scholars believe it to be a sister of Tamil like Telugu or Kanarese, others regard it as a highly developed dialect of old Tamil, while a few Indian scholars of Malabar are prone to think that it is a dialect of Sanskrit and that it had nothing to do with Tamil from its very origin. The last seems an extreme view prompted by a false sense of patriotism; and the subject is interesting and important enough to deserve an examination at some length.

The etymology of the term 'Malayalam' which properly applies to the territory and not language, seems obscure. It does not occur either in early or mediæval Tamil literature. The people of the West Coast call their home-speech as Malayazhma or Malayayma. These are compounds of two Malayalam or rather Tamil words *mala*, a 'mountain' and *alam* or *alma*, 'government'. The latter are verbal nouns formed by postfixing the noun terminations *am* (அம்) and *ma* or *mai* (மை) to the verb *al* (ஆள்) to rule. 'Azhma' may be a mistake for 'alma'. It is not right to accept the meaning that Malayalam is a 'deep (ஆழம்)mountainous region'.

The Chera or Kerala country, called also the Malai-nadu and Malai-mandalam in Tamil and Malayalam works, was known to the early Greeks as Dimurike or Tamilakam and 'Kerobothros' or the Chera country, and to the mediæval nations as 'Malabar' (Skt. *Malavar*, Ar. *Mala-barr*) or the 'region of mountains' From about the beginning of the sixteenth up to the early years of the last century, Tamil was known to Europeans as the 'Malabar' language. But it has been considered by Western scholars as an instance of misapplication of the term 'Malabar' to Tamil. However, I am inclined to think otherwise, though with reference to the present condition of the Malayalam language it might be an undue extension of its signification. When the term 'Malabar' was first applied to Tamil by the early European travellers or missionaries there was not, as will be shown hereafter, much difference in the colloquial or rather the vulgar forms of the two languages, and they were justified in calling both as the 'Malabar' language.

The people of Kerala or Chera Desa in the third century called themselves Tamilar and even thought it proud to be known by that 'sweet' name as the following quotation will show :—

வணடமிழிகழ்ந்த
காய்வேற் நடக்கைக் கனகனும் விசையனும்
செங்குட்டி வன்றன் சினவலேப் படுதலும்.—*Sil.*

The work which we have reviewed in the tenth essay is probably the earliest literary record relating to the Chera kings and their subjects whose home-speech was Tamil. And it might conveniently be taken as containing the origins of the Malayalam language. Another Tamil work of about the same period is the Ainkurunuru 'or the 'Five short Hundreds'. It was written by five different poets of the Kerala country and compiled under the orders of the Chera king Yanaikkat-chey-Mandaram-Seral-Irum-porai. A third work of greater importance, but belonging almost to the same period is Silappadikaram. It was composed by Ilango-Adikal, a younger brother of the Chera king Senguttuvan, and forms one of the five Tamil major epics. All these teem with 'Malabaricms' or usages peculiar to Malayalam, but which are considered as slang or provincialisms in pure Tamil. Words like ஒல்லா (must not), போத்து (he-buffalo), கைநிலம் or கைநிலே (camp), வட்டி (basket), &c., which occur in these Tamil works of the Kerala country, are still current in the spoken language of Malabar and Travancore when they had become obsolete in Tamil.

The later Tamil authors of Kerala were Aiyanaritanar, Cheraman Perumal and Kulasekara Perumal. Aiyanaritanar flourished about the seventh or eighth century A. D. He was a prince of the Chera dynasty and wrote a treatise on grammar entitled the 'Venba-Malai.' The other two were kings of Malabar and flourished during the eighth or ninth century. For their literary remains we must refer the reader to the eleventh 'Tirumurai,' of the Saivas, to Mr. Govinda Pillai's 'History of Malayalam Literature' and to our chapter on the Alvars. It must, however, be pointed out here that the proportion of Sanskrit words in the early Tamil works of the Chera country, namely, Ainkurunuru, Paditruppattu, Silappadikaram and Venbamalai is comparatively very small, while in the later writings of the Kerala saints—Cheraman and Kulasekara—it is perceptibly higher, mainly owing to Brahmanical influence. Kulasekara was also a Sanskrit poet. The latest Tamil poet who, according to a current tradition, visited Kerala and lectured on the Ramayana before large audiances was the famous Kamban (A. D. 1145-1205). Lectures in 'Tamil on the Ramayana were evidently popular and much appreciated in Kerala during this period, and it is interesting to note that even today Kambaramayanam is recited and commented upon by special minstrels or a class of wandering preachers. The first works in the early Malayalam language are accordingly the 'Ramacharitram' and the 'Ramayanam' which are more after the model of Kamban's great work.

In ancient Tamil literature Chera or Kerala is invariably spoken of as a Tamil country; and from the Tolkapyam it might be inferred that this kingdom had at least seven Nadus or provinces, namely—Venadu, Puzhinadu, Karka Nadu, Sitanadu, Kuttanadu, Kuda Nadu and Malayama Nadu, in all of which Kodum or vulgar Tamil was spoken. In later Tamil literature Malabar, Travancore and Cochin are called Malainadu or Malai-mandalam. Hence the Chera kings were also called Puzhiyan, Kuttuvan, Kuda-Nadan, Malayaman and Kolli-chilamban (Lord of the Kollimalais). For sometime the Kongu country (Salem and Coimbatore districts) was under them, and hence the people of the country were known also as Kongans. Two Tamil inscriptions in a Jain temple on the Tirumalai hill inform us that Adigaman Ezhini of Tagadur (Salem district) belonged to the Chera or Vanji family. Sita-Nadu is the Nilgiris and it is needless to say that it was within the Chera dominion.

The names of villages in Malabar and Travancore which have suffixes like, *seri, ur, angadi* (a bazar), *kodu* or *kod* (summit of a hill), *kadu* or *kad* (a forest), *tod* or *tottam* (a garden or canal), *padi, karai, turai, kulam, kuricchi, kalam, vayal, eri, pattu, kundu, tali, iruppu*, &c., are all pure Tamil words and indicate that they were originally built and occupied by the Tamils. The names of Malabar villages like

Mel (west or upper)-muri, *Mel*-attur, *Tamir*-kadu, and *Kazham*-paramba support the theory that the ancient inhabitants of Kerala were Tamil Dravidians. Again, from the existence of Tamil words *kizhakku* (east) and *merku* (west) in the Malayalam language, Dr Caldwell argues that 'the Malayalam is an off-shoot from Tamil, and that the people by whom it is spoken were originally a colony of Tamilians'. This argument confirms beyond a shadow of doubt the Tamil origin of the Malayalam people, though it seems to Mr. Logan fanciful and ingenious. Prior to the fifth or sixth century A. D. the Tamil words குணக்கு, குடக்கு, வடக்கு and தெற்கு expressed the four directions, while கிழக்கு and மேற்கு then meant 'downward' and 'upward.' In all these the particle கு is a dative case termination meaning 'direction.' Later on குணக்கு and குடக்கு became classical or used only in literature, and their place was taken by கிழக்கு and மேற்கு which acquired that significance with reference to the position of the Tamil country lying east of the Western Ghauts. Notwithstanding the strikingly reverse configuration of the modern Malayalam and Tamil countries, the Tamil word கிழக்கு has come to denote the 'east' on both sides of the Ghauts and in both languages. This is no doubt an anomaly and can be explained only by accepting that the early inhabitants of the Malayalam country were Tamil immigrants from the East coast districts.

The word மேற்கு has, however, retained in Malayalam its ancient Tamil meaning 'upward', and its modern significance is expressed by a Tamil compound படி-ஞாயிறு or the 'setting sun.' Doubting the correctness of Dr. Caldwell's argument Mr. Logan suggests that the terms கிழக்கு and மேற்கு were coined with reference to the rise and setting of the sun. This seems to be very ingenious, because, if that had been the case, the words for 'east' and 'west' should be cognates and found in all the Dravidian languages; and the necessity to coin a compound Tamil word *padi-jnayiru* in the place of a simple one, *merku*, should never have been felt by the early inhabitants of Kerala.

Among the towns of the West coast Tondi (modern Kadalundi), Mandai, Musiri and Vanji occur frequently in early Tamil literature. Tondi was a famous sea-port and capital of a division of the Chera country ruled by Poraiyan, while Vanji or Karur was the metropolis of the other division; Musiri (Gr. *Mouziris*) was a famous emporium of the West and centre of the pepper trade in India. The following quotations from ancient Tamil literature will be found interesting :—

(1) செங்கோற், குட்டுவன்றெண்டி.—*Ain*. 178.
(2) கலந்தநத பொற்பரிசம், கழித்தோணி யாற்கரைசேர்கருங்து மூலத்தாரமுங் கடற்றாரமுந், தூலப்பெய்து வருநந்தீயும் புனலங்கள் என்பொலந்தார் குட்டுவன், முழங்குகடன் முழவின் முசுறி.—*Pur.* 343.
(3) இயற்றேர்க் குட்டுவன் வருபுனல் வாயில்வஞ்சி.—*Pat.* 3.

The above are cities of commercial and political

importance. Tamil religious literature is replete with descriptions of Hindu shrines visited by the Saints, who composed on the spot hymns about them. Among the towns of religious celebrity come first Gokarnam and Tirucchengunrur (near Quilon). These are seats of famous Siva shrines which were visited by the Tamil saints Appar and Sambandar in the seventh century. Tiruvanjaikulam seems to be a later one, because only one saint, Sundarar, a contemporary of the Chera king Cheraman Perumal sang of it. Among the Vaishnava shrines of the Tamil-Malayalam country Tirumuzhikalam, Tirunavoy, and Tiruvallavazh, were visited by Tirumangai Alvar about A.D. 750, Nammalvar (A.D. 920) mentions in addition to these Trivandram, Tiruvanparisaram, Tirukatkarai, Tirupuliyur, Tiruchengunrur, Tiruvanvandur, Tiruvattaru, Tirukkadittanam and Tiruvaranvilai. Kulasekhara Perumal has sung only Vittuvakkod. The Vishnu shrine at Tiruchengunrur could have come into existence only after the time of Tirumangai Alvar, that is after A D. 750.

This last town which was built on the Chittar river was an important Brahman settlement in the days of Nammalvar (A. D. 920) wherein, as described by him, 3,000 Brahmans lived.—அமர்ந்த சீர் மூவாயிரவர் வேதியர்கள் தம்பதி (VIII, iv. 10.) We have therefore every reason to believe that the Nambudri [1] (or Nambi-sri, Nambi-tiru or Nambi, Tamil நம்பி meaning 'a

---

1. Compare தம்பிரான் which has become in Malayalam தம்புரான் and தம்புராட்டி.

noble man') Brahmans settled in Malabar and Travancore between the sixth and eighth centuries of the Christian era. According to Keralolpatti, a mythological account of the Malayalam country composed probably by a Nambudri Brahman during the eighteenth century, Brahmans were brought down by Parasurama from the Punjab and made to settle first at Gokarnam in South Kanara, where they were made to shave their hind lock and to grow it on the front, perhaps as it is said, to prevent their going back to their original home. But we learn from other sources that this king was Mayurasarma—the founder of the Kadamba family and not Parasurama.

The date of Mayuravarma is about the early part of the sixth century. The Namburi Brahmans must, therefore, have settled in and around Gokarnam, during this period and their migration to the south from this centre must have taken place during the sixth and seventh centuries. The example of Mayuravarma was followed by the Chola and Pandya kings of the time, who invited small colonies of Brahmans now known as the Soliya Brahmans.

But this does not mean that there were absolutely no Brahmans in the Tamil country before the sixth century.

The country was deeply plunged in Buddhism and Jainism. The non-Brahman Saivas and Vaishnavas, of course instigated by the few Brahmans, were contending against these religionists. There were not many Brahman religious institutions;

nor were there many powerful inducements for Brahmans to migrate to the south. Politically the Tamil countries were in a state of turmoil. The Kalabhras, the Kadambas, the Pallavas, the Chalukyas, the Cholas, the Pandyas and the Cheras were fighting with one another. Religion suffered from the ills of political unrest. There was no definite state religion ; each king professed the religion which suited his whims and caprices. Better days dawned during the seventh century when Brahmanism, *i.e.*, the cult of Siva and Vishnu, came out triumphant in the religious struggle. The Tamil countries became more or less quiet. And the very Brahmans who had served as messengers and domestic servants under the wealthy Dravidians, as now, became priests and *purohits* to the Tamil kings, thus securing for themselves a wider influence in the country. All these led to the construction of a large number of temples to Siva and Vishnu, and to the invitation of more Brahmans from the Aryavarta during the seventh and the early part of the eighth century A. D. for purposes of worship in temples and to serve as purohits to Dravidians.

These Brahmans have since been known honorifically as 'Nambis' in all the three Tamil countries—Chera, Chola and Pandya—in contradistinction to later Brahman immigrants usually styled as 'Bhatta.' The former wear the tuft of hair in front, while the latter keep it at the back of their head. They are called the Purva-sikhai or Puraschudakula

Brahmans. All the Brahman saints—Vaishnava and Saiva—and some of the Brahman ministers under the ancient Tamil kings belonged to this Purvasikhai or the 'front-locked' Brahmans. The early Tamils were indebted to them for their civilisation, which developed steadily under the influence of the later Brahman immigrants from the north. These later immigrants who were specially invited by Tamil kings from the middle of the eighth century downwards, kept themselves distinct as a class and formed no social alliance with the Dravidians. They, therefore, came to be considered superior to the Nambis, Nambudris [1] or the Soliya Brahmans. Most of the land grants to the Bhatta or the later colony of Brahmans belong to this period. The early or Nambi Brahmans seem to have entered the Tamil-Malayalam districts from the north-west, while the Bhatta or later Brahmans appear to have taken the southern route through the Telugu country.

When the Nambudri Brahmans settled in Kerala the country was not uninhabited. All the lands were not wholly theirs, nor were they the sole *jenmis*; and we see no special reason why it should be so only in Kerala when such has not been the case in the Tamil or Telugu country. From the Paditruppattu we learn that the Chera kings lavished presents upon Tamil poets and Brahmans of Malabar and Travan-

---

1. It is said that the Cherumars called the Nambudris as 'Chovvar' which may be a corruption of Sabhaiyar or Savaiyar a name usually applied to the ordinary or plebeian Brahmans of the Tamil districts

core. Imayavarman is said to have given 500 villages in the district of Umbarkadu to the Brahman poet Kannanar ; Senguttuvan the revenues of Umbarkadu to Paranar ; Selvakkadunko all the country within his view from the top of the hill Nanra to poet Kapilar ; while another king gave a portion of his country to Kappiyanar. How could then such enormous land grants be made, had the country been the exclusive property of the Nambudri Brahmans ? Moreover, all these had occurred before the Nambis or Nambudris settled in Malabar and Travancore. The fact seems to be that the whole Kerala country belonged to its kings, and they had a right to dispose of it as they pleased. And out of reverence to learned Brahmans, whom they brought from Upper India from time to time, lands were granted free of tax as Brahmadayam for their maintenance.

But the total neglect of the native Tamil literature by the Dravidian inhabitants of Kerala, their general ignorance and their respect for Nambudri Brahmans gave the latter an undue advantage which in course of time showed itself in the Nambudri's exclusive ownership to all the Kerala country. And to support the theory of their ownership, the Nambudris even fabricated false traditions.

The Chera, like the Chola and Pandya countries, was inhabited by all the early Tamil tribes and castes. The identity of some of these minor Malabar castes with those that occur in the inscriptions of Rajaraja Chola (A. D. 985—1013) has been noticed before. Of the remaining castes of Kerala, the numerically most important are the Nayars, the Tiyans, the Iluvans and the Cherumans, none of which are now to be found in the east, though the names of villages like Vellancheri, Idacheri, Ayancheri, Valayanad, Parayancheri and Pallipuram in the Kurumbranad, Valluvanad, Ponnani and other taluks of the Malabar district clearly prove that Kerala was once inhabited solely by the Tamils. Then, how did these castes come into existence and how are they ethnically related to the corresponding castes of the Tamil districts?

About a thousand or more years ago all the modern Tamil castes were not in existence, the Tamil people were divided into tribes according to the nature of the soil in which they lived and the conventional tribal names like the Vellalas, Maravas, Idaiyans, Mallars, Pallars, and Kuravas survive to this day in the Tamil districts.

The word Nayar, like Vellala which includes a large number of cultivating castes, is a vague name, The present Nayar caste has grown by the gradual accretion to it of Chakkan (oil-presser), Vaniyan (trader or oil-monger), Eruman or Kol-ayan (Tamil shepherd), Kanisan and Panikkan (sub-division of the Tamil Iluvans), of Pallichan and Urali (Tamil Pallis), and lastly of the Vellala castes. Among the important sub-divisions of Nayars, 'Sudran' has no meaning; Agattucharna and Purattucharna are only later innovations introduced after Hyder's invasion.

THE ORIGIN OF MALAYALAM

Attikkuricchi [1] and Vattakadan are only territorial names, Kiriyattils alone seem to be the descendants of the pure Velirs or Vellalas [2] of the West Coast. As late as A. D. 1320 we find the Vellalas as the cultivating caste of Malabar. Thus, none of the ancient Nayars are of Telugu extraction as believed by some scholars.

The armies of the Chera kings were recruited from the people of the Kongu country who were a race of fine stalwart warriors:—(1) நர்மபடைக்கொங்காகோவே ; (2) சோரலாதற்கு திகழொளி ஞாயிற்றச் சோழனமகளீன்ற மைந்தன் கொங்கர் செங்களம்வேட்டுக கங்கைப்பேர் யாற்றுக் கரை போகிய செங்குட்டுவன்.—*Sil.* xxix. 1-3.

And this is confirmed by the fact that some of the feudal chieftains of Malabar and Travancore, like the Zamorin of Calicut, belonged to the Pogondan subdivision of the Coimbatore Idaiyans. 'Kunnala-kon', one of the titles of the Zamorin, is a pure Tamil expression (*kurunila-kon*) meaning ' chief or king of a small country,' and ' Konatiri' or Konan-tiru, or *konan* is a title of the Idaiyans of Coimbatore, Madura and Tinnevelly districts. In Malabar, Idaiyans are called Kol-Ayan[3] and Eruman (buffalo-men) ; and these are among the sub-castes of Nayars. The name

---

1. We are not convinced of the correctness of the etymology of ' Attikurichi' from Sanskrit *Asti* bone, and Tamil *kura* to cut.

2. The Cherumars or the natives of the soil address the Nayars as Ilankoil, which is precisely the same title as ' Ilankokkal ' given to the ancient Vellalas of the Tamil districts

3. *Kol* is a contraction of 'Golla' which is the name of the Telugu shepherd caste, while 'ayan' is that of Tamil Idaiyans.

Eruman appears in the Tanjore inscriptions of the eleventh century. It is not surprising that the Tamil Idaiyars are treated as a sub-caste of Nayars, when we find some of them elevated even to the rank of Kshatriya Samantas. The Siviyar (palankeen bearers) and the Agattu-Charna sub-divisions of the Tamil Idaiyan[1] caste are note-worthy, as affording a connecting link between them and the Samantas and Nayars of Malabar. The words குட்டி and கிடாவு and கிடாகள், which in the Tamil districts signify the 'young ones of cattle', denote in Malabar 'children.' This shows that the Idaiyars held a dominant place in the constitution of the Nayar and the Samantā castes. Idaiyans, especially of the Kongu country, had their own chieftains and they were good cavalry men. They contributed soldiers and commanders to the Chera army after the conquest of the Kongu country by the Chera kings about the first or second century.

பொருமுரா ணெய்திய கழுவுள் புறம்பெற்று
கால்வல் புரவி யண்டரோட்டி.—*Pad.* 88.

(Defeated the Idaiya chieftains who opposed him and routed the Idaiyans of the swift-footed cavalry.)

The word Cheruman or Chiruvan means a small man, and the Cherumans were really so in comparison with the robust Kongu Idaiyans and Vellalas who constituted the Nayar or the Nayakar caste. In a Malayalam deed of 1523 A.D. the name of this caste appears as Valli-Alar or Valli-Sattanmar, but not as

---

1. It will be curious to observe that in one sub-caste of Idaiyans in the Madura district, called the Pendukku-mekki, the Marumakkattayam law of inheritance is followed.

herumars. 'Valli' seems to be a mistake for 'Villi'. 'ome interesting sub-divisions of this agrestic tribe, like Eralan (ploughmen), Idangai (left-hand), Kaladi (irrigators), Pallan, Paraiyan, Rolan (Irulan or Villi), Valluvan and Vettuvan are found among the Tamil Pallans also. Moreover, the customs and manners of these tribes both in Malabar and the Tamil districts, including their laws of inheritance, agree so completely that one might conclude that the Cherumas and Pallans belonged to one and the same tribe of Naga-Dravidian field labourers and soldiers. As for the Tiyans and Iluvans of Kerala, the latter of whom are found in the Tamil districts as well, we feel some difficulty. Whether they are strangers or autochthones to Southern India it is not possible to discuss here. That the great numerical strength of the Tiyans of Malabar as well as their homogeneous nature seem strictly to point to the latter. Further, the oxogamous groups of the North Malabar Tiyans and the Izhavans of Madura and Tinnevelly are called *illams*, and one of the former goes by the name of Pazhayar which is a Tamil word meaning 'toddy drawers'. A note on Tiyan has, however, been appended to this volume and it will give some interesting facts concerning this question. We need not go further into this problem of ethnical affinity between the peoples of Kerala and the two other ancient Tamil provinces. None of the early Malabar castes had any connection whatever with the Telugus, as is believed in some quarters.

If at all there is any Indian province in which little or no real archæological work is done, it is Kerala. Besides the publication of a few copper-plate grants and some stone inscriptions at irregular and long intervals of time by Burnell, Gundert, P. Sundram Pillai and others, no systematic explorations have yet been made and no regular epigraphical[1] researches undertaken. With the very few materials at our disposal we shall attempt to trace the growth of the Malayalam language.

Some scholars seem to think that the copper plate grants from Malabar should not be utilised for tracing the growth of the Malayalam language, as the grants are in Tamil and the donors were Perumals or kings of foreign extraction, invited by the Numbudri Brahmans to rule the Kerala country They are also of opinion that the colloquial Malayalam was quite distinct from the language of inscriptions and that 'the early poets of (Malabar) were no doubt much affected by influence of the early Tamil poets, who formed a literary school and developed a court language'. The difference between the literary Tamil and the colloquial Tamil—a difference due certainly to the antiquity of its literature and the settled form of the language—cannot be a reason for the disparity between the colloquial language and the language of public documents. For, while literature, chiefly classical

---

1. In Travancore the archæological Department seems to be. doing useful work under the direction of Mr Gopinatha Rau, M. A.

literature, is intended only for the educated few, copper-plate grants, stone inscriptions and similar public records are meant for all classes. A comparison of the inscriptions of Rajah Raja Chola (A. D. 985-1013) with the literature of that period would illustrate the above principle. The Kerala inscriptions cannot be an exception to this plain philological truth. Moreover, how are we authorized, in the absence of any work written in the colloquial Malayalam of that period, to say that the colloquial Malayalam was quite distinct from the language of inscriptions? Do the Malayalis really possess any literature anterior to the tenth century A. D. written in the so-called Malayalam language? If at all there be any record written in colloquial Malayalam it must be the inscriptions.

As for the Perumals being foreigners to Kerala, we might say that, till about the ninth century A. D., some at least of the Kerala kings were foreigners, because they inherited the Kerala throne by right of succession in accordance with the Marumakkatayam law, but they were never invited by the Nambudri Brahmans as these would have us believe, in order to enhance their importance and establish their authority in the Kerala country. On the contrary, many Chola and Pandya kings married Kerala princesses and their sons became lawful heirs to the Kerala kingdom :—

(1) நெடுந்தணேகேள்வியந்துவற்கொருதந்தை
யீன்றமகள் பொறையன் பெருங்கேதயீன்றமகன்
செல்வக்கடுங்கோவாழியாதன்．—*Pad*. 70.

(2) குடவர்கோமா னெடுஞ் சேரலாதற்குச்
சோழன் மணக்கிள்ளியீன்றமகன்
கடல்பிறக்கோட்டியசெங்குட்டுவன்.—*Ib*. 50.

(3) The Chola king Parantaka I (A. D. 907-946) married a Kerala princess.

(4) Kulasekhara Pandya took with him ... all the forces of the two Kongu countries that belonged to his mother's two brothers.—*Mahawanso,* 239.

Matrimonial alliances among the three Tamil dynasties seem to have continued until about the down-fall and extinction of the ancient Pandya and Chola houses between the 11th and 13th centuries, when the influence of the Nambudri Brahmans began to extend even into the Kerala royal households. The latest alliance of this kind was between Ravivarma *alias* Kulasekhara and a Pandya princess in A.D. 1299. This Kerala king defeated Vira Pandya and was crowned on the banks of the Vaiga. He ruled over Kerala, Pandya and Chola countries till about 1316. Probably this was the period when the communication between Kerala and the other two Tamil countries began to decline ; and this was the period when the Nambudri Brahmans laid the foundation stone for the ill-planned tottering edifice of the Malayalam tongue, by their closer touch with the Nayar and other high caste Dravidian families.

The statement that the early Malayalam poets were affected by the early Tamil poets seems rather surprising, the term 'early' not referring to the same age, as both are of unequal antiquity. Malayalam had scarcely any literature worth the name before the middle of the thirteenth century, whereas Tamil literature dates from the opening years of the Christian era. Tamil has a grammar written three centuries before Christ, whereas Malayalam had none till so late as A. D 1860. Tamil, at least the literary phase of it, had been well defined and formed two millenniems ago, while Malayalam is even to-day in a state of formation. It is inconceivable, therefore, how the early Malayalam literature could have been influenced by the early Tamil poets, particularly when we remember that all social intercourse between Kerala and the Tamil country had ceased at least one century before the birth of the Malayalam literature, unless it be that early Tamil literature was the literature of the early people of Kerala also.

The statements of Dr. Caldwell that the separation of Malayalam ' from Tamil evidently took place at a very early period, before the Tamil was cultivated and refined', and that Tamil 'bids fare to supersede the Malayalam' are thus opinions which need stronger evidence before they could be accepted.

Returning now from our digression to the copper-plate grants of Malabar, we find in the Mamballi inscriptions of Sri Vallavan Kodai (A. D. 973) the language used is pure colloquial Tamil interspersed with a few Malabaricms like ஒன்ன for உள்ள, சங்சரன் for சங்கரன், எடம் for இடம் &c. Verbs are inflected as in அட்டிகெகாடெத்தான் [1] ; and the datives of அமுது and

1. The word அட்டி in the expressions அட்டிக்கொடுத்தல் and

அவன் as அமுதினுக்கு and அவன்க்கு but not as அமுதின்னு and அவன்னு as now. And in the Kottayam plates of Vira Raghava Chakravarti (A. D. 1320) the language is also Tamil freely intermixed with Malabar idioms like வாதில் for வாயில், படிஞூஞாறு for படிஞாயிறு, ஒள்ள and ஒண்டாயில் for உள்ள and உண்டாகில், இருந்தருள for இருந்தருள, எழுங்கள்ளி for எழுந்தருளி &c., and verbs were still inflected We find also caste names like வெள்ளாளர், ஈழவர், தச்சா and தீயர். All these will be made more clear in the following section which deals with the linguistic evidence of the growth of the Malayalam language.

To illustrate the development of the Malayalam language and the peculiarities of each period of its growth, typical selections are given below from Panikkar's Ramayanam, Krishna-gatha, Adhyatma Ramayanam and Nala Charitam, each of which may be taken as representing a particular period in the growth of the Malayalam language together with short explanatory and philological comments:—

(1) கொண்டலிங்கேரிருண்டே சுருண்டே நீணடொளிவார்ந்து திங்ஙும், குந்தளபாரமோடு முகில்குலத்திட மிங்கலபோலே, புண்டரீ கேகூடணங்கரி கெப்பொலிந்தவள் வீதசொங்நாள்.

அட்டிபபேறு is not correctly understood in Malabar. The Malabar Gazetteer explains அட்டிபபேறு (attiperu) as 'a parcel of rights'. Prof. Wilson thinks that *atti* is the less accurate reading of *otti* (ஒத்தி) a mortgage. I think both are incorrect *Atti* is a pure Tamil word meaning 'poured' and it corresponds to the Skt. *Udagapurvam* *Attikoduttal* is to give by pouring water and *atti peru* is the acceptance of a gift made as above. During the 17th century its exact meaning was, however, forgotten and the redundant expressions like நீராடேகூடி அட்டிப்பேறும் நீரும் கொடுத்தான் came into use

THE ORIGIN OF MALAYALAM

(2) அம்மதா நங்நேரம் தங்மகந்தங்நேயும்
செம்மெயெடுத்துக்கொண் டங்குபோவான
சாரதது நிங்நொரு நேரததுச் சொல்லிநாள்
நீலக்கார் வேணிமா ஒெல்லாரோடெம்
வாய்ப்பாங்நு நிங்நுள்ள கார்ப்பாஸம் கொண்டெளள
கூர்ப்பாஸம் மேநியில் சேர்த்தெபபோழும்.

(3) நூறுயிரம் கபி வீரங்மா போகணம
ஒரோதிசிபட நாயகங மாரோடெம்.
ராகவாஸ்தலோ பாங்தே ஸஞ்சரிக்குமபோள்
ராகேந்து முகிவிஸ்த கண்டு விஸ் மயம்பூணடாள்
க்ருத்ர ராஜதுமொரு பதரவா நாயுள்ளொரு
குத்ர ராஜெகபபோலே பத்தவைரத்தோடதி
கருத்த நாயக்ரோ செங்நு யுததவும் துடங்கினெ

(4) பூததும் தளிர்த்துமல்லாதே பூருஹங்களில்
பேர்த்துமொங் நில்லி விடெகாண்மான்
ஆர்த்து நடககும் வண்டிங் சார்ததும் குயில் குலவும்
வாழ்த்துங்நு மதநங்நே கீர்த்திேய மற்றெங்நில்ல. [ளே
அபத்ரவிச் சீடெண்ட ஞாெனாருவநத்தில் மேவங் நாண
ஆெங்நாலும ரக்ஷிபபாநிநி அபரங்வருமோ கேணளே.

The first quotation is from the Ramayana of Kannassa Panikkar (A. D. 1350). It does not appear that there was any real literature in Malavalam before this period. The language of this work is wholly Tamil, with of course Malayali peculiarities. In this extract குநதளபாரம் and புண்டரீகேக்கூணன் are the only two Sanskrit compounds, and the rest are all Tamil words. The grammatical terminations இன், ஒடி, அத்து, ஆள் and the tense particles are all Tamil. And the only Malayalam usages are வார்கது for வார்ந்து, இட for இடை, போலே for போல and அரிகே for அருகே ; and

திங்கும் (dense, thick) is only a vulgar form of Tam. திணு ங்கு. Most of the Tamil words used in this extract, which are still current in Tamil, have become obsolete in Malayalam giving way to words of Sanskrit origin. Here the verbs are always inflected and the practice of dropping the personal endings has not yet come into existence. It is a translation of a Sanskrit work and Sanskrit words and expressions are freely used to the extent of about 50 per cent, though the grammar is throughout Tamil. On account of these peculiarities which bring it closer to Tamil, the author has been styled by Malayalam scholars rightly, perhaps wrongly, the Chaucer of Malayalam literature.

The second extract is from the Krishnappattu of Cherusseri Namburi (A D. 1550). The author uses only one Sanskrit word (வேணி) in the first quotation, which is written in pure colloquial Tamil. The only Malayalam peculiarities are தனே்ே for தன்னே, அங்கு for அங்கு and சொல்விஞன் for சொனனுன். A Tamilian may not use அம்ம and செம்மே in poetry, because they are colloquial and considered slang in Tamil. In the second passage, the writer uses two Sanskrit words கார்ப்பாஸம்(cotton) and கூர்ப்பாஸம (coat), which no Tamil writer will ordinarily use. The rest are Tamil words, some being slightly modified. எபோழும் is எபொழுதும, ஆர்ந்து is ஆர்ந்து. Though the author was a Brahman Sanskrit scholar he has not used so many Sanskrit words as Kannassa Panikkar, because the work was primarily intended for females and ordinary readers. The Krishnagatha is written in the colloquial Tamil or a Tamil dialect of the Kerala country known as Malayalam. In this work verbs are mostly inflected, while neuter verbs have invariably dropped their inflexional terminations. The clipping of personal endings in verbs must have already commenced during the early part of the 16th century. And the forms of Tamil words used here are mostly those that we find in the vulgar conversation of the uneducated Tamilians. செய்ச்ச for செய்விதது, பச்சோடம for பச்சைப்படம், வேணுன்ன for வேணுமென்ற &c. He has largely used colloquial Tamil words like அஞ்சுக, மசசு, மாடி, தென்னல், சேவடி, தின்மை, &c. which have become obsolete in modern Malayalam. The dative case in ன்னு or நது has also come into usage along with other Tamil grammatical forms. The author is now gratefully remembered by all the non-Brahman classes of Kerala as the pioneer of liberal education; he was the first Brahman who wrote for the benefit of the Sudra castes in their own tongue, the Malayalam, in spite of the fact that the Nambudris despised their dialect; and he is justly called the 'Morning Star' of modern Malayalam literature.

The next author we have to consider is Tunjat Ezhuttachchan who flourished about A. D. 1650. All his works are translations from Sanskrit, and he has freely used Sanskrit words and expressions, more abundantly than any other writer who preceded him. He was the first to use the Sanskrit case endings as in *orodisi, sthalopante,* and adverbs like *ittham, iti, pura* &c.; relative pronouns like *tat, mat, tava,* &c He has even added Sanskrit case terminations to Tamil nouns as in கேர, இவ்விடே ; and locatives in ங்கல (correctly, ஙகு + இல் = in the place) make their first appearance. Awkward combinations of Sanskrit and Tamil words like சித்தகாம்பு, கார்வெண்ணி, வசத்வேனசெயுந்து &c., and the arbitrary construction of Tamil words so as to obscure their derivations as in தருக்கண், எழுங்கெள்ளி, உரியாகே, எழுநீற்று, &c., were introduced by this writer. He followed no rules of grammar or vocabulary, because there was no grammar neither before nor after him in the Malayalam language. It is in his works that we find uninflected verbs largely used, though occasionally appear verbs with personal endings. It would be difficult for any one to read his works without a good knowledge of Sanskrit. To him the study of Malayalam meant the study of Sanskrit. We might boldly say that Ezhuttachchan was the first Malayalam writer who gave a death blow to Tamil his mother-tongue. For this act of vandalism he is admired by the people of Malabar as the 'Father of the Malayalam classical literature.'

The latest writer we have to deal with is Unnayi Variyar who lived about A.D 1750. His Nalacharitam is an admirable production Though he was a good Sanskrit scholar like Ezhuttachchan, he has not spoilt his work by introducing into it too much Sanskrit. His setting of Sanskrit *slokas* is choice and his use of the Manipravala style is graceful. In the two passages given above there are only about half a dozen Sanskrit words, while the rest are pure Tamil. The negative particle அ, the case post-positions இல், இன், எ or ஐ, றெ (உடைய) and verbal endings மான், பான, ஆல் (ஆன in கேளேன்) are all Tamil. In மேவுன்றுளேன் the particle ன்ன is only a contraction of கின்ற, கின்ன or இன்ன which is a sign of the present tense; similarly ன்று is an abbreviation of கின்றது. Thus if the Sanskrit passages are not taken into account, his vocabulary and the structure of his composition are mainly Tamil.

It may be assumed that grammar and dictionary tend to contribute to the fixity and permanence of a language. The early Tamil inhabitants of Kerala were mostly merchants, cultivators and soldiers, and they did not care for literary excellence or even to improve their mother-tongue. Nor did the later Malayalis care to write one, because the Dravidians were most of them uneducated and the Brahmans cared little for a Dravidian tongue. That work was reserved for a foreigner—Dr. Gundert, who was at once their Agastya and Divakara. Owing to the curious mixture of the agglutinative Tamil with the inflectional Sanskrit, the work of bringing out a satisfactory Malayalam grammar has become a super-human task. The language has not yet reached its classic stage; and it is still in a state of formation. Neither its grammar nor its vocabulary is settled; and the very fact that it still retains the peculiar Tamil letters ழ and ற proves its very late separation from Tamil.

GRAMMAR :—To determine what words are of pure Tamil origin and what not, we have definite grammatical rules giving the letters which should come at the beginning, middle and end of words. This is not possible in the case of Malayalam which has freely borrowed words from Sanskrit and foreign languages and incorporated them in its vocabulary.

The coalescence of letters or *sandhi* in Malayalam, owing to the influence of Sanskrit, follows wholly neither the rules of Sanskrit nor of Tamil. Sometimes the one, sometimes the other is followed, and in some cases neither. Sanskrit rules are sometimes applied to Tamil words. The expression வில்முரிஞ்-ஞூச்ச, if the Tamil rules are applied, must be வினமுறிஞ்ஞுவொச்ச and சொல்ல + இல்ல will become சொல்லவில்ல and not சொல்லீல்ல, nor are they according to the Sanskrit rules. பல + இடம் will be in Tamil பலவிடம் and not பலேடம் as in Malayalam. In the last example the Sanskrit rules are applied to pure Tamil words. Many of the Tamil *sandhis* which existed in early Malayalam or Tamil have now become obsolete, as in விண்டலம், எண்டிசை, மேற்றாம் (now மேததாம்), பொற்றுடி (பொல்த்துடி), &c. In Malayalam ண் + ச becomes ஞ்ச, ம் + க becomes ங்க, ள் + த becomes ள்த்த or த்த, but these are not allowed by the Tamil rules of *sandhi*. The Malayalis cared more for ease and always tried to avoid difficulties instead of facing them boldly. Hence, they have abbreviated several compounds : thus, செயது + கொள்ள + ஆம் has become செய்தோளாம்,

செய்ய + வேண்டும் = செய்யேண்டு, அங்கு + நின்று + அங்ஙுந்று, போக + வேண்டும் = போகணம் and so on.

Most of the differences between Tamil and modern Malayalam as regards grammatical endings and formation of words are attributable to this principle of laziness or phonetic decay ; and the dropping of personal suffixes in finite verbs is partly due to this cause and partly to their redundancy. In the Tamil sentence நான் அடித்தேன், either நான் or ஏன் in அடித்தேன் may be safely omitted without impairing the idea expressed by that sentence. Thus, Malayalam may be said to be passing through, like English, the analytical stage. In Malayalam அடிசச will be vague without the nominative which should be made explicit.

From the early Malayalam literature, which extended down to the sixteenth century, we find that verbs were inflected, and that the pronominal terminations disappear in the succeeding two hundred years. In a Malayalam sale deed of 1756 A. D. expressions like எழுதிக்கொடுத்தான் and எழுதிசசகொண்டான் were freely used. In the Tamil of the infant and the illiterate the idea of 'I beat' is expressed even to this day by நான் அடிசசே (Cor. அடித்தேன), ' you beat ' நீ அடிச்சே (Cor. அடித்தாய்), and ' he beat ' அவன் அடிச்சா (Cor. அடித்தான்). Thus, the subjects நான், நீ and அவன் are clearly given out and the personal endings ஏன், ஆய் and ஆன் are, as a rule, contracted or dropped. In the East coast, however, this Tamil of the populace has been constantly subjected to corrections and modifications with reference to the approved literary Tamil of the learned section. The same process was certainly in operation among the early Tamils of the Kerala country who were mostly illiterates; but since these grammatical and lexicographical forms were left unrestrained by any fixed rules, and since this process of phonetic decay was aided by the indifferent attitude of the Nambudri Brahmans who were quite ignorant of literary or classical Tamil, they had come to be eventually accepted as correct usages in their later corrupt Sanskritized Tamil or Malayalam literature.

This was how the personal terminations of Tamil verbs were dropped in Malayalam. There are yet some traces of verbal inflexions in the second person plural as in சொன்னவீன் and in the first person plural as in தாரம்—we will give, &c. It is not, therefore, correct to say, as some Malayalam scholars seem to assert, that there are no traces of inflexions in the colloquial Malayalam or that Malayalam verbs were never inflected.

We may explain the vagaries of Malayalam language, which is technically called the "levelling" of inflections, and its grammar by taking one or two specific instances :—

(1) அஹிசசத் ரத்திஙகல் இருந்து...இதி நது வருத்தியெநது சொல்லுந்து,

(2) ரக்ஷிசகுந்து தனியாதிரிமார்.—*Ker.*

In the first quotation the termination 'ந்து' serves different purposes; நது in இருந்து is a modified form of

Tamil ந்து (particle of past tense); நது in இதிந்து is a contraction of ன்கு (dative case suffix); ந்து in யெந்து is an abbreviation of என்று; and ந்து in சொல்லுநது is a modification of கின்றது, குன்னது or உன்னு (present tense). In the second example குநகது is the same as கின்றது, but here the neuter inflexional ending is retained. We have reasons to believe that the high-caste personal endings in verbs were gradually dropped in Malayalam, the neuter endings taking their place regardless of gender; and these also in course of time disappeared. There are many such grammatical irregularities and fluctuations, but only a few are quoted here as illustrations.

VOCABULARY :—The same uncertainty exists in the matter of vocabulary also. It has no dictionary like the Divakaram and the Pingalandai of Tamil or like the Amarakosh of Sanskrit. The following are some of the irregularities which might be noticed in the Malayalam vocabulary.

(1) The same word is used in various forms. For example, the Tamil word கமுகு (areca-nut) appears in Malayalam as கமுக and கவுநகு; கமுகு (vulture) as கமு வந, கமுக, கமுங்கு; கயிறு (rope) as கயறு and கமறு; பருத்தி (cotton) as பரிந்தி and பாத்தி &c.

(2) Words of different origin appear in the same form. Tamil உவர் becomes ஓர which is apt to be confounded with ஓரம் (margin); Tamil இயக்க as எக்க, while எக்கம் means sighing, வெக்கை (heat) as வெக்க and வைக்க (to put) also as வெக்க; தளி is a 'temple' as well as to 'sprinkle' (தெளி) &c.,

(3) Sometimes த, ற and ர are indiscriminately used as in அகத்துக and அகற்றுக, உறவு and உரவு &c. This is very common in the vulgar Tamil of to-day

(4) Compounds are so contracted and joined together that none of its component words can be identified. Tamil தேய்+பிறை becomes in Malayalam தேவற; அக்கி த்திரி is 'agnihotri', 'patteri' is 'Bhattasri' &c.

(5) Vowels which necessitate the use of the lips are usually changed or omitted; இரு becomes இரி; உரை, உரி (as in உரியாடு) ; தீல, தல ; உயிர்ப்பு, வீர்ப்பு ; புறவு (pigeon) பராவு ; &c.

(6) Probably for the same reason when two vowels of the same class come together either of them is altered. Thus கநா becomes கிணவு ; கடா, கிடாவு ; பலா, பிலாவு, &c. In all these examples the final is short or குற்றுகரம்.

(7) Sanskrit words when adopted are so far distorted by the Dravidian Malayalis that it would be difficult to discover their correct forms:—*chite* is 'jata'; *chattam*, 'srarddham'; *kotamba*, 'godhuma'; *chetu*, 'Sakatam'; *chirta*, 'Sridevi'; *vakkanam*, 'vyakyanam'; *veli*, 'bali'; so forth. It cannot be ascertained on what principle *mesham* becomes *medam* and *vesham* as *vezham*, which in Tamil means an 'elephant'. The unnatural partiality of the Kerala people to Sanskrit has induced them to derive some pure Dravidian words from Sanskrit ; பச்சில or பசுமை இல (green leaf) is derived from Sanskrit *patram*; மடு or மட்டு (honey) from Sanskrit *madhu* ; மை from Sanskrit *mashi* &c.

(8) Surds in most cases are changed into nasals. குஞ்சி becomes குஞ்ஞி ; குன்று, குன்னு ; நாம்பு, நாமபு ; நாறு, ஞாற்று ; அங்கு, அங்ஙு ; தாழ்ந்த, தாண ; பஞ்சு, பஞ்ஞி ; &c.

This change is noticeable in the early Tamil works of the Chera poets. Malayalam has a softer and more nasalized sound than Tamil. And this may be due to the climatic conditions in the Kerala country, which has an unusual rain-fall of 116 inches in a year. The peculiarities of the Malayalam language may be stated curtly thus : ' it is the home-speech of a Brahman-oppressed Dravidian race, whose vocal organs were affected by an incessant cold'. Highly cultivated languages like Sanskrit or Tamil are always free from such confusions which characterize the lower stages of a human speech.

We shall conclude this short essay with a statement of the circumstances which led to the origin of the Malayalam language. It must not be difficult to determine them as the change has taken place within the past six or seven hundred years.

(1) The natural facilities for communication between the East and the West coasts of the Indian Peninsula were very little. The lofty ranges of the Western Ghats, with only a few passes between, and the impenetrable and extensive forests down the sides cut off the two regions.

(2) The marriage connections between the Chera and the two other Tamil dynasties had ceased partly on account of the extinction of the

ancient line of the Pandyas in the twelfth and of the powerful Cholas in the thirteenth century, and partly owing to the wars of succession which resulted from a conflict of the ordinary and the nepotic laws of inheritance. The latest alliances on record are the marriages of the father of Kulasekhara Pandya (A. D. 1190) with a Kongu or Chera princess and of the Chera king Ravi Varma or Kulasekhara (A. D. 1300) with a Pandya princess. To this should be added the union of the aggressive Nambudris with the Chera princesses to prevent foreign intervention in their social and political affairs.

(3) The study of Tamil literature was neglected in the Chera country owing to the dominating influence of the Nambudri Brahmans, which kept the non-Brahman Dravidians of the country perfectly ignorant of their rich literature, and owing to the extinction of the ancient Chera line of kings who patronized it.

(4) The introduction of Judaism, Christianity and Muhamadanism direct from Western Asia at a very early period, the frequent internal troubles among the feudal chiefs of Kerala, and the constant wars between them and the Pandyas and Cholas for nearly four centuries from the eighth gradually tended to diminish their intercourse. The Chola king Ko-Chengannan is said to have defeated the Chera Kanaikkal Irumporai and taken him prisoner. This forms the subject of 'Kalavali Forty' of the poet Poigaiyar. During the middle of the eighth century the Pandya

king Parankusan or Ko-Maran Jatavarman defeated the Chera kings in a series of battles at Vilijnam, Pulandai, Kottar, Chevur and other places. All these are mentioned by the commentator of Iraiyanar's Agapporal. We need not enumerate here the other wars in which the Cheras suffered defeat, as they are given in the *South Indian Inscriptions.*

(5) The customs and manners of the Nambudri Brahmans and their sexual connection with the Sudras, which in course of time spoiled both Sanskrit and Tamil, were looked upon with disfavour by the East Coast Brahmans or *Bhattas*, who always regarded the former as an inferior class on that account, though to a lesser degree than they did the Nambi or the 'front locked' brethren of their own country.

(6) For this reason none of the later religious reformers—Ramanuja, Madhva and others—did not care to introduce their reforms in Kerala. In a vast country of 14,250 square miles there were in the days of the Tamil Saints (650-950 A.D.) only one Siva shrine and thirteen Vishnu temples, whereas during the same period there were at least 300 temples dedicated both to Siva and Vishnu in a small area of 3,259 square miles—we mean in the Tanjore district. Hinduism, as it was understood and practised in the North and East, was evidently at a great discount in Kerala during that period. Even now pilgrims from the Tamil land rarely visit these shrines in Malabar and Travancore, excepting one or two, as they are practically unknown to Hindu devotees.

(7) Last of all comes the climate of Kerala with its incessant rain throughout the year and its dampness and heat on account of the proximity of mountains, which make the country uninhabitable for the East Coast people.

To summarize: Tamil, Vadugu (Telugu) and Karunatam (Canarese) are the only Dravidian languages which are mentioned in the early Tamil works. Malayalam as a distinct language does not appear in any Tamil work anterior to the fifteenth century. From the fact that Tamil has not been influenced to such an extent like the other two, and that it alone has a grammar and literature from the earliest times, we have very strong reasons to believe that it is the oldest of the South Indian vernaculars. We are not prepared to accept the opinion of Mr. Rice that ' Kannada was the earliest to be cultivated of all the South Indian languages', as he himself says in another place that none of the extant works in Canarese go earlier than the ninth century. It is quite natural to scholars, who have made a special study of some particular vernacular, like Dr Gundert, Mr. Logan or Mr. Rice to speak highly of it to the disparagement of the other languages of the same group. But to get a comparative estimate of them it would always be safer to follow the views of Dr. Caldwell, who has made a critical study of all the Dravidian languages without any bias towards any one of that group. The map will explain graphically the order of migration of the several Dravidian races and the degree of relationship among their languages. The grammar and vocabulary of Tamil and Telugu are quite different, and the age when they had parted from each other goes back to pre-historic times. These considerations would favour our regarding them as sister languages. And the greater affinities of grammar and vocabulary which exist between the early Canarese and the early Tamil seem to point out that the former was the first born daughter or rather the youngest sister of Tamil ; and this seems to receive an additional support from the fact that the northern limit of Tamil (Tirupati) which is bounded by Telugu has for the last two thousand years remained unaltered, while its north-western boundary had even before the fifth century A. D. been encroached by Canarese from Dvarasamudram and Coorg down to the Coimbatore district.

As regards Malayalam which was scarcely in her womb prior to the thirteenth century, we might say without any fear of contradiction for the reasons set forth above, that it is the latest dialect of Tamil which has come largely under the influence of Sanskrit. It is to be observed that at no period in historic times Sanskrit was a spoken language, and it is most unlikely that it could have been so among a non-Aryan people as the inhabitants of Malabar and Travancore Many Sanskrit words and idioms they might have borrowed ; but both in genius and in structure Malayalam remains, in spite of its Sanskritic saturation, a Dravidian tongue in close alliance with other chief non-Aryan languages of South India. And in the words of a Travancore statesman 'one could hardly help concluding that Malayalam is nothing more than old Tamil with a good admixture of Sanskrit words'; or, as Dr. Caldwell has said in one place, ' it might perhaps be regarded rather as a very ancient dialect of the Tamil than as a distinct language'. This must be the opinion of all impartial scholars, and it must no longer be a matter of dispute whether Malayalam s an "old and much altered off-shoot" of Tamil or its sister language, because it is evidently neither.

CONCLUSION

A line drawn from Mercara on the west to Tirupati on the east marked the northern limit of the ancient Tamil country; that portion of the Indian Peninsula to the south of this line, with the sea on the three sides was called *per excellence* the Tamilakam or Dravida-desa. It was inhabited by three distinct races—the Nagas, the Dravidians and the Aryans. The non-Aryan Tamils belong to this great Naga-Dravidian race.

Evidence points to Nagas as the aboriginal inhabitants of this country. They were divided into two sections—the earlier or the savage section, and the later or the semi-civilized section. The former belonged to the Negrito race and the latter to a mixed one. Apparently both migrated to India from the south when it was connected by land with Australia, the earlier tribes being driven to the interior hills and forests and the later immigrants occupying the east coast from Cape Comorin to Vizagapatam and extending as far as Nagpur in the Central Provinces. These were the *vanaras* and the *rakshasas* of the Ramayana. It is by no means easy to say when these races entered India.

Then came the Dravidian Tamils, the word 'Dravidian' being used in this work chiefly in a restricted sense to denote only the Velir or the Vellala tribe of the ancient Tamils, who were regarded as Kshatriyas, Vaisyas or Sudras according to their occupations, and this seems to be countenanced by Manu's definition of 'Draivda' as a man of an out-cast tribe descended from a degraded Kshatriya. The Dravidians were like the Brahuis and the Todas a fine stalwart race probably of the Aryo-Mongolian extraction. They were not dark complexioned, but their colour has been described in early Tamil works as that of the tender mango leaf. Their original home was somewhere in Asia Minor where the ancient Accadians lived. They had entered India by the North-western passes long before the Aryan migration. During the time of the Mahabharata War, say about the fifteenth century before Christ, they lived in Upper India, occupying small detached areas. Immediately after the 'Great War' the Dravidians trekked south wards by the way of western India halting for a time at Dwarasamudram in the Mysore (buffalo) Province. From thence they proceeded in three separate bands to the east, south and west, and established three small kingdoms known as the Chola, Pandya and Chera. The Cholas and Pandyas had very often to contend with the half-civilized Nagas, while the Cheras seem to have quietly taken possession of a country along the West coast almost uninhabited by any semi-civilized section of the Naga tribe. In the east the close contact of the Nagas and Dravidians led to a fusion of races. In the west that could not have happened at so early a period. And I am inclined to think that the Nayars of Malabar and Travancore are not the modern representatives of the ancient Nagas, but hybrid descendants of the early Naga-Dravidians and Aryans. The original Dravidians were a warlike race of hunters and cattle-breeders, and their partiality to the buffalo may be observed in the Todas of the Nilgiris, a pure Dravidian tribe, who must have found their way on these mountains simultaneously with the other tribes at the time of their dispersion from Dwarasamudram, probably about the ninth or tenth century before Christ.

Lastly came the Aryans, who were mostly Brahmans. The earliest band of them might have migrated to the Tamil country about the fifth or sixth century before Christ; and from this period down to the fourth or fifth century A. D. a thin stream of Aryan emigrants seems to have flowed southward. Sometimes it assumed larger proportions, which it did when a large number of them came from the north-west and spread evenly in all the Tamil-Malayalam districts. These Brahmans are known as Nambis in the Tamil districts and as Nambudris in the Malayalam or Chera country. All these Brahmans keep the lock of hair on the top of their head. Their migration took place between the sixth and seventh centuries A. D., when Buddhism and Jainism were receiving mortal blows from the federal army of the Aryo-Dravidian theologians, and when innumerable temples began to be erected for the Brahmanical gods in the Tamil districts The latest band of the Brahman settlers were known as the Bhattas, and their migration from the northeastern Telugu country must have taken place between the eighth and tenth centuries, that is sometime after the downfall of the great empire of Harshavardhana. Before the arrival of the Bhatta Brahmans the Nambis or Namburis of the west coast had developed themselves into an exclusive and influential community in the midst of the uncultured Kerala Dravidians with peculiar social and religious customs. The Bhatta Brahmans who had formerly lived on the banks of the sacred Ganges, Godavari, Kistna and Cauvery did not care to cross the Western Ghats. Few families did, however, go. They are still known there as Bhattatiris, while the latest Bhatta immigrants from the Tamil country are called simply Pattar. The Brahmans of the East coast, though they consider themselves purer in blood, are generally darker in complexion (like the Brahmans of Bengal) than the easy going wealthy and infragamous[1] Namburis, which is no doubt due to the

[1]. I have called them 'infragamous' as there has been a kind of social sanction to the loose marital connection of the younger male members of the Aryan Brahmans with the women of the Dravidian castes in the Kerala country.

climatic conditions and the hardships they had been subjected to during the previous ten centuries of residence on the scorching plains of the unprotected East.

There was no caste system among the Nagas and the Dravidians. It is an institution introduced by the 'cow-loving' Aryan settlers. The Tamils or the Naga-Dravidians were first divided into tribes, not castes, according to the territory wherein they happened to live when the earliest Aryans colonized the Tamil country. The numerous Tamil castes of modern times, with the exception of a handful of Vellalas, must have grown out of a few territorial tribes of Nagas. The Velirs or Vellalas alone were Dravidians. The Viswa-Brahmans and the Dravida Kshatriyas had no place in this system.

The home-speech of all these people, including the Brahmans, is Tamil. It is ignorance of the elementary principles of philology on the part of Tamil pandits that has led them to attribute divine origin to their mother tongue. Tamil is an ancient member of the Dravidian family. What language the Nagas spoke we have no means to find out. Tamil belongs to the agglutinative group of languages and it has no relation whatever with the inflectional Sanskrit. We may however find some remote affinities between it and the Indo-European languages—both in their grammar and vocabulary—a fact which indicates that the Tamils lived with the Aryans in Upper India before their downward march to the Dekhan. Tamil is a living tongue ; and so the early Tamil differs slightly from the mediæval and the modern forms of it. Owing to its great antiquity and its classic perfection with a settled grammar and vocabulary, so early as the second or third century B. C., literary Tamil differs very much from the colloquial ; and colloquial Tamil differs from the vulgar Tamil which gave birth to the Malayalam language about the eleventh or twelfth century A. D.

The phonetic system of Tamil is very defective ; and though defective, it has three sounds ∴, ற and ழ which are peculiarly its own and which are not to be found in any other language. It had an alphabetic writing called the Vatteluttu, which the people borrowed direct from the Phœnician or Himayaritic merchants six or seven hundred years before Christ ; and it was supplanted by the Grantha-Tamil characters during the ninth or tenth century A. D. when Brahman influence was at its zenith in the Tamil country. The first extant grammar of the Tamil language was written by a Brahman about B. C. 350.

We have no data to settle what the religion of the Nagas and Dravidians was before the arrival of the Brahmans in Southern India. As early as the tenth century there were in each village a Pidari or a Sasta (Tam. சாத்தன்) temple besides one or more for some of the puranic gods, then known as Sri Koil. All the Siva and Vishnu shrines whose glories were sung by the Nayanars and Alvars, belong to the latter class. The ancient Naga-Dravidians appear to have been animists or demonolators when they first came in contact with the Aryans. Till about the third or fourth century A. D. Brahmanism of the Vedic type, Buddhism and Jainism were professed in the Tamil districts. Or, as Dr. Pope has 'said the prevailing religion of this period was a most remarkable mixture of Saivism, Jainism, Buddhism and the ancient demonolatry'. I must add to these Indraism and Vishnuism. During the puranic period when Brahmanism came out triumphant, that is between the fifth and eighth centuries, the cults of Siva and Vishnu alone survived. Siva is said to have nipped the head of Brahma, given a kick to Yama, knocked out the teeth of the Sun, and so on ! Such was the fate of the Vedic deities.

All the extant Tamil works on religion and ethics bear clear marks of Aryan influence, and it would be obviously untenable to hold with Dr. Pope that the Tamils have developed a religion of their own independent of Brahmanism from the earliest period and that 'Saivism is the old pre-historic religion of South India essentially existing from pre-Aryan times.' It is urged by the same scholar that evil spirits and blood-thirsty gods were worshipped by the early warlike Naga-Dravidians with rude and cruel ceremonies; and before the time of Sankaracharya even human sacrifices seem to have been offered to them. But this shamanism or demonolatry was surely no Saivism, any more than hydrogen is water, though it had some of its essential elements similar to those of the Vedic

Rudraism. Moreover, the words Siva and Siddhanta are not of Dravidian origin. The Saivism or the Saiva Siddhanta of the modern non-Aryan Tamilians may therefore be defined as an eclectic religion composed of the hydrogenous demonolatry of ancient Naga-Dravidians and the oxygenous Rudraism of the Vedic Aryans colligated together by later philosophic Brahmanism of the Pauranic period.

The sixty-three Nayanars or Saiva Saints including Appar and Trignana Sambandar seem to have flourished between the sixth and ninth centuries; and the Saint Manikka Vachakar, who is out-side that bead-roll flourished about A. D. 875. It was after the twelfth century A. D that the Saiva Siddhantam of the Dravidian Tamils was given a philosophic basis in imitation of the great systems of Sankaracharya and Ramanujacharya; and its authors were again Saiva Brahmans.

The cult of Vishnu was equally powerful and not less ancient than Sivaism. It has been in existence since the Vedic times. But this humanitarian religion did not attempt to take converts from among the demonolatrous Naga-Dravidian tribes of hunters and warriors, nor was it in their nature to embrace such a catholic religion despite the teachings of the Vaishnava *alvars* or saints, who with the Saiva Nayanars actively worked for the expulsion of Buddhism and Jainism from the Tamil country. Nammalvar was the last of the Vaishnava Saints, A. D. 925; then came a line of Vaishnava *acharyas* or religious teachers commencing from Sri Nathamuni (A. D 905—1025) and ending with Manavala-Mamuni (15th century). It is to Ramanuja and Vedanta Desika (14th century) that Vaishnavism owes its stability and greatness, while the other *acharyas* only popularized it by their lectures and comments. Thus, Dr. Pope's statement that the 'Vaishnava system has been a formidable rival of Saivism since the twelfth century,' and Dr. Caldwell's assertion that the *alvars* were the disciples of Ramanuja are either perversions of the true history of Vaishnavism, probably put into their heads by interested Tamil Saivas, or hasty and one-sided views formed without regard to historical accuracy.

In Tamil there is no literature unconnected with ethics or religion and there is no ethics or religion in India without the Aryan influence. The earliest literary work in Tamil to which any definite date could be assigned is the Kural of Tiruvalluvar, which goes up to the opening years of the Christian era. There must have surely existed some works anterior to that period, since the age of the first Tamil grammar is believed to be the third or fourth century B. C., and the Tamilians have been acquainted with the art of writing at least from the sixth or seventh. But none of the pre-Tolkapyam works are now extant, probably with the exception of a few short poems included in the Agananuru and the Purananuru.

The history of Tamil literature may be divided

into six periods, namely,— the academic (B. C. 500— A. D. 150) ; the classic (A. D 150—500) ; the hymnal (A. D. 500—950) ; the translations (A.D. 950—1200) ; the exegetic (A. D. 1200—1450) and the modern or miscellaneous (A. D. 1450—1850). Original works in Tamil are not very many and they can be counted on one's finger's ends The bulk of its literature comprises metrical translations from Sanskrit *itihasas* and *puranas*. Short ethical poems, like Eladi and Tirikadukam, intended for school children, and the huge mass of religious hymns and songs of the Saiva and Vaishnava devotees are honourable exceptions. There was no prose literature before the last century, if the prose commentaries on ancient authors be excepted.

Alone among the Dravidian languages Tamil possesses a literature, ancient as well as interesting. Every Tamilian must esteem it a grand and noble heritage, which he can call his own only by approaching the study of it in a scientific spirit. Let us all join hands lovingly in the sacred task of reconstructing the best history of this people and their language, and tracing the continuity of their development. And in this let us follow the examples of Dr. Latham, Pro . Skeat and others, whose work for their English language and literature stands unrivalled.

APPENDIX I

THE EARLY PANDYA KINGS

The materials for writing a history of the Pandyas will be found in (1) current traditions and legends, (2) some of which are distorted and interlarded with miracles in the local *puranas*, (3) in early Tamil literature, and (4) inscriptions. Of these the first and second are unreliable, chiefly owing to their antiquity and the variety of narrow channels through which they had passed before they attained the present form. The local puranas, most of them being obviously mythical, put us on the wrong scent, and in some cases operate as counter-acting agents in our researches. The third is entitled to some credence; but on account of the repetition of some names and the absence of dates, they have to be corroborated by other independent testimony. Inscriptions alone, when they are not forgeries, yield accurate and reliable data, as they cannot easily be tampered with like the *puranic* or other records.

It is intended in this note to compare and contrast Tamil traditions, legends and local *puranas* with early literature and inscriptions and show their worthlessness for historical purposes. As the annals of Tamil literature prior to the eleventh century is shrouded in obscurity, it will be useful to take for consideration the history of the Pandya kings from the earliest times up to A.D. 950.

The earliest available information about the Pandya kings is that which is contained in the Pattuppattu, the Agananuru and the Purananuru. From the various names of Pandyas which occur in these poems Mr. Kanakasabhai has constructed the following genealogical table :—Nedum Seliyan I (50-75)—Verri Vel Seliyan (75-90)—Nedum Seliyan II (90-128)—Ugra Peruvaludi (128-140)—Nanmaran (140-150). The exact relationship of these kings and the data on which this table is based are not clearly understood. At any rate Ugra Peruvaludi in whose reign Tiruvalluvar and Auvai flourished could not have succeeded Nedum Seliyan II who won the battle of Talai-Alankanan Further, the dates assigned to these kings seem to be half-a-century too early. His table has, therefore, been slightly modified and improved as given below. It is only tentative and must remain so until epigraphy discloses new facts some day or other :—(1) Vadimbalamba Ninra Pandya, B C. 450—(2) Nilandaru Tiruvir Pandya, B. C. 350—(3) Palsalai Mudukudumi Peruvaludi, B. C. 25—(4) Ugra Peru Valudi A. D. 125—(5) Nedum Seliyan I, A. D. 150 —(6) Verrivel or Ilam Seliyan, A. D. 175—(7) Nedum Seliyan II, A. D. 200—(8) Nanmaran I, A. D. 225—(9) Maran Valudi, A. D. 250—(10) Nanmaran II, A. D. 275 —(11) Peruvaludi, A. D. 300. The name of the first king means ' he who survived the deluge'. According to the Mahawanso a tidal wave from the Indian ocean washed off the southern shores about B.C. 450. The above may be a reference to this. In the reign of the second Pandya the Tamil grammarian Tolkapyar lived. The third and the most famous among the early Pandyas was Palsalai Mudukudumi [1] Peruvaludi. He was a great patron of learning and Brahmans and performed many *yagas* or sacrifices. He might have been the king who sent an embassy to Augustus Cæsar in B. C. 25 ; and this fact has been alluded to in the Velvikudi grant as 'going as ambassador to the gods'. Ugra Peruvaludi is said to have engraved the fish on the Himalayas. Nedum Seliyan I constructed many tanks for irrigation, which fact has been commemorated in a poem by Kuda Pulaviyanar. He committed suicide for having, without a proper enquiry, ordered the decapitation of Kovalan an innocent merchant of Kaveripatam at the instigation of a crafty goldsmith. The merchant's wife Kannaki committed *sati* and was deified as a Goddess of Chastity. To appease her wrath the king's son Verri Vel Seliyan sacrificed one thousand goldsmiths. Nedum Seliyan II while yet a boy defeated the two Tamil kings and five chieftains at Talaiyalamkanam. Sattanar the famous author of Manimekalai and a stanch Buddhist lived in the reign of Nanmaran I and the poet Nakkirar flourished probably in the days of Nanmaran II

With the discovery of the Chinnamanur copper plates in 1906 and of the Velvikudi grant in 1908, the mist that enveloped the early history of the Pandyas may be said

---

1. The custom of keeping a tuft of hair on the head was purely Indo-Aryan. In Southern India no non-Aryan tribe or caste had it. Hence the early Brahman settlers were called குடுமி செளவியர் (*Kal.* 71) This Pandya king was perhaps the first Dravidian who adopted this Aryan custom on account of his having performed many *yagas* or sacrifices like the Brahmans.

to be disappearing. They have brought to light several facts hitherto unknown, and furnished valuable data to fix the different stages in the progress of Tamil literature. The genealogical table which has been constructed from the materials supplied by them goes up to the beginning of the seventh century, causing a lacuna of nearly three hundred years between it and the one given above. Perhaps this was the period of the Jaina ascendancy; and the Jains might have been instrumental to the occupation of the Pandya country by the Kalabhras or the Jaina rulers from the Carnataka country.

Before giving the actual pedigree of Pandya kings, the plates proceed to mention the achievements of the real or mythic kings in the past without mentioning their names. Among these may be stated,—the churning of the ocean for nectar, appearing on the throne of Indra, mastering the Tamil language, bringing back the sea, obtaining the titles of Puzhiyan and Panchavan, founding the city of Madura, excelling pandits in learning, leading elephants into the Bharata country after the death of the great charioteer, absolving Vijaya from the curse of Vasu, engraving the fish, the tiger and the bow on Mount Meru, constructing many tanks, defeating two kings at Talayalankanam, translating the Mahabharata and establishing the College of poets at Madura. To these the Sanskrit portions of the bigger Chinnamanur plates and the Velvikudi grant add that Agastya was their family priest, that one of the Pandyas induced Ravana to sue for peace, that one of them went as ambassador to the gods and that the god Brahma requested the Pandya who had survived the 'deluge' to take up the protection of the three worlds.

APPENDIX I

Then comes the following genealogy :—

Mudukudumi Peruvaludi.
|
Kalabhra occupation
|
1. Kadungon A. D. 600.
|
2. Maravarman Avani Chulamani, A. D. 620.
|
3. Jayantan or Sendan, A. D. 650.
|
4. Maravarman Arikesari, fought at Nelveli, A. D. 680.
|
5. Jatavarman Ranadhiran A. D. 710.
|
6. Arikesari Parankusan Rajasimha I, Ter Selvan or Termaran, A D. 735.
|
7. Jitila Varman Parantakan Srivara, A. D. 770.
|
8. Rajasimha II, A. D. 785.
|
9. Varaguna I, A D. 810.
|
10 Srimaran Sri Vallabha Deva, A. D. 835.
|
┌──────────────────────┬──────────────────────┐
11. Varaguna Varman   12. Parantakan Viranarayana
A. D. 862—3   A.D. 885 m a Kerala princess.
|
13. Rajasimha III, Abhimana Meru; defeated by Parantaka Chola in A. D. 910.

Among these kings Palsalai Mudukudumi Peruvaludi was a remote ancestor of Kadungon. The name of Kadungon occurs in the commentary on Iraiyanar's Agapporul as the last king in whose reign the first *Sangam* was abolished. In the reign of Jayantan (*Tam.*

Sendan) Chulamani a Jaina Tamil classic was composed by Tolamoli Devar in memory of the king's father Maravarman Avani Chulamani. Maravarman Arikesari (No. 4) who boasts of having won the battle of Nelveli (நெல்வேலியில் வென்றமாறன்) must be identified with Sundara or Kun Pandya. Had the impaling of 8000 Jains by Trignana Sambanda—an event so much exaggerated and described with pride in the Saivapuranas—been an accomplished fact it must have been referred to in the plates. Arikesari Parankusan had the title of Ter Seliyan—a name which occurs in the above commentary as Ven-Ter Seliyan and as the founder of the second Sangam. Jatila Varman Parantakan, known to the Tamils as Komaran Sadaiyan, was a famous king and the donor of the Velvikudi grant. He had the title of Srivara and granted the village of Srivara-Mangalam in the Nanguneri taluk, Tinnevelly district, to a Magada Brahman named Sujjata Bhatta. He was a devout worshipper of Vishnu. His minister Marankari built a temple and an *agrahara* in A. D. 770 to God Narasimha at the foot of the Elephant hill or Yanaimalai near Madura. Varaguna I might have been the builder of the Vishnu temple at Varaguna-Mangalam. His grandson was a staunch Saivite, converted probably to that faith by his minister and Saiva saint Manikka Vachakar, while his great-grandson Rajasimha III or Srivallabha Deva was a Vaishnava owing to the influence of the Vishnuvite Selva Nambi, his purohit and religious preceptor. In the reign of this last Pandya lived the Vishnuvite saints Periyalvar and Andal.

Some of these facts will be found stated in early

APPENDIX I

Tamil literature and in the Madura *stalapurana*. The copper plates refer also to the founding of a college of poets at Madura and the translating of the Mahabharata. The first has been considered in our essay on the Tamil academies. As regards the Mahabharata which in the opinion of Prof. Macdonell attained its complete form in Sanskrit about A. D. 350, there appears to have been more than one Tamil translation. All the Tamil versions must have therefore been made subsequent to A. D. 400. The first of these versions is probably the one referred to in the grants. The translator's name is at present unknown and the very existence of the work is doubtful. Whether it was identical with the Bharata-Venba of Perundevanar (A.D. 750) or altogether different cannot be ascertained owing to the paucity of information. Provisionally, however, it may be assumed that the Bharata-Venba of Perundevanar was a second translation. The third was by the Saivite Aranilai Visakan Trailokyamallan Vatsarajan of Arumbakkam (1) in the reign of Kulottunga Chola III (1178-1215) This translation of the epic, though it does not survive to this day, might have been undertaken when Kamban was engaged in translating the Ramayana. The fourth rendering of the epic into Tamil was by Villiputtur Alvar, a Vaishnava poet of the fifteenth century. It is only a fragment or an epitome, but completed by Nalla Pillai in A.D. 1732-1744.

So far the history of the early Pandyas from Tamil literature and inscriptions. From both the sources the

(1) Madras Government Epigraphist's report, dated 2nd July 1906, p. 74.

number of Pandya kings does not exceed twenty. On the other hand, the Madura Stalapurana gives a long list of some seventy-three Pandyas beginning with Kulasekara and ending with Madhuresvara, besides another list of some forty-one illegitimate Pandyas. The *purana* narrates miraculous events connected with the local deity. Most of the names in the lists seem to be fanciful or mythical, corroborated neither by literature nor by inscriptions. Before proceeding to compare and examine them it will be necessary to give an outline of the salient points from the Halasya Mahatmya so far as they relate to the Tamil academies and the early poets, first according to the order of the 'sacred sports' or the deeds of Siva and secondly according to the succession of the Pandya kings.

I. The 51st 'sport' was the establishment of the Madura College during the reign of Vamsasekara Pandya ; (52), in the reign of Champaka Maran the pride of Nakkirar was subdued by Siva ; (53 and 54) Siva directs Agastya to teach Tamil grammar to Nakkirar ; (55) Nakkirar's commentary on Iraiyanar's Agapporul recited before the dumb Brahman child, Rudra-Sarman ; (56) refers probably to Tiruvalluvar's contest with the members of the academy , (57-61) miracles concerning Manikkavachakar which occurred in the reign of Arimardhana Pandya ; and (62, 63), the Jains were persecuted by the Saivite apostle Trignana Sambanda during the reign of Kubja, Kun or Sundara Pandya.

II. The fourth king was Ugra Pandya. He is said to have performed ninety-six Asvamedha or horse sacrifices, and he was the founder of a Sangam or academy. The seventh was Vikrama Pandya. In his reign the elephant that came to destroy Madura at the machination of the Jains was metamorphosed into a hill by Siva with the help of Narasimha. In commemoration of this event the Pandya king built a temple for the Vishnu God Narasimha in the Yanamalai hill. 'மேவரு நரசிங்கத்தை யிருத்திஞன் வேழக்குன்றில்'. The tenth in succession was Anantaguna Pandya. In this reign Sri Rama visited Madura while searching for his wife Sita. The nineteenth was Varaguna. He went to Tiruvidaimarudur in the Tanjore district to expiate his sin of *brahma-hatti*. The forty-sixth was Vamsasekhara in whose reign the third academy was established, Nakkirar, Paranar, Kapilar &c. being its members. Nakkirar composed the கைலைபாதி காளத்திபாதியந்தாதி. Rudrasarma listened to Nakkirar's commentary on Iraiyanar's Agapporul. The sixty-first was Arimardhana. The saint Manikkavachakar flourished in this reign. The last but one and the seventy-second king in the list was Kubja or Kun Pandya. In his reign 8000 Jains were impaled by Trignana Sambandha.

Stripping the above miraculous events of their mythological garb and considering them together it will be seen that they are most of them stern historical facts ; only the order of time has not been observed. The 'sacred sports' of Siva at Madura are narrated in three or four Sanskrit puranas namely, Uttara Maha Purana, Kadamba Vana Purana, Sundara Pandyam and Halasya Mahatmyam—all which were composed some time after the tenth century A. D. out of the current traditions and legends. And their Tamil translations must have been made long after that period. These accounts differ as regards the order and description of 'sports'. Some of the accounts are conflicting in other respects. The Tamil names of kings are sanskritized and are not arranged in chronological order as will be seen later on. Thus, the Tiruvilayadal Purana, like all other puranas, is a compilation of traditions, miracles and other stories, all jumbled together regardless of any time sequence and without any order. It would, therefore, be extremely injudicious to use them for historical purposes without caution.

The only king who is mentioned in Tamil literature as having performed many Yagas or sacrifices is Palyaga (salai) Mudukudimi Peruvaludi. He was an ancestor of Nedum Seliyam of the Talai Alanganam fame. He must therefore have flourished about the beginning of the Christian era. Nowhere is it laid down that Ugra Pandya conducted any sacrifices; but one Ugra Pandya or Ugra Peruvaludi is said to have attended a Rajasuya sacrifice performed by the Chola king Perunarkilli who lived about the first century A. D. The fourth king in the list is Vikrama Pandya in whose reign the Narasimha temple at the foot of the Anaimalai hill was built. From the inscriptions discovered in that temple, we learn that it was constructed by Maran Kari, a minister of the Pandya king Parantaka or Nedum Sadaiyan in A. D. 770 (No. 7). The age of Manikka Vachakar, who is said to have lived in the reign of the 61st king Arimardhana, but actually in the reign of Varaguna the 19th Pandya king, was the second half of the ninth century; and the date of Trignana Sambanda has been determined to be the latter half of the seventh. As he is believed to have been a contemporary of Kun or Sundara Pandya, who is known in Tamil religious literature as Nedumara Nayanar of Nelveli, he might be identified with No 4, Maravarman Arikesari (A. D. 680) given in our genealogical table. Thus, we find the *pauranic* accounts of these historic facts are grossly anachronous and at variance with those which one might glean from early Tamil literature and the epigraphical reports.

APPENDIX II

NOTE ON AGASTYA'S GRAMMAR

Quite recently there has appeared a small book, entitled Per-Agattiya-Tirattu, which profeses to be a collection of aphorisms from 'the great grammar of Agastya.' It contains, besides, a set of rules which Pandits believe were composed by Kazharamban at the bidding of his revered teacher Agastya. Both these collections of excerpts seem to be for the following reasons forgeries foisted, like so many other works, upon that great mythical sage.

1. The style is simple and very modern; it contains too many Sanskrit words; and the difference between the language of this work and that of Tolkapyar, his direct disciple, is patent in every one of its Sutras.

2. In the days of Agastya the number of Sanskrit words in Tamil must have been very small, and the necessity for framing rules for the loan of Aryan words could not have been felt, as it was in the days of Buddhamitra and Pavanandi. It was on this account that Tolkapyar did not give any definite rule under that head, except in a vague manner thus :—

சிதைந்தன வரினுமியைந் தனவரையார்.

On the other hand, this Per-Agattiya-Tirattu devotes one whole chapter of some 24 Sutras to Sandhis and word formation, which have been explained in the seventh essay as the peculiar characteristics of Sanskrit. Evidently it includes in the Tamil vocabulary of Agastya's age pure Sanskrit words and foreign or *desiya* words borrowed by modern Tamil as the following aphorisms will show:—

(1) ஞகரம் அ ஆ எ ஒவ் வோடாம்.

(2) யகரம் அ ஆ உ ஊ ஒ ஔ வுடனும்.

With this compare the corresponding *sutras* in (a) Tolkapyam and (b) Nannul.

(a) (1) ஆ எ ஒ எனு மூயிர் ஞகார்த்துரிய.

(2) ஆவோடல்லது யகாமூதலாத.

(b) (1) அ ஆ எ ஒவ்வோர டாகுரும்முதல்.

(2) அ ஆ உ ஊ ஒ ஔ யமமுதல்.

3. The author of this grammar seems to think that the Tamil letter Aydam, ஃ, is borrowed from Sanskrit as will be inferred from the following *sutras*.

(a) முதலுயிர் மெய்யாய்த மூப்பாளென்றே. (7)

(b) எ ஒவ்வும் முறனவுந்தமி ழெழுத்தென்க. (54)

(c) ஐந்தொழி யெழுத்தெலாம் வடவெழுத்தாகும். (55)

It is usual to say that ழ, ள, ற, and ன, which are purposely placed last in the Tamil alphabetic system to indicate their speciality to that tongue, and the letter ஃ, which has neither the sound of *visarga* nor that of *jihvamulya* but a sound peculiarly its own, are the distinguishing marks of Tamil. To call Aydam a Sanskrit letter is absurd. Moreover, the author of this work seems to derive Tamil from Sanskrit.

4. The பேரிசைச்சூத்திரம் attributed to Agastya's

disciple Kazharamban purports to give us an outline history of the Tamil language. It is divided according to this writer into eight periods, namely, (1) Pre-alphabetic, (2) Alphabetic, (3) Grammatic, (4) Academic, (5) Monastic, (6) Jaina, (7) Pauranic, and (8) Modern. This classification, which on the face of it is unhistorical and anachronous, has been adopted with but slight modification by Mr. Damodaram Pillai in his introduction to Virasoliyam ; and it has been criticized at some length in the eighth essay. The last or modern period may be taken to commence in the fifteenth or sixteenth century A. D. A classification, which refers to phases of literary activity of the sixteenth century, to have been made by a disciple of Agastya in the second or third century B. C. is a hard pill to swallow, even should it come from the best of scholars. But Tamil Pandits will readily believe it to be the work of a disciple of Agastya. And the reader can easily understand that this work is a clear instance of forgery. What seems probable and believable is that Per-Agattiyam is a composition of a learned member of one of the Saiva *mutts* or monasteries in the Tanjore or Tinnevelly district written for the use of the Saiva students of Tamil, who may have had in the beginning a prejudice against the use of Nannul (being the work of a Jain) though it was decidedly the best grammar, and that it may have come into existence long after A. D. 1250.

5. In the prefatory *sutra* to Tolkapyam it is said of its author Tolkapyar as follows :—

......தமிழ்கூறு நல்லுலகத்து
வழக்குஞ் செய்யுளு மாயிருமுதலி
னெழுத்துஞ் சொல்லும் பொருளுநாடிச்

செந்தமிழியற்கைச் சிவணிய நிலதொடு
முந்துநூல்கண்டு முறைப்பட வெண்ணிய
புலநதொகுத்தோன்......
மல்குநீர்வரைப்பி ஊனந்திர நிறைந்த
தொல்காப்பியன்.

For the purpose of dealing with the Tamil letters, words and rhetoric as used in the ordinary speech and in poetry, the author clearly says that he observed the usages of the Sen-Tamil men (செந்தமிழியற்கைச் சிவணியநிலம்) and carefully studied the early literature (முந்துநூலகண்டு) before collecting, collating and arranging facts for methodical treatment in his grammar (முறைபபடவெண்ணிப் புலந்தொகுத்தோன்) after the model of the Sanskrit *Aindram*. He has not said anywhere in his grammar one word about Agastya, his reputed teacher. It has been at least the Tamil custom for an author to begin his work with a salutation for his teacher or Acharya. In this case the teacher was a divine Rishi and the supposititious writer of the first Tamil grammar Both of them flourished at the same period. It is not understood why Tolkapyar should have taken so much trouble to observe the usages, to study the Tamil authors, and to deduce therefrom the grammatical rules, or why he should have recited his work for the approval and edification of the academy before a fellow student—Athangottasan—while Agastya was its president. Was it to pick up flaws in his master's great work, and was he such an ungrateful pupil? Tamil pandits would easily believe that the two divine rishis were always at loggerheads. But, all these throw serious doubts as to whether Agastya had really written a Tamil grammar and whether Tolkapyar was ever his disciple. The comment on the prefatory sutra by Sivagnana Swami in confirmation of the facts that Agastya had learnt his Tamil from Siva, that he had been the author of the first grammar of the Tamil language and that it had served, before it was lost, as the model for all the later works on grammar, seems to me very unsatisfactory and even fanciful. No man has ever seen the Agastya's grammar, and the statement of Mr. Damodaram Pillai that it was a jumble of rules relating to the three kinds of Tamil is purely a creation of his powerful imagination. What I am inclined to believe is that every myth and tradition connecting Agastya with the Tamil language should have come into existence subsequent only to the seventh or eighth century A. D.

APPENDIX III
THE AGE OF MANIKKA VACHAKAR

The only Tamil poet whose date has called forth a good deal of controversy from pandits and scholars is Manikka Vachakar. It is, in my humble opinion, mainly due to their sectarian bias, their superstitious belief in the *pauranic* stories, their want of confidence in epigraphy and their incorrect understanding of the historical trend of the Tamil language, literature and religion. One writer thinks that Manikka Vachakar belonged to a period subsequent to the third academy, another puts his date long anterior to it, while a third brings it down to the thirteenth century. Dr. Pope, the Editor and translator of Manikka Vachakar's works, believes that he lived ' somewhere about the seventh o:

eighth century of our era,' while yet in another place he writes that his date 'may reasonably be assigned to the tenth century.' Thus the age of Manikka Vachakar remains still unsettled. It is not intended to waste some more ink and paper by launching into any elaborate discussion (or by seriously attempting to refute their arguments, but to briefly indicate certain grounds for a correct determination of his date.

(1) The traditional order of enumerating the four famous Saiva saints—Appar, Sambandar, Sundarar and Manikka Vachakar and the position assigned to Tiruvachakam and Tirukkovai in the Saiva *tirumurais* seem to support the view that the last mentioned poet-saint lived later than Appar. And this theory is confirmed by the fact that Manikka Vachakar and Kalladar have described in their works a considerably larger number of Siva's sports than that referred to by Appar or Sambandar, who must have visited Madura—the far famed capital of the Pandyas and a stronghold of Saivism in the South.

(2) As a rule the best annotator would quote illustrative passages from the contemporary writers or from those who preceded the author whose work he annotates. The commentator of Manikka Vachakar's Tirukkovai—Perasiriyar, Nacchinarkiniyar or whoever he might be—cites authorities from Iraiyanar's Agapporul, Tolkapyam, Kural, Kalittogai, Appar's Tevaram and Naladiyar. Since the authors of all these works had lived long before Manikka Vachakar, he must have understood that Appar was his predecessor.

(3) In his Koil-padigam Manikka Vachakar speaks of

APPENDIX III

Ponnambalam or the 'Golden Hall' at Chidambaram. According to traditions this hall was first built by Hiranya Varman, probably a Pallava king, during the sixth century; and we have no reason to believe that this shrine was in existence before the days of the Chola king Kocchengannan who is said to have built several temples to Siva and Vishnu, and also gilded the hall at Chidambaram.

செம்பொன்னணிந்த சிற்றம்பலத்தை.—T. T. 82.

This Chola king lived probably in the latter half of the sixth century.

(4) Manikka Vachakar refers to Pey Ammaiyar, the Saiva lady saint and poetess of Karaikal, who could not have flourished earlier than the sixth century for the simple reason that the *andadi* form of Tamil poem, in which her திருவிரட்டைமணிமாலை and அற்புதத்திருவந்தாதி were written, did not come into use before that period, as explained by Nacchinarkiniyar in his commentary on the Tolkapyar's *sutra* விருங்தேத்தானும்.

(5) A careful and candid study of the present work will convince the reader that the religious doctrines expounded by Manikka Vachakar in his Tiruvachakam, the general tenor of his writings and his contempt for other religions and sects may not enable him to take the poet's age beyond the hymnal period, *i. e.* A. D. 500—950.

(6) One of the 'sacred sports' of Siva at Madura was the send-off of the Pandya king Varaguna to His *loka* or heaven; and this act of divine grace has been alluded to by Manikka Vachakar:—

நாடொடு சுவர்க்கநானிலம்புகாமற்
பாகதிபாண்டியற் கருளினே.

Again in his Tirukkovaiyar he refers to that king thus :—

... வரகுணனுந்
தென்னவனேன்றஞ்சிற்றம்பலத்தான். (306)
... சிற்றம்பலம்புகழு
மயலோங்கிருங்களியானைவரதுணன். (327)

It is thus evident that our saint lived in or after the reign of Varaguna Pandya. Epigraphical researches have up to now brought to light only two Pandya kings of that name, the earlier of whom lived in the first quarter of the ninth century. And the Varaguna alluded to by Manikka Vachakar must have been the Varaguna Varman mentioned in the Ambasamudram inscriptions (*Ep. Ind.* Vol. IX., Pt. ii). He was a devout worshipper of Siva and granted donations of money and land for his worship in many Siva temples.

But the Halasya Mahatmya informs us that Manikka Vachakar lived in the reign of one Arimardhana Pandya who was forty-second in succession from the only Varaguna given in the Mahatmya list. This is one of the many shocking anachronisms which one may find in the above *stala-purana*.

(7) In the sacred sports of Siva at Madura as narrated in this *purana*, the 'jackal miracle' which is erroneously connected with Manikka Vachakar and which is stated to have occurred in the reign of Arimardhana Pandya, the sixty-first in the list, comes after the sport of turning into rock the Elephant that came to destroy Madura in the reign of the seventh Pandya, and the hearing of Nakkirar's commentary on Iraiyanar's *Agapporul* by the dumb child, Rudra Sarman, in the reign of the forty-sixth king. The slender data on

APPENDIX III 405

which the first of the above sports rests did actually take place in the reign of Jatila Varman Parantakan, A D. 770. Nakkirar's commentary contains an illustrative *kovai* addressed to the Pandya king Arikesari Parankusan who reigned about A. D. 740.

It is admitted by Tamil pandits that the Tirukkovai of Manikka Vachakar was composed in accordance with the rules given in Iraiyanar's Agapporul, and that our saint must have read Nakkirar's commentary. The date of Iraiyanar's *Agapporul* could not be earlier than A. D. 650. and that of the commentary by Nakkirar about A. D. 740. Manikka Vachakar must have therefore lived after A D. 740. If, now, we admit that the sports or miracles are narrated chronologically in the *stalapurana*, the 'Jackal miracle', coming after the metamorphosis of the Elephant, must have happened after A. D. 770 Thus even according to the writers of the Madura *Stalapurana*, Manikka Vachakar must have lived after A. D. 770.

(8) The religious propagandism of Manikka Vachakar, his visit to Ceylon and his conversion there of many Buddhists and their king which are narrated in the Vadavur *Stalapurana*, are confirmed by Rajaratnakari of Ceylon. This occurred in A D. 819 or more correctly about A. D. 869.

(9) The language of Manikka Vachakar and the various metres employed by him do not take us so far back as the sixth or seventh century. Sanskrit words and phrases like இயமானன, உரோமம், சோரன், தோயம், விமலன், அமுததாரைகள், சண்டமாருதம், சிநதாகுலம், திக்கசாகரம் and மாதாவுதரம் were not used by the poets of the academic period. The resemblance between the works of

Periyalvar, Andal, Nammalvar and Manikka Vachakar in thought, language, style and form is so close as to suggest their being contemporaries more or less. The above Vaishnava saints lived between A. D. 850 and 925.

(10) In the Tiru-tonda-togai (திருத்தொண்டத்தொகை) of Sundarar, the last of the sixty-three Saiva saints, who lived about the first quarter of the ninth century no mention is made of Manikka Vachakar. Yet like the Vaishnava acharyas who twisted and misconstrued texts to fix the beginning of the Kaliyug as the age of Nammalvar—the last of their saints—some of the more recent pandits and scholars have attempted to put the date of our Saiva saint long anterior to that of Appar and Trignana Sambandar, interpreting the expression பொய்யடிமை யில்லாத புலவர் in the திருத்தொண்டத்தொகை as a reference to the saint, and supporting it by two vague allusions found in the following lines from Appar's Tevaram :—

(1) நரியைக் குதிரை செய்வானும்.
(2) குடமுழங்கீசனே வாசகனுக்கொண்டார்.

Here the first quotation proves nothing, as the miraculous transformation of Jackals into 'horses' though traditionally connected with Manikka Vachakar, is an old 'floating myth', like many others of that kind. It was one of the many miracles performed by Siva, and to which our saint himself refers thus,

நரியைக்குதிரையாக்கியநன்மையும்.

There is a reference to this miracle in the Kalladam also. Had Kalladanar, its author, lived posterior to Manikka Vachakar, which seems to me to be more probable, the Jackal miracle should be taken as one of the many

APPENDIX III

floating myths current during the hymnal period of Tamil literature (A. D 600—950), as he has not mentioned Manikka Vachakar in that connection.

In the second quotation the word வாசகன் has been misinterpreted as Manikka Vachakar, and in support of this fanciful meaning the pandits quote two Sanskrit puranas whose authority might be as questionable as that of Halasya Mahatmya and other puranas Here வாசகன் (Skt. *vachaka*) means a ' servant ' or 'messenger' and nothing more.

Now coming to the Tiru-tonda-togai, it might be asked —Why should Manikka Vachakar alone be referred to in this indirect and vague fashion while the other sixty-one saints, some of whom were comparatively less notable, have been mentioned by their names or titles? There is no answer to this question. Both Sundarar and Manikka Vachakar were Brahmans of the same sect; and the latter was the minister of a Pandya king and a great religious disputant who did much for the propagation of Saivism. If Sundarar had to refer to him, he would have with pride mentioned the *name* of this saint instead of using this round-about expression, which may be applied to any sincerely pious poet. He must have also read Appar's Tevaram and noticed in it the incident of the 'Jackal miracle' as well as the word வாசகன். If Manikka Vachakar had really lived before Sundarar and if the latter saint had interpreted வாசகன் to mean Manikka Vachakar, could he not have referred to our saint at least by that holy name in his Tiruttondattogai? This clearly shows that Sundarar had never heard of the name of Manikka Vachakar—the fourth great saint of the Saivas, because he had not yet been born in this world.

Nambiyandar Nambi, the Vyasa of the Dravidian Vedas, has correctly understood the expression பொய்யடி மையில்லாத புலவர் to mean collectively the forty-nine professors of the third academy at Madura.

தாணியிற் பொய்மையிலாத் தமிழ்ச்சங்கமதிற் கபிலர் பரணர் நக்கீரர்முத ஒற்பத்தொன்பது பல்புலவோர்.

Do the modern Tamil scholars claim to be more learned and better informed in this matter than Nambiyandar Nambi who lived within one hundred and fifty years after Sundarar or Manikka Vachakar?

It has been urged by a recent writer that Nambiyandar Nambi has misunderstood the above expression, and that he has wrongly calculated the total, forgetting that the 'traditional sixty-three' was the number of the individual saints sung by Sundara Murti. A grand discovery indeed! But was our poet so ignorant of the rudiments of arithmetic as to merit the critic's condemnation? Has Sundara Murti or any writer anterior to Nambiyandar Nambi stated that the number of individual saints was *sixty-three*? And, if not, how could he call it 'traditional'? Perhaps, he forgot that most of the names of the Saiva saints were almost unknown before the time of Nambiyandar Nambi, who for the first time collected and arranged the Devara and other Saivite hymns, and that their apotheosis was mainly due to his works. If we add Sundara Murti, as our poet has rightly done, to the 62 individual saints enumerated in the திருத்தொண்ட த்தொகை we get the *now* traditional 63. But, if we take the above expression to mean Manikka Vachakar, we get in all 64 which is not the traditional number of Saiva saints, as we cannot by any means omit Sundara Murti from the list.

It is therefore plain beyond any shadow of doubt that the saint Manikka Vachakar must have been an elder contemporary of Periyalvar and Andal of the Vaishnava sect and lived in the reign of the Pandya king Varaguna II (A. D. 870), that is two centuries later than Appar and Trignana Sambandar, half a century later than Sundarar and about one generation earlier than Nammalvar. And this is the view accepted by every student of epigraphy.

KALLADANAR.

The Kalladam is an erotic poem of some one hundred *agavals*, describing mostly the 'sacred sports' of Siva at Madura. Its author Kallada Deva Nayanar was a Saiva poet of the *pauranic* or hymnal period Tamil pandits very often confound him with Kalladanar, an earlier poet of the academic age. The former was a Saiva devotee and author of திருக்கண்ணப்ப தேவார்திருமறம் and a commentary on the Tolkapyam besides the Kalladam, while the latter was a bard and wrote only a few eulogistic verses on the Pandiya king Nedum Seliyan, second century A D Thus Kallada Deva Nayanar and Kalladanar were two distinct poets like Poigai Alvar and Poigaiyar.

Both must have been natives of Kalladam, once a flourishing sea-port near Quilon on the West Coast. In the days of Manikka Vachakar, it was probably the seat of a Saiva shrine, கல்லாடத்துக் கலந்தினிதருளி—T.V. II. 11, which must have come into existence during the ninth century A. D., as no mention is made of it in the

Tevaram of Appar or Sundara Murti. It would only be a vain subterfuge of pandits if it was said that their hymns on that place had been lost along with several others at Chidambaram.

In the Kalladam one may find references to Tiruvalluvar, Nakkirar, Kannappar, Chakkiyar and Murti Nayanar. Concerning the last it says,—

 படைநானகுடன் பஞ்சவற்றுரந்து
 மதுரைவவ்விய கருநடர்வேநத
 நருகர்ச்சார்ந்து நினனருட்பணியடைப்ப. (57)

This event happened, as we have said in Appendix I, about the beginning of the seventh century, which must be taken as the earliest limit of the age of Kalladam.

Again the same work refers to the commentary of Nakkirar on Iraiyanar's Agapporul and to the commendatory verses of the forty-nine professors of the third academy on the Kural of Tiruvalluvar.—

(1) மாறனுமபுலவரு மயங்குறுகாலே
 முந்துறபடபெருமனற மூளேத்தருள்வாக்கா
 லன்பீனநதிணை யென்றறுபதருத்திரங்
 கடலமுதெடெத்துக் கரையில்வைத்ததுபோல். (3)

(2) அருநதமிழ்க்கீரன் பெருநதமிழ்ப்பணுவல்
 வாவியிற்கேட்டகா வியங்களத்தினன். (52)

(3) ஐந்திணைவழுவாத கபபொருளமுதிணேக்
 குறமுனிசேறவும் பெருமுதற்புலவர்க
 ளேழேழுபெயருங் கோதறபபருகவும். (65)

(4) சமயக்கணக்கர் மதிவழிகூறு
 துலகியல்கூறிப பொருளிதுவென்ற
 வள்ளுவன்றனக்கு வளர்கவிப்புலவர்முன்
 முதற்கவிபாடிய முக்கட்பெருமான். (15)

The above quotations show clearly that the Kalladam

is a repertory of old traditions, ghoulish legends and mixed miracles relating to the Saiva religion and literature, narrated in such a form as to allure the Dravidian mind. It is one of those religious books which are highly valued by the Tamil Saivas ; and it has given rise to the proverb—கல்லாடம் கற்றவேறு மல்லாடாதே. (Venture not to argue with one that has studied the Kalladam).

They prove further that the author of Kalladam was not unacquainted with Nakkirar's commentary on Iraiyanar's Agapporul and that he must have lived several years after Perundevanar, one of the forty-nine professors of the Madura College. In our essay on the Tamil academies it has been shown that this commentary on Agapporul was written sometime after A. D. 750 and that Perundevanar, the reputed author of the Tamil Mahabharatam, lived somewhere about A. D. 785. Further, the number of sports played by Siva at Madura came to be definitely fixed as 64 during the time of Kalladar, while it was not so in the days of the last four great saints It is thus pretty evident that Kallada Deva Nayanar lived between A D. 850 and 950, and that he may have been a younger contemporary of Manikka Vachakar whose Tirukkovayar served, according to a traditon, as the model for his Kalladam.

APPENDIX IV

NOTE ON THE WORD TIYAN.

The word Tiyan designates a class of toddy drawers in Malabar, Travancore and Cochin, and it is commonly supposed to be a synonym for Izhuvan, which is the name of another caste of palm-cultivators found in the Tamil and Malayalam countries. The traditions current in Malabar represent them as immigrants from Ceylon, and in accordance thereto the words Tiyan and Izhuvan are derived by the old-school philologists of Malabar and their European supporters, like Drs. Caldwell and Gundert and Mr. Logan, from 'dvipam' (an island) and Simhalam (Ceylon). This etymology, though advocated by such high authorites and confirmed also by Malabar traditions, seems to be rather fanciful and devoid of any historical or ethnological foundation. It is needless to mention here the utter worthlessness of Keralolpatti and Keralamahatmya as historical records. For the purposes of ethnological investigations no reliance can be placed on either of these, because they are only later compositions of the Nambudri Brahmans of Malabar, who *de facto* had in their hands the destiny of the Chera kingdom. It is not the only instance in which the Malabar people have shown their primitive knowledge of the modern sciences of language and ethnology. 'Embran' is derived from *hebrahman*; 'Nambi' from *nambu*, to believe; 'Kuric'chan' from *kuri*, to mark, 'Variyar' from *varuka* to sweep and so on. Of course, these etymologies were supported by strange traditions, short or long, which the Nambudri Brahmans were ever ready to invent. For these vagaries of etymology the language is responsible, not the people. The mother-tongue of the non-Aryan tribes. of Malabar was purely a Tamil dialect, and about fifty per cent. of the words found in the Malayalam vocabulary are of Tamil origin As, however, Sanskrit had and even now have an undoubted preference in matters social and religious, the natural tendency has been to derive the Tamil words from Sanskrit.

The arguments advanced by the upholders of the 'Simhala' or 'Dwipa' theory are,—

(1) 'The Keralolpatti says that at one-time five artificers having provoked the Perumal's wrath emigrated and found refuge in Ceylon, from whence they were brought back by the intercession of foreigners, and in their train came the caste of cocoanut tree cultivators'. (2) The cocoanut tree is not indigenous to India but was introduced by the southern islanders of Ceylon. It is suggested by some that the connecting link between the words Tiyan and Dvipan survives in 'Divar' of Canara. One writer goes even to the length of tracing the Kadamba chiefs of Humcha to the children of the islanders, 'Divara Makkalu'. (3) Mr. Logan points out that since cocoanut is not mentioned in the list of exports from Malabar given in the Periplus in the first century A.D., it is probable that the palm was introduced by the Tiyans (Dvipans) and Izhuvans (Simhalese) from Ceylon before the sixth century A.D.

As to the first argument it may be remarked that the *South Indian Inscriptions* inform us that the toddy-drawing classes of the country from Cape Comorin to Tirupati were called Izhuvans. In none of the ancient works Sanror or Shanan is used to denote the modern caste of Tamil toddy-drawers. Granting then, that all the Shanans of the Tamil country and the Tiyans and Izhuvans of Malabar and Travancore are the descendants of the original immigrants from Ceylon, we have at present nearly two millions of this guild following the same trade and occupation in both the countries. The population of Ceylon according to the Census of 1891 was nearly three millions. Although there had been several invasions and occupations of the northern part of Ceylon alternately by the Cholas and Pandiyas, the annals of that island from the first century to the ninth do not speak a word about any irruption or civil war that could have led to the evacuation of the island by nearly two-thirds of its useful inhabitants. We read in the Mahawanso that a branch of the Pandiyans was ruling for a short period in Ceylon. Moreover, the relationship between the Singalese and Keralas was, in fact, so little that it is scarcely possible that such a large immigration directly from Ceylon to Malabar could have taken place during that remote period. In the copper plate grants of the Syrian Christians the names Izhuvan and Tiya-alvan, occur; and it is evident that the Tiyans (not Dwipans or Tivans) were then (A. D 1320) an organisedguild with headmen or *alvans*, and that the Izhuvans were later immigrants from the Tamil country. The difference in the customs observed by the two toddy-drawing castes confirms the truth of the statement. The Izhuvans follow the Makkatayam rule of inheritance while the Tiyans of North Malabar follow the nepotic law of Bhutal Pandiya. Being later immigrants, the Izhuvans of Malabar are regarded by the Tiyans as of very inferior status, just as their Cherumas and Pulayas hold the Paraiyas of the Tamil country in low estimation. The name Izhuvan is derived by Dr. Caldwell from Simhalam, Sihalam, on the analogy of the Greek word Indoi from Sindhu. There can be no necessity for thus dragging a Sanskrit word through many stages, when there is already in the Tamil language the simple word Singalam.

APPENDIX IV

With regard to the second argument, it may be said that the word in 'Divara Makkalu' is not ' Divara' or Divar, but it is 'Deva or Devara' an ordinary title assumed by the South Indian kings ; The Kadamba kings had it; the Kallan and Marava castes of Madura still have it; and a section of the Todas called the Palals style themselves 'Der-mokh' or the sons of God. The Kadambas are said to have been toddy-drawers, because toddy-drawing was, and even now is, the special occupation of several primitive tribes who are found in various parts of India bearing different local names. As subjects of the Kadamba kings, the palm cultivators of Canara assume with pride the name 'Devara makkalu;' the Kallans and Maravas are called Tevans or Devans, because their ancestors are believed to have been kings, and in the last Census several of them have returned their caste name as 'Tevan' simply ; the Palals are called ' Dermokh ' because they are the high priests of the Todas. According to the ' Dwipa' theory all these castes and tribes may be said to be the descendants of the ' islanders'! The important caste of toddy-drawers who bear the name of Tiyan or Dvipan in Malabar is considered in their land of nativity, Ceylon, as strangers or ' Duravar'. How then can we say that the palm cultivators and toddy drawers of South India are immigrants from Ceylon? It is probable that a few families of toddy-drawers may have returned from Ceylon with the artificers, but not in such large numbers as to give a territorial name to an immense caste consisting of two millions or more members and living in various parts of Southern India.

Now coming to the third argument, it may be urged

that either the cocoanut might have been omitted to be mentioned by an oversight, or might not have been an article of export. In Southern India it was certainly valued and much used by the Tamils for drink and food during the first century A. D.

ஒதெங்கி னிளனீ ருதிர்க்கும் வளமிருகன்றுடி.—*Pur*.

At any rate this argument is not strong enough to support the theory of the migration of such a numerous caste from the tiny island of Ceylon. It is also contrary to the general law of migration from the north to south India during the historic times.

The argument from the Tamil name of the cocoanut palm is more imaginary than real. The word *tengu* found in the Dravidian languages, as *tenkaya* in Telugu and *tengina* in Canarese, is derived from the root *tem* or *ten* which means 'honey' or 'sweetness.' *Tengu* is the sweet or honey tree and not the southern tree as some philologists would have us believe. And *ten-disai* is the sweet direction where Tamil or the 'sweet' tongue is spoken. This direction is called in Tamil *ten* with reference to the habitat of the Tamilians, just as *mel* (merku) and *kil* (kilakku) denote 'west and east' with reference to the lofty mountains of their country. Since *ten (r) ku* and *tengu* are derivatives of the same root *ten*, it is not right to say that *tengu* (cocoanut) is derived from *terku* and call it *par excellence* the 'southern tree', as if there had been no cocoanut trees in India before the introduction of that useful palm from Ceylon by the Tiyans.

What then is the etymology of the terms Izham, Izhavan and Tiyan. 'Izham' means the land of Kubera or the Indian god of gold (Izham) for which the island of

APPENDIX IV

Ceylon or Lanka was renowned in the Puranas. This word is quite distinct from 'Izham' which means 'toddy.' The latter is derived from 'Izhu,' to draw, and it may be found in Telugu as 'Idiga'. It is highly probable that 'Izham' has come to denote toddy also, as a number of synonyms for toddy indicates the high importance of this beverage which was esteemed in early times as valuable as gold. On these grounds we are far from agreeing with Dr. Caldwell and other scholars in tracing the word 'Izham' or 'Izhavan' from 'Simhalam' which had already found its way into the Tamil language in the form of Singalam.

Similarly we would derive Tiyan from *ti-an*, which means a 'sweet man,' or one whose occupation is the manufacture of the *ti* or 'sweet' drink. It is an occupational but not a territorial name applied to this class of toddy drawers. When most of the Drvidian castes, like Nayadi, Pulayan, Cheruman, Kammalan and Panikkan, who are supposed to carry pollution with them, possess Dravidian names, why should Tiyant and Izhavads alone be called by Sanskrit appellations?

INDEX

(*Names of Tamil authors and works are printed in Italics.*)

Aborigines, 19, 377
Academies, the traditional account of the, 252, later, 254; work of the, 257.
Accadian, its affinity with Tamil, 34, 121
Accent in Tamil, 135.
Adiyarkunallar, annotator, 189
Adjectives, not declined, 165
Agapporul, Nakkirar's commentary on Iraiyanar's, 253, 403
Agastya, 45, 150, 390, age of, 118, grammar, 188, 397, priest of the Pandyas, 52, students of, 237.
Agglutinative languages, 147.
Ainkurunuru an early Chera-Tamil anthology, 342
Alapedai or prolation, 133.
Alphabet, the Tamil, 113 *et seq.*
Alvars, or Vishnuvite saints, 218, names of, 295, the 'first,' 299.
Ambalakkaran, a caste, 69.
Ambalavasis, a caste, 103.
American languages, 172
Anaimalai inscriptions, 319.
Audal, a lady saint, 323
Anthologies, Tamil, when compiled, 254, 257
Anthropometry, doubted, 14
Anti-brahmanical literature, 225.
Appar, a Saiva Saint, 217, 305.
Archaeology, 16.
Arisil kizhar a Tamil poet, 269.
Arunachala kavi, 190.
Arunandi Sivacharya, a Tamil poet and philosopher, 222.
Artizans, social position of, 74.
Aryans, original home of the, 35, conquest of South India, 51
Aryan theory of the Tamils, 20
Asoka, 126.
Assyrians, 11

Ativira Rama Pandya, a poet king, 225, 255.
Atti-peru, meaning of, 359 *f.n.*
Augustus Caesar, an embassy to, 389
Aynai hill, 266.

Bedar, a caste, 101.
Beschi, Father, 225, on vowel signs, 131
Betel-leaf, use of, 329
Bharatam, when translated, 247
Bhatta or later colony of Brahmans, 349, 380
Biographies of saints, 296.
Bitti Deva, of Mysore, 111.
Brahma-Aryan, a title, 65
Brahmans civilizing the Tamils, 42, invited by Tamil kings, 59; their exclusiveness, 89; their influence in Tamil literature, 186, in Malabar, 318, when migrated, 379.
Brahmanism, early, 285-288, in Kerala, 373.
Brahmi characters, 115; used by Brahmans and Buddhists, 126, and Vatteluttu compared, 123, all South Indian alphabets traceable to, 127; except Vatteluttu, 128.

Brahuis, a Dravidian tribe, 50, 378, and the Dravidians, Dr. Grierson on, 37, 38.
Bray, Mr. Denys, 33; on the Dravidians, 37
Brihat Katha, 243.
Buddhamitra, a Tamil grammarian, 119,128, on mispronunciation, 137
Buhler, Dr G., on Vatteluttu, 120, 243.
Burnell, Dr. A. C., 116, on Vatteluttu, 120.

INDEX

Caldwell, Dr. 33, 412, on the word 'Dravida', 5: on the aborigines, 19, on Tamil civilisation, 50; on the Paraiyas, 81, on the Tamil alphabet, 120; on Tamil diphthongs, 156, on Tamil literature, 201—204; on the Alvars, 281, on Malayalam, 345, 359

Case terminations, 164.

Castes, Tamil, 58, regional classification of, 62, in Raja Raja Chola's time, 66; origin of, 67; increase of, 73, disputes, 74; the right and left-hands 95

Caste system, 61 ; Vellalar's position in, 61; introduction of, 75 ; among the Naga-Dravidians, 381.

Cattle-lifting, before a war, 40

Ceylon and Tiyans, 415

Chakkiyar Kuttu, 190.

Chera customs, early, 275.

Chera kings, dates of certain, 265, genealogy of, 270.

Cheruimars and Pallans, names of castes, 354.

Chidambaram, temple at, 318

Chinese, 161.

Chintadripetta, 93

Chintamani, a Jaina work, 219, 298, age of, 255

Chudamani Nigandu. Tamil dictionary, 219.

Chulamani, a poem, 219, 392.

Coimbatore, derivation of, 31

Combination of letters, 140.

Commentators, Tamil, 196 ; names of, 223,Vaishnava, 223.

Commentaries, need for, 223

Communication between the East and West Coasts, 371

Compound words in Tamil, 158, and in Sanskrit, 161

Conjeeveram, religions at, 290

Consonants, Tamil, 134, softening of Sanskrit, 161.

Copper plate grants, 115 , early Malabar, 356

Cow, its importance 73.

Cox, Prof. H., quoted, 15.
Critical spirit, 196.

Damodaram Pillai's division of Tamil literature, 198-200, 399.
Dancing women, 190
Dandi, a grammarian, 220.
Dead, disposal of the, 39, 214
Dependant letters in Tamil, 133.
Der-mokh, 415.
Deva Nagari alphabet, 29.
Devar (Aryans), 10.
Devara-makkalu, a title. 415.
Devara hymns, 190; and Divya prabandam, compared, 292
Divakaram of Sendan, a Tamil dictionary, 65,219
Dots, use of, in Tamil letters, 122.
Drama, 187; works on the, 189.
Dravida, explained, 1, Manu's definition, 5, Dr. Caldwell's use of, 5, etymology of, 6, and Gauda contrasted, 3
Dravidas, the five, 2, the custom of, 3, proper, 4, Nambudries not included, 4 f. n.
Dravidins. 61, in Upper India, 36, not a dark race, 378, civilisation of, 60 , religion of early, 283 , various theories concerning, 17 *et seq*, connection with Australians, 18
Dravidian, linguistic and ethnological applications, 37; family and Uralo-Altaic languages, 170, 171 ; languages, degree of relationship among the, 374 , their influence in Sanskrit, 168, 169 , interchange of letters in, 151 ; migration, not by sea, 47 ; thought, 186.
Drinking, 74.
Dual termination, 163.
Dvarasamudram, 378

Early Tamil, 173-177
Enadi Nayanar, a Saint, 66.
Ethical literature, 193-195
Etymology, Tamil, 162
Exegetical period, 222-224

INDEX 421

Eyinas, an ancient tribe, 12, 76.
Ezhuttacchan, a poet, 361.

Faction disputes, not in Malabar, 98
Final letters in words, 139
First academy, described, 235, age of, 239
Food and the caste system, 73.
Forbes, Capt., on the North Indian Nagas, 27.
Frazer, Mr. J G., 200
French academy, compared with *Sangam*, 260.

Gait, Mr. G A., quoted, 15
Gandaraditya, a king, 255, 292.
Gandharvam, a form of marriage, 104; gandharvis, dancing women, 190.
Gaulamanai, a poet, 217, 200
Gender, rational, 103.
Geography, the Tamil's ignorance of, 142
Gnana Vettiyan, a Tamil work, 197.
Grammars, the Tamil, 114
Grantha-Tamil characters, 114; why introduced, 128, rules for naturalisation of, 128
Grierson, Dr, 17, 39, on Tamil literature, 207
Gunabhara, a Pallava king, 305
Gunadhya, age of, 243.
Guruparamparai, or the lives of Vaishnava reformers, 220.

Haddon, Dr., 19.
Haeckel, Dr, 18.
Hill tribes, 68.
Hinduism, history of, 282, 285.
Hiranya Varma, a king, 402
History, foreign to Hindus, 195.
Hovelacque, Dr, 35, 172, 195.
Hunter, Sir W. W., on Dravidian migration, 23, 108; on Tamil literature, 204.
Huxley, Prof T., 18
Hymnal period, 217.

Idaiyan, history of, 71, 76, 103, in Malabar, 353.
Ilakkana Vilakkam, 224.
Ilakkana Kottu, 224.
Ilango-Adigal, a Jaina poet, 216.
Images of Saints, 338.
Indo-Europeanisms in Tamil, 167, 168.
Inflection of verbs in Malayalam, 368.
Initial letters in words, 138
Inscriptions, on social position of certain castes, 75, 77; giving a Paraiya's decision, 80; on the Kaikolas, 82 *et. seq*; use of Vatteluttu and Grantha-Tamil in, 127.
Interchange of letters in, 136
Ir or *r*, as plural suffix, 163.
Irrigation tanks, 43, the system borrowed from the Babylonians, 43
Islamism and Brahmanism, 186.
Isolating languages, 147
Iyakkan or Yaksha, a Marava chieftain, 55.
Iyal Tamil, 187.
Izham, meaning of, 416.
Izhavas, a caste, 66, 72, 77, 413.
Izha-putchi, a tax, 72

Jains, position of, in the caste dispute, 110; a right-hand caste, 112.
Jaina, Sangam, foundation of, 251, Tamil works, 219.
Jespersen, Dr., quoted, 261.
Johnston, Mr. C J, 86 *f. n.*

Kacchiyappa, a Tamil poet, 220
Kadars, a forest tribe, 13,22,56
Kadunkon, a Pandya king, 252.
Kaikolan, 65, 95, as temple servants, 97, were Eyinas, 82, origin of, 82, 83, not good weavers, 83.
Kalabhras, foreign invaders, 250.
Kalingam, meaning of, 83
Kalingattuparani, a poem, 221.
Kalittogai, an anthology, 216.
Kalladanar, 3, 216, age of, 409.

Kallan, a caste, 29, 69.
Kamban, 219, 262, date of, 54, lectured in Malabar 343.
Kammalas, thread wearing by, 75, 77, 108; in Malabar, 104, origin of the, 85,-88; their version of caste disputes, 97.
Kanakasabhai, Mr V., his etymology of the word Tamil,7; his theory of Mongolian origin, 13, 25, 192, on Early Chera kings, 272; on the Pandiya kings, 388
Kanchipuram, description of, 76, origin of caste disputes at, 99.
Kannappa Nayanar, a saint, 29.
Kannassa Ramayanam, 360.
Kapilar, 45, 216, 268, 270, 271; as name of three different poets, 197, not a Paraiya, 248.
Kappiyanar, a poet, 266.
Karaikkalammai, a saint, 403
Karaiyan, a fishing caste, 72
Karanam, a caste, 75.
Katantra, a grammar, 118
Kaveripatam, destruction of, 60.
Kaysina Valudi, age of, 252
Kazharambhan, a student of Agastya, 397
Keane, Dr, A H, 19, on Tolkapyam, 138
Kerala, a Kodum-Tamil country, 264, 341 Nambudris ownership of 350
Khonds, a hill tribe, 90.
Kings, duties of Hindu, 108
Kocchengannan, age of, 250,319.
Kodum-Tamil, where used, 142
Kol-Ayan, a shepherd caste, 353
Koliyans, weavers, 80.
Konatur, meaning of, 353.
Kottayam plates, 360.
Krishnagala, a poem, 360.
Kshatriyas, 59, 103.
Kudumi or tuft of hair, 389.
Kulasekharalvar, a Chera-Tamil saint 309, 343
Kundalakesi, a Jaina work, 219
Kunnalakon, meaning of, 353
Kural, 113, Sanskrit influence in the, 194.

Kurichan, a hill tribe, 91.
Kurumbas, a tribe, 13, 69.

Language, no safe test of race, 13, changes in its growth, 145, morphological classification of, 147
Left-hand castes, 95.
Lemurian theory, the, 21, 33
Letters, number and order in Tamil, 132, 137; peculiar to Tamil, 134, combination, 117, 'levelling' in Malayalam, 368.
Linguistic affinity, 153
Literary forgeries, very common in Tamil, 197
Loan words, how to detect, 155
Locality and communities, 73
Logan, Mr., on the derivation of 'Kizhakku,' 345, 412.
Long ள and ழ, 51, 61
Lydekker, Prof., 18.

Macdonell, Prof A A, 118.
M'Crindle, Mr J W, 44
Madigas, leather workers, 101.
Madura, the Southern, 240, seat of Tamil learning, 256, Sangams, 232. purana, 394-6.
Mahabharata, 1; interpolations in the, 51, its popularity, 52; translated, 256, 393; date of the war, 239.
Mahawanso, on the caste disputes, 102
Mahishyas, a mixed caste, 75.
Makkal (Dravidians), 10.
Malabar, a Kodum-Tamil country, 344, castes and the Tamils, 351, temples in, 347.
Malaiman, a caste, 101.
Malasar, a hill tribe, 56.
Malayalam, a dialect of Tamil, 9, 375, not an inflectional language, 149, meaning of, 341; early literature in, 357; and vulgar Tamil, 367, grammar, 365, 366-369, levelling process in, 368; vocabulary, 369-371; why separated from Tamil, 371-6.

INDEX

Mamballi, copper plates, language of, 359.
Manavalamamuni, a Vaishnava reformer, 222, 385
Mangudi-kizhar, a poet, 78, Marudanar, 216
Manikka Vachakar, 392, et seq
Manimekalai, a Chera-Tamil epic, 39
Manipravala, 229.
Maran, etymology of, 31.
Maravas, a caste, 11, 70.
Maraignanasambanda, a Saivite philosopher, 222.
Marayan, a caste, 66
Marriage, the Rakshasa form of, 55, among the early Tamils, 314, connection amongst the Tamil kings, 372.
Marumakkatayam law, 103
Mathematics, Tamil, 192
Mauryan alphabet, 125
Max Muller, quoted, 258
Mayura Varma, a king, 348
Mediæval Tamil, 177-180
Meykanda Deva, a Saivite philosopher, 222.
Middle letters in words, 140
Modern Tamil, 180-183, characters, 129, why angular, 131
Modern, Tamil prose, 230
Molony, Mr. J C, on Tamil, 135
Monastic learning, 224.
Mongolian theory, 24.
Moods, 163
Mosiyar, a Tamil poet, 243.
Mulattama Kanniyar, 217
Mudukudumi Peravaludi, a Pandiya king, 388, 391.
Mudattirumaran, a king, 252.
Mukundamalai, a poem, 310
Mussalmans, attitude towards foreign literature, 186, 187.
Music, 187, works on, 189, history of, 189, 191.
Musiri, an ancient town, 346.
Muttarasa, feudal chiefs, 69.
Muttiriyans, a caste, 69.
Muttollayiram, a poem, 217.

Nacchellar u a poetess, 268.

Nacchinarkiniyar, a Tamil commentator, 45, 118, 123, 328, on Vowel-consonants, 129
Nagas, 10, their connection with the Pallis, 10 f n, with the Cholas 11, described, 27; in S. India, 28, 69, tribes, 61
Naga-Dravidians, 377.
Nagakumara kavyam, a Jaina work, 219
Naidatam, a Tamil classic, 225.
Nakkiar, 216, 393, his account of Academies, 252
Naladiyar, date of, 69, 219, 254.
Nalayiraprabandam, 291.
Nallanduvanar, author of Kahttogai, 216.
Nambis or Nambudris, early Brahmans of Tamil country, 349, 379.
Nambudris, 108, meaning of 347, not the sole Jenmis, 350, influence of, 358, and Bhatta Brahmans, 373
Nambiyandar Nambi, a Poet, 220, 407, age of, 293
Name giving, 337
Nammalvar, a Vishnuvite Saint 65, Sanskrit words in his works, 128, life and writings of, 324, age of, 327-338, on the Chera temples, 347.
Nannul, a Tamil grammar, 161.
Napputanar, a poet, 217
Nasalisation in Malayalam, 371.
Nathamuni, 220, 291, 327, 334.
Nattattanar, a poet, 216
Nayadis, a low caste, 90
Nayanars or Saiva saints, 218.
Nayars, 103, composition of the caste, 352.
Negritos, 56
Nemnadam, a grammar, 219.
Nelson, J. H, 111.
Nilakesi, a Jaina or Buddhist work, 269
Nouns, 162, of quality, 162.

Occupation and castes, 78

Orthography, Tamil, 113; Sanskrit and Tamil compared, 155. *Ottaikkuttan*, a poet, 84, 220.

Padirruppattu, a Chera-Tamil work, 342.
Pallan, a low caste, 70, 71
Pallava, meaning of, 65, 69, 70, 214, not liked by Tamil kings, 105, downfall of their kingdom, 106.
Palli, a caste, 70
Pans or Tamil tunes, 188, 332.
Panans, 11, 84, 102, 235
Panchalas, the (see Kammalas)
Pandya kings, 48; early, 387; genealogy of, 391.
Panini, a grammarian, 117
Panmrupadalam, a work, 217.
Panmrupattiyal, 136.
Paranar, a poet, 216, 267, 271.
Paraiyas, etymology of, 78, origin of the people, 77, their former greatness, 79-81; Dr. Caldwell on the, 81, 101.
Parani, a war song, 221.
Parts of speech, 162, difference in Tamil and Sanskrit, 163.
Particles (Idai-chol), 162.
Pattanavan, a fishing caste, 72.
Pavanandi, on letters, 113, 128
Pazhamoli, a poem, 219
Per-arayan, a title, 65.
Periyalvar, 320, age of, 321.
Periyavacchan Pillai, a Vaishnava commentator, 322
Perumpanarruppadai, 76.
Perundevanar, a Tamil poet, 219, age of, 247, 254
Perunguurur Kizhar, 269.
Perunkausikanai, a poet, 217.
Philology, principles of, 143.
Phonetics, Tamil deficient, 134
Pidaran, caste, 66.
Pillai Perumal Aiyangar, 225.
Pingala Nigandu, a Tamil Dictionary, 219.
Poigaiyar, a poet, 250.
Poli or change in letters, 136.
Poll-tax, 107.
Polluting castes, 65

Polysynthetic languages, 147
Pope, Dr., on Saivism, 383, 401.
Poyyamozhi Pulavar, a poet, 255
Prabhulinga lila, a poem, 225.
Prayoga Viveham, 153.
Pre-academic period of Tamil literature, 212.
Pre-Aryans, the three types of, 61
Presents to Tamil poets, 260.
Pronouns, relative, 165.
Pronunciation, of ற, 133; of ழ (Zh), 134
Prose literature, 228-230, need for, 184.
Pugazhendi, a poet, 220.
Puranic Hinduism, 288.
Purapporul Venbamalai, a poem, 55, 217, 313.

Quantity in Tamil letters, 133

Racial varieties, data for determination of, 13.
Rajaraja Chola's inscriptions, 77, 83, castes of his time, 66
Rakshasas, the, 9, 378, ancestors of Paraiyas, Pallas etc., 54, Rakshasam, a form of marriage, 55, 104
Rama, a typical Aryan, 53.
Ramanuja Charya, 111, 222.
Ramayana, the, 51
Rangacharya, Prof. M, on caste disputes, 101
Ravana, 52, not a Dravidian Tamil, 53
Relations, Tamil words to denote, 105.
Religion, broke up castes, 73, 74; in the academic period, 251, of the Tamils, 382.
Rhetoric, 166
Rhys Davids, Dr, on the Tamil alphabet, 119
Rice, Mr. L., 102
Right-hand faction, 92 et seq; castes, 95; army mentioned in inscription, 106, 107
Risley, Sir H H, 12,13, 17, 24, 32.
Roman colony at Madura, 48, 244.
Rudran Kannanar, a poet, 217.

INDEX 425

Sacred hymns, collection of Tamil, 292.
Saints, the Tamil, 218
Saiva activity, early, 292-294.
Saiva mutts, learning in 224.
Saiva philosophy, not Dravidian, 192.
Saiva Siddhantam defined, 384.
Saivism, 383
Sakkai, a caste, 66.
Sakti workship, 96
Sambandam or marriage, 108.
Sandhi or coalescence, 160.
Sangam, references to, 231, 392, meaning of, 23, origin of, 234, age of the second, 241, 243, Buddhistic origin, 252.
Sankaracharya, 2
Sanskrit compounds, 159, poets and Tamil Sangams, 238, and Tolkapyam, 128.
Sattanar, 216, 389; a Buddhist poet, 251, 258.
Sekkilar, age of, 220, 293.
Selva Nambi, a Brahman, 320.
Sembadavan, caste, 72
Semman, leather-workers, 85.
Sen-Tamil, where spoken, 141
Sewell, Mr R., on South Indian people, 20, on the Tamil alphabet, 124.
Shanan, a caste, 71
Ship, Tamil words for the, 48
Siddhar school 226.
Silappadikaram, an early Chera Tamil work, 342.
Siragnanamuni, on letters, 133; on usage, 144; on the origin of Tamil, 149
Siravakkiyar and Tirumalisai Alvar, 306
Smith, Mr Vincent, 39, 49, 265.
Social life in Kerala, 274.
Soligas, a forest tribe, 56
Sourashtras, a weaver caste, 60
Siivaramangalam, 331.
Sundaramurti Nayanar, 407.
Suryanarayana Sastri, 200
Swaminatha Desika, on Tamil and Sanskrit 152· on Tamil letters, 170

Tamil, the word explained, 6; Mr.Kanakasabhai's derivation, 7, affinity with Uralo-Altaic languages, 14, 34, an agglutinative language, 148, 381; changes in, 145, the Divine origin of, 149, not the only Dravidian language, 150; its relationship with Sanskrit, 152, 153; and Sanskrit compared, 163, 166, affiliation of, 169, 172; history of early, 173; mediaeval, 177, modern, 180, peculiarities of early, 267-280, Nambudris' attitude to, 368.
Tamils, the three racial types among the, 10, 56, a warlike race, 41, 185, 261; their culture, 42, their foreign trade, 47-50, in Sanskrit epics, 51, probable date of their migration, 47; their acquaintance with the Romans, 48, and the Assyrians, 121; their commerce with the Egyptians, 121, religion of the, 215, 382
Tamil-akam, boundaries of, 8.
Tamil alphabet, history of, 114; when introduced, 115, before Agastva, 122, Mr. R Sewell on the, 124, defective, 124, 134; origin of, 136.
Tamil castes, 67.
Tamil civilisation, 240; Mr. Kanakasabhai on, 192, Dr. R Caldwell on early, 193; due to Agastya, 237
Tamil Dictionary, copiousness of, 261.
Tamil kings, and the Mahabharata war, 44, are Kshatriyas, 61; of Malabar, 357; none in Rama's time, 54
Tamil learning, how encouraged, 255, 259.
Tamil letters, origin of, 136, 382.
Tamil literature, extent of, 191; division of, 187; posterior to Aryan contact, 195; Mr. Damodaram Pillai's division of, 193-200· Mr. Suryanara-

yana's,200, 201;Dr. Caldwell's, 201—204; Dr. Hunter's, 204; M. Julien Vinson's, 207-210; proposed division, 211-213; periods of, 386, 399 ; pre-academic period, 212 ; academic period, 213; hymnal period, 217; exegetical period, 222-224 ; modern period, 224, 226; and by Nambudri's, 372.
Tamil research, the new School of, 46, 51.
Tamil Scholars, self-sufficiency of, 195.
Tamil words inSanskrit, 154, 161.
Tamil works, approved by the Sangam, 216.
Tayamanaswami, 65.
Tembavani, a poem, 225.
Temple building begun, 290.
Tengu or cocoanut, 415.
Ten Tamil Idylls, The, 88.
Ten Tens, the, 264.
Ter-Chelian, age of, king, 253.
Tevan, a title, 415.
Third Sangam, described, 245 ; dissolution of, 248, 251.
Thomas, Mr. E., on the Indian alphabets, 119.
Tiruchengunrur, a Brahman centre in Kerala, 347.
Tirumalisai Alvar, 302-307.
Tirumangai Alvar, 29, 311 ; age of, 317.
Tirumurais, a collection of Saiva religious hymns, 220.
Tirunakkarasar, same as Appar.
Tiruppanalvar, 307.
Tiruttakka Deva, 255.
Tiruttonda-Togai, a list of Saiva Saints, 406.
Tiruvalluvar, an ethical poet, 216, 285; malai, 247-249.
Tiyans, a Malabar caste, 103, 411, and Izhavans, 355, 417.
Todas, 13, 38, 379.
Tolkapyar, age of, 116, 400; describes only Vatteluttu, 122, 126; Mr. A. H. Keane on, 138; on final letters, 139.
Tomb stones, 16.

Tondaradippodi Alvar, 307.
Topinard, Dr., 18.
Toti, meaning of, 80.
Trade with Babylon, 47 f.n. 48.
Traditions, 16; value of, 387.
Translations, Tamil, 219.
Travancore, a Kodum-Tamil country, 344.
Turkic and Tamil, 165.
Trignana Sambanda Nayanar a Saiva saint, 396, 207.

Udayanakavyam, a poem, 219.
Ugra Peruvaludi, a king, 249; age of, 252.
Ula, a kind of poem, 221, 222.
Umapati Sivacharya, a Saivite divine, 222.
Umaru Pulavar, a poet, 225.
Unnayi Variyar, a Malayalam poet, 361.
Uralo-Altaic languages and Tamil, 14; group and the Dravidian family, 170.
Usimuri, a work on Tamil prosody, 217.

Vaidya, an extinct caste, 64.
Vaikhanasa Dharmasutra, 87.
Vajra Nandi, a Jain teacher,251.
Valaiyapati, a Jaina work, 219.
Vali and Sugriva, 56.
Valluvas, Paraya priests, 99.
Vanamamalai Mutt, 331.
Vanniyan, a caste, 69.
Vanaras, the, 51, 56, 377.
Vannans, a caste, 77.
Varagunamangai, 330.
Variyan, a Malabar caste, 66.
Vatteluttu, 114 ; history of, 116 ; introduced, 119 ; Dr. Burnell on, 120 ; Drs. Buhler and Caldwell on, 120 ; and other alphabets compared, 123 ; independant origin of, 121; borrowed from Semites, 124; Tolkapyar's description of, 126 ; not borrowed from Brahmi, 128, 131.
Vedan, a hunting caste, 29, 101.
Vedas, unwritten, 234.

INDEX

Vedanta Desika, 222, 385
Velaikkarar (infantry), 106.
Vellallas, the, 38, 61, etymology of the name 42; their position in the caste system, 61; account of, 63-65, in Malabar, 353
Velirs (Vellalas), 61, 62
Venbamalai, a Chera-Tamil work (See *Purapporul*.)
Venkayya, Mr V., on the Tamil alphabet, 125.
Villiputturar, a poet, 225
Vira Pukka Raya, 112.
Virakkals or tombstones, 40
Vinson M Julien, 207-210.
Virasoliyam, 65 *f n*, 161, 220.
Vishnuism, early history of, 288; Dr. Pope on, 385,
Vishnu temples, ancient, 289
Vishnuvardhana, a king, 336.
Vocabulary, Tamil, 153, Malayalam, 369-371.

Vowel-consonantal signs, 129-131
Vulgar Tamil and Malayalam, 367.

Wars with the Cheras, 372.
West-coast towns in Tamil literature, 316.
Whitney, Prof W. D, on the growth of language, 115-117.
Word-formation in Tamil and Sanskrit, 157
Words, rules for Tamil, 137-110, coining not allowed, 262.

Yakshas or Rakshasas, 54.
Yanadis, a forest tribe, 88
Yavanas, 59 *f. n*, 211, 265.
Yazh, described, 188.
Yesodarakavyam, a poem, 219

Zh (ழ), 30, 134

THE END.

The Guardian Press Madras

4

Milton Keynes UK
Ingram Content Group UK Ltd.
UKHW050028211124
2986UKWH00055BA/90